'From the dangerous days of Elim's breaking days of the martyrdom of Maldwyn's book traces a path of lear mountains and valleys of our Movem reminder to us that it is all too easy for movements to become monuments. He highlights the challenges of poor leadership and competitive spirits. He reminds us that our Movement is first and foremost, or should be, a Movement from God for God and held by God. This volume is not an act of nostalgia but an act of defiant remembering.

Like any good historian, Maldwyn offers us the victories and mistakes of the past as a salutary warning that we must not make the same mistakes again and we must not allow our past victories to become our crowning glories. All the way through this work, I am nudged and challenged by the Holy Spirit to see the threads of Divine Grace and Providence alongside the human threads of obedience, courage and faithfulness. However, I also see how things unravel when obedience is replaced with control, when courage is replaced with fear and when faithfulness is replaced with seeking to hold on to position or to please the crowd. Maldwyn's book is a prophetic call to Elim - beckoning us to continue to be the Movement that God has called us to be through bold, brave and Pentecostal passion and warning us not to become a has-been movement that once shone brightly but could become nothing but an ember - a dying coal of what was once a powerful fire.

This book is explosive in its implications. We ignore it at our peril. We can either live in the past or learn from it. We can ignore it or be shaped by it. My deep prayer is that every leader in Elim, at every level and in every sphere, will read this book and be changed by it. We need an Elim that is not afraid to be what God has called us to be, led by women and men who put the Kingdom above their positions and the glory of God above their reputations. This book calls us to be a Movement on the cutting edge of what God is doing rather than on the back foot of our fears and insecurities. Buy it. Read it. Pray through it, and be changed by it, for the glory of God.'

Rev Malcolm Duncan F.R.S.A.
Lead Pastor Dundonald Elim Church

'In this second volume, Maldwyn continues to express his devotion to the Foursquare Gospel as expressed through the Elim Pentecostal Church. He carefully reveals the places and the people who played vital roles in the maturity and the multiplication of this missional church and organisation.

He writes, not only as an historian, but as a practitioner; as someone who has demonstrated significant commitment to Elim over many decades, as well as having exhibited a deep love for the One who is the focus and foundation of that Movement.'

Rev Duncan Clark,
Coventry Elim Church.

'Maldwyn Jones' first volume 'And they came to Elim' on the early history of the Elim Movement made for compelling reading. This second volume covering the post Second World War period is no less so. Drawing on archive material that as Elim's Official Historian he has been able to access, he reveals the crises and recovery of the Movement during that period with all its challenges and struggles. He writes with perception and reflection on the events and of the individuals involved during that time. I highly recommend this very valuable and inspiring record for anyone interested in knowing more of the development and history of the Elim Pentecostal Church.'

Rev Trevor Harris

And They Came to Elim

A History of the Elim
Pentecostal Church
Vol 2 1940-1980

Maldwyn Jones

British Library Cataloguing in Publication Data. A catalogue
record for this book is available from the British Library.

Published for Maldwyn Jones by Verite CM Limited Worthing UK
www.veritecm.com

ISBN 978-1-914388-43-9

Printed in Great Britain.

Dedications

With grateful thanks to my Lord and Saviour who having saved me at the age of 14 has kept me in his grace these past 60 years and brought these special people into my life:

Gwenda Lewis, my lovely sister who has always been there for me.

William Evans, my pastor, together with his wife Mary, helped establish me in the faith.

Len Cowdery, a valued friend and mentor.

Acknowledgements

In writing this, my second volume, I have received the assistance, encouragement and advice from a number of colleagues and friends. My close friend Stuart Blount, Elim's Director of Ministry has been a treasure-house of encouragement to me in writing this volume. He has very kindly written the Foreword and in this he stresses the importance of this and the final volume. He rightly points to the previously undocumented material and personal knowledge which have not been made available in book form.

It has taken me twice the length of time writing this second volume than it took to write the first. There is not the abundance of readily available material to hand as was the case with my first volume. Long hours reading through hundreds of copies of Evangels took its toll. The annoying thing is that having finally come to the end of the book I am aware of so much that I have left out. Some of this will be covered in the third volume.

Chris Cartwright, Elim's General Superintendent has been a constant encouragement to me and has spurred me on to write. His father, Desmond, was Elim's first Historian and his contribution to the Elim Archives is legendary. Were it not for his meticulous keeping of records and materials, I doubt that Elim would have such a magnificent archives as it has today. Indeed, it could be argued that we would have no archive at all. Des was a valued friend and a great mentor. I miss him.

To my friends Phill and Sally Thompsett and Mike and Peggy Greenway, my sincere appreciation for your help and encouragement. Phil was appointed Elim's Official Archivist in 2013 and has continued faithfully in this role ably assisted by his wife, Sally until very recently. I am sure that the whole Movement would wish me to mention this and to express our gratitude for their work in the archives.

Sally Gibbs, the College Librarian has for the past couple of years been involved with moving and reorganising the archives which now contain five Pentecostal collections. Sally has been a great help in showing me where to find various documents and books. Special thanks again to my friend David Butcher for providing some photographs which are included in the book.

I continue to be grateful to the National Leadership Team for the honour of being Elim Historian and in allowing me the privilege of writing this book.

I wish to thank my friends Malcolm Duncan, Trevor Harris and Duncan Clark for their kind and perspective reviews.

I also wish to express my appreciation to Chris Powell and the team at Verite CM Limited for their work in printing this book and making it ready for publication. Deep appreciation also to Dr Neil Hudson who has edited the book. Being an acknowledged Pentecostal Historian, Neil was extremely helpful in getting me to format my material systematically and chronologically. He was brilliant at highlighting my repetitions. Thank you Neil

To my wife Ruth, a huge thank you. You have been by my side for these past fifty years. Without you these books would not have been written and any positives that I have accomplished throughout 53 years of ministry would have been negatived without your wisdom, patience, understanding, encouragement and love. The past few years when the Parkinson's has begun to take its toll have added further pressure for you are no longer just my wife, but my carer also. From the bottom of my heart, thank you.

Finally, I thank and praise my Lord and Saviour, Jesus Christ for saving me 63 years ago and for keeping me by His grace all these many years. It is indeed, a great privilege to serve Him.

Contents

Foreword

I have known of Maldwyn Jones for most of my life, but really got to know him well when I moved to lead an Elim affiliated church less than a mile from the Elim church he was pastoring. Though the two churches had a less than glorious history, Maldwyn and I struck up a friendship that has lasted for nearly 30 years and deepened as those years have rolled by.

I've learned a lot of things about this book's author, but two stand out that are entirely relevant to this important work. Maldwyn loves Elim. He and Ruth have given their lives to serve our movement diligently and faithfully. But he also loves the history of our movement. His first volume in this series plotted the remarkable first 25 years of Elim's growth as revival fires were lit across this nation.

This second volume however, is, in my humble opinion, of greater significance. Several other authors have written of Elim's earliest years but in this book, Maldwyn writes the history of a period so far uncatalogued. The post second world war era for Elim was one of huge change. Not only was the movement affected by the massive cultural shifts of an impoverished nation battling with the aftermath of the war, but the men leading Elim were also battling with the challenges created by the painful split with George Jeffreys its charismatic founder. The way in which Maldwyn charts this journey is captivating and the biographical accounts of those who took up the challenge will hopefully inspire you too.

I grew up in Elim hearing many of the names of those whose stories are brought to life in these pages. You will discover that they were ordinary men, but like Peter and John who faced the Jewish

Sanhedrin for sharing the gospel of Jesus, these too were men who, "had been with Jesus" (Acts 4:13).

Maldwyn's work is always well researched and articulately written. You will feel the energy with which he writes and the passion he has for these stories to be told. There are those who may wonder why it is necessary to look back and record sauch a history when the current needs of our world should engage our attention more fully. I would have to disagree. George Santayana, the American philosopher, said, "Those who do not remember the past are condemned to repeat it." In this way, Maldwyn's work is a reminder to us that the errors of the past can too easily be repeated in the future. They may have a different face and a different name, but we are foolish if we do not learn from what has preceded us.

This book should be read by all who want to understand why the Elim movement is what it is today and who we should be grateful for. As you read let it light a fresh fire in you to be committed to the great commission of Jesus just as those men and women that have carried the flame before us were.

Stuart Blount

Introduction

In this, the second of the trilogy on the history of the Elim Pentecostal Church, the book will feature the immense problems faced by the young denomination following the rift caused by the resignation of its leader and founder, George Jeffreys. The enormous difficulties confronted by Elim at this time were massively exacerbated by the Second World War. The war affected Elim more than most other Christian denominations, not just because Elim was such a young organisation,[1] but as an organisation with evangelism at its heart, its evangelistic outreach was seriously hindered during the conflict.

In the introduction to the first volume, I stated that: 'The story of the Elim Pentecostal Church in the UK is an inspirational, and at times, a miraculous one.'[2] Reference is made to the outstanding miracles that occurred during the campaigns of George Jeffreys. In chronicling the history of the Movement,[3] the facts of its survival after the twin traumas of schism and world war and its subsequent expansion in the period 1950-1980 is nothing short of miraculous.

The first volume dealt with the birth and early years of Elim. This volume will seek to trace the survival, establishment and growth of Elim in the incredibly challenging period of the Second World War and the immediate post-war years. Attention will be given to the different type of leadership that the Movement developed in the early post-war years. There was need for structures to be put in place that would help the young denomination recover from the trauma of the schism that occurred resulting in the resignation of its founder and leader, which were added to by the horrors of war.

'Knowledge of the past matters to societies, whose customs, inherited attitudes, laws and institutions are normally explicable only in terms of their earlier history.'[4] This is true, not only of societies, but countries and nations whose culture tradition and religion have historically helped form the identity of said countries and nations. The same is true of religious organisations and especially Christian denominations. In the case of Elim, knowledge of our history is essential in helping us understand our present situation. This is particularly so as regards our constitution. The previous volume revealed how the Deed Poll of the Elim Pentecostal Church became the central document for the governance of the Movement.[5] The establishment of the Deed Poll, largely the work of E J Phillips, with the full agreement of George Jeffreys, is still the bedrock of Elim's governance to this very day. The action taken in changing and amending constitutions and laws requires a historical knowledge of the times and challenges that were behind the establishment of such documents in the first place.

The first volume clearly established the fact of Elim being an evangelistic movement. This was due largely to the evangelistic campaigns of George Jeffreys and the Elim Evangelistic Band. Following Jeffreys' departure, other evangelists needed to carry on the work of evangelistic campaigns. This form of church planting remained the major national approach to Elim's expansion right throughout the period that this volume covers.

The 'swinging sixties' saw the rise of the Beatles' generation and a reaction to the strictures imposed by a previous generation. This was also the period of the 'cold war' and the ever-present threat of a nuclear holocaust. The book will trace Elim's development during these revolutionary times. It had been my intention to conclude this volume with the challenges faced by Elim with the rise of the Restoration Movement and the vibrancy of charismatic worship in non-Pentecostal groups and churches. This will now be covered in the third volume. This volume will show Elim's missionary expansion and recount 'Elim's darkest day'.

So, let the story continue.

Notes

1 By the time of the outbreak of the Second World War, the Elim Pentecostal Church had only been in existence for 24 years.

2 Jones, Maldwyn, *And they came to Elim: Volume 1, 1915-1940; An official history of the Elim Pentecostal Movement in the UK* (Rickmansworth: Instant Apostle, 2021), p17

3 This is a generic term that will be used to describe the Elim Pentecostal Church throughout the book. This will be in place of referring to it as a denomination.

4 Thomson, David, *The Aims of History: Values of the Historical Attitude* (London: Thames and Hudson, 1969), p12.

5 1934 Deed Poll; Deed of Variance 1942.

1
Before the Storm

Adolph Hitler

In 1933, Adolph Hitler became the Reich Chancellor of Germany. From this time onwards, it was almost inevitable that there would be a Second World War in which Britain would once more line up against Germany. Churchill, on many occasions referred to him as 'Corporal Hitler'.[1] Hitler mobilised Germany for war. Britain, in the meanwhile, much to Churchill's despair, did not do so. Neville Chamberlain declared war on Germany on Sunday, 3rd September 1939.

The impact of the first months of the war was huge. Sweeping measures were put in place to avoid loss of life: nightly blackouts were instituted, cinemas and theatres closed, hospitals were cleared to make room for civilian casualties that were anticipated to reach into tens of thousands. It was the evacuation programme that really brought home to people the reality of war. This had a tremendous effect upon churches of all denominations, but it affected Elim particularly. The churches were depleted by the large number of men that were conscripted, the blackouts affected the main Sunday services in Elim, which were the evening Gospel services. In addition to this was the evacuation of children and vulnerable adults from the cities. This greatly affected Elim's children and young people's work which was a vital part in the Movement's ministry.

It is important to understand the attitude of the British government and people in the years prior to the outbreak of war.

The 1931 General election resulted in a coalition government headed up by Ramsey MacDonald, the country's first Labour Prime Minister. He took office as Prime Minister for the second time despite great hostility from the majority of his fellow Labour Members of Parliament. He was helped by the support of Stanley Baldwin. Churchill's verdict on this coalition government is worth noting: 'The British Government which resulted from the General Election of 1931 was in appearance one of the strongest and in fact one of the weakest in British records.'[2] After severing himself from the Labour Party, which he had helped create, MacDonald found himself at the head of an administration that was very largely Conservative. There is no doubt that Stanley Baldwin was very influential in the formation of government policy during this period. The greatly reduced Labour Party was led by the extreme pacifist, George Lansbury.

Lansbury's pacifism seems to have affected the government because whilst Germany was rapidly re-arming itself, 'The MacDonald-Baldwin Government felt bound to enforce for some time the severe reductions and restrictions which the financial crisis had imposed upon our already modest armaments and steadfastly closed their eyes and ears to the disquieting symptoms in Europe.'[3]

The Elim Evangel records the first meeting held during the war under the heading of 'London's First Air-Raid Warning'. The writer describes how the congregation were asked to gather in the main part of the church, leaving the gallery and filling the part of the building under the gallery so that they would be protected from falls from the roof. He goes on to state that all this was done with speed but with calmness as the congregation knelt in pews to pray. There was not a trace of panic. In nearby Stanley Road, Croydon, a baby was dedicated between the 'Take cover' and the 'All clear' signals. 'Services were held as usual and there was no undue alarm, but much of the presence of God.'[4]

To some, all the preparations and warnings appear to have been over-emphasised in light of the first six months of the war when almost no action occurred. This period is often referred to as 'the phoney war'.[5] This period seems to have had a profound effect on the psyche of the British people. The moods of anticipation, fear, anxiety, suspicion on the part of some, together with that of excitement and preparation for mobilisation by others all mixed together must have had quite an effect on the stoic British temperament. The following lengthy quotation sums up the thinking and action of the average British person during this time.

> For those on the home front, the early months are defined by exceptionally rapid change and accompanying panic. Pre-emptive stockpiling (and the ensuing shortages) drive panic-buying. Many are re-located hundreds of miles from home – separated from parents, children, friends and family – and feel terribly displaced. For others the unfamiliarity of the situation is invigorating with the war a welcome change from the months and years of uneasy peace that preceded it. But as 1939 hurries to a close with no sign of the promised dangers, many find themselves trying to get back to… normal life again. The public are at odds over what is the "correct" behaviour and the right level of caution. Their scrutiny of each other is close and often merciless. For every person angered by a mother recalling her children from the countryside there is another irritated by being ordered to bring their gas mask to the theatre or livid at the thought of digging up a prized lawn for potatoes…humour and stoicism are typical, thriving on the benign novelty of what will later be called "The Phoney War"'.[6]

Notes

[1] He was an Austrian who fought for Germany in the Great War and was deeply distressed by Germany's defeat and also by the Treaty of Versailles that, in the opinion of most fair-minded people, was far too harsh on Germany and provided a fertile ground for those German people who felt a deep sense of injustice in the terms of the Treaty.

[2] Churchill, Winston, *The Gathering Storm, The Second World War, Volume 1,* (London: Penguin Classics, 2005) p60.

[3] Churchill, Winston, ibid, p64.

[4] *Elim Evangel,* 29th Sept 1939, p619

5 The term was coined by journalists to derisively describe the first six months period of the war during which no land operations were undertaken by the Allies or the Germans after the declaration of war on 3rd September, 1939, following the invasion of Poland by Germany.

6 Brown, Becky, *Blitz Spirit: Voices of Britain Living Through Crisis 1939-1945* (London: Hodder & Stoughton Ltd, 2020) pp10-11.

2
Parting of the ways

The 1939 Conference resulted in George Jeffreys' resignation from the Elim Pentecostal Church which he had founded in 1915. It was at this Conference that E J Phillips made a blistering attack on the competence of Jeffreys' ability to lead the Movement. The speech is outlined in the last chapter of my first volume. Suffice to say here is that Phillips made it clear that Jeffreys was unsuited for the work of leading the Movement.[1] Jeffreys made demands that he felt were essential for the Movement but, bizarrely, refused to attend the Conference and insisted on negotiating through a group of ten ministers appointed by himself. The following were appointed: Pastors Barton, Brewster, Gwilym Francis, Mercer, McAvoy, Morgan, Taylor, Stoneham, Steward and Tweed. The minutes state that this 'committee was to co-operate with him (Jeffreys) and represent him and his views at the sessions of the Conference.'[2] The composition of this committee is very interesting. Francis, Mercer, Stoneham, Steward and Tweed were very much in Jeffreys' camp and, in fact, left Elim in support of the Principal.[3] McAvoy and Morgan's sympathies were very much with the Executive Council. The appointment of Brewster is a very intriguing one. He was a great admirer of Jeffreys and a great deal of pressure was placed on him to secede from Elim and join the Bible Pattern. It is probable that Jeffreys saw Brewster as his successor in leading pioneer evangelistic campaigns. He had already led a number of successful campaigns in which good churches were established. Chief among these was Neath, which he pioneered out of Swansea when he was the pastor there. But Brewster was strongly committed to Elim and was elected to the Executive Council in 1952.[4]

At the Conference, George Jeffreys presented eight points that he wanted the ministers to accept if he was to continue as leader of the Movement.[5] One of the most contentious issues was Jeffreys' insistence on allowing lay representatives[6] to be members of Conference. This would result in a Ministerial session and a Representative session of Conference, with the Representative session being the governing body of Elim.

The Conference made many concessions to Jeffreys' eight points. It was quite a long-drawn out procedure, but eventually, the Conference agreed to most of Jeffreys' proposals including the vexed question of lay representation. There was a caveat to this in that it would be introduced providing there was a two-thirds majority for it at the Conference. There was a compromise proposed by the Conference over the ownership of church buildings. Jeffreys wanted each church to have control of its property under the Model Trust Deed, and so jointly own the church with the Movement.[7] The Conference proposal was:

> That a Deed Poll of Trust be executed by the Elim Trust Corporation covering every church building of which the Corporation is Trustee and that this Deed Poll of Trust provide that no such church property be sold or mortgaged without the approval of at least a majority of the members of the local church. Also, that no games, bazaars, entertainments, dances, whist drives, and the like be introduced into the local church unless approved by at least a majority of the members of the local church as well as the Ministerial Conference.[8]

The Conference expressed its clear support of all church property included within the Model Trust Deed being owned by the Elim Trust Corporation, of whom the Executive Council were the trustees or appointed trustees to act on their behalf. The ownership of Alliance property was thus placed firmly in the hands of the Alliance. A concession was made making it obligatory for any building to be sold only by a majority of the members of the local church. This proved to be unacceptable to George Jeffreys as he tried to negotiate further concessions from the Conference. Jeffreys' advisers asked for more time to consider. Kay states that Jeffreys asked for 28 days to give his final view to the Conference and at this point patience snapped.[9] It was clear that the obstacle between Jeffreys and the Conference was on the issue of the Model Trust Deed.[10]

The other issue that would have been a concern to Jeffreys was the last one made by the Conference: '10. That matters of doctrine be decided by the Ministerial Conference and not by the local church.' This would have prevented Jeffreys from bringing the doctrine of British Israelism into the Movement. The Minutes record the following decisions made by the Conference:

> On the question of the Declaration of Trust, the Principal would not agree and sent word to say he would only be satisfied if the concessions made by the Conference on the eight points would satisfy his laymen advisors. It was seen that further negotiations were valueless. It was then "RESOLVED that this ministerial Conference having gone to the limits in their attempts to meet the Principal's demands are determined at the expiration of seven days from the date of this resolution to withdraw all the concessions agreed upon and to abide by the Deed Poll of 1934, unless the following conditions are complied with by the Principal during the said seven days:

> [1] That he sign an agreement embodying the terms agreed at this Conference.

> [2] That he limit the number of laymen whom he consults on these matters to six.

> [3] That he undertake not to contend with the Constitution of the Alliance by means of circular letter, printed matter, or organised effort.[11]

The Conference went on to pass a proposal calling on the Principal 'to transfer to the Elim Trust Corporation within three months of the passing of this Resolution all Alliance property in Great Britain of which he is Trustee or Joint-Trustee.'[12] In his first brief appearance at this Conference, Jeffreys informed the members of his decision to withdraw as his nominees, Joseph Smith and Charles Kingston and replace them with William Barton and Gwilym Francis. Smith and Kingston were supportive of E J Phillips and Barton and Francis were very much 'Jeffreys' men'. This did not affect things in so far as the Conference representatives still held a majority on the Council.

Whilst a division in the Movement was seemingly inevitable, E J strived for a situation that would result in Jeffreys becoming the spiritual leader of Elim whilst the Executive Council led the Movement. Hudson viewed this as being totally unworkable arguing that in the light of Phillips' devastating attack on Jeffreys at the 1939 Conference, there was no way in which a man so totally discredited could possibly have the necessary qualities to be a spiritual leader. However, E J concentrated his attack not on the spiritual integrity of Jeffreys, but on his administrative and business failures. Hudson made the following summation of Phillips' speech:

> It was during this Conference that Phillips began to outline the exact gravity of the situation facing the Movement. Whilst Jeffreys refused to join the Conference, preferring to make occasional appearances and statements, Phillips began the Conference by refuting each of Jeffreys' contentious points, as he had promised he would. He then outlined all the changes that Jeffreys had proposed throughout his time as leader. Whilst the stated purpose in this exercise was to help ministers 'get a proper perspective', *the underlying aim seems to have been to discredit Jeffreys in the eyes of the ministers so that any further proposed changes would be rejected.*[13]

It is clear that Phillips was out to discredit Jeffreys and therefore, it was not incongruous of him to suggest that Jeffreys became the spiritual leader of the Movement without any constitutional authority. Furthermore, Phillips had long been of the opinion that Jeffreys had abandoned his main gift of evangelism, concentrating instead on reforming the Movement. The minutes of Tuesday, 21st November records the nub of Phillips' speech and reveals something of the impact that E J had on the ministers:

> Pastor E J Phillips made a statement in reply to the Principal's circular letter of 11th July, 1939, answering point by point the Principal's statement and showing where many of them were inaccurate. He gave a resume of the various changes made in the work at the instigation of the Principal and also replied to several points in the Principal's circular letter.[14]

It is clear from the Conference minutes that there was considerable frustration felt by the ministers at Jeffreys' absence from the discussions. In response to this, it was 'RESOLVED that the Conference appoint a deputation of four men to wait on the Principal to impress on him the necessity of his being present on Tuesday evening. Pastors W L Brambleby, J J Morgan, G H Thomas and F G Cloke were appointed to form this delegation.

In his speech to the Conference on Tuesday afternoon, 21st November, E J presented a General Survey of the changes and decisions brought about at the behest of George Jeffreys over the years. He appealed to his longevity claiming that he had 'had much more than anyone else to do with the organisation of this work, and have been on the governing body longer than anyone else – apart from Principal.'[15] Phillips pointed out that when he went to Belfast in 1919, there was absolutely nothing by way of accounts, lists of properties and virtually non-existent administration. To a trained and organised mind such as E J possessed, such a situation was, in his own words 'hopeless'. He then launched into the constant changes in the Constitution. The first was drawn up in 1922 by George Jeffreys without consulting the Overseers, of whom he was one. This was amended the following year. A new Constitution was written in 1925, amended in 1927 and yet another new Constitution and new rules in 1929. In 1934 a Deed Poll was drawn up, together with new rules. Phillips was at pains to point out that this was not done in a hurry. Discussion around a Deed

Poll had been going on for a number of years. E J made it clear that the late Pastor Henderson who died three years previously had been deeply involved in the proposed Deed Poll. In 1938, according to Phillips, Jeffreys began agitating for a new Deed Poll. E J's conclusion was that there was a new Constitution on average every three years.

Resignation

Just before Conference, Jeffreys sent a somewhat rambling and confused letter to the delegates. The last paragraph of his letter gives us some idea of his mindset at this time:

> In my pamphlet 'The Pattern', which represents the basis for my future ministry, you will see that I have destroyed all bridges behind me, and there can be no going back. If at this Conference we could really overcome and forget the past, and concentrate on a constructive policy which would bring more interest to the members of our churches, there is no reason why we should not work together to bring revival to our land. If this is not done, I cannot see anything before us but the drying up of the work. Impossible to go ahead if the people who are the mainstay of our Movement are not with us. I am retiring from the Conference because physical and mental strain of the last few months have taken toll of my strength. I will be at No. 10 and will endeavour to answer any questions in writing by the Ministers. I am prepared to meet any Ministers or others for the purpose of consultation and advice. The day has come when I (Jeffreys) must know where each minister stands because issues are at stake. So farewell! May God bless you all, and give you wisdom and foresight in your.......The Lord bless you.[16]

These minutes are fuller and easier to follow than the summary minutes that were sent out to the delegates. They record the days and dates that the various discussions were held. The Conference did its utmost to meet Jeffreys' policies. As noted above, the Conference, in response to Jeffreys' proposals made three provisional statements as a basis for the agreement to the eight points submitted by him. Jeffreys took exception to the third point in which he would be required not to contend against the Constitution of the Alliance either in written form or public speech. The minutes record his reply:

> I will not contend against the Elim Alliance Constitution if and when legally amended along the lines already suggested, and should I ever have cause to change my mind on this point, then I will first of all acquaint the Ministerial Conference in Session.[17]

He further promised to alter 'The Pattern'[18] to conform to the wishes of the Conference on the plurality of Elders, also other points. 'The Conference regarded this statement as sufficient ground for negotiations on the other two points.'[19]

The minutes of the 1939 Conference reveal the strong disapproval of the lay advisors that seemed to be influencing the Principal. Jeffreys wanted to ensure that either a Model Trust Deed or a Deed Poll of Trust be executed by the Elim Trust Corporation, 'so as to cover each local church, and that this matter and the matter of what powers, if any, shall be delegated to the local church, shall be left to the Executive to work out a proportional scheme to be confirmed or otherwise by a postal vote of the Ministerial Conference.'[20]The Conference made one final attempt to meet Jeffreys' proposal by proposing that a Deed Poll of Trust be executed by the Elim Trust Corporation giving the local church a veto on activities to be held in connection with their local work. E J reported that he had failed to persuade the Principal on this point. The Conference came to the reluctant conclusion that further negotiations would be valueless.

The timing of the actual resignation of Jeffreys is difficult to ascertain from the minutes. The Conference was scheduled to end on Friday 24th November, but the minutes clearly state that the Conference was prolonged for another week and finished on Friday 1st December. However, the minutes seem to indicate that the Conference concluded shortly after Jeffreys' resignation. It seems that the last three pages of the minutes of the 1939 Conference cover the deliberations that took place during the second week, after the resignation of the Principal. On Friday morning, 24th November, Jeffreys attended the Conference and read out a statement announcing his resignation from the Alliance, and also from the Elim Church Incorporated, after which he handed letters of resignation to E J Phillips in his role as Secretary-General of the Alliance and to W G Hathaway as Secretary of the Elim Church Incorporated, after which he left the meeting.

Notes

[1] Jones, Maldwyn, ibid, pp391-393

[2] 1939 Ministerial Conference Minutes, Monday afternoon, 27th November 1939, (Elim Archives).

[3] This was the title that George Jeffreys took on himself and it was this that was used throughout Elim when referring to him. Even in the Conference debates following his resignation, he was referred to by this title.

[4] This was the year that Brewster was appointed President of Elim for the first time. He, in fact tied with J J Morgan, each having 116 votes. The Constitution at the time called for lots to be taken in the event of a tie. The result was that Brewster was elected on the casting of lots. (Conference 1952, Minutes of the Representative Session).

[5] The 8 points were the demands for: 1 The Ministerial Conference to be the governing body of Elim, with the Executive Council being the functioning arm of the Conference. 2. District Presbyteries to include an equal mix of ministers and lay representation. 3. Lay representatives to be included into the Conference. 4. Mortgages to come under the control of the Governing Body, with legal exemption being granted to those who had previously controlled them. 5. A sustentation fund to be established for disabled, widows and orphans; a subsidy fund to be established for poorer churches. 6. A Book of Order to be made available to everyone to show how the Movement was governed. 7. Each church to have control of its property under the Model Trust Deed, and so jointly own the church with the Movement. 8. Each church to have elders and deacons. (Conference Minutes 1939) Ibid.

[6] Lay Representatives were members of local Elim church leaderships. The Conference acceded to Jeffreys' wishes with regards to lay representatives. Each church was allowed to appoint a representative to attend the Conference and take part in the discussions and vote. There were two sessions of Conference: Ministerial and Representative. It was the Representative Session of Conference that was deemed the Governing Body of the Movement.

[7] No 6 of the 8-point plan presented to Conference by Jeffreys.

[8] Minutes of the Ministerial Conference of the Elim Foursquare Alliance, 20th November to 2nd December 1939. (No 9 of the Conference response to the 8 proposals made to the Conference by George Jeffreys). The official Conference Minutes are kept at the Elim Archives, Regents Theological College, West Malvern.

[9] Kay, William, *George Jeffreys: Pentecostal Apostle and Revivalist*, (Cleveland, Tennessee: CPT Press, 2017), p347

[10] George Jeffreys had come to believe that each Elim church should own its property.

[11] Minutes of the 1939 Ministerial Conference.

[12] Minutes of the 1939 Ministerial Conference.

[13] Hudson, Neil, *A schism and its aftermath. An historical Analysis of denominational Discerption in the Elim Pentecostal Church 1939-1940.* (PhD Dissertation, King's College, 1999) Author's Italics

[14] Minutes of the 1939 Conference, Tuesday 21st November, 1939.

[15] E J speech to 1939 Conference, Tuesday, 21st November, (Malvern: Elim Archives)

[16] This letter was included with the notes that the Stenographer, Mabel Dalton, and that formed the minutes of the Conference. The minutes included in these series of papers that are titled 'MINUTES OF ANNUAL MINISTERIAL AND GENERAL CONFERENCES AND ANNUAL PREBYTERY MEETING HELD AT ELIM TABERNACLE, PARK CRESCENT, CLAPHAM, LONDON, S.W.4. NOVEMBER 20TH – DECEMBER 1ST 1939

[17] 1939 Conference Minutes, ibid.

[18] The Pattern was a pamphlet that was published in November 1939 outlining Jeffreys' views on Church government, in particular that of establishing deacons and elders in the local church and allowing lay representatives to be admitted onto the governing body of the Alliance. This became a monthly magazine published by the Bible Pattern Movement.

[19] 1939 Conference Minutes, ibid.

[20] 1939 Conference minutes, Thursday morning, 23rd November.

3
Fallout

Following the 1939 Conference when George Jeffreys resigned from Elim, strenuous efforts were made to effect a reconciliation. The idea had been mooted during the Conference debates that Jeffreys should cease to be involved in the business side of the work and devote himself to the spiritual leadership of the Movement.

In his devastating speech to the 1939 Ministerial Conference, E J referred to 'the scores of schemes drawn up by G J – schemes (he) never troubled you with, but troubled us (the Executive Council) for years. In addition, literally hundreds if not a thousand letters during past years arguing and setting out all kinds of schemes.'[1] Phillips made it clear that in his opinion, Jeffreys was not fighting for a principle, rather, he was fighting for his own way. Phillips felt that he had submitted 'more than enough evidence to suggest that G J is totally unfitted for the business side of the work of God.'[2] The final few lines of Phillips's speech make it clear that although he considered Jeffreys to be totally unsuited to the business side of the work things would dramatically improve if Jeffreys were to lay aside the business side of the organisation and concentrate upon his evangelistic giftings.

> In Acts 6, the twelve called seven men for the business side of the work, and said "We will give ourselves continually to Prayer and to the ministry of the Word."[3] If the Principal would only take his hands off the government of the work, we would forget the past and I believe there would be a new lease of life for Elim. Left to ourselves, without interference, even

now by the grace of God we can solve Elim's problems. I believe we could evolve a scheme that could bring the whole work together. We might even manage to solve the Irish problem. Apart from this I see disaster and we may as well face up to it. But if he (G J) would give up his power to appoint nominees, and promise not to interfere with the government of the work in any way, the work could be saved. If he would remain head of this work but with no more to say as to its government than King George VI has to the government of this land, then we would gladly work with him, and I believe once more the blessing of God would rest on the Elim work which we love and for which we have almost given our life's blood.[4]

Phillips realised that the parting of the ways between Jeffreys and Elim was virtually inevitable, but he provided a formula by which Jeffreys could remain as spiritual leader of the Movement, but be excluded from having a major say in its business affairs. It is worth noting that in the copy of his speech, E J underlined some of his words but crossed out others. In the above quotation, for example, he underlined the words 'give up his power', but had crossed out the immediate phrase prior to that which read 'withdraw from the Executive.' This shows that Phillips was not out to destroy the Principal, but to get the work on an even footing. His longing was always that Jeffreys should return to Pioneer Evangelism, a work that he had sadly neglected since 1935.

One can imagine how the ministers that were present at the 1939 Conference felt on returning to their home assemblies. Many of them had come into the Elim work through Jeffreys' ministry. He had established a great number of the churches that they presently ministered in. Whilst there was a strong majority in agreement with the comments and observations of E J they would have been extremely saddened by the loss of the founder of Elim. Their spirits rose slightly when it seemed that a role was being created for Jeffreys that would see him lead in a non-executive role. On 5th December, they were given the following information by Elim Headquarters in a circular letter:

Principal George Jeffreys, who for some time has intimated his desire along these lines, has resigned from the Executive Council, and is thus released from the business side of the work. This will free him more fully for his spiritual ministry in the work of the Lord, which God has so signally blessed in the past.[5]

The fact was, that in resigning as a minister of the Alliance, Jeffreys automatically lost his place on the Executive Council. There had been some discussion around the possibility of him taking the position of Moderator and the Executive Council, now led by Phillips, certainly hoped that this would take place. However, a few days after the 1939 Conference, Jeffreys published an article under the heading of 'Why I resigned from the Elim Movement'. This was followed by a reply from the Executive Council, published on 20th December.

George Jeffreys in his reasons for resigning from the Movement that he had founded, made the issue of local church government and property the main reasons for his resignation. In his view, it was the last of these eight points that he considered the cause of division.[6] In Jeffreys' opinion, as expressed in the article concerned. 'The division came on the above question, for I wanted every church to have a Model trust deed, so that its interests would be safeguarded for all time by the church members themselves. To my mind, this Model Trust Deed was essential if justice was to be done to the people of our churches.'[7]

Phillips was always of the opinion that the main reason for Jeffreys' desire for reformation was not so much on the local ownership of church property, but Jeffreys' determination to allow local churches the right to include secondary doctrinal issues into their local constitutions. This would pave the way for Jeffreys' pet doctrine of British Israelism to be taught freely in Elim churches.

Jeffreys was determined that local churches be allowed freedom of expression on matters of secondary doctrinal issues. The Minutes of the 1939 Conference revealed that the delegates gave careful consideration to each of Jeffreys points. On the second point: the Minutes record the following: 'The question of Property was then discussed, and the proposal of the Principal that a committee of laymen be appointed to meet the Executive and discuss the property question was negatived.'[8]

The following section of Phillips' reply to Jeffreys' many demands is important in our evaluation of Jeffreys' reasons for leaving Elim, as it gives credence to Phillips' firm opinion that the real reason behind the resignation was Jeffreys' desire for British Israelism to be taught as a secondary doctrine in Elim:

> On point No. 2, the Principal agreed, but stated it was not sufficient, each church he claimed should include (a) that a Church Membership be appointed with power to vote its officers. (b) No sale of property or change of doctrine or procedure to be enforced upon any local church apart from a majority vote of the members. (c) No change of doctrine or procedure to be adopted by the church apart from the consent of the governing body.[9]

'The Principal said the grounds given by the Conference virtually contained a censure and a restriction of free expression in the governing body (the Conference). He claimed ministers should be free in a constitutional manner to contend for principles which are considered to be vital.'[10]

Pamphlets

One of the saddest and inglorious actions of the very sad division within Elim occurred shortly after the conclusion of the 1939 Conference. It came in the form of a pamphlet issued by George Jeffreys under the heading: 'Why I Resigned from Elim'. This was published after the Conference. In this pamphlet, Jeffreys claimed that he had 'no quarrel with anyone'. He states his disagreement with the form of government that prevailed in Elim:

> 'For some years I have been at variance with the system of government in Elim which is, in my opinion, most unfair to our people. I have tried and failed to change the system

because unfortunately a majority on the Executive Council and also a majority in the Conference regarded my continual efforts to bring about certain reforms as being uncalled for.'[11]

It is somewhat disingenuous of Jeffreys to have written that he had been at variance with the system of Church government in Elim for 'some years'. He was the one who commissioned E J Phillips to draw up the Deed Poll and of which he, personally, was the signator. Phillips consulted with Jeffreys on every point of the Deed Poll and nothing was finalised without the Principal's permission.

An interesting fact in Jeffreys' antagonism to the governance of Elim at the time is that he recognised that there was a majority in the Conference who did not want the changes that he was advocating. He referred to the all-embracive power granted to the Executive Council regarding ownership of church property. He expressed his disappointment at the failure of the Ministerial Conference to introduce lay representation to the churches. This would have resulted in a balanced government of ministers and laymen on a 50-50 basis. According to Jeffreys, this was turned down by a large majority of the ministers. Yet, commenting on this, the third of his eight points presented to Conference, he states: 'The above will not be granted until a two-thirds majority of the Ministerial Conference votes for it.' Having been a minister of the Elim Pentecostal Church for fifty-four years, I can attest to the fact that major changes to the constitution have always required a two-thirds majority, and where changes to the Deed Poll are made, the required majority is 75% in two successive years. The 1939 Conference did not reject lay representation at Conference, it merely expressed the fact that it would require a substantial majority for the legislation to be approved. Indeed, just three years later, the Deed Poll was altered and a Representative Session of Conference was provided for which allowed laymen to be part of the governing body of the Elim Movement. The same decisions were made concerning the creation of District Presbyteries and the appointment of local church sessions comprising of deacons and elders.

Jeffreys argued that the real cleavage came between himself and the Conference when negotiations commenced on a proposed Deed of Trust or a Model Trust Deed. Jeffreys stated that he wanted sufficient time to meet with a responsible body of representative laymen from the churches to consider the clauses that should be placed within the deed.[12] It was at this point that the Conference seemed to lose patience with the Principal and presented him with their own ultimatum which required him to an agreement embodying the terms agreed at the Conference; the number of laymen to be limited to six and that he would undertake not to contend against the Elim Constitution by means of circular letter, printed matter or organised effort.

Following the decision of Conference, George attended the morning meeting on 1st December and made the following statement:

> Today I feel led of God to resign my position as your Leader, both in the Elim Foursquare Gospel Alliance and also in the Elim Church Incorporated. I do so because I can no longer subscribe to the policy you are following in the work. The Leader of any movement should be one with the policy of the movement he leads.[13]

Jeffreys goes on to acknowledge the decision of the Conference to place on record 'its deep and heartfelt gratitude to him under God, for his untiring and loyal service during the 25 years of his labours as Founder and Leader of the Alliance.'[14] He also acknowledged a further proposal: 'that this Ministerial Conference wishes to record its earnest desire that Principal George Jeffreys should forthwith accept office as Moderator of the Elim Alliance and remain Principal of the Elim Bible College.' As reported in the pamphlet, E J Phillips, the Secretary-General made a personal appeal to George Jeffreys to remain on as head of the movement, without Executive work, as desired by the Conference. Jeffreys was again unable to commit himself to a decision until he had consulted with 'a few lay brethren'. According to Jeffreys, these

34

brethren did not deal with the governing body of the Elim, but simply concentrated on the needs of the local church.

The eight points that they presented, were very much the same as those debated at the Conference and which were to be approved by the 1942 Deed of Variance. But the eighth point was different to the one presented to Conference. It read: 'A majority vote of the Church to reject or accept any change in Doctrine and Procedure proposed by the Governing Body.' Phillips had been adamant in his opinion that the underlying reason for Jeffreys wanting to dramatically alter the Deed Poll was to give local churches the right to be the final arbiters on matters of secondary doctrine. This would have given Jeffreys the green light to push his British-Israelite views. This was the crux of the whole issue as far as E J was concerned. The last of these 'new' eight points seems to indicate that he was absolutely correct in his understanding of the real reason for Jeffreys' departure from Elim.

A Reply

Elim's reply to Jeffreys' pamphlet has E J's fingerprints all over it. Regret was expressed as to the necessity of such a response. A summary of Elim's organization was provided and an explanation given for the requirement of the Deed Poll in 1934 which was signed by the Principal, in which the Constitution of the Alliance was set out. Reference was made to the Principal's response to the Deed Poll which had been set out in the Elim Evangel:

> The Constitution of the Elim Foursquare Gospel Alliance has now been set out in a Deed Poll which has been duly enrolled in the Supreme Court of Judicature. Thus in the event of the home-call of any of its present leaders, suitable and satisfactory provision has been made for the continuance of the activities of the work. The whole Movement is now governed by an Executive Council which is elected by the Ministerial Conference. A new Trust Corporation is being formed for holding property in trust, and, as in the past, no Church building for which any money has been subscribed

or given will be held by any individual personally. Thus it will be seen that the hitherto foundation upon which the Elim Alliance has been built is being strengthened, and the magnificent work of the past is more than ever being consolidated and conserved.[15]

Elim's reply makes it clear that the Executive Council considered that George Jeffreys' strongly held British Israelism teaching was at the heart of the schism between himself and the Movement that he had founded. Apparently, the Principal threatened to resign if the subject was not allowed to be debated in Conference. The other concern that was raised in Elim's reply was that Jeffreys took up and advocated a system of local government. 'The Executive knowing full well that such systems in other denominations had led to divisions and disruption, opposed the scheme, but in order to meet the Principal, they sanctioned the formation of a Local Government Section in Elim. The results of this experiment fully justified the fears of the Executive Council.'[16]

It must be understood that nearly all of Jeffreys' requests for reformation of church government within Elim had been accepted. He acknowledged this when he wrote: 'The Executive Council of Elim has now agreed in principle, to the seven points I had previously laid down as a basis for an agreement between themselves and the Elim churches under their control. For this we are truly thankful to God in answering the prayers of the large family of praying warriors in our beloved Elim.'[17] This is quite a remarkable statement written just a month after he had announced his resignation from Elim. In the previous month's edition of the Pattern, he wrote: 'Since I wrote PATTERN No 1, I have been led of God to resign absolutely from the Elim Movement.'[18] Having tendered his resignation, he was still intent on calling the shots as far as church government within Elim was concerned.

Notes

[1] Phillips, E J, *General Survey*, Notes of speech to the 1939 Ministerial Conference, (Malvern: Elim Archives)

2 Phillips, E J, *General Survey,* ibid.

3 Acts 6:4, A V.

4 Phillips, E J, *General Survey,* ibid.

5 Cartwright, Desmond, *The Great Evangelists, The Remarkable lives of George and Stephen Jeffreys,* (Basingstoke: Marshal, Morgan and Scott, 1986) p155.

6 The wording of the eighth point is as follows: 'Each church to have reasonable control of its own Church property, under a proper Model Trust Deed, so that the building would be held jointly by the Church and the Governing Body of the Movement, like other denominations.'

7 Jeffreys, George, *Why I resigned from the Elim Movement,* (Malvern: Elim Archives)

8 1939 Conference Minutes, ibid.

9 1939 Conference Minutes, ibid.

10 1939 Conference Minutes, ibid.

11 Jeffreys, George, ibid.

12 Jeffreys, George, ibid, p3.

13 Jeffreys, George, ibid, p3.

14 Minutes of the 1939 Elim Conference, ibid.

15 *Elim Evangel* 15th June, 1934: quoted in *A Reply to the Pamphlet by Principal George Jeffreys entitled: "Why I resigned from the Elim Movement."* (Malvern: Elim Archives, 1940)

16 *A Reply:* ibid.

17 Jeffreys, George, *Changes in the Elim Government* (*The Pattern:* Vol 1, No. 2, February 1940) p3.

18 Jeffreys, George, *Can I accept the Office of Moderator in Elim?* (*The Pattern:* Vol 1, No 1, December 1939) p4.

4
At War

Civil War

On the 10th May, the reality of war came crashing upon the consciousness of the British people when it was learned that Germany had invaded Holland and Belgium. It was in the same months that the reality of the internal division within Elim began to dawn upon the thinking of Elim members. It is too easy to come to the conclusion that Elim was so taken up with its internal problems that the second world war was secondary in the minds of Elim ministers and members. An examination of the Elim Evangel during this period shows that this was not the case. There was very little mentioned in the Evangel concerning the division between George Jeffreys and the Executive Council. Whilst there is some justification in criticism of the Elim leadership in its somewhat scant reporting of the war, it must be remembered that there were strict regulations on what could or could not be printed during the war years. There were obvious restrictions placed on war-time publications. The war-time Evangel was quite different in appearance from its pre-war production. There was no colour in them and a lack of photographs.

The Evangel did record some aspect of war-time activity in nearly every edition. An article appeared in the June 24th, 1940 edition under the title 'The Invasion of Belgium'. Belgium was invaded by Germany in the previous month and Elim's missionary to Belgium, Pastor Archie Scott wrote an account of their escape from Belgium. He recalled the siren sounding on the morning of invasion and realised that their work in Belgium would be curtailed and finally terminated. Scott refers to the rapid advance of the enemy. What was unleashed upon France and the Low Countries was 'blitzkrieg', a form of warfare that was unknown in previous wars. As a result of a pact with Stalin, Hitler had been able to concentrate all his attention on the western front. On 10th May, 1940, Hitler unleashed his massive forces which amounted to one hundred and fifty-five divisions, of which ten were the armoured 'Panzer' divisions. 'Hitler was therefore in a position to deliver his onslaught on France (and Holland and Belgium)[1] with 126 divisions and the whole immense armour-weapon of ten Panzer divisions, comprising nearly three thousand Panzer divisions, comprising nearly three thousand armoured vehicles, of which a thousand at least were heavy tanks.'[2]

British citizens had very short notice of the need for evacuation. Scott gives the following account of the evacuation of himself and family:

> On Wednesday, after the invasion, at four a.m., we were obliged to leave all and flee to France. It was with heavy hearts that we said 'Good-bye' to the one or two around us. We were now in reality some of those of whom we had read so often – refugees. Oh, what a God we have! Although our train was attacked three times not one hit was registered, there being at one instance thirty German bombers over our head. The Saturday evening, we were welcomed at Victoria Station by Pastor J. Smith, and what a joy it was, dirty and tired as we were, to be received with such kindness! Never shall we forget that service of love. When we were in our room at the College the door was continually knocked by one friend or another with, 'Would this comb and brush be any help'…etc.[3]

The same edition of the Evangel reported a special service for the troops at a camp 'somewhere in Wales'. The report was by P S Brewster the Pastor of the City Temple, Cardiff. The report states that Brewster and others with him went to the camp and requested to see the Commanding Officer, and offered to send a number of double decker buses if he would rally his men and allow them to come for a great service of Prayer and Thanksgiving. Some of the soldiers at the camp were recent survivors of Dunkirk and some had seen action in Norway. The C.O. consented and there was great interest within the camp for such a service. No doubt, the provision of a light supper for the men was an added attraction.

> On Sunday, the huge City Temple at Cardiff was packed to suffocation and the singing was an inspiration. To see row after row filled with soldiers singing heartily and looking as though they were enjoying the house of the Lord was very gratifying. There is undoubtedly a seeking after God. At the close of the meeting seven hands were raised to accept Christ as personal Saviour. These were all prayed with and handed a convert book, and we believe their names were recorded in heaven. The way is gradually opening so that regular services can be held in the camps, to the obvious delight of the men.[4]

This was just one example of how Elim responded to the changed conditions for evangelism even as they coped with the privations caused by the attacks on the major cities.

The Unity Conference

Great efforts were made both within and outside Elim to bring about a reconciliation between George Jeffreys together with the Revival Party and the Executive Council. Hopes were high that such reconciliation could be achieved. Ludwig Naumann, 'a consecrated Pentecostal business man of London'[5], had tried on a number of occasions to bring before the leaders of the various Pentecostal movements in the British Isles the need for a greater sense of unity. His efforts were unsuccessful due largely to the fact that most of the leaders were taken up with concerns in their own particular areas of responsibility. 'By 1938, however, there had come imperceptibly, a definite change of attitude; and to the surprise of all, a renewed invitation by Mr. Naumann to a Pentecostal Unity

Conference brought a favourable response from brethren from every section of the Movement.'[6] Gee speaks glowingly of this first Unity Conference and writes:

> Embarrassment vanished as soon as the assembled company dropped on their knees in worship and prayer. The Spirit of God fell upon them immediately, and great grace came upon all. The brethren realised that beneath all their different strong convictions upon many important matters there existed the eternal fundamental unity of the Spirit as Christ's own gift to the members of His Body. The Rock was there, and our feet felt it.[7]

A Second Unity Conference was held at the Kensington Temple, London 22-25 January 1940. Gee is of the opinion that the second conference did not attain to the spiritual unity of the first one and expresses the opinion that human weaknesses presented many difficulties in the hope of achieving true unity within the various British Pentecostal streams.[8] He does conclude, however, that the opportunity for the various leaders to enjoy personal fellowship was enhanced by the presence of the Spirit in their midst.[9]

The Unity Conference, which had representatives from Elim, Assemblies of God, The Apostolic Church and the Bible Pattern Fellowship, was well received by George Jeffreys and a full report of it was published in the Pattern. Alongside the report, there is an article written by Jeffreys under the heading: 'Comments on the Unity Conference'.[10] He highlighted the fact that a 'So-called Layman' (Ludwig Naumann) was the Chairman'. Jeffreys noted that there were representatives from 'practically all the Apostolic and Pentecostal bodies in the land gathered together for Conference.'[11] The purpose of the Conference was laid out as follows: 'Under the big-hearted Chairmanship of Mr Naumann these brethren had gathered with the object of uniting the forces of Christ – not with the idea of merging many organisations into one, but of creating a United Spiritual Fellowship, which would function for the Glory of our Lord in these days of international strife and supernatural revival.'[12] The writer of this particular report on the Unity Conference is not mentioned, although it is most likely that it was written by Jeffreys. The reference to 'supernatural revival' as though the heady days of the 1920's and early 30's were continuing seems somewhat unsubstantiated at this time when the Movement that Jeffreys had planted was in the midst of great turmoil. After commenting on the need of locally appointed elders, Jeffreys comments on the crisis in Elim. Considering that he had resigned from Elim some seven weeks prior to this Conference, Jeffreys writes as though he is still very much a part of Elim. His comments are included in full:

> Some of us who had been called to the Conference wondered what effect the crisis in Elim would have upon the Unity Conference. The crisis had brought to the notice of the whole of the Pentecostal Movement such questions as Church Government; Church Procedure; Church Property; Church Finances, and the questions of Doctrine and Prophecy; some of the very things that had been the cause of division amongst Pentecostal people for years. Yet one breathed freely as discernment registered sympathy for Elim from the hearts of the brethren from the other Movements.
>
> It was a touching moment and one that can never be forgotten, as one after another from the different Movements offered their services as mediators between the two sides of the situation in Elim. There was also a sigh of relief when the Elim Executive made advances towards a settlement and produced their Statement, 'A basis for Unity in Elim'. Quite a few of the brethren told me afterwards that their prayers would follow us as we sought to clarify the necessary points to be put before the Elim people for acceptance.[13]

The statement 'A Basis for Unity in Elim' did not gloss over the difficulties that were existent in the Movement and a robust defence was made by the Executive Council of their position. Mention was made of three pamphlets that had been printed, 'the first by Principal Jeffreys, followed by a reply from the Executive

Council, and another Reply to our leaflet by Principal Parker.'[14]The Executive Council had taken exception to Mr. Parker's 'attempts to prove there were a number of inaccuracies in the statement issued by the Executive Council'. The following statement made the stance taken by the Executive Council on Mr Parker's 'Reply' very clear: 'In that pamphlet Mr. Parker attempts to prove there were a number of inaccuracies in the statement issued by the Executive Council. While the Executive is prepared to prove to the hilt every statement in its pamphlet, and to show conclusively that Mr. Parker's pamphlet abounds in statements which are absolutely contrary to facts, we do not desire to publish a reply, as we feel that only harm is being done to the work by flooding our Churches with conflicting pamphlets.'[15]

Reference was made in the statement by the Executive Council to the Seven Points published in The Pattern, dated January 1940[16]. The Elim Unity Pamphlet highlighted the main point on which there was acute difference of opinion and it was Lay Representation from the Churches on a large Governing Body of the Alliance.

> There were two reasons why the Ministerial Conference did not accept this proposal.
>
> [1] There was no general demand for it in our churches.
> [2] It was considered to be another method, of which there had been a number in recent years, whereby the Principal hoped to introduce British-Israel teaching into the work.
>
> The above arguments no longer apply, for –
> As regards the first point, there is now evidence that a very strong demand has been created by the publication of the Principal's pamphlet.
> As regards the second point, the reference to the British-Israel situation in our pamphlet has revealed a strong opposition amongst laymen to the introduction of British-Israel teaching to our churches.[17]

This clearly shows the willingness of the Executive Council to be persuaded by the laymen in the churches to bring into the General

Conference, lay representatives on a 50-50 basis. They were, however, determined in their resolve not to allow British Israelism to be included as a secondary doctrine in the Elim churches.

The other note of concern within the Unity pamphlet was the issue of each local church having its own Trust Deed. The last two paragraphs are quoted in full because it shows the Executive Council's concerns as to the Principal's terms for creating the Trust Deed and also it summarises the Executive Council's desire for unity.

> To this Trust Deed we have agreed in principle. Cleavage came on the question of the terms of the Deed and the manner in which these terms were to be decided. The Principal now requests that it shall be decided by a representative body of ministers and lay brethren from the churches. We suggest that these terms shall be decided at the full meeting of the new Governing Body with ministers and laymen on a 50/50 basis. The position can then be fully gone into, and their decision will be final.
>
> From the foregoing it will be seen that agreement can be reached on all these points, and we now submit our views, praying that the threatened division in Elim may yet be avoided and that peace and unity may prevail, that the work of Christ among us may go forward, and that the future of Elim may be bright with the promise of a still greater outpouring of the Holy Spirit upon Ministers, Church Officers, and congregations, as well as on the Principal and member of the Executive Council.[18]

The Final Parting

A day of prayer for all Elim ministers was held on 6th February at the Bible College before two days of meetings between Jeffreys and the Executive Council on 9-10 February.[19] There were very high hopes of there being a settlement to this dispute. We must not underestimate the steps that the Executive Council went to in order to make room for Jeffreys' demands. Once they had agreed to a

General Conference consisting of ministers and lay representatives, they went ahead with changing the Deed Poll in order to cater for this. Although the Revision of the Deed Poll was not completed until 1942, the Council made provision for lay representatives to be present at all future General Conferences from 1940 onwards.

There were strong hopes for a renewing of fellowship with brethren that had almost been lost to each other. 'And then without warning at all these hopes were dashed when Jeffreys conjured a new requirement and circulated it in a pamphlet.'[20] Jeffreys now demanded that all supplementary doctrines should be decided by the local church. This latest demand was a clear vindication of E J Phillips' oft repeated view that the real kernel of Jeffreys' demand was to allow British Israel teaching to come into Elim via the local church.

W G Hathaway, sent a letter to each minister and asked them to call an immediate meeting of their deacons to discuss this latest demand by Jeffreys. This was the point of no return as far as the Executive Council was concerned. That the letter came from Hathaway who had a record as a peacemaker in the ongoing dispute is very significant. In his letter, dated 17th May, 1940, Hathaway refers to the coming Conference in which mutual recommendations had been agreed upon at a meeting between the Executive Council and the Principal and his Advisory Committee were agreed upon and were to be placed before a General Conference consisting of ministers and lay representatives. An Agenda had been drawn up and agreed upon. Hathaway comments: 'Now, in addition to the Mutual Recommendations, this question of supplementary doctrines has been imposed as a fresh condition to unity.'[21]

The 1940 Elim Conference was a landmark in the Movement's history. For the very first time, the Conference admitted lay representatives into its ranks. The Conference Minutes record that there were 'About 75 ministers and About 75 lay representatives... '[22] The first item that came under discussion was concerning supplementary doctrine. The Minutes record the following: 'Finally, it was RESOLVED "That all questions of Doctrine outside of the Fundamentals be decided by the Governing Body, with liberty of expression for different interpretations of prophecy in the churches." The voting conducted by ballot, supported the motion: 83 for the motion, 75 against.[23] This surely met Jeffreys' perennial concern since British Israelism was customarily classified as a form of prophetic interpretation. By a narrow margin he had secured the option to teach what he wanted.'[24] The closeness of the vote revealed the unease that existed within Elim concerning the right to grant liberty for the teaching of various prophetic interpretations. However, the reason that it was passed at all, is undoubtedly down to the first part of the proposal which clearly gave the authority of changes to supplementary doctrines firmly to the Conference. The legislation passed by the Conference meant that in any proposed changes on supplementary doctrines would have to be approved by the Conference.

One of the most complex decisions that the Conference had to address was that of the Office of Moderator. It must be remembered that Jeffreys was no longer an Elim minister, he had resigned the previous year. The lengthy minute reveals that there must have been a great deal of discussion and debate on the issues. It reads as follows:

> The Conference gave very careful consideration to this point (The office of Moderator)[25], and there was a desire in the interests of unity that Principal Jeffreys should return to the Movement. The Principal expressed his wish to return to the Movement as an Evangelist, to continue revival work, but not to take office as Moderator. There was a sincere desire among those present that a basis of agreement should be reached on this point. It was eventually RESOLVED 'That Principal George Jeffreys be asked to withdraw his resignation as President of the Elim Church Incorporated, and return in that capacity to the Elim Movement. The voting of the whole Conference, including those in attendance was as follows: For the motion, 158: Against, 10. Principal Jeffreys thereupon intimated in the Conference his acceptance of

the proposal, and verbally withdrew his resignation from the Elim Church Incorporated.[26]

However, within a few short months, Jeffreys made his final break with the Movement that he had founded. He resigned a second time in November 1940 on the very dubious grounds that nothing had changed since his resignation a year earlier. One can only assume that he did not consider the very significant decisions of the Conference with respect to Lay membership and Trust Deeds etc. to be of such triviality that they were not worthy of being referred to as 'changes. It is clear that the Principal was determined to get his own way. The final break had come. George Jeffreys, the founder of the Elim Movement, resigned finally in November 1940 never to re-join.

Notes

[1] Author's parenthesis.

[2] Churchill, Winston, *Their Finest Hour: The Second World War, Volume II*: (London: Penguin Classics 2005), p27.

[3] *Elim Evangel: The Invasion of Belgium* (W Archie and E Scott), Vol 21, No.26, p411.

[4] *Elim Evangel, Special Service for the Troops*: P S Brewster: 24th June, 1940, Vol 21, No 26, p406

[5] Gee, Donald, *The Pentecostal Movement*: (London: Elim Publishing Company Limited, 1949), p169.

[6] Gee, Donald, ibid: p170.

[7] Gee, Donald, ibid: p170.

[8] Gee, Donald, ibid: p171.

[9] Gee, Donald, ibid, p171.

[10] *The Pattern*, Vol 1, No 2: February 1940, p7.

[11] The Conference was held in the YMCA, Great Russell Street, London, but the evening rallies were held in Kensington Temple.

[12] *The Pattern*: ibid: p6.

[13] *The Pattern: Comments on the Unity Conference* by George Jeffreys, ibid: p7.

[14] *A Basis for Unity in Elim*: A Statement by the Executive Council of the Elim Foursquare Gospel Alliance: January 1940: (Malvern: Elim Archives)

[15] *A Basis for Unity*: ibid.

[16] Actually, there is no mention of the seven points in the January 1940 edition of the Pattern. The seven points are mentioned in Jeffreys' pamphlet: *Why I Resigned from Elim* December 1939, (Malvern: Elim Archives).

[17] *A Basis for Unity*: ibid.

[18] *A Basis for Unity*: ibid.

[19] Kay, William, *George Jeffreys*, p356

[20] Kay, William, ibid, p357.

[21] Hathaway, W G: Letter to Ministers: CL.21. 17th May, 1940: (Malvern: Emil Archives).

[22] Minutes of the Elim Conference: May, 1940.

[23] Minutes: ibid: Item 2.

[24] Kay, William; ibid: p359.

[25] Author's parenthesis.

[26] Minutes of the Elim Conference: May 1940.

5
Guernsey Occupied

The 1940 Elim Conference was held at a very grave time in the history of the United Kingdom; the dates of the Conference being 20-24 May. By this time, the 'phoney war' spoken on in an earlier chapter had well and truly ended. The German army had swept across the low countries and had entered France. It became clear that the British Expeditionary Force would have to be withdrawn. Churchill, being aware of the plight of over 300,000 British and Commonwealth troops crowding the beaches of Dunkirk ordered the British Admiralty to arrange as many ships as possible to cross over to ports and inlets of the north-eastern coast of France in order to evacuate the British Expeditionary Force from total annihilation.

On the 18th May Antwerp, Belgium's main port, fell to the Germans. Churchill, just a few days after becoming Prime Minister, telegraphed President Roosevelt to 'show how seriously the interests of the United States would be affected by the conquest and subjugation not only of France, but of Great Britain.'[1] Germany had conquered Holland and Belgium and Churchill was fearful that a similar fate awaited the United Kingdom. In all his correspondence with Roosevelt, Churchill referred to himself as 'Formal Naval Person'. It was in this manner that he addressed the United States President on the evening of 18th May.

> I do not need to tell you about the gravity of what has happened. We are determined to persevere to the very end, whatever the result of the great battle raging in France may be. We must expect in any case to be attacked here on the Dutch

model before very long, and we hope to give a good account of ourselves. But if American assistance is to play any part it must be available soon.[2]

In a further communication with Roosevelt that same day, Churchill firmly expressed the determination of the war cabinet that 'our intention is, whatever happens to fight on to the end in this island.'[3]

National Day of Prayer

Whilst the Elim Conference was in session, there was an overwhelming sense of foreboding in the country due to the plight of the British forces on the beaches of Dunkirk. The German High Command boasted that its troops were about to annihilate the British Army. The Prime Minister found himself preparing to announce to the public an unprecedented military catastrophe involving the death or capture of a third of a million soldiers. That this did not happen is, in the minds of very many people, not just Christians, an amazing answer to prayer. On 23rd May, the King, George VI, encouraged by the Prime Minister, requested that the following Sunday, 26th May, should be observed as a National Day of Prayer. The nation responded and devoted itself to prayer in a way that it had not done so previously. Churches, chapels and other places of worship were filled to capacity with people praying for the nation.

The 'Miracle of Dunkirk' was just that! At the Cabinet meeting of 20th May, Churchill expressed the following suggestion: 'The Prime Minister thought that as a precautionary measure the Admiralty should assemble a large number of small vessels in in readiness to proceed to ports and inlets on the French coast.'[4] Subsequently, a conference was held in Dover that same day to consider 'the emergency evacuation across the Channel of very large forces.'[5] The plans for a massive evacuation of the British and allied forces from the beaches of Northern France was named 'Operation Dynamo'. A very rare and special Emergency Bill was presented to

Parliament that 'would give the Government practically unlimited power over the life, liberty and property of all His Majesty's subjects in Great Britain. In general terms of law the powers granted by Parliament were absolute.'[6]

The Elim Conference concluded its business on 24th May. Disappointment was expressed that no time had been available for discussion of efforts to extend the work due to the heavy programme that had been dealt with. Elim had been born as a result of evangelism, it was in the very fabric of the Movement. The Conference recognised that in spite of the throes of disunity and division that it had gone through, it was vital for the Movement to return to its core principle of reaching the nation with the Foursquare Gospel. 'It was therefore RESOLVED 'That the Conference approves the discussion from year to year and with a view to exploring all avenues for the extension of the Elim work in future.'"[7] The final matter that was discussed at the Conference was the Day of Prayer for the nation. The minutes record the following:

> The Conference expressed its appreciation of the attitude of the King in calling for a day of prayer for Sunday, May 26th, and the following telegram was sent to His Majesty:
> 'In view of the Day of Prayer which your Majesty has graciously commanded, we would respectfully request that in these grave times your Majesty consider the closing of Cinemas, places of amusement and public houses on this Day of Prayer, and that thus in contrition and prayer the whole nation may seek the face of God for His help and guidance.' From the Annual Conference of the Elim Foursquare Gospel Churches now in session in Clapham, London.'[8]

These last two resolutions of the Conference may not, at first, appear of any great significance, but it brought a sense of continuity into the minds of the delegates present. It reminded them of Elim's justification for existence: evangelism. Their founder and prime evangelist had been lost to them, but determination was expressed to continue with the task of reaching the nation with the Gospel. This was very much in the mind of the Executive

Council and at their quarterly meeting in April 1941, the following minute was recorded: 'RESOLVED that S. Gorman be appointed as Evangelistic Secretary.'[9] To some extent, this was a strange appointment as Samuel Gorman was not a renowned evangelist. He was recognised throughout the Movement as an outstanding Pastor and Teacher. Having said that, there was no-one on the Executive Council at that time who was renowned for conducting evangelistic campaigns, certainly not in the manner of George Jeffreys.[10] However, evangelism was very much in the mindset of Elim pastors at that time and it was expected of them to devote much of their energies in seeking to reach people with the Gospel of Christ.

In sending a telegram to the King at the end of its business session, the Conference was following a trend that had been established at its great gatherings throughout the twenties and thirties. George Jeffreys had, on a number of occasions sent greetings to the King on behalf of the Elim Movement. Although a seemingly small matter, such an action of sending a telegram to the King would have brought a sense of continuity to the delegates at such an uncertain time both in the Movement's and Nation's history.

Occupation

One of the chief concerns of the nation during most of 1940 was the imminent threat of invasion by Germany. The Dunkirk evacuation did not lessen the fear of invasion. However, the Dunkirk evacuation brought a sense of great relief to the British people. It is difficult to over-estimate the importance of the Dunkirk evacuation. The prayers of the British people, including thousands of Elim members, were answered in a quite remarkable manner.

> By midnight on 2nd June 1940 the Dunkirk evacuation was completed: 338,226 men had been evacuated in the space of seven days. British, Dutch and French ships, including 665 British civilian craft, had assisted in the evacuation. Hundreds of soldiers had been killed by German bombs during the

evacuation. The worst single disaster was the death of more than three hundred men when the Waverley, a paddle steamer that had been previously converted into a minesweeper, was subjected to half an hour of unremitting air attack.[11]

There is no doubt that the one factor that saved Britain from occupation by a ruthless and powerful enemy was the fact that she was an island nation. Churchill wrote movingly of the armada of little ships that made their way to and from Dover to Dunkirk saving hundreds of thousands of lives. He recognised that the protection of the sand dunes and Britain's prowess in the air would have been in vain without the sea:

> The sea was calm. To and from between the shore and the ships plied the little boats, gathering the men from the beaches as they waded out or picking them from the water, with total indifference to the air bombardment, which often claimed its victims. Their numbers alone defied air attack. The Mosquito Armada as a whole was unsinkable. In the midst of our defeat glory came to the island people, united and unconquerable; and the tale of the Dunkirk beaches will shine in whatever records are preserved of our affairs.[12]

The threat of invasion, however, was still very much in the thinking of the Cabinet. Time and again, Churchill emphasised that Britain would continue to fight on alone, with only her colonies to fight alongside her. The British Government were prepared to wage war from the New World, if through some disaster England herself were laid waste.'[13] Preparations were made for the defence of the nation including Anthony Eden's plan of raising Local Defence Volunteers. This met with an immediate response in all parts of the country. Churchill renamed this vital core of defence 'The Home Guard'. Herbert Morrison, one of the Labour members of the Cabinet had suggested the use of the term 'Civic Guard' but Churchill preferred the term 'Home Guard'.[14] Many Elim men signed up to serve in the Home Guard and a number of Elim pastors based in London were involved in supervising service during enemy aircraft bombardment when the underground stations were used as shelters when the bombs were falling.

Although mainland Britain resisted occupation by the German forces, one part of the British Isles suffered greatly in this respect – the Channel Islands. As far as the wider picture was concerned, the occupation of the Channel Islands was not a major episode in the Second World War, but to the islanders themselves, it produced all the problems and difficulties that people faced in the larger occupied countries. 'How far to collaborate with the enemy, what to do about resistance and sabotage, how far to endure isolation from friends and allies, how to tolerate extreme hunger and cold, how to face illness with inadequate medicines, how year after year to sustain morale when there was no certainty that they would be delivered.'[15]

The Elim Churches in Guernsey

When war broke out, there were three Elim churches in Guernsey: Eldad, Vazon and Delancey. Of the three, Vazon was the first established and considered to be the main Elim church on the Island. Vazon, in fact, was one of the first Elim Churches outside Ireland. Although, originally a Brethren Assembly known as the Cobo Mission, it gave birth to the Vale Mission and a small group within that Mission accepted the Pentecostal message. A meeting was set up in the home of Mr. Batiste who was to become one of the leaders of the fellowship. Meetings were held in the packing shed of Mr Batiste's tomato exporting business, the group met initially under the name of Vazon Mission. In 1921, the Vazon Mission joined the Elim Movement with Joseph Smith as its first pastor. [16]The Vazon Church planted a second church on the Island – Delancey, in 1934. A third Elim Church was established in 1936 in Eldad.

The occupation of the Channel Islands, was a great challenge to the people who lived there. It became clear that Britain was not going to be able to protect the islands from occupation. An evacuation plan was put into motion at the very last moment.

Thousands of people were evacuated from Guernsey, especially families. 'The transport of the evacuees, first to Weymouth, and then on to their wartime homes further north, was well managed, considering how short the notice was.' [17]

There were three Elim ministers in Guernsey at that time: John Woodhead at Vazon, Gilbert Dunk at Eldad and Arthur Jackson at Delancey. The three worked well together and there was close harmony between the three churches. This is clear from the Elim Evangel report of the Whitsun Convention on the island:

> It is acknowledged by all that the greatest Elim convention ever held on this island was this Whitsuntide, and every meeting has drawn record attendances. Owing to the limited accommodation at the Vazon Elim Church, a large canvas Tabernacle was hired and pitched near the sea at Vazon Bay. The Misses Virr of Bradford were the special speakers for the Convention and both their preaching and singing were a great inspiration to everyone. From all over the island, people thronged to hear these messengers of the Cross. The largest congregations ever registered at Vazon were those of the Sunday evening. On Monday a united convention of the three Elim churches was held in the tent when Pastors Dunk and Jackson and the Virr sisters were the speakers…Pastor Woodhead convened all the services and was very happy amongst such scenes of revivalism. [18]

Just a week after this report was published, the Channel Islands were invaded by Hitler's troops. Guernsey was invaded on 30th June. This had been preceded by bomb attacks on the islands where a total of 44 people had been killed, 23 of them in the raid on Guernsey. Philip Dunk, however, states that 'The final toll, (of casualties)[19] released the next morning was reported as: 29 deaths in Guernsey, 9 in Jersey with many more badly wounded.'[20]In the meanwhile, a swiftly organised evacuation plan was put into motion. On Sunday, 16th June, the Chiefs of Staff put forward a recommendation to the War Cabinet that the Channel Islands be demilitarised. The decision to abandon the Channel Islands was totally repugnant to Churchill. He was of the opinion that British Naval power could frustrate the invasion of the islands. 'If there was the slightest chance of a successful resistance, the Royal Navy must give battle.'[21]

It is estimated that almost one half of the population of Guernsey were evacuated. This included British Forces personnel and about 3,000 young men of call-up age who chose to serve in the British forces. But it was the evacuation of children and their mothers that caused the greatest heartache. The Elim churches, like all the churches in Guernsey were denuded of their Sunday School population overnight. Irene Dunk (Gilbert's wife), wrote:

> It was estimated that 5000 children were transported safely from the Island in 31 hours. An amazing effort, but many were the sad scenes in those hours. Men holding their children as if they could never let go: tears flowing freely as parents took their children to the boats: some panicking and rushing back home with them to reconsider then rushing them back to the boat once more…sometimes several times: anguish registering on faces, reflecting the turmoil within. They were days that one would never wish to see again.[22]

Gilbert and Irene Dunk made the decision to remain in Guernsey. It was hoped, and thought that the occupation would only last a few months. 'If the enemy did occupy the Islands the British government hoped that it would not be for long.'[23] Arthur Jackson, the Pastor of Delancey Elim Church sent his wife and two small children back to England whilst he stayed in Guernsey for a short time until he felt it was right for him to leave. Circumstances meant that once that decision had been taken, the 'short time' lasted for the duration of the war. Arthur Jackson was transported to a prisoner of war camp close to the Russian frontier in 1942.

> The Pastor of the Elim Church at Vazon, on the west coast, was Rev John Woodhead. After much prayer, John had taken his wife and two daughters on one of the boats back to England, intending to return alone, and continue his ministry. He was

due on the next return-sailing of the mail boat '*Isle of Sark*', however, due to the actions that followed in the next two days, was prevented from doing so.[24]

Churches across Britain were deeply affected by the impact of the Second World War. Their young men and women joined the forces and ancillary services which impacted greatly on numbers attending the services. The blackout, air-raids causing widespread destruction of home and church buildings, the evacuation of children from urban areas and the fear of invasion and ultimate defeat caused great challenges for Elim people as it did for all churches throughout the nation. 'But no churches in Britain experienced the difficulties of wartime to the same extent as the three Elim churches on the tiny Channel Island of Guernsey.'[25] The Elim churches on the Island not only survived, but thrived during the period of occupation by the German forces. That this was the case, was due in no small measure to the remarkable work of Gilbert and Irene Dunk, together with the sacrifice and courage of Arthur Jackson. More will be said concerning the ministry and legacy of Gilbert and Irene Dunk in a later chapter, but mention must be made here of the stoic heroism of Arthur Jackson. Having bid farewell to his young wife and two small children, in the hope that their separation would be comparatively short, he devoted himself to the work at Delancey and jointly with Gilbert Dunk, he helped pastor the Vazon church for over two years.

> Arthur Jackson was sent to a prison camp in September 1942, one of more than 1,000 men, women and children deported from Guernsey and Sark during 1942 and 1943 to Germany. Gilbert Dunk and his wife were only spared that fate because a Methodist minister, Rev Donald Stuart offered to go to Germany in his place. Rev Stuart and his wife had no children and he was close to retirement, his act of sacrifice which allowed Gilbert Dunk to stay with his young family led to Rev Stuart's death from malnutrition in Germany. Pastor Dunk became the minister of all three churches and led them through five years of isolation, oppression and fear.[26]

Notes

[1] Churchill, Winston, *Their Finest Hour: The Second World War, Volume 2* (London: Penguin Books 2005), p49.

[2] Churchill, Winston, *Their Finest Hour*, ibid, p51.

[3] Churchill, Winston, *Their Finest Hour*, ibid, p51.

[4] Churchill, Winston, *Their Finest Hour*, ibid, p52.

[5] Churchill, Winston, *Their Finest Hour*, ibid, p53.

[6] Churchill, Winston, *Their Finest Hour*, ibid, p56.

[7] Elim Conference Minutes: May 1940.

[8] Elim Conference Minutes: May 1940.

[9] Minutes of the Executive Council: 7th April, 1941: (Malvern: Elim International Offices).

[10] The Executive Council, elected by the Conference, at that time consisted of the following men: Pastors E C W Boulton, J T Bradley, F G Cloke, S Gorman, H W Greenaway, W G Hathaway, C J E Kingston, E J Phillips, and J Smith.

[11] Gilbert, Martin: *A History of the Twentieth Century, Volume Two 1933-1935:* (London: Harper-Collins Publishers 1998), p314.

[12] Churchill, Winston, *Their Finest Hour*, ibid, p92.

[13] Churchill, Winston, *Their Finest Hour*, ibid, p99.

[14] Churchill, Winston, *Their Finest Hour*, ibid, p147.

[15] Cruikshank, Charles, *The German Occupation of the Channel Islands* (Stroud: The History Press 2019) Preface: p.vii.

[16] Jones, Maldwyn: *And they came to Elim, Volume 1:1915-1940* (Rickmansworth: Instant Apostle, 2021): pp149,150

[17] Cruickshank, Charles, ibid, p46.

[18] *Elim Evangel*, Vol 21, No 26, 24th June, 1940, p406.

[19] Author's parenthesis.

[20] Dunk, Philip, *Occupation: Pastor, the Early life and times of Gilbert T S Dunk,* (Copyright, Philip M Dunk 2012) p69.

[21] Cruickshank, Charles, ibid, p23.

[22] Dunk, Philip, ibid, p.60.

[23] Cruikshank, Charles, ibid, p23.

[24] Dunk, Philip, ibid, p72.

[25] Cartwright, Chris with Holdaway, Jan and David, *Defining Moments, 100 years of the Elim Pentecostal Church* (Malvern: Elim Pentecostal Church, 2014), p73.

[26] Cartwright, Chris, ibid, p73.

6
A Slow Recovery

Elim, like every other Christian organisation had to adapt to war-time conditions. As mentioned in the previous chapter, it was a greater challenge to Elim than most other denominations because of the challenges caused by the blackout. The Gospel service, which was geared to attract non-church people, was held in the evenings. The effect of the blackout during the winter months had a dramatic impact on the Sunday evening Gospel service. Elim has always been traditionally strongest in the urban conurbations of the country. Elim's main churches were often located in the most dangerous areas – large industrial towns and cities. Whilst London was the main target of enemy bombing, port cities such as Liverpool, Hull, Portsmouth, Southampton, Plymouth, Bristol, Cardiff, Swansea and Belfast were particularly vulnerable as were the Midlands industrial centres such as Birmingham, Coventry, Leicester and Nottingham. Canty gives a somewhat depressing description of the chaos caused in Elim churches at this time. The effects of the war and schism within Elim meant that the crowds just melted away.

> Sometimes no more than half a dozen gathered, perhaps around a coke stove in some wretched hall close-curtained to emit a chink of light in the total blackout. Four-fifths of the world were eventually engulfed in the conflict. The lights of Europe did not go out one by one as Sir Edward Grey's too often quoted words put it, but all at once, literally. Church

goers groped their way with shielded electric torches, if they could get a battery, often breathing acrid smoke-screen protecting industrial plants.[1]

The evacuation of children and the call-up to the armed forces or to other aspects of national service, placed many young people in strange places and jobs far removed from an Elim Church.[2] In a very short time, a church might be reduced of three-quarters of its Sunday evening congregation.

The evacuation of children had a profound effect on the youth activities of the churches, particularly in London. G H Thomas, the pastor of the Thornton Heath Elim Church, recorded the loss through evacuation of many of their Sunday School children. 'On Sunday we had to say goodbye to many of those whom our teachers had been privileged to instruct Sunday after Sunday.'[3] He goes on to express his encouragement at the fact that some of the scholars had said they would teach the choruses they had learned in Sunday School to the people with whom they were going to live. Prayer was offered for the protection of the children and their parents who were to be separated from them.

Evangelism re-aligned

Evangelism continued in Elim after the departure of George Jeffreys. The huge campaigns of the twenties and thirties were no more, but other ministers took up the challenge of reaching the nation with the Gospel. Others took up the challenge of pioneer evangelism. George Backhouse pioneered in Lowestoft during the summer of 1939 with a total number of 750 decisions recorded with many healings being testified to.[4] New churches were opened in Andover and Christchurch during this time. The church at Christchurch was opened by P N Corry, a member of the Executive Council. The Evangel reports the unusual circumstances at the dedication of the new building. It was opened during a blackout. 'There is a stillness in the air, and people's minds are full of war news and the destruction of human lives.'[5] Both these churches came into being as a result of local evangelistic enterprise.

Whilst George Jeffreys is rightly credited with the establishment of most, if not all, the larger Elim churches, up until the late thirties, many smaller churches were established as a result of local initiative. An example of this was the establishment of the Selly Oak Elim Church in 1936. It came into being as a result of the work and ministry of Mr. Yardley, who was converted during the great campaign in Birmingham in 1930. He started meetings in his home in Selly Oak in 1935 and a permanent work was established there the following year. W G Hathaway, the Field Superintendent at the time is reported to have commented on the fact that two thirds of all the Elim Churches had, by 1939, been opened as a result of the actions of other people, rather than directly by George Jeffreys.

Elim Evangel

The Executive Council minutes of meetings held during the Second World War, show that there was virtually no reference to the war which is quite incredulous. There are a few oblique references to war-time conditions. The first is with reference to a request from an Elim Pastor, Jack Tetchner to take up work in France in connection with the British Forces. It was decided to put this to the Conference for consideration if there was time for such a discussion.[6] A second reference was to the Executive Council's discussion of the date for the 1943 Conference and the following minute was written: 'Resolved that the date of the Annual Conference be August 9-13, 1943 in order to take full advantage of the light afforded by the New Moon.[7] I would have thought that they would have meant, the full moon, as a new moon gives no direct light.[8] This resolution would have been passed due to a consideration of the blackout that was enforced during the war.

Letters to and from the Executive Council at this time seemed to be focused almost entirely on the schism within the Movement.[9] The Elim Evangel, on the other hand, gave some valued consideration to the difficulties and situations caused by the outbreak of war. A series was commenced under the title 'Clippings and Comments', these were a short reprise of situations, mostly abroad, caused by the war. It included a comment from 'The Times' newspaper, quoted by 'The Christian' magazine which reported the shooting of the first conscientious objector in Germany for failing to carry out his military duties. He was described as 'a fanatical member' of the Society of Earnest Bible Students.[10] The same edition carries a comment on the plight of Jews in Germany:

> The Jewish community is dwindling to vanishing point in Germany. If the alleged census taken in Germany on the 17th May this year be correct, then the Jewish tragedy stands revealed. It is affirmed that out of the 650,000 Jews who lived in Germany in 1933, only 300,000 are at liberty: 200,000 emigrated; 30,000 are detained in prisons and concentration camps;20,000 committed suicide; 8,000, it is alleged were murdered and 90,000 died. Of the 300,000 Jews in Austria, only 140,000 are still at liberty; 130,000 have emigrated; 10,000 are in concentration camps; 10,000 have committed suicide, and 5,000 were murdered. These figures need no comment.[11]

'News and Views on the world today' was an article anonymously written under the pseudonym 'Puritan'. It was a collection of comments based on situations current at the time.[12] One such comment referred to Germany and France as 'Fields of blood and bones'. 'Such is the terrible, yet true description of the lands of France and Germany. On these fields, battles without number have been fought by these two enemies, and probably more human blood has been shed there than in any other part of the world.'[13] It goes on to briefly summarise the historical conflicts between the two countries commencing with Attila the Hun in the fifth century down to the First World War. 'What horrors the fields of France and Germany could recall! What will the present Carnival of Hell bring forth?'

Frequently, the Evangel carried articles or reports that compared the spiritual war that Christians were engaged in with the actual war in Europe. Military words and expressions were used in connection with the work of evangelism. An example of this is the following report of the ongoing work of the Kingstanding Elim Church under the heading 'A SPRING OFFENSIVE'.

> The introduction of the black-out cancelled many of the church's winter plans at Kingstanding. Nevertheless, this was made the opportunity for consolidating the work. Now under the leadership of the pastor the church is carrying on aggressive warfare. The enemy territory is constantly attacked, and men and women are being delivered from the Devil's concentration camps. Each Sunday souls are saved, numbers increasing. It thrills the heart to see converts coming with such regularity.[14]

In the same edition, the Crusader Commissioner, Pastor D B Gray made an appeal for Elim members to contribute to the cost of sending Evangels to Crusaders serving in the Forces. He noted that there were between one and two hundred Crusaders in the forces with whom he regularly corresponded. 'Already scores of replies are being delivered from these brethren telling of the keeping power of Christ, and the assurance of His presence with them in their new and in some cases dangerous surroundings. Join with us daily in prayer that they will be kept and their lives preserved.' He goes on to stress the importance of these Crusaders receiving regular copies of the Elim Evangel in response to requests from them. 'So far the members of the London Crusader Choir are undertaking to meet this need. Should others wish to help or contribute towards this effort, perhaps you will write us.'[15]

Under the leadership of George Jeffreys, much importance had been placed on literature in the form of tracts, booklets and books. This was made much easier by the Movement's own printing press in Clapham. The schism and the war meant that the printing and publishing of Gospel literature was greatly constricted. An appeal was made through the Evangel for monetary gifts to produce Gospel literature for H M Forces.

> We would again like to draw the attention of Evangel readers to our campaign for reaching the men in H M Forces by means of the printed page. Since bringing this matter to your notice in March last, many thousands of tracts have been sent out from the Publishing Office, in response to applications from friends in all parts of the British Isles eager to serve their Master by the thoughtful and prayerful distribution of Gospel literature. These are dark days – days fraught with anxiety and danger; days, however, in which the light of the Gospel message can shine all the more brightly by reason of the darkness around. We pray that the little Gospel leaflets distributed may be used in God's hands to bring many out of the darkness of sin into the glorious light of the Gospel of Christ.[16]

Canty was dismissive of such efforts. He mentions a front-page Evangel piece under the title. 'Elim Plans a Forward Move'. He describes it as 'A wistful mixture of glorious aims and pathetic means, suggesting ways of contacting Forces' personnel, evacuees and children, adding that 'a grant has been made by the Foursquare Gospel Testimony for leaflets to be distributed "in every military camp in the country". The grant was £75! As a hope that the Gospel would look more relevant to the desperate days it was promised that "a Union Jack in the corner of each tract" would adorn them. Canty contrasted this very meagre figure with the war costing £120 per second.[17]

E J Phillips, in his role as editor of the Elim Evangel was not afraid to step out into uncharted waters in comments, editorials and articles during the Second World War. One of the December 1941 editions has on its front page an article about Martin Niemoeller, the German theologian. It is titled: 'The Reason Niemoeller Lives'.[18] The article refers to its 13th October edition where the story was related of Dr Leo Stein, who was released from a German concentration camp where he had close contact with Pastor Niemoeller. 'This

Jewish doctor of law paid a remarkable tribute to the Christian faith of Niemoeller and gave the world more information concerning him than has come from any other source.'[19]

Many people asked why the Nazis allowed Niemoeller to live. Dr Stein gave an interesting answer: 'It is a classic illustration of "having the bull by the tail." It is bad for them to have him alive because he is not afraid to speak against them. But it would be worse for them to have him dead.'[20] The remainder of the article is quoted at some length:

> In a remarkable article, Dr Stein passes on a message from Niemoeller in which he tells how he visited Hitler to protest at the turning of the Nazis against the Church. Said Hitler in reply: 'If the Christian Church wants to fight me, I shall annihilate it as I have crushed all my other enemies. I don't mind walking over corpses as long as I reach my goal. I need no Christianity. Whoever won't obey will be destroyed, and that goes for you too. You are a deserter, and you know that for desertion there is only one punishment – death.'
> 'I have only deserted to Christianity,' the pastor replied, 'and I am willing to take on myself the suffering it involves.' You will regret it.' These were Hitler's final words to Niemoeller.
> 'During the last four years of my imprisonment I have never had any cause for regret,' Niemoeller concludes. 'As long as I have my cell where I can pray, I am still happier that Hitler, the promise-breaker and incorrigible liar, who hardly dares go out alone for fear that a bullet might hit him from behind.
> 'To the people the world over I send this message: *Keep the Faith!*'[21]

The Editor of the Evangel at this time was E J Phillips. The inclusion of articles such as the above was something that he obviously felt deeply about in view of his strong Jewish background.

It was not just the war that occupied the minds of Elim people. The departure of George Jeffreys caused great concern within the churches. Philips felt it necessary to explain the changes to the Deed Poll to the Evangel readers. The 25th August, 1941 edition of the Evangel carried an article explaining Elim's New Constitution. Virtually nothing had been said about the departure of George Jeffreys from Elim, although, this article did mention him by name, and he is even referred to in one place as 'Principal'. This silence was to continue for many years. The Executive Council felt, however, that an explanation of Elim's new Constitution should be provided for the readers of the Evangel. It was stated that in the early days of Elim, the government was an entirely autocratic one, 'but with the passing of the years a form of government has been developed which has become more and more democratic.'[22] The article went on to outline the development of Elim's government from the early days up to the present time. 'Last year a Conference of Ministers and Laymen representative of the whole Movement was called, and that Conference unanimously decided what was to be the future government of the Elim work.'[23]

An explanation was given of the absolute control of Principal George Jeffreys who, in time, appointed three Overseers with himself assuming the title of 'Principal Overseer. But these Overseers only held office at his will and he could at any time deprive them of their office. The effect of this, however, was that the work was still entirely governed by the Principal. This form of government continued until 1934. The article goes on to say:

> Some years prior to 1934, Mr. Jeffreys had evolved a plan whereby the responsibilities and powers resting on his shoulders should be passed on to an Executive Council, and considering the draft for many months, he executed in 1934 a Deed Poll transferring the government of the work to the Executive Council.[24]

Constitutional changes to the Governing Body, the Local Church and to Church Buildings are outlined in this article. The writer is slightly disingenuous when he states that: 'This form of government is to pass away…' Although the Executive Council would no longer be the governing body, it would still remain the governing body in between Conferences. That which is totally new, is the introduction of laymen into the Conference, this would be the legislative assembly within the Movement. The writer then goes on to explain the formation of a Ministerial Session of the Conference:

As in the Methodist Church, there will be a separate Ministerial Session to deal with matters particularly affecting the ministers, but this session will neither discuss nor decide any matter relating to the churches or the work as a whole. Such matters will be decided by the whole Conference on which there will be an equal number of ministers and lay representatives from the churches.[25]

As the years have progressed, the above has proved to be inaccurate on both points. Matters relating to both ministers and churches have been discussed and debated on in the Ministerial sessions of Conference prior to them being debated and voted upon in the Representative Session of Conference. The reasons given for this has been the fact that some issues have had a direct bearing on ministers, although they could only be approved by the General Conference and it was therefore felt justified for the matters to be discussed at the Ministerial Session first. On the issue of an equal representation of ministers and lay representatives, this has not occurred in the time of the author who has attended fifty-five Conferences. This equal distribution of ministers and lay representatives only occurred in the first few years of the Revised Constitution. It became costly and unworkable for every church to be able to afford to send a minister and a lay representative to Conference.

Changes to the governing of the local church was also explained in the article. Again, there is some ambiguity in the opening statement of this section where it states that for the first twelve years or so of the history of the Elim Movement, the minister was completely in control of the local church. Every minister was subject to the rules and regulations laid down by his superiors. Before 1934, although George Jeffreys was in control of the Movement, he had a Council and then a number of overseers were appointed and every minister was subject to their rule. Besides this, at one time ministers were moved on an annual basis. What the article refers to is the appointment of local church officers, deacons and, in some cases, elders. 'Under the new Constitution the local church is to be controlled by the "Church Officers," who will consist of the deacons together with the elders (if any) and the minister.' Elders were to be appointed by the minister in conjunction with the District Superintendent but it was made clear that no such appointment could be ratified without a confirmatory vote of the church members every two years.[26]

The final point in the article concerned the trusteeship of church buildings It was explained that there were at the time two trust corporations in Elim – the Elim Pentecostal Alliance Council and the Elim Trust Corporation. It was made very clear that these trustees have been merely 'holding trustees,' i.e. they have not had any powers of management. 'Until 1934 the managing trustee of the buildings was Principal George Jeffreys, but since 1934 the managing trustees have been the Executive Council.'[27] The following lengthy quotation explains the new set-up:

> Under the new Constitution the Executive Council will cease to be the managing trustees of the church buildings. The managing powers will be divided between the Directors of the Elim Trust Corporation and the local Church Officers, and it is interesting to note that the Directors of the Elim Trust Corporation will be appointed by the Annual Conference, three of them being ministers and three laymen. The respective powers of the Elim Trust Corporation and the local Church Officers are set out in the Deed of Trust, but suffice it to say that under the Deed the property is held for the local church and for the denomination, and that the church cannot take it away from the denomination nor can the denomination take it away from the church.[28]

With the progression of time, it became harder to appoint local trustees and eventually, almost every building in Elim came under the management of the Elim Trust Corporation. Currently there are no lay members on the Elim Trust Corporation and neither is it any longer appointed by the Conference. The Directors of the Elim Trust Corporation are the National Leadership Team.

Notes

1 Canty, George, *Unpublished manuscript on History of Elim*: p142

2 Canty, George, ibid, p142.

3 Thomas, *Elim Evangel*, 29th Sept 1939, p619.

4 *Elim Evangel*, ibid, p620.

5 *Elim Evangel*, 20th Oct 1939, p660.

6 *Executive Council Minutes*, 20th Nov 1939 (Malvern: General Superintendent's Office, Elim International Offices).

7 *Executive Council Minutes*, 7th Dec 1942

8 The full moon occurred on 15th August, 1943. From the 9th of the month onwards, it was a waxing moon, therefore the light from the moon would have been getting stronger.

9 This was especially the case during the early part of the war.

10 *Elim Evangel*, 20th Oct 1939, p660.

11 *Immanuel's Witness quoted by Elim Evangel*, ibid, p660.

12 *Elim Evangel*, 13th May 1940, Vol 21, No 20, p309.

13 *Elim Evangel*, ibid.

14 *Elim Evangel*, 20th May 1940, Vol 21, No 21, p326

15 *Elim Evangel*, 20th May 1940, Vol 21, No 21, p334

16 *Elim Evangel*, 17th June 1940, Vol 21, No 25, p397

17 Canty, George, ibid, p144.

18 *Elim Evangel*, 29th Dec 1941, Vol 22, No 52, pp729-730.

19 *Elim Evangel*, ibid.

20 *Elim Evangel*, ibid.

21 *Elim Evangel*, ibid, p730.

22 *Elim Evangel, What is Elim's New Constitution?* 25th August, 1940, Vol 22, No 34, pp521,523.

23 *Elim Evangel*, ibid.

24 *Elim Evangel*, ibid, p521.

25 *Elim Evangel*, ibid, p251.

26 This was many years later changed to a four-year period which currently applies.

27 *Elim Evangel*, ibid, p523.

28 *Elim Evangel*, ibid, p523.

7

Elim Conference 1941

Repercussions from the 1940 Conference

Reference has been made in a previous chapter to the pamphlet war between the Bible Pattern Movement and Elim. 'The pamphlet war was damaging to both sides and, as is often the case in inter-church argument, caused numbers of people to walk away from both sides.'[1] Both sides made strong attempts to win the votes of ordinary church members. Jeffreys needed the members from the Elim churches that he had established in order to help build and establish the new Bible Pattern churches. Equally, Elim had to put forward a strong case to keep the loyalty of their members. Kay points to the fact that whereas the pamphlets written on behalf of the Bible Pattern Movement were almost always written by Jeffreys, Elim's pamphlets were almost entirely anonymous, although there is little doubt that the chief author of Elim's pamphlets was E J Phillips. This resulted in Jeffreys being in the firing line whereas no personal criticism could have been hurled at an individual in the case of Elim's pamphlets.[2]

Having lost the battle with the ministers on the floor of the Elim Conference, Jeffreys turned his attention to the deacons of local Elim churches. In fairness to Elim, the Executive Council sought, in the first place to address issues raised publicly by Jeffreys in the Pattern magazine by corresponding privately through the ministerial circular with Elim ministers. Following the Conference, 20-24 May, 1940 Mr Jeffreys made a request 'for a small committee to be set up to deal with matters that were not dealt with at the Elim Conference…and also to deal with events that have since transpired.'[3] Jeffreys is somewhat disingenuous in his claim that since the Conference, some churches had taken a stand against coming into the Alliance (Elim) under the arrangements of the May Conference until the position is clarified. He claimed that 'the Executive know as well as I do'.[4] The statement was incredulous because the churches he was referring to were already Alliance churches! Because the Executive Council had turned down the Principal's request, he took it on himself to acquaint the readers of the Pattern of the difficulties that had been raised (with him) by ministers and churches since the Conference. It needs to be pointed out that at this time, George Jeffreys was still an Elim minister and, as such, was bound by the decisions of Conference and in writing as he did in an open forum, he damaged his ministerial integrity.

In the circular sent out to members of the Conference, the Executive Council were at pains to point out that the decisions made concerning the constitution and make-up of the Conference were clearly in the hands of the Conference, not the Executive Council and that the Principal himself publicly promised to abide by the decisions taken. 'Now, the Principal, in direct contradiction to his promise takes objection to these things which were actually decided by the Conference, but to endeavour to bring within the scope of the new Constitution the few churches which were then outside the Alliance.'[5]

The pamphlet and circular war between both parties was to continue for some considerable time until the Elim Executive Council made the decision not to issue any further pamphlets in reply to those penned by Jeffreys and the Bible Pattern Movement. Hudson makes the following comment on the pamphlets: 'From the first resignation of Jeffreys in 1939, there were around forty pamphlets and numerous letters circulated by Jeffreys and Elim, each defending their own priorities and attacking the other. For both sides, the pamphlets were weapons in the battle for the loyalty of the churches.'[6] This war of written words did not reflect well on either party, especially in the midst of the raging hostilities of the Second World War.

In considering the writing and circulation of the pamphlets, together with the ministerial circulars that were sent out from the Executive Council during this time, the author wishes to pay tribute to Pastor William Evans who kept a copy of each pamphlet and circular from both sides. These, he gave to my predecessor, Elim's first Official historian, Desmond Cartwright. This collection was passed on to the Elim Archives in Malvern. William Evans was, for many years, the Pastor of my home church in Porth, Rhondda, South Wales. He was, for a short time, George Jeffreys' chauffeur and pastored the Elim churches at Hendon and Coulsdon before engaging in a period of full-time evangelism with John Woodhead. He was later appointed assistant pastor at Cardiff City Temple under the leadership of P S Brewster. It was there that he met and married Mary, the widowed daughter of Alderman George Williams who became Lord Mayor of Cardiff in 1950. Because Alderman Williams was a widower, his daughter Mary stood by his side as Lady Mayoress while he undertook his role as Lord Mayor.

William Evans was my pastor and throughout the many years that I knew him, I always used the designation 'Pastor' whenever I spoke to him. He and Mrs Evans contributed greatly to my spiritual development. He was hard working, conscientious and diligent as the keeping of the pamphlets shows. He had a very clear understanding of the schism in Elim and he carefully and prayerfully weighed up both sides of the dispute. William Evans was, in my opinion, one of Elim's unsung heroes and I would ask the readers' indulgence in paying this short, but heart-felt tribute to an outstanding pastor who was faithful to the end of his days to His Lord and to the Movement that he had been called to serve.

The 1941 Elim Conference

The Conference met from the first to the fifth of September, 1941 at the Elim Church Hall in Carfax Lane, Clapham. It was the first Conference held under the new rules where there was a Representative Session which was responsible for legislation and a Ministerial Session in which matters relating exclusively to pastors were discussed. The first Ministerial Session took place on Thursday afternoon, 4th September. The Representative Session comprised of an equal number of ordained ministers and laymen. The Minutes record that: 'There were present about 48 lay representatives and 48 ministers, members of Conference, there were also present some 56 others.'[7] A limit of 150 voting members of Conference had been set by the Executive Council and confirmed by Conference. The reason for this was to ensure, as far as possible, an equal representation of ministers and lay representatives. This number was later increased to 250 and a limit was completely removed in the last decade of the previous century. The Conference Chairman was Charles Kingston, a member of the Executive Council.

The reason for a reduced number of attendees was given as follows: 'Following the calling of the Roll, a discussion ensued on the membership of the Conference. Owing to many being engaged on work of national importance, the church representatives were less than would have been the case in normal times, and consequently the number of minister members was reduced to conform to the number of lay representatives.

Following the 1940 Conference, the Executive Council sent out an undated Circular,[8] but from its contents, it is obvious that it was sent out in late August or early September 1940. The Circular outlined the four points that were considered by the Principal were not satisfactory:

[1] The Annual Conference which is the Governing body shall consist of a number of ministers (or at the discretion of the District Presbytery, Probationary Ministers), and elected laymen from the District Presbyteries as shall from time to time be decided by the Conference itself.

[2] After the debt is cleared each local church is free to allocate the remainder of its surplus offerings either to any of the recognised funds of the Alliance or to any funds listed for

that purpose at the Annual Conference as the Conference may decide, later.

[3] That all questions of doctrine outside the Fundamentals shall be decided by the Governing body.

[4] The Stationing Committee to appoint the Minister after consultation with the Church Officers as the type[9] they advised. The appointment to be for an indefinite period and to be at the discretion of the Stationing Committee.[10]

These changes to the Constitution were huge and they came, in part, as a result of the agitation for reform of the Movement's government by George Jeffreys. The circular pointed out that these changes were not put together by the Executive Council but by the democratic vote of the Conference. Jeffreys had given the Conference his promise to stand by the Conference decisions and not only that, but he had further promised that he would endeavour to bring within the scope of the new Constitution the few churches which were then outside the Alliance.[11] The Executive Council was incensed by the failure of Jeffreys to fulfil the promises that he had made to the May Conference. A letter was sent to all Elim ministers dated 23rd August, 1940 with the instruction to 'Kindly read this letter to an early meeting of your Diaconate.' This was underlined and placed at the top of the letter.[12]

The letter expressed the regret of the Executive Council to have to send yet another letter to the churches concerning the situation in Elim. It was felt that they (the Executive Council) had no option but to write to the diaconates yet again following a letter sent out from Norwood,[13] the contents of which appeared in the August edition of 'The Pattern'. The Executive Council expressed its distress at having to 'spend time, paper, and postage in replying to these circulars which are being sent to the churches.' The letter sets out Mr Jeffreys' misinterpretation of the decisions of the May Conference and then sets out what it (the E C) sees as the ways in which he (Jeffreys) broke his promises made to the delegates at the May Conference. The following lengthy quotation sums up the exasperation of the Executive Council at George Jeffreys' failure to live up to the promises he made to the Conference.

> It is complained that our letter of 15th August deals with personalities. But how can we avoid this when we are dealing with an attempt by one or two individuals to upset the decisions of the Conference? What does the Principal really want? Some years ago,[14] of his own free will he made the Executive Council the governing body of the Alliance. After a time, this did not satisfy him, and he pressed for the Ministerial Conference to be the governing body. Shortly afterwards he pressed for the governing body to consist of ministers and laymen on a 50/50 basis. Now within three months of their first Conference, it is evident that he is not willing for that body to govern.
> The letter to which we are replying further states that at the May Conference minorities were silenced. This is not a fact. It was an open Conference and everyone was free to state his opinion. The reason why the Principal and those with him were asked to stand to their feet to signify that they would abide by the decisions of the Conference was because the Conference was called in the interests of unity. The churches and ministers opposed to the Principal's policy were about to make concessions for the sake of unity, and they naturally wanted to know at the beginning of things whether after they made these concessions the Principal and party would abide by the decisions. The Conference also asked the members of the Executive Council similarly to stand to indicate their willingness to abide by whatever the Conference decided, and they immediately did so without any hesitation. *Everyone present at the Conference remembers full well the difficulty they had in inducing the Principal's party to stand.*[15] The lay brethren in particular were exasperated, and some of them were about to leave the Conference declaring they were not prepared to waste their time there if all were not willing to abide by the decisions of the majority. Finally, the Principal's party stood.[16]

The note of sheer exasperation felt by the members of the Executive Council is clearly revealed in the last sentence of the above paragraph. There is a sense of incredulity in it: 'Can it be true that those who pleaded for the Conference representative of all the churches to decide the future of the work should now repudiate its decisions?'[17]

In ensuring that the Representative Conference was combined of an equal number of *laymen and ministers, a large number of ministers were disenfranchised.* Jeffreys picked up on this and commented: 'No church or minister in the Alliance is assured of the right to representation at the Conference.'[18] The members of Conference were aware of this discrepancy and the minutes record the following: 'It was unanimously agreed that some adjustment of the proposed new Constitution should be made so that ministers be not disenfranchised as a result of Lay Representatives not attending.'[19] A further proposal was also unanimously agreed upon that allowed everyone present at the meeting to take full part in the discussion and voting, 'but that on all vital matters confirmatory votes be taken of the Representative Conference consisting of an equal number of ministers and laymen.'[20] The minutes record that there was considerable discussion before the Conference approved the Draft Deed of Variation (Deed Poll) circulated in May 1941.

The Conference then turned its attention to the General Rules. These dealt with the formation of Presbyteries and rules for the appointing of District Superintendents. District Secretaries and Treasurers were to be appointed in each presbytery and Foursquare Gospel Testimony funds raised in each District to be allocated to such districts for the extension of the work minus 10% which was to be sent to Headquarters for printing and any special grants.

The attention of the Conference was then turned to the vexed issue of property. It was decided that the Conference approved the Model Trust Deed of the Elim Foursquare Gospel Alliance dated 23rd May as a Model Trust Deed. This meant that all properties in the Trust was owned by the Movement and not by individual churches. This had been drawn up by E J Phillips with the full consent of the Executive Council and signed by George Jeffreys. 'The Elim Conference of ministers and laymen passed a resolution with an overwhelming majority authorising the Executive Council to take such steps as might be considered necessary to ensure that the rights of Elim church members and their buildings were properly safeguarded.'[21] The Conference went so far as to consider taking legal action in order to enforce Jeffreys to transfer his trusteeship of all Elim property over to the Elim Trust Corporation. 'It was eventually resolved that this Conference considers it is not contrary to the Scriptures for the trustees to take legal proceedings where necessary to protect the interests of charities and it approves of the Executive Council taking such proceedings at its discretion in order (1) to enforce the relinquishing by Mr George Jeffreys of the trusteeship of Elim properties, and (2) to prevent certain Elim Church buildings being used for purposes other than those of the Elim Foursquare Gospel Alliance.'[22]

The ministerial session of Conference, deputed the discipline of ministers who had joined the Bible Pattern churches to the Representative Session. The Representative Session acted as an official Board of Enquiry. This was to be the first and only time when the discipline of ministers was considered by both sessions of Conference. It was reported that Pastors R Mercer, H M Strange and A S Gaunt had already resigned prior to the date of the Enquiry, their cases were not considered. The cases of three ministers – Lemuel Morris, Gwilym I Francis and E O Steward - was then considered in their absence. They were charged with the following charges: (1) Fostering dissension within the Elim Movement, (2) Breaking the solemn agreement they made when entering the Elim Ministry, and (3) joining an organisation actively opposed to the Alliance.

Such was the significance of the 1941 Elim Conference that a whole edition of the Elim Evangel was devoted to it (22nd September, 1941). The leading article was written by Pastor James Hardman under the title 'Days of Inspiring Conference'.[23] He made little mention of the enormous constitutional changes that were passed, nor of the removal of ministers who were loyal to George Jeffreys. He wrote that the unity on the decisions reached made it clear that God had indeed answered the prayers of the delegates that they might have 'the mind of Christ'. 'Although there was such important business discussed, the Holy Spirit was manifested in a wonderful way, and the whole Conference was gripped by the power of God.[24] Reference was made to the very impressive Ordination Service which took place on the final day of the Conference.

A Declaration was made at the Conference which was of such significance that the Executive Council took the decision to have it printed in the Conference edition of the Elim Evangel. The Declaration by the Elim Conference, 1941 made it very clear that it was the unanimous opinion 'that the strife and contention that has lately arisen among us has not been engendered by the Spirit of God, *but rather by the Adversary*,[25] in an endeavour to divert and distract our attention from the main purpose for which God Himself brought this work into being, namely the preaching of the Gospel of the Grace of God to all men, the dissemination of the Pentecostal doctrines for the edifying of believers, the proclamation and practice of the highest standard for Christian discipleship, the teaching of Divine healing, and the quickening among true believers of the Blessed Hope of the Return of our Lord and Saviour Jesus Christ.'[26]

This was a vitally important declaration for the Conference to make because it re-affirmed the Foursquare Gospel ethos of the Movement. The Conference went on to make the following six declarations:

[1] To put God first in all things and to give Him the place which His glory and majesty demand and to allow no personality to have the pre-eminence and priority which alone belong to the Lord Jesus Christ.

[2] To allow no consideration, whether of policy or procedure, to deter us in our earnest endeavours to extend the Kingdom of our Lord Jesus Christ.

[3] To seek to maintain in our churches both in precept and practice the highest standard of scriptural and spiritual holiness.

[4] To seek to promote the closest co-operation between the Church Diaconates and the Conference, and to keep the

members of the Churches in close touch with all matters of importance which affect their spiritual and moral welfare.

[5] To endeavour by all means possible at our disposal to spread the message of the fulness of Christ, and to seek to establish a permanent witness to this Pentecostal message in as many cities, towns, and villages in this and other lands as time and opportunity permit before the close of the Day of Grace.

[6] To cease to endeavour to please man in our policy or procedure and to seek only God's will and mind as revealed in His Word, and to accept that and that alone as our Standard and Guide.

We further call upon all members of Elim congregations in all the Churches to stand loyally behind the Conference in its endeavour to maintain unity, progress, and, above all, brotherly love, being fully assured that if this is done then the blessing of God will rest on us all and His smile will ever be upon us.[27]

This was, undoubtedly, a momentous Conference as far as the Elim Movement was concerned. It was the beginning of a comeback to those principles and policies that had envisioned the birth of the Movement. True, they no longer had their charismatic Founder leading them to battle against the forces of darkness, but they declared emphatically that despite the strife and contention of the preceding four years, they had drawn a line in the sand and Elim would not only survive, but by the grace of God grow and continue to evangelise and open churches both home and abroad.

Notes

[1]   Kay, William, *George Jeffreys*, ibid, p372.

[2]   Kay, William, *George Jeffreys*, ibid, p372.

[3]   Jeffreys, George, *Since the Elim Conference of May, 1940, The Pattern*, August 1940, Vol 1, No 8, pp3,4.

[4]   Jeffreys, George, ibid.

[5]   Copy of Circular letter sent by the Executive Council to the members of the Elim Conference, (Des Cartwright Archives, Regents Bible College, Malvern), August 1940.

[6]   Hudson, Neil, *A Schism and its aftermath, An historical analysis of Denominational Discerption in the Elim Pentecostal Church, 1939-1940*, (Ph.D., dissertation, Kings College) p298

7   Elim Conference Minutes 1941, Representative Session, (Malvern: Elim Archives)

8   Circular sent out by the Executive Council, August or September 1940, (Desmond Cartwright Archives, Malvern).

9   Author's italics.

10 It was intended at first, that non-Executive Council ministers should be included in the personnel of the Stationing Committee, but this was soon discovered to be impractical and within a very short period of time, the Executive Council became the Stationing Committee.

11 Ministerial Circular, August/Sept, 1940, ibid.

12 Circular letter from the Executive Council to the Diaconate of each Elim Church, 23rd August, 1940 (Malvern: Elim Archives).

13 Jeffreys' centre of operation at this time was 19 Beulah Hill, Upper Norwood, London, SE 19.

14 1934

15 Author's italics.

16 Letter to the Diaconates, ibid.

17 Letter to the Diaconates, ibid.

18 *The Pattern*, 8 August 1940, Vol 1, No 8, p3.

19 Elim Conference 1941, *Minutes of the Representative Session*, p1.

20 Elim Conference 1941, ibid, p1.

21 Kay, William, *George Jeffreys*, ibid, p375

22 Elim Conference 1941 ibid, p3.

23 *Elim Evangel*, 22nd September 1941, Vol 22, No 38, p561.

24 Hardman, James, *Elim Evangel*, ibid, p561.

25 Author's italics.

26 Declaration, *Elim Evangel*, ibid, p569

27 Elim Conference Minutes, 1941, ibid, pp6,7 printed in *Elim Evangel*, ibid, p569

8
Crisis

1941 was to be a momentous year in the history of the Second World War. It was during this significant period that Britain was joined by two major allies – Russia and the USA. For almost eighteen months, Britain had shouldered the huge burden of the conflict against the most powerful and tyrannical enemy that she had ever encountered. After Dunkirk and the Battle of Britain, it was hoped that the imminent fear of invasion by the Nazi forces had receded and that the British nation was safer than she had been in 1940. But, the sense of isolation and having to fight on alone against such incredible odds weighed heavily upon the Prime Minister: 'Looking back upon the tumult of the war, I cannot recall any period when its stresses and the onset of so many problems all at once or in rapid succession, bore more directly upon me and my colleagues than the first half of 1941...Greater military disasters fell upon us in 1942, but by then we were no longer alone and our fortunes were mingled with those of the Grand Alliance.'[1]

The blitz on London continued throughout 1941 and other cities and industrialised areas throughout the country were devastated by enemy bombing. In addition to the onslaughts of the Luftwaffe, Elim had its own battles to fight. Its main battle, however, was not with George Jeffreys and The Bible Pattern movement, it was a fight for survival. In the thirties, Elim had a dozen of churches with Sunday Evening congregations numbering around the thousand marks. After the war, Elim only had one church in that category – Cardiff City Temple, under the leadership of its greatest post-Jeffreys evangelist – Percy Stanley Brewster. More will be said of him in later chapters of the book, suffice to say that at this point, he was already a seasoned evangelist. In 1936, whilst pastoring the church in Swansea, he held a campaign in the Brangwyn Hall, Neath and established a thriving Elim Church in this South Wales Town. In October 1941, he held a pioneer campaign in Aberystwyth where he was assisted by Ken Matthew and Cyril Hadler.[2] He, along with John Woodhead, held some memorable war-time evangelistic campaigns which brought some hope to the beleaguered Elim Movement. But, Elim's woes continued and despite a strong and united Conference, Elim was in great crisis during the first four years of its history without its Founder, George Jeffreys, at the helm.

Disputes over Buildings

Concern was expressed at the 1941 Conference over the failure of George Jeffreys, despite many promises, to transfer his trusteeship of Elim Church properties to the Elim Trust Corporation. We have already noted that the main area of dispute as far as George Jeffreys was concerned, was the right of local congregations to own their own property. The 1934 Deed Poll which was signed by Jeffreys, firmly placed the ownership of church property under the control of the Conference with the Executive Council being its agent. It would appear that between the years 1936-1938, Jeffreys had a complete change of mind on the ownership of Church property. But did he? The fact is that he and members of the Revival Party held the trusteeship of a number of churches. The justification for this was that these properties had been paid for directly by George Jeffreys. The author is of the opinion that without Elim, Jeffreys would not have had an independent income. The contrast must be made between Jeffreys and Phillips in this respect. Phillips came from a wealthy family, yet, when he retired, he had no personal property to live in. He and his wife lived in rented property in Eastbourne. Phillips refused to acquire property whilst he was an

Elim minister. Jeffreys, when he died in 1961 had an estate worth just short of £21,000. Unlike Phillips, he did not come from a moneyed background.

In the dispute over buildings, neither party brought honour to themselves and sadly, many Elim members were damaged by the situation. The problem arose in those congregations that remained loyal to Jeffreys and, naturally, wanted to retain the building that they worshipped in. Jeffreys maintained that the local congregations had, by their sacrificial giving, bought these buildings and, therefore, should be allowed to retain them when they broke away from Elim to join the Bible Pattern organisation. Jeffreys had a valid argument but it was almost impossible to establish how much of each property purchased had been given by those members loyal to Jeffreys. Elim certainly had the law on its side and, as we shall see, was prepared to go to law in order to retain its rightful property. Elim clearly stated its case at the 1941 Conference as recorded in the Conference report published in the Elim Evangel.

> On the subject of properties, there was considerable discussion, particularly in view of the fact that Mr Jeffreys, after many promises to transfer his trusteeship of Elim Church properties to the Elim Trust Corporation, still refuses to carry this out. Time and time again he has enumerated certain conditions which he required to be fulfilled before he would transfer his trusteeship. When these conditions have been carried out, other reasons have been given for a refusal. Consequently, the Conference felt that it was necessary to take stronger action, and *after careful and prayerful consideration, during which Bibles were open and many Scriptures quoted*,[3] the following two resolutions were passed:
>
> 'That this Conference calls upon Mr George Jeffreys forthwith unconditionally (1) to sign the necessary Deeds appointing the Elim Trust Corporation as trustee of all Elim Foursquare

Gospel Alliance properties of which he is a trustee, and (2) to resign as a Director of the Elim Pentecostal Alliance Council.'
'That this Conference considers it is not contrary to the Scriptures for Trustees to take legal proceedings where necessary to protect the interest of charities, and it approves of the Executive Council taking such proceedings in order (1) to force the relinquishing by Mr George Jeffreys of his trusteeship of Elim properties, and (2) to prevent certain Elim Church buildings being used for purposes other than those of the Elim Foursquare Gospel Alliance.
The former resolution was passed unanimously by all present and also unanimously by the Representative Session consisting of Ministers and Laymen in equal numbers. The latter resolution was passed by a large majority, only eight voting against the motion. This was confirmed by a vote of the Representative Session of Ministers and Laymen, when only seven voted against, no one abstaining.[4]

Jeffreys responded to the Elim Conference Report (1941) in which he expressed his willingness to give up his trusteeship of Church property, 'When I am asked to do so in a resolution passed by the congregation worshipping in the building.'[5] This was, to say the least, a disingenuous reply from Jeffreys seeing that in at least four properties, the final say was not given to the Congregation, but by the trustees that he had appointed. He took the Conference to task over their justification of going to law in order to settle property disputes. 'As Christians, there should be no question of legal proceedings. Surely it is the Scriptural way to get the decision of the Church rather than go to law.'[6] Again, he was referring to the local congregation.

Congregational Crisis

There were four church buildings that Jeffreys had appointed his own trustees to. They were: Kensington Temple, Brighton, Blackpool and Glasgow City Temple. The trustees appointed were himself, Ernest Darragh, James McWhirter and Robert Tweed.

In the case of Blackpool, Robert Tweed gave the trusteeship of the building over to Elim in the mid-seventies. He did not levy a charge. The ownership of Glasgow City Temple reverted to Elim ownership in the late fifties and was sold for £15,000. The three trustees of the Glasgow building were Ernest Darragh, James McWhirter and George Jeffreys. The Brighton church building, situated in the Lanes and known as the Glynn Vivian Hall[7], was transferred to the Elim Trust Corporation in the early part of the nineteen sixties. The trustees of Kensington Temple were Darragh and McWhirter. Jeffreys maintained that the local congregation should have the last say concerning the building in which they worshipped and that 'until Elim changed the (Trust) deed in line with the wishes of the congregation and its officers, he would not surrender his trusteeship.'[8] Elim was not prepared to modify their trust deed, but, following the death of Darragh and Jeffreys, James McWhirter sold the building back to Elim.

Worthing

By the autumn of 1941, George Jeffreys was determined to influence churches to leave Elim and join his new organisation. The Worthing church, under the leadership of E O Steward, a staunch supporter of Mr Jeffreys, was one of the first Elim churches to align with the Bible Pattern movement. When the Worthing minister moved to take over the pastorate of the Jubilee Temple, Blackpool, a minister was appointed who, in Jeffreys' words 'was fresh to the Elim controversy'.[9] It would appear that the new minister, E A Prangnell, was not an Elim minister and the circumstances surrounding his appointment are unclear. According to the Pattern account of his induction service, he had been 'duly appointed by the members of the church to the pastorate'.[10] Who presented his name to the Worthing Church is not revealed, but it was more than likely on the recommendation of the Advisory Board of the Bible Pattern Movement. The new minister 'examined the claims of both sides and decided to stay in Elim'.[11] In a pamphlet reprinted in the Pattern magazine, Jeffreys claimed that the Pastor of the Worthing Church received a threatening letter from Elim Headquarters which resulted in him going to London to meet with Elim's leaders.[12] Elim's response to what they considered an untrue statement was to clarify the situation as follows:

> The reason he (Pastor Prangnell) went to Elim Headquarters to discuss the position of the Worthing Church were (1) because there was a good deal of unrest and strife in the Church consequent to their affiliation with the Pattern; (2) because he had reason to believe that the new Elim Constitution was being misrepresented in the pages of *Pattern*, and (3) because he had received a friendly letter inviting him to come and discuss the matter.[13]

The outcome of the meeting between Worthing's pastor and Elim leaders was that Pastor Prangnell was offered a credential as an EFGA minister with a guaranteed minimal salary on the condition that the Worthing church returns to Elim. A church meeting was held on 26th October, 1941 when the decision was made to return to Elim. This meeting was 'properly called by seven days' notice and was representative of the church'.[14]

A meeting was held by Mr Jeffreys in Worthing on 12th November, 1941. About 200 people were present. According to the Elim Pamphlet only 47 were Worthing people, and not all of that 47 were members of the Worthing Church. 'The reader will naturally ask: Who made up the remainder of the congregation? Although this was a Worthing meeting to deal with Worthing affairs, over seventy-five per cent of the congregation consisted of people who had been brought over from Brighton, Southampton and other towns. It is not the first time the Pattern has adopted such methods. A request by the Worthing Pastor that these people should be asked to retire, as the meeting was to deal with the business of the Worthing Church, was promptly refused.'[15] At this meeting, Mr Jeffreys made it clear that he was determined to establish a Pattern Church in Worthing.

Elim and Portsmouth

Probably as a result of their experience over the Worthing conflict, Elim decided to be more robust in their handling of disputes over church buildings that were owned by the Movement. In situations where local congregations meeting in buildings owned by the Elim Trust Corporation, decided to leave Elim and join the Bible Pattern Movement, there was great controversy, wrangling and dissention that did not enhance the spiritual integrity of either of the parties involved. The decision of the 1941 Conference to consider legal action to force George Jeffreys to relinquish his trusteeship of Elim properties and to prevent certain Elim Church buildings being used for purposes other than those of the Elim Foursquare Gospel Alliance, though duly passed by a large majority, caused some consternation in the Movement.

In the pamphlet 'Elim and Portsmouth', the leaders of the Alliance stated that on Sunday, 7th December, 1941, a party of five ministers from London arrived at the Elim Church, Portsmouth. The purpose of this visit was to induct Pastor Gerald Ladlow as the new Minister and 'recommenced Elim services in the Church building which legally and morally belongs to the Elim Foursquare Gospel Alliance.'[16] The Portsmouth Elim Church, with the encouragement of their Pastor Robert Mercer had taken their stand with George Jeffreys in his demands for certain changes in the Elim Movement, particularly when he first resigned in 1939. 'After the 1940 May Conference when unity seemed to be reached and Mr Jeffreys returned to the Elim Movement as President, the Portsmouth Church followed his example and strengthened the bond of fellowship with the rest of Elim.'[17] However, when Jeffreys resigned a second time, the Portsmouth Church again followed his lead, and decided as a Church not to recognise Elim's new Constitution and to stand with the Founder.

The pamphlet states that George Jeffreys, after forming his new Bible-Pattern Church Fellowship had influenced a number of churches to secede from Elim and join this new group.

'Portsmouth Church did not take the formal stand with the Bible-Pattern Fellowship until Pastor Mercer resigned from Elim. By this time many of those members who had stood loyally by Elim were being made to feel they were not wanted in the Portsmouth meetings. The deacons who remained loyal to Elim were voted out of office and replaced by "Pattern" supporters. Consequently many of the members sought Christian fellowship elsewhere.'[18] Elim faced a considerable dilemma. Pro-Elim members were leaving churches because the pastors and leaders of those churches had decided to go along with Jeffreys. Although initially, only five churches left Elim to join with the Bible-Pattern Fellowship, the feeling within Elim Headquarters was that the time had arrived to take a stand against Jeffreys and to re-claim the buildings that legally belonged to Elim.

There can be no doubt that the Portsmouth Church building and properties belonged to the Elim Foursquare Gospel Alliance. Jeffreys and his supporters made much of the claim that as a result of a local building being paid for largely by the members of the local church, those said members should have the right to decide whether or not they wanted to leave Elim and join the Bible-Pattern Movement. Such an argument is disingenuous because it would be impossible to prove what percentage of any local Elim Church membership had given their money for a building with the purpose in mind of following George Jeffreys. Elim leaders rightly pointed out that under the Deed Poll which was executed by George Jeffreys in 1934, the Executive Council of nine ministers, George Jeffreys himself being one, were made trustees of all Elim buildings as well as all other monies, and legally charged with the task of seeing that these properties were used only for the purposes of the Elim Foursquare Gospel Alliance.[19]

It was stated that the Executive Council were faced with two alternatives: (1) To allow non-Elim ministers to continue to preach in these five Elim Church buildings, or (2) To take steps to see that the Elim buildings were secured for the use of the loyal Elim people, for which purpose they were intended. The Executive

Council were adamant that as trustees, they had no alternative but to go with the second option. In order to achieve their objective in securing Elim properties for rightful Elim congregations, there were three possible options open to them

    (a) They could appeal to a court of law to give them possession of these buildings unlawfully retained by the Pattern supporters.

    (b) Step into the buildings and take charge of the services, instal a loyal Elim minister and trust that in addition to the loyal Elim members in these places many others would remain and become again an Elim congregation.

    (c) Take other steps to secure the rights of the Elim members and friends to retain the privileges of membership of their own church and to secure for them the use of the Elim building for worship.

The Elim leaflet states that after carefully weighing up the situation and seeking carefully to be guided the right path, the Executive Council decided to go for option (b). Details are then provided of the manner in which the five Elim ministers went to the Church in Arundel Street Portsmouth and took possession of the building. It proved to be a stressful situation that resulted in two separate services being conducted in the same building, one by Elim under the leadership of Joseph Smith in the main building, and one by the Bible Pattern under the leadership of Robert Mercer, with Principal Parker being the speaker, in the minor hall. It was a wholly unsatisfactory situation that did not reflect well on either party.

Adding to the deep sense of grievance felt by the Bible Pattern people was the fact that the Elim party were accompanied by a 'detective'. 'The fact that the taking of the building occurred on a Sunday morning when a communion service was due to be held and in the presence of a police officer, who had been brought along in case of trouble, aroused anger in the Pattern group and confirmed their worst fears about the strong-armed dictatorial nature of the Elim Executive.'[20] Actually, it was a private detective, not a policeman that accompanied the Elim ministers to Portsmouth. In its own version of the proceedings of that day, the Pattern states that Phillips and Hathaway handed Mr Mercer a letter as soon as he entered the building. The letter informed Mr Mercer that Gerald Ladlow was being installed as the new minister of the Portsmouth Church. The letter contained the following statement: 'As you are aware, this Church building is held in trust for the purposes of a Church of the Elim Foursquare Gospel Alliance, and it is the duty of the Executive Council to see that these trusts are carried out. We regret that recent events have made it necessary to take this step.'[21] It was stated in the Pattern that the Elim Executive members warned Mr Mercer that any public opposition would be dangerous. This warning was explained later by the fact that the Executive had a detective with them. Elim's explanation of the presence of a detective was as follows: 'As we had been previously warned that some physical resistance might possibly be offered to any attempt by Elim to take over the services, a private detective and his assistant were brought into the meeting to act as witnesses should any attempt be made physically to interfere with the Elim party taking the service.'[22]

There were internal disputes in a number of other Elim churches including Carlisle, York, Southampton and Barking. George Jeffreys tried to get these congregation to join the Bible-Pattern Movement. He opened a Free Elim Church in Carlisle and encouraged members of the Carlisle Elim Church to leave Elim. At that time, the Carlisle Church was pastored by John Woodhead, one of Elim's leading evangelist. He ensured that the Carlisle Elim Church prospered despite Jeffreys starting his own church in the border town.

Notes

[1] Churchill, Winston, *The Grand Alliance – The Second World War Volume 3*, (Penguin Books, London 2005), p3.

[2] *Elim Evangel*: 14th October, 1941, Vol 22, No 41, p600.

[3] Author's italics

[4] A Report of the Conference of September, 1941, *Elim Evangel*, 22nd September 1941, Vol 22, No 38, pp566,567.

[5] *The Pattern*, October 1941, Vol 3, No 19, p2.

6 *The Pattern,* ibid.

7 Kay, William, *George Jeffreys,* ibid, p169.

8 Kay, William, ibid, p.379.

9 *The Pattern, The Elim Headquarters and the Worthing Church,* Mid-November 1941, Vol 2, No 22, p6.

10 *The Pattern,* October 1941, Vol 2, No 19, p3.

11 Kay, William, ibid, p376.

12 *The Pattern,* ibid.

13 *Worthing and Elim, Exposure of a false Publication,* Pamphlet published November 1941, (Malvern: Elim Archives)

14 *Worthing and Elim,* ibid, p4.

15 *Worthing and Elim,* ibid, p1.

16 *Elim and Portsmouth,* A pamphlet published by Elim, dated December 1941, (Malvern: Elim Archives).

17 *Elim and Portsmouth,* ibid.

18 *Elim and Portsmouth,* ibid.

19 *Elim and Portsmouth,* ibid.

20 Kay, William, ibid, p377.

21 Parker, Percy, *Elim Executive's Amazing Act at Portsmouth: Pastor Mercer and his Church driven out!* (*The Pattern,* Mid-December 1941, Vol 2, No 24, p3)

22 *Elim and Portsmouth,* ibid.

9
Two Resignations

It is difficult for those of us who were born after the Second World War to imagine the horrors that the war brought upon the inhabitants of these islands, and indeed of the population of most of Europe. The Blitz continued until May 1941. Churchill stated that the Blitz of 1941 fell into three phases.[1] The first phase in January and February, the weather came to Britain's aid. Whilst Cardiff, Portsmouth and Swansea were heavily bombed during these months, London had a temporary reprieve from the nightly air-raids. Steps were taken during this time to strengthen the Civil Defence Service and more active methods of Defence were initiated. 'Smoke-screens, highly unpopular with the local inhabitants whose homes they contaminated, were prepared, and later proved their worth in protecting Midland industrial centres.'[2] Decoy fires were started in port cities and industrial centres with the aim of protecting naval, military and industrial buildings and yards that were vital in the on-going conflict with a ruthless enemy.[3]

The second phase began in early March 1941 when harbours and dockyards on Merseyside and the Clyde were attacked. 'On the 8th and for three succeeding nights Portsmouth was heavily attacked and the dockyards damaged. Manchester and Salford were attacked on the 11th.' The heaviest blows fell in April. Massive air-raids were concentrated on Coventry and the Cathedral there was totally gutted. Over two thousand, three hundred people were killed and more than three thousand were seriously injured on the resumption of attacks on London on the 16th and 17th of the month. This was the third and final phase of the Blitz in which the enemy went on trying to destroy most of Britain's principal ports. Plymouth came under attack each night from April 21 to 29. Although decoy fires helped to save the dockyards in Devonport, this was at the expense of the city. The city centre was destroyed and over three and a half thousand Plymouth civilians were killed. 'The climax came on May 1, when Liverpool and the Mersey were attacked for seven successive nights. Seventy-six thousand people were made homeless and three thousand killed or injured. Sixty-nine out of a hundred and forty-four berths (in the docks)[4] were put out of action, and the tonnage landed for a while was cut to a quarter.'[5] Hull and Belfast were heavily bombed during this third phase.

Donald Gee writes of the enormous strain on the British people during the early years of the war. The morale of the people was severely tested.

> In the midst of all this stood the hundreds of Pentecostal churches that had come into existence through the Revival. They stood. They were worthily active in a variety of ways. They justified their existence in the severest testing of national crisis that could be imagined. Their sister churches on the Continent passively and heroically carried on. The fiery trial revealed how genuinely they had become established in the grace of God. Many had deemed the Pentecostal Movement a 'flash in a pan' – just a passing phase of effervescent 'revivalism'. The war proved otherwise. The Movement had come to stay.[6]

The Executive Council circa 1940

Elim, quite apart from its trauma caused by the separation between George Jeffreys and the Movement that he had founded, was to experience further turmoil from within its own ranks that must have rocked its very foundations and most certainly would have vexed the hearts and minds of its leaders at that time. Before going on to deal with the two resignations of members of the Executive Council, it would be pertinent at this point to profile the Executive

Council of 1940. It must be borne in mind that at first, two members of the Council were ex-officio – Jeffreys and Phillips by virtue of their office. Jeffreys was allowed to nominate three members and the Conference appointed the other four members. The three members appointed by George Jeffreys were: Gordon Tweed, Robert Ernest Darragh and James McWhirter. These three joined the Elim Evangelistic Band when Elim's Head Offices were situated in Belfast. They had been very close to George Jeffreys from the very early days and were intensely loyal to him. They were later to be associated with the World Revival Crusade, a very small group who accompanied Jeffreys on most, if not all his campaigns.

Ernest Darragh[7] was Jeffreys' oldest and closest friend. They first met at Thomas Myerscough's Bible School in Preston in 1913. Darragh was the first person to join up with the Elim Evangelistic Band. He was Jeffreys' song leader at the latter's evangelistic campaigns. Blessed with a rich tenor voice, and this Welshman concedes that there is scarcely a sweeter melodious sound than an Irish tenor, Darragh was the soloist at Jeffreys' meetings. He was also a fine preacher and conducted a number of evangelistic campaigns under the Elim banner in Ulster and the South of England. Margaret Streight was the second member of the Elim Evangelistic Band and she accompanied Darragh on his evangelistic campaigns. She married Robert Mercer who was also from Northern Ireland. Mercer replaced Robert Tweed as one of Jeffreys' appointees on the Executive Council. James McWhirter, came under heavy criticism at the 1937 Conference where his position as Crusader President was questioned. 'A cutting was read by Mr F B Phillips from the Eastbourne Gazette, Wednesday July 14th 1937, which made a plain statement that "Professor McWhirter, one of Principal Jeffreys' Ministers, had completed a new book – 'Britain and Palestine in Prophecy', published by Methuen", and Mr Phillips considered that Mr McWhirter was in honour bound not to have published the book.'[8] No doubt being aware of the controversy over McWhirter's British Israel views strongly expressed in the book, Jeffreys decided to withdraw his nominated members for that year. This resulted in McWhirter and Darragh losing their positions as members of the Executive Council. However, at the 1939 Conference, Jeffreys decided to exercise his right to nominate once more. The Conference minutes of 1938 seem to indicate that there were six ministers appointed by the Conference and not four; E C W Boulton, W G Hathaway, J Smith, P N Corry, R Mercer and S Gorman. This is the order in which they appear in the minutes, therefore one may assume that this was the voting order so that Boulton would have received the highest number of votes and Gorman the least.

At the 1938 Conference, Jeffreys appointed Smith, Kingston and Mercer as his appointees. 'He said he wished to put in as his nominees the three men who came next in voting for the Council, so that they would carry out the wishes of the Ministerial Conference.'[9] At the very difficult and contentious Conference of 1939, Jeffreys changed his appointees yet again. He withdrew the names of C Kingston and J Smith from being his appointees and replaced them with two men who he considered were totally loyal to him. They were William Barton and Gwilym Francis.

When the dust finally settled and the split had occurred, Robert Mercer joined the Bible Pattern Movement and his place on the Executive Council was taken by F G Cloke. The Conference minutes of 1938-41 are not altogether clear about who were elected, removed and reinstated. Barton and Francis went with Jeffreys. It appears that Smith and Kingston were reinstated. Voting for the Council was arranged in such a way that five members would be appointed in one year and four in the following year. Members therefore served a two-year period but were allowed to stand for re-election. There is no record of voting at either the 1940 nor the 1941 Conferences, but looking at the Elim Evangels of that period, it would seem that J T Bradley was elected to the Executive Council in 1940 and most likely took the place of Robert Mercer.

At the beginning of the forties, the Executive Council consisted of the following nine men: E C W Boulton, J T Bradley, F G Cloke, P N Corry, S Gorman, W G Hathaway, C J E Kingston, E J

Phillips and J Smith. There is no record in the Conference minutes to the election of J T Bradley, but he is reported in the minutes of the 1943 Conference to have been re-elected. The same is said of Greenway who was also re-elected. It is the Author's opinion that Bradley was elected to fill the vacancy caused by Mercer leaving to join Bible Pattern and that Greenway was elected or possibly, co-opted to fill the vacancy caused by the resignation of P N Corry.

The First Resignation

Whilst it must be the duty of a historian to publish the whole account of the historical survey within his orbit, the question must always be asked: 'Why am I doing this?' There are certain names that have to be mentioned because their sudden disappearance from the written history demands an explanation. Such was the case with the first Dean of the Bible College, P N Corry. He was at the Pentecostal Missionary Union Bible school in Preston at the same time as George Jeffreys and Ernest Darragh. He served as an officer in the British Army. There is no record of the exact date that he joined Elim, but within a very short time of his acceptance as an Elim minister, his gifting as a teacher and leader were recognised and he was appointed to the position of Dean of Elim Bible College.[10] He was Dean of the College from 1926 to 1938. He was elected to the Executive Council on 21st October, 1934.

He stepped back from the position of Dean in November 1938. The following statement was written in the Executive Council minutes: 'Resolved that the proposal laid before the Council by Pastor P N Corry that he be released from the Deanship of the Elim Bible College and be allowed to conduct Bible School campaigns be accepted. The Council wish to place on record their high appreciation of Mr Corry's services as Dean and lecturer at the Elim Bible College over the past eleven years.'[11] Corry continued in his role as a member of the Executive Council and was chairman of the 1939 Conference.

It would appear from a reading of the Executive Council meetings that Corry was appointed chairman after the split with Jeffreys. In the April 1940 minutes, he is present for the first day's meetings. The second day's minutes record: 'It was resolved that the resignation of P N Corry be accepted.' Corry is not mentioned again other than that he is mentioned among others who were not be allowed to preach in Elim churches. His resignation was sudden. He was arrested, charged and later imprisoned for gross indecency. He was sentenced to 12 months imprisonment. Some years later he was again arrested and was sentenced to serve a four-year term of imprisonment. It was the view of my predecessor Desmond Cartwright that Corry appears to have been arrested at the Executive Council meeting. Having read through the Executive Council meetings I have come to a similar conclusion.[12] The understandable policy of the Executive Council was to maintain a strict silence about the situation, but over the years it filtered through to many of the Elim ministers of that period.

This would have been a shocking situation for the Executive Council to have faced. Their troubles, however, were compounded by the fact that the conduct of four young ministers was such that the Council had to take action. At a special meeting of the Executive Council held on 4th June in order to consider disciplinary action against three young ministers, a Court of enquiry was set up to investigate the charges against them. The charge was: 'You are charged with conduct inconsistent with your calling as a Minister of the Gospel.' The author has seen the full report of the Court of Enquiry and strong evidence of misconduct was placed before them.[13] The three admitted their offence, although there was denial by one of certain specific offences. 'The Court in the absence of all three of the accused proceeded to consider the verdict, which was unanimously decided as follows.'[14] The names of the three are recorded and against each of them, the following appears: The Charge was considered to be proved.

A fourth minister was called to a Court of Enquiry set up by the Executive Council under a resolution dated 13th December

1943. The Court, consisting of the same five members from the previous hearing met on January 26th 1944 to consider 'Conduct inconsistent with his calling as a Minister of the Gospel.' The minister was presented with evidence of his failure which, at first, he denied. At the meeting on December 13th the Minister was accompanied by a church officer from the church that he was pastoring. 'He was questioned concerning his statement and confirmed that he was guilty.' The Council took a different approach to this fourth minister. The report records: 'Pursuant to the power vested in it by Resolution of the Executive Council, the court suspended (the minister) until the end of the 1944 Conference.' At that Conference whilst the Conference upheld the removal of the three other ministers, it decided to reinstate the fourth minister.

The forced resignation and arrest of Corry, together with the disciplining of the four young pastors shows that there appeared to be a problem as to personal sanctification within Elim at this time. There were other issues that fed into the mindset of some of the younger ministers that caused unnecessary problems. With the changes to the 1934 Deed Poll that saw deacons and church sessions elected in local churches and the appointment of lay representatives to the Conference, questions were asked of ministers to a far greater degree than previously. Young ministers were required to wait five years from the commencement of their ministry before they were allowed to marry. The subject of annulment, divorce and fornication were debated in Conference.

The Second Resignation

Fred Cloke was a Plymothian, who, along with his brother-in-law Leon Quest, went as students to the Elim Bible College in 1927. Both were appointed Elim pastors and Cloke was appointed to Southport where he had a successful ministry. He was a regular contributor to the Elim Evangel and had a reputation for being an excellent Bible teacher. Cloke emphasised personal holiness time and time again in his preaching and in his writing. He viewed personal holiness as being 'The summit of Christian Experience.'[15] He saw holiness as a peak which the believer could climb and reach. Starting in the lowlands of initial Christian experience, the believer, much like Christian of old, sets out, but not to the Celestial City which would be reached when he gets to Heaven, but to the summit of Christian experience which Cloke interprets as 'practical holiness'. In reading Cloke's articles, I have come to the conclusion that he viewed holiness as something that a new believer cannot possibly enter into. 'We do not regard the standard of perfect holiness to be one that can be entered into immediately by the earnest, sincere believer.' He also taught that there was coming a great world-wide Pentecostal Revival which would be the answer to prevailing conditions. He saw himself as being a key player in the coming revival.

He resigned his membership of the Executive Council at a special meeting of the Council held in Letchworth on 15th October, 1943. The following minute appears in the Council minutes:

> Mr Cloke's Statement. As promised, Mr Cloke read to the Council a statement outlining his views expressing disagreement with the present Constitution of Elim and deploring the lack of spirituality and holiness in Elim, as well as the drift from Pentecost. He also expressed in this statement his firm conviction that God would raise up a new Movement, partly from the present Elim work, and that God would raise up a new Leader, indicating that from this Movement which would begin in England the work would spread throughout the country and become world-wide in its extent. While agreeing with the urgent need for Elim and other Pentecostal Bodies in this country to return to a fuller and more virile Pentecostal witness, the Council did not agree with Mr Cloke that the situation as far as Elim was concerned was irretrievable, but that where there was a wholehearted turning to Him, He would cleanse, renew, and inspire, still held good if it were believed and obeyed.

With the exception of Mr Cloke, all the members were agreed on this point. It was particularly stressed at the meeting that the Council were doing everything in their power to raise the standard of truth and holiness in the Movement *as evidenced by recent action taken with the purpose of cleansing the Movement from things that would militate against its best interests.*[16]

On 20th October, Cloke sent a letter to all Elim ministers informing them of his resignation from the Executive Council. Because of his opposition to the revised Deed Poll, some may have thought that Cloke was going to align himself with Mr Jeffreys. That he had no intention of doing so becomes apparent when he writes: 'For many years before the crisis over the constitution there was a definite slump in our spiritual state to which I called attention, and when God would have purged the Movement, He was withstood, until today the state of the Movement is appalling.'[17] Cloke clearly felt that Elim had completely lost her spiritual strength, she had soft-peddled on the truths of Pentecost, had declined in holiness and was far removed from the truth and blessing of earlier days. One portion of his letter must have exploded with similar force and was intended to cause the same utter devastation within the Movement, in the same way that enemy bombs had so impacted the nation. Writing about the current state of the Movement, Cloke stated the following:

It has drifted away from the fundamental standards of the New Testament, and the declension from holiness, and from Pentecostal truth and blessing is gathering momentum under the present management of the Movement. Confused in doctrine, degenerating in conduct, bereft of spiritual power, and encumbered with a form of government too unwieldly to be practicable, too unscriptural and unspiritual to be respected, and too weak to stem the rising tide of iniquity, the time has come for men of the Book to declare their convictions, and, standing themselves against the reactionary forces of our time, to invite others to return to the truth and blessing which once dominated their vision.[18]

Cloke's resignation could have caused great damage to Elim at a time when the Movement was still reeling from the resignation of its Founder, facing the huge difficulties that the war caused their evangelistic policy and by moral problems which Cloke, being a member of the Executive would have been fully aware of. That he did not have much of a following is, in the author's opinion down to the fact that he overstated the perilous state of the Movement and also attacked the integrity of his fellow Council members, especially E J Phillips.

Notes

1. Churchill, Winston, *The Grand Alliance*: ibid, p38.

2. Churchill, Winston, *The Grand Alliance*: ibid, p38.

3. Churchill, Winston, *The Grand Alliance*: ibid, p38.

4. Author's brackets.

5. Churchill, Winston, *The Grand Alliance*, ibid, p39.

6. Gee, Donald, *Wind and Flame*, ibid, p197

7. He was always referred to by an abbreviation of his second name – Ernie.

8. Elim Conference Minutes, 1937 (Malvern: Elim Archives)

9. Elim Conference Minutes, 1938 (Malvern: Elim Archives)

10. This was the title that was used for the person who led the Bible College. He was, in effect, the principal of the college, but the title 'Principal' was not used for many years because George Jeffreys used that particular title and it was felt that it would cause confusion if the head of the Bible College had the title 'principal'.

11. Executive Council Minutes, 21st November, 1939 (Elim International Offices, Malvern).

12. Corry never linked up with Elim after his imprisonment, but he went on to make a useful contribution to society in his role as Recorder for Nantwich.

13. The Court of Enquiry consisted of Boulton, Kingston, Gorman, Smith and Hathaway, Executive Council members, together with two ministers, W F South and G H Thomas. They were given the option to have their case heard by all seven members as constituted, or by the five members of the Council only.

14. Elim Foursquare Gospel Alliance, Courts of Enquiry Book (GS office, Elim International Headquarters, Malvern)

15. *Elim Evangel*, 5th May, 1941, Vol 12, No 18, p283.

16. Author's italics

17. Letter, F G Cloke to all Elim Ministers, 20th October, 1943

18. Letter, F G Cloke to all Elim ministers, ibid.

10

The Executive Council 1940-1950

Leadership was never more crucial than in the dark days of the Second World War. Winston Churchill was appointed Prime Minister by His Majesty, King George VI on 10th May, 1940 in succession to Sir Neville Chamberlain. He was sixty-five years old. He formed an all-Party coalition government, the first in Britain since Lloyd George's First World War coalition had broken up in 1922.[1] Her Majesty's Opposition called for a debate on the war situation and this commenced on 7th May, 1940. On the second day of the debate, 8th May, Mr Herbert Morrison, on behalf of the Opposition, declared their intention to have a vote on what had now become a vote of Censure.[2] This day saw Lloyd-George make his last decisive intervention in the House of Commons. 'In a speech of not more than twenty minutes he struck a deeply-wounding blow at the head of the Government.'[3] In this final, devastating speech, David Lloyd George, the Prime Minister that saw a successful allied victory in World War I, made the following appeal for leadership: 'It is not a question of who are the Prime Minister's friends. It is a far bigger issue. He has appealed for sacrifice. The nation is prepared for every sacrifice so long as it has leadership, so long as the Government show clearly what they are aiming at, and so long as the nation is confident that those who are leading it are doing their best.' He ended his speech with these words: 'I say solemnly that the Prime Minister should give an example of sacrifice, because there is nothing which can contribute more to victory in this war than that he should sacrifice the seals of office.'[4]

Although the Government had a majority of 81 in the vote, over 30 Conservatives voted with the Labour and Liberal Oppositions, and a further 60 abstained. As a result, Chamberlain felt that his position as Prime Minister was untenable. He called Churchill and Lord Halifax to a meeting with two Labour leaders, Clement Attlee and Arthur Greenwood. The Prime Minister expressed the paramount need of a National Government and sought to discover whether the Labour Party would serve under him. It became clear that they would not. Chamberlain was in favour of Lord Halifax being his successor but Halifax felt that it would be almost impossible for him to lead the Government from the House of Lords. Chamberlain then advised the King to call on Churchill to form a government. Churchill's self-reflection is worthy of note at this point in our observation of Elim's leadership at this time:

> Thus, then, on the night of 10th May, at the outset of this mighty battle, I acquired the chief power in the State, which henceforth I wielded in ever growing measure for five years and three months of world war, at the end of which time, all our enemies having surrendered unconditionally, or about to do so, I was immediately dismissed by the British electorate from all further conduct of their affairs.
>
> During these last crowded days of political crisis my pulse had not quickened at any moment. I took it all as it came. But I cannot conceal from the reader of this truthful account that as I went to bed at about 3 a.m. I was conscious of a profound sense of relief. At last I had authority to give directions over the whole scene.
>
> I felt as if I was walking with destiny, and that all my past life had been but a preparation for this hour and for this trial. Ten years in the political wilderness had freed me from ordinary party antagonisms. My warnings over the last six years had been so numerous, so detailed, and were now so terribly vindicated, that no-one could gainsay me. I could not be reproached for either making the war or with want

of preparation for it. I thought I knew a great deal about it all, and I was sure I should not fail. Therefore, although impatient for the morning, I slept soundly and had no need for cheering dreams. Facts are better than dreams.

Ernest John Phillips (1893-1973)

Elim's leadership was vested in the Executive Council. They took collegiate responsibility for the affairs of the Movement between the Annual Conferences. But there is no doubt that among this group of nine men, one man took the unsought for place of leadership around the table. I refer to the Secretary-General, Ernest J Phillips. He refused the position of President and was not even chairman of the Executive Council nor the Conference, until he became the President in 1956, by which time he had retired from his position as Secretary General. A comprehensive account of the ministry of E J and his significance to Elim is given in my first volume.[5]

For many years Jeffreys and Phillips had worked together and the drawing up of the Deed Poll in 1934 in order to widen the base of Elim's leadership and to give birth to the Executive Council and the Annual Conference was a joint affair by the two men. E J drew up the Deed Poll and Constitution, but Jeffreys was consulted at every point. 'Although E J was the architect, it is clear that throughout the consultation with solicitors regarding the 1934 Deed Poll, he was in close touch with Jeffreys and consulted with him throughout the whole procedure. He made it clear in his correspondence with the solicitors that he conferred with Principal Jeffreys on constitutional matters.'[6]

That E J Phillips became the de facto leader of Elim following the resignation of its founder is very clear. This, in itself, is quite remarkable when one examines the differences in their roles and ministries. Jeffreys was a charismatic leader in every sense of the meaning of that word. He was a powerful preacher, a brilliant evangelist and had a powerful healing ministry that attracted crowds of thousands of people to his campaigns. The Birmingham campaign of 1930 is indisputably his greatest. The culmination of that campaign saw the great Bingley Hall with a seating capacity of 17,000 filled every night for two weeks. But the campaign started in a most discouraging manner as far as Jeffreys was concerned. The campaign commenced in Ebenezer Chapel, Steelhouse Lane on the 26th March. Jeffreys expressed his discouragement in a letter to Phillips.[7] The tide turned, however, and larger premises had to be hired to carry on the work. These included Birmingham Town Hall and the Embassy Ice Rink in Sparkbrook before moving on to the Bingley Hall. Over 10,000 converts were registered and 1,100 baptised in water.

In stark contrast to Jeffreys, Phillips was seen as a 'desk man'. He was an administrator of the very highest calibre but that did not resonate with some historians. One asserts that Phillips usurped Jeffreys' leadership within Elim.[8] 'It is evident that E J did not see himself as a figurehead, but as a leader among others.'[9] One current writer on the subject of leadership makes the startling claim that leaders are neither born nor made, they are summoned.[10] Sweet goes on to assert that leaders 'are called into existence by circumstances. Those who rise to the occasion are leaders.'[11] It is in this respect that Phillips rose to leadership within Elim. The dire circumstances of the time summoned Phillips to leadership and he responded to it in a calm, dignified and hard-working manner. His colleagues were astonished at the long hours he put into his work as Elim's Secretary-General. He was known to have been working in his office very late at night.

The author would argue that Phillips never set out to wrestle Elim's leadership out of the hands of the founder. Others saw the division in Elim being the result of a power struggle between Phillips and Jeffreys: 'As Jeffreys gained notoriety and attracted the spotlight of success, their close friendship dissolved into a power struggle over the organisation they led.'[12] The implication here is that E J was somehow jealous of the success and ministry of Jeffreys: that is not the case. E J was not a platform man. He was not an outstanding preacher and seldom preached at national events or conventions. He was a man who seemed at ease with his own personality and ministry. He was a man who was completely comfortable in his role and was content in carrying out the work for which he was best suited.[13]

William George Hathaway (1892-1969)

If Phillips was the de facto leader of Elim following the resignation of George Jeffreys, William Hathaway emerged as the next most prominent member of the Executive Council. Hathaway came into Elim as a result of meeting George Jeffreys during the Glasgow campaign in 1927. Hathaway was one of the ministers working for the Apostolic Faith Movement under the leadership of William Hutchinson. He had been given the impressive title of National Overseer for Scotland, but in reality this amounted to very little. He, like E C W Boulton, another former associate of Hutchinson who became a member of Elim's first Executive Council, opposed Hutchinson's teachings on British Israelism.[14] This was quite ironic, because George Jeffreys himself subscribed to similar eschatological views relating to Israel and Britain.

Hathaway's gifting as an organiser gained him a position at Elim Headquarters in Clapham. According to Malcolm Hathaway, his grandfather helped organise Jeffreys' campaigns. It is clear that he took over the main administrative duties whilst Phillips was incapacitated due to hospitalisation as a result of tuberculosis. He was one of the nine signatories to the Deed Poll 1934.[15]

It is obvious that Hathaway soon made a favourable impression with his ministerial colleagues in that he was one of the five men elected to the first Executive Council. The minutes of the 1934 Conference do not include the votes cast, but the following year, the votes were as follows: Boulton (sixty-eight votes), Hathaway (sixty-three), Corry (forty-eight), Smith (forty-one). In the following year, Hathaway gained the highest number of votes (seventy-four). Phillips was unable to attend the 1937 Conference due to him being in a hospital in the Isle of Wight. The minutes of the Conference clearly reveal that Hathaway deputised for Phillips.

The Minutes of the 1941 Conference show that Hathaway was appointed 'Chief Secretary'.[16] Phillips was appointed Secretary-General, Boulton – Field Superintendent, Smith – Dean of Elim Bible College, D B Gray – National Crusader Secretary. The same Representative Session confirmed Phillips as Editor of the Elim Evangel. In 1942, the nominations for Headquarters Officers changed in that Boulton was appointed Editor of the Elim Evangel and Hathaway became the Field Superintendent. From the years 1941 to 2000, Elim operated with a Field Superintendent. His role was to relate to the ministers, to bring to their attention matters relating to them in their work. He was there to give help, support and guidance. However, he was often the first or second cog in the wheel of discipline. Once the Presbytery system had been inaugurated, the District Superintendent would often be involved in the settlement of church disputes. In many cases, the problems ended at that point. However, if the problem between a pastor and his local church was of a certain severity, the District Superintendent would contact the Field Superintendent. Over the years, this position became to be seen as that of a first assistant to the Secretary-General/General Superintendent. The role of Field Superintendent was abolished in 2000 and his work divided between the Regional Leaders.[17]

W G Hathaway was a very gifted individual. He was in great demand as a Convention speaker. He was an adept theologian, and a fine College lecturer. He was also a talented musician and was the compiler with Frank Birkenshaw of the Elim Chorus Book. The importance of the Elim choruses cannot be overlooked. Hathaway and Birkenshaw tuned into the secular music scene and based many of their songs on the popular music culture of the day. Some of the tunes seemed to have been lifted straight out of the music halls and Gospel lyrics added to them. During George Jeffreys campaigns where people in their thousands attended, buses to and from the Campaign halls would have been filled with people singing the Elim Choruses. These songs would often proclaim the Foursquare message of Jesus the Saviour, Healer, Baptiser and coming King.

Hathaway was an author of a number of books. Two subjects in particularly caught his imagination: The Gifts of the Holy Spirit and the Second Coming of Christ. He lectured on both of these subjects at the Elim Bible College and I can recall the sheer enthusiasm with which he delivered his lectures on the Return of Christ and the End Times. The 1967 Israel-Arab war got him particularly excited. He referred to notes that he had written a number of years prior to the six-day war and showed how his particular prophetic view-point had been correct all along.

His book "A Sound from Heaven"[18] is a Pentecostal Classic. He gives an accurate but brief account of the Pentecostal Revival that occurred at the commencement of the last century. Whilst reading books of this nature, we must bear in mind that the writers were first-hand witnesses of, and partakers in, that great Pentecostal Revival that has left its mark on the universal church of Jesus Christ in a radical and profound manner. Pentecostalism has influenced every stratum of the Christian Church. The Archbishop of Canterbury, Justin Welby, in a video greeting to the Elim Pentecostal Church on the occasion of the celebration of their Centenary testified to the fact that he spoke in tongues on a daily basis.[19]

On the subject of speaking in other tongues being the initial evidence of the baptism in the Holy Spirit, Hathaway addressed the controversy over the question as to whether speaking in other tongues was or was not was the evidence of a person having received the baptism in the Holy Spirit. He outlined the three schools of thought and gives arguments in favour and contention on each one. The Three schools of thought are:

> SCHOOL ONE: Those who believe that the baptism of the Holy Spirit is always accompanied at the outset by the person speaking with other tongues and it is always the initial evidence of having received the baptism.
>
> SCHOOL TWO: Those who believe that it is generally accompanied by speaking in other tongues, but that

allowance must be made for exceptional cases where a person may have received the baptism but may not actually have spoken in tongues.

SCHOOL THREE: Those who believe that some physical manifestation will always accompany the baptism, but this may be speaking with tongues, prophesying, or some other supernatural physical manifestation.[20]

Hathaway gives a detailed and comprehensive summary of Scriptural accounts on behalf of the first school. He skims over the second school of thought in a few short sentences, but gives more time and space to the third school. In his summation, Hathaway is at pains to show that his views are proved by Scripture and backed by experience. His summation is a brilliant exposition of the classical Pentecostal view on Initial Evidence. It comes down firmly on the side of speaking with other tongues being the classic evidence of the baptism in the Holy Spirit, but leaves a slight opening for other supernatural manifestations under the anointing and inspiration of the Holy Spirit to be evidenced also.[21]

All three of these schools admit that in the majority of cases speaking with tongues is the evidence of the incoming Spirit, they agree there must be some definite manifestation; they must allow also some latitude for exceptions if they can do so without breaking down the whole case. I am fully convinced that here we can find bedrock, and that the Scriptural position is as follows:

The normal New Testament experience of the baptism in the Holy Spirit brings with it the power to speak with other tongues as the Spirit gives utterance, and this gift ought to be, and generally will be, in evidence. The manifestation of other clearly defined gifts of the Holy Spirit, such as prophecy, healings or the working of miracles can be regarded as additional visible evidence of the indwelling of the Holy Spirit.[22]

Hathaway's contribution to the Elim Pentecostal Movement was enormous. He served as Field Superintendent and Editor of the Elim Evangel. The former position, he held on two separate periods.[23]

Notes

1 Gilbert, Martin, *Churchill, the Power of Words,* (London: Transworld Publishers, 2012) p239.

2 Churchill, Winston, *The Gathering Storm,* ibid, p594

3 Churchill, Winston, *The Gathering Storm,* ibid, p594

4 Churchill, Winston, *The Gathering Storm,* ibid, pp594-595

5 Jones, Maldwyn, *And they came to Elim – An official history of the Elim Pentecostal Movement in the UK, Vol 1, 1915-1940*, (Rickmansworth: Instant Apostle, 2020) pp136-142, 353-361.

6 Jones, Maldwyn, ibid, p 354

7 Letter, Jeffreys to Phillips, 25th March 1930, quoted by Desmond Cartwright, *The Great Evangelists*, Basingstoke: Marshall Pickering, 1986), p104

8 Jones, Maldwyn, ibid, p364 and Liardon, R, *God's Generals: The Healing Evangelists* (Sarasota, FL: Robert Liardon Ministries), p82

9 Jones, Maldwyn, ibid, p368.

10 Sweet, Leonard, *Summoned to Lead,* (Grand Rapids: Zondervan, 2004), p12.

11 Sweet, Leonard, *Summoned to Lead*, ibid, p12.

12 Liardon, R, *God's Generals*, ibid. p82.

13 Jones, Maldwyn, *An Analysis of the Role of E J Phillips and an Assessment of his Leadership in the Establishment of the Elim Movement as a coherent Christian Denomination:* (MA Dissertation, Bangor University, 2011), p39.

14 Information received from a telephone conversation with Malcolm Hathaway, W G's grandson; 7th March, 2022.

15 The following is the order of the names that appear on the Deed Poll; George Jeffreys, R E Darragh, Robert Tweed, Ernest J Phillips, James McWhirter, Joseph Smith, Ernest C W Boulton, Percy N Corry, W G Hathaway. These men formed the first Executive Council. Jeffreys and Phillips were ex-officio members of the Council due to their positions in the Movement. George Jeffreys nominated three of the remaining seven members (he had wanted the right to nominate four but had to settle for one less) and the other five were to be elected by the Conference.

16 Elim Conference September 1941, Minutes of Representative Session, (Malvern: Elim Archives), p4.

17 Following the election of Chris Cartwright to the position of General Superintendent in 2016, He created the office of Director of Ministry, which position is currently occupied by Stuart Blount. This office has taken on some of the roles of Field Superintendent.

18 Hathaway, W G, *A Sound From Heaven*, (Clapham, London: Victory Press 1947).

19 Westminster Hall, London, September 2015, Celebration of Elim's Centenary.

20 Hathaway, W G, ibid, p58.

21 Hathaway, W G, ibid, p57.

22 Hathaway, W G, ibid, pp61,62. Original italics.

23 He was Chief officer 1941-1942, Field Superintendent 1942-1950 and 1957 to 1960; he was Editor of the Elim Evangel 1953-1956. He was the President of Elim 1948-1949.

11
The Executive Council: Continued

As pointed out in my previous chapter, good leadership is vital in any organisation. In the realms of organisational leadership, no situation is as hazardous as when moving from a Founder-led Movement to one with elected officers. This was the enormous challenge that faced Elim in 1940 after the departure of George Jeffreys. We continue in this chapter to profile the remaining members of the Executive Council during this critical period of time in Elim's history.

Samuel Gorman (1904-1983)

The sons of Ulster have served the Elim Movement incredibly well throughout its history and continue to do so to this day. Apart from England no other country in the United Kingdom has provided as many members of Elim's National Leadership Team as those born in Northern Ireland. The list is pretty impressive: Ernest Darragh, Robert Tweed, James McWhirter, Robert Mercer, Samuel Gorman, Joseph Smith, James Morgan, James Kennedy, Wesley Gilpin, John Smyth, Eric McComb, Gordon Hills, James Glass and Edwin Michael. Seven of these men served as President of the Alliance (Gorman, Smith, Morgan, Kennedy, Gilpin, Smyth and McComb), one of them, Joseph Smith, served in this capacity on two occasions. In addition, the Irish Superintendent at the time, Sandy Wilson, served as President of Elim in 1978-79.

Samuel Gorman entered the Elim ministry in 1927. Coming from the Belfast area, his home church was Ballysillan Elim Church which was situated at the top end of the Shankill Road, a strong Loyalist area.[1] The first church that he was appointed to after his marriage was Greenock The Sunday evening congregation in Greenock at the time often exceeded 1000. He was just 24 years of age.

In my first volume, I have given an account of the many incredible evangelistic campaigns led by George Jeffreys from 1915 through to 1938. There is not a doubt that there was a spirit of revival in the air. In a period of twenty-five years Elim grew from virtually nothing other than a handful of young men who felt a call from God to evangelise Ireland along Pentecostal lines, to a denomination of 215 churches with an International Missions that had representatives ministering in various parts of the world. 'That which characterised and galvanised (these) campaigns was the emphasis placed on divine healing. There were many reports of people being miraculously and supernaturally healed...'[2] George, and his brother Stephen, were amongst that small company of ministers and evangelists who were referred to as 'the Children of the Revival'. 'They were both very much products of the Welsh Revival. They associated themselves with people who were anxious to keep the revival fires burning. This affected the ministry of both brothers throughout the course of their lives. They were looked on as "Revivalists".[3] It was into such a 'revival' atmosphere that Gorman commenced his ministry in Greenock.

Samuel Gorman was looked upon by huge numbers of Elim people as a superb pastor. His very pleasing Ulster tilt was heard on many convention platforms throughout the British Isles. He was in demand as a preacher. Strongly evangelistic in his Gospel sermons, he was also a great devotional speaker. His calm and loving temperament was often required when strong discordant notes were sounded around the Executive table. Gorman pastored a number of large Elim churches. As well as Greenock he led the churches in Portsmouth, Letchworth and Birmingham Central Church (Graham Street). He served the Movement in the following capacities: Field Superintendent, Editor of the Elim

Evangel and Missionary Secretary. He was the second person to be elected to the role of President which, from 1946 was an annual appointment. From 1940 to 1945, George Kingston had filled the post of President of Elim Church Incorporated and, in such role, he chaired the Conference. E C W Boulton became the first president appointed on an Annual basis, an honour which was given to him a second time.

Gorman commenced his Presidential year of Office on Monday 16th June 1947 when the retiring President, E C W Boulton, presented him with a Bible. His Presidential address was printed in the Evangel and it clearly shows the depth of his spiritual experience and also his ability in Biblical exposition. He based his thoughts on Acts 26:16-18 where Paul gives an account of his conversion. His two main points reveal Gorman's philosophy of the calling and work of a pastor. He was conscious of the fact that this service was not just the induction of the Movement's President, but also it was the occasion of the ordination of a number of Elim pastors. He declared that this passage of Scripture, (1) Sets forth the majesty of the Christian ministry and (2) Reveals the power of the exposition of truth.[4] In this powerful sermon, Gorman showed clearly the reasons that he was a model for young ministers setting out on their pastoral pilgrimage. Sam Gorman remained a member of the Executive Council for 23 years and retired in 1960 due to ill-health.[5]

E C W Boulton 1884-1959

Ernest Boulton, like Hathaway, was a minister of the Apostolic Faith Church founded by William Hutchinson having previously been a Salvation Army officer. Born in Hampstead, London, Ernest Charles William Boulton was a prominent figure in the early British Pentecostal Movement.[6] He became a Christian on the 10th August 1901. Boulton joined up with Elim following George and Stephen Jeffreys' campaign in Hull in 1922.

He had preached for George Jeffreys at Elim conventions in Northern Ireland on a number of occasions and had obviously made quite an impression on Elim's Founder, so much so that Jeffreys appointed him as one of Elim's overseers in 1923, just one year after he joined Elim. Although siding with Elim in the dispute with Jeffreys, it would appear that Boulton was more sympathetic towards the Principal than any of his fellow Executive Council colleagues. His almost sycophantic biography of George Jeffreys,[7] reveals the depth of his admiration of the Principal.

Boulton was one of the four members of the first Executive Council voted in by the 1934 Elim Conference. He served the Movement as Editor of the Evangel and Dean (Principal) of Elim Bible College. Boulton is one of only five men who were appointed by the Conference to serve as President on two separate occasions.[8] He served on the Executive Council until 1954 and retired in 1956.[9]

Joseph Smith 1890-1980

Joseph Smith served as an Elim minister for almost seventy years. He was one of the four Conference appointed members of the first Executive Council (1934) and remained a member of the Council until 1960. He was Elim's President on two occasions. He was Dean (Principal) of the Elim Bible College from 1939 to 1947. He also served as Irish Superintendent for two terms. Joseph Smith was greatly loved and highly respected throughout the Elim Movement. Students would hang on his every word as he talked to them in informal gatherings outside the lecture halls. Young ministers would do their utmost to get him to come and speak in their small churches. Smith never refused an invitation based on the size of the congregation nor by the meagre ministry gift that he was likely to receive. He was renowned throughout Elim for his evangelistic fervour and anointed prophetic ministry. He was as close as Elim ever came to having a national prophet. 'He was a tall, striking-looking man with sharp features and bushy eyebrows which he was able to raise when making a pertinent point that he wanted to emphasise.'[10] His faith was irrepressible and it certainly galvanised the students at the Bible College. His students soon learned that they, too must abound in faith.

Joseph Smith was a keen personal evangelist and seemed always to have a pocketful of Gospel tracts to hand out. He would target cinema and theatre goers waiting for the doors to open. He rarely, if ever, missed an opportunity to share the Gospel. 'Joseph Smith was an inspiration to all and sundry. He lived the faith in an exciting and Christlike way. He never wasted a moment of his life. He was a great personal soul-winner. The students could not have had a better teacher in the things of God and the ministry.'[11]

Joseph Smith was very much a pastor. In the early days of Elim, ministers were moved on an annual basis. In all he pastored 24 Elim churches, two of them on three separate occasions.[12] He was often used as the first pastor of new, large congregations that had been formed as a result of George Jeffreys' great pioneering campaigns in the twenties and thirties. He was the first pastor of the Glasgow church when founded in 1930. From there he went to the new church in Cardiff and then Swansea. He was also the first pastor of the Grimsby Elim Church and the Plymouth Church which was founded by Stephen Jeffreys campaign in October 1924.

Smith was a firm critic of George Jeffreys after the schism in the Movement. He had no time for Jeffreys' change of heart over church government. 'Before I came to Elim, I was a member of a Pentecostal church where doctrinal matters were judged by the local assembly and I know how the church was rent asunder because of that very thing...For God's sake let us keep these things out of our local churches...Conference is the place to settle disputes – a church is a place to worship God.'[13]

Charles Kingston

Charles Kingston was the son of George Kingston who invited George Jeffreys to conduct an evangelistic campaign in Leigh-on-Sea, Essex. The result of this campaign saw the establishment on the first Elim Church in England. George Kingston pioneered a number of churches in Essex and although his group of churches were an important part of the Elim Church Incorporated, the work did not fully affiliate with Elim until 1964. The Essex churches as they were referred to, carried the official name of 'Elim Pentecostal Church'.[14]

Charles Kingston joined the Elim Evangelistic Band in 1920 and served for a short period in Northern Ireland. It is interesting to note that he was baptised in the Spirit a year after he joined the Band. Elim has never insisted that those applying to enter its ministry should be baptised in the Holy Spirit. The Movement has insisted, however, that those accepted into the Elim ministry but have not been baptised in the Spirit, seek that blessing. Charles Kingston's first appointment in England was to the newly established church in Clapham. This church was opened in 1922 when an old disused Methodist building was rented for a twelve-month period. Ernest Darragh and Miss Adams commenced the meetings and Kingston was brought across to help them. His evangelistic ability was recognised at a very early stage in his ministerial career. He went on to lead some of Elim's prominent churches including Croydon.

Kingston's appointment to the Executive Council is shrouded in mystery. The 1936 Conference minutes record that he received six votes and was therefore not elected to the Executive Council.[15] The 1937 Conference minutes, however, record the following: 'Those present: Principal George Jeffreys (in the chair), Pastors E C W Boulton, W G Hathaway, J Smith, R Tweed, P N Corry, R Mercer, C J E Kingston (members of the Executive Council) and 76 other members of the Ministerial Conference, 31 Probationers, 33 sister Evangelists and wives of ministers, and about eight others.'[16] The same minutes record that all eight members (including Kingston) were re-elected and Samuel Gorman was also elected. But according to the 1936 Conference minutes, Kingston failed to be elected. The only possible explanation is that Kingston was one of Jeffreys' 3 nominations to the Council. His first nominations were Robert Tweed, Ernest Darragh and James McWhirter. In the list of Executive Council members in 1937, Tweed and Darragh are excluded and Mercer and Kingston appear in their place.

At the 1938 Conference, the minutes record the following, 'He (the Principal, George Jeffreys) announced C J E Kingston, J Smith and R Mercer as his nominees, and said he wished to put in as his nominees the three men who came next in the voting for the Council so that they would carry out the wishes of Conference.'[17] The following year, he rescinded two of his nominations, Kingston and Smith and replaced them with W Barton and G I Francis. Incredibly, Gwilym Francis had only been accepted as a full minister of the Alliance at the 1938 Conference and his ordination occurred in 1939. It is the only occasion in Elim's history where a minister was ordained and appointed to the Executive Council (NLT) in the same year. A further irony is that Charles Kingston was the Chairman of the 1939 Conference and was in the chair when Jeffreys read the statement to the Conference removing him from the Executive Council.

Kingston remained on the Executive Council following Jeffreys' resignation and remained on it until he resigned his position in 1950. His father, George, died in 1949 and the burden of his father's business activities fell upon Charles. George Kingston owned a chain of butchers' shops throughout Essex and the East End of London. Charles remained as an Elim minister and was in great demand as a convention speaker and Bible teacher. He was elected President in 1964. He chaired the Conference business meetings from 1939-1946 and 1966.

J T Bradley 1905-1998

James Thirlwall Bradley came from the city of Carlisle. He was present at the George Jeffreys campaign in Carlisle in 1926. He was at the time, a member of the Railway Mission in the city. He was so impressed by the campaign that he joined Elim and was very quickly appointed as a pastor. His sharp, intuitive mind, together with a depth of Biblical knowledge and a proven ability as a Bible teacher soon brought him to the attention of his colleagues. He was elected to the Executive Council in 1940 when he replaced Robert Mercer who resigned from Elim and joined the Bible Pattern Movement.

Bradley pastored some of Elim's larger and significant churches which included Croydon (1961-64), (Clapham 1947-52) and Sheffield (1944-46). He was Crusader President (1944-45). He served the Movement in some of its most significant positions. He was Principal of Elim Bible College (1952-58), Editor of the Elim Evangel (1964-70) and Secretary General (1970-1974). His appointment as Secretary General was somewhat controversial and was reflected in the number of votes that he received. At the time, a simple majority was required to confirm the nomination by the Executive Council. The votes cast were 130 for and 73 against.[18] Under current legislation which requires a two-thirds majority approval, he would not have been appointed. He replaced Greenway who retired at the 1970 Conference. Bradley was three months older than Greenway.

There was a wide perception within the Movement that Bradley was not as 'Pentecostal' as perhaps he should have been. A number of ministers who knew him well conveyed to the author that he (Bradley) had never spoken in tongues and this was a source of great personal disappointment to him. Does that mean that he was not baptised in the Holy Spirit? J T Bradley certainly proclaimed the truths of Pentecost and those who knew him well had no doubt that he was baptised in the Holy Spirit.

H W Greenway

Billy Greenway served as Secretary-General (General Superintendent) of Elim for a period of thirteen years (1957-1970). He succeeded the highly respected E J Phillips having worked closely with him for a number of years. Greenway was appointed to the Executive Council in 1940 in place of Percy N Corry. He remained a member of the Council until 1973, a period

118

of thirty-three years. He continued to attend Council meetings in a non-voting capacity until his death in 1977.

Greenway's home church was Clapham. He was one of Clapham's earliest members having been introduced to the Pentecostal meetings by a godly lady in the Baptist church that he attended along with his friend Herbert Court, who also became an Elim minister.[19] Greenway pastored some of Elim's larger churches including Bradford, Swansea, Greenock and Hull. He served the Movement as Field Superintendent (1954-1957) and Editor of the Elim Evangel (1946-1953). Under his tenure of office as Secretary-General, Elim experienced a steady, if unspectacular growth. Over a hundred churches were added to Elim during his leadership of the Movement. He was elected to the office of President of Elim and served as such in 1956-1957.

J J Morgan

James (Jimmy) Morgan, was yet another Ulsterman who made a great impression on Elim and was a member of the Executive Council for a number of years. He was a much-loved pastor and a popular convention speaker. It seems that he was appointed to the Executive Council to fill the vacancy caused by the resignation of Fred Cloke in 1943. The first reference to him in terms of being voted on to the Council was in 1944 where he received fifty-five votes and elected to the Council. He remained on the Council until 1952 when a most unusual situation occurred. The minutes record the following: 'It was reported that there was a tie between Pastors P S Brewster and J J Morgan, who both had 116 votes, and therefore lots were drawn according to the provisions of the Constitution, as a result of which Pastor P S Brewster was declared elected. Tribute was paid in reference to the work of J J Morgan on the Executive Council for the past eight years.'[20] This is the first, and only time in the history of Elim that lots were drawn to choose a member of the Executive Council.

Morgan was re-elected to the Council two years later in the place of Boulton. Morgan was a respected and loved Elim minister and his appointment as Field Superintendent in 1960 was considered a popular one by his colleagues. He served in that capacity for six years and was then appointed pastor of the Clapham Elim Church. He remained a member of the Council until 1968. He served as Elim President 1953-54. It was somewhat ironic that he succeeded Brewster as the President. J J Morgan was a fine preacher.

Notes

[1] This refers to those who saw themselves as being loyal to the Crown and wish to remain within the United Kingdom of Great Britain and Northern Ireland. In dealing with 'The Troubles' in Northern Ireland in the third volume this is the terminology that I shall be using.

[2] Jones, Maldwyn, *And they came to Elim, Vol 1*, ibid, p219.

[3] Jones, Maldwyn, ibid, p 72

[4] Gorman, Samuel, *The Presidential Address, Elim Evangel*, 7th July, 1947: Vol 28, No 25, pp392-394.

[5] He, like E J Phillips, suffered for many years from tuberculosis.

[6] Jones, Maldwyn, ibid, p126.

[7] Boulton, E C W, *George Jeffreys – A Ministry of the Miraculous*, (London: Elim Publishing Company), 1928.

[8] The other three were: Joseph Smith (1949 and 1956), P S Brewster (1952 and 1965), W R Jones (1970 and 1982)

[9] A fuller biography of Boulton is included in my first volume, pp126-129

[10] Jones, Maldwyn, ibid, p129.

[11] Lewis, Wynne, *A History of Elim*, (Unfinished transcript, Author's personal copy).

[12] Clapham and Ulster Temple, he was also pastor of the Brighton Elim Church on two separate occasions.

[13] *Elim Evangel*, 1941, pp267-8, quoted by Jones, Maldwyn, *And they came to Elim, Vol 1*, p130.

[14] This name was later adopted by Elim as the name that the Movement would be known. However, the official name of Elim remains as 'The Elim Foursquare Gospel Alliance'. The reason that this name was chosen to describe Elim churches was to accentuate the fact that Elim was a Pentecostal movement.

[15] General and Ministerial Conference of the Elim Foursquare Gospel Alliance, 7th to 11th September, Conference Minutes, p4.

[16] Elim Foursquare Gospel Alliance, Annual Ministerial and General Conferences 13th to 17th September 1937, Conference Minutes, p1.

[17] 1938 Conference Minutes, pp4,5.

[18] Elim Conference 1970, Minutes of the Representative Session (Author's copy).

[19] For further details see, Jones, Maldwyn, *And they Came to Elim, Volume 1*, pp159-163

[20] Minutes of the Representative Session of Conference, 1952, p1.

12
International Missions in the Forties

Elim International Missions or the Elim Missionary Society as it was then known, commenced in 1923. Up until this time, Elim used other missionary organisations through which to send and support those Elim workers who felt a call to the mission field. Miss Dorothy Phillips is recorded to have visited India with the possible intention of returning at a later date. At this time, Miss Phillips was not a member of an Elim Church and there is no record of her being seconded as an Elim Missionary. It is quite clear from her correspondence she was exploring a possible call to the mission field in India.[1]

First Elim Missionaries

The first ordained Elim missionary was Cyril Taylor who joined the Congo Evangelistic Society after his ordination at Dowlais in April 1920. His son, Sir Cyril Taylor (1935-2018) the renowned educationalist writes of the influence that James Salter[2] had on his father:

> My father's inspiration was a remarkable character called James Salter, who had been born into poverty in Preston, Lancashire in 1890. Despite the difficulties of travel during the Great War, Salter managed to get himself to the Congo in 1915, driven largely by a faith in the Pentecostal cause. His followers in the Elim Pentecostal Mission claim that as a result of a constant struggle with malaria, he was raised from

his deathbed six times. It was on his return to Britain to recruit more followers that my father heard this message.[3]

Miss Adelaide Henderson, the sister of William Henderson, one of Elim's early leaders, was one of the missionaries who worked alongside Taylor in the Congo. She went out to the Congo in 1922 in the company of her fellow missionary Miss Elsie Brooks from Tunbridge Wells. On the long journey by train and river boat from Cape Town, they both contracted Malaria. Sadly, Elsie died a few miles from the settlement where the two ladies were to minister. Cyril Taylor was a medical doctor and he was one of the workers who helped Adelaide recover from her own illness. She stayed in the Congo for two years before having to return to the UK due to recurring illness. Adelaide Henderson was a key figure in the establishment of the Elim Missionary Society. She was the Secretary of the Society from 1925-1944. She remained a member of the Elim Missionary Council until 1950.

The Establishment of the Elim Missionary Society

According to Canty, George Jeffreys did not have a great deal of enthusiasm for missionary enterprise.[4] This would have been understandable in that he poured most, if not all, his energy into conducting revival campaigns in the UK. There is a total absence of any reference to overseas missions in the Conference minutes until 1942 when the office of Foreign Missionary Secretary is included in the list of Headquarters' Offices. George Thomas, a former missionary to Mexico and Spain succeeded Adelaide Henderson as Foreign Missionary Secretary in 1944. The very first reference to the activities of Elim missionaries in the Conference minutes occurred in 1944.

> Foreign Missionary Work. An encouraging report was given by G H Thomas in which special reference was made to the continued increase in missionary donations. Mention was also made of Elim Missionaries in enemy occupied territory. After some discussion on the missionary work, it was decided that

a committee be set up to investigate fully the position of Elim Missionaries and Elim Associate Missionaries in their relation to other Missionary Societies with a view to commencing an Elim Foreign Missionary Society. It was also decided that the members of the Elim Foreign Missionary Council be appointed annually by the Conference and that the number of members be 9. Elim Missionaries on furlough being invited as a usual practice to sit on the Missionary Council, such Council to have power to co-opt a representative from the Elim Pentecostal churches (previously known as the Essex Elim churches). Those elected as members of the Council were: G H Thomas, Miss A Henderson, E C W Boulton, W G Hathaway, S Gorman, C J E Kingston, E J Phillips, J Smith and Miss M Barbour.[5]

The above minute is confusing, to say the least. It is generally accepted that the Elim Missionary Society was commenced in 1923. It appears, however, that between the two world wars, Elim Missionary activity was conducted largely on the basis of Elim Missionaries being seconded to other societies. One society, in particular, was a favourite with Elim through which to second candidates – The Congo Evangelistic Society. From the above minute, it seems that this arrangement was to be radically changed, if not stopped altogether. This was to cause some existing missionaries working with other organisations considerable difficulties. Although the Elim Missionary Society was successfully initiated with Elim having its own distinct fields in various parts of the world, some Elim missionaries were to continue working in partnership with other missionary organisations.

The Remarkable McGillivrays

John McGillivray went out to China in 1910 under the auspices of the Pentecostal Missionary Union, five years before Elim came into being.[6] He was the head of a family of remarkable missionary-evangelists who were connected with Elim for many years. John showed some sympathy towards George Jeffreys and this was viewed with some disapproval by former members of the PMU. The reason for this, more than likely, was the fact that the PMU amalgamated with the Assemblies of God and became the missionary arm of that organisation. There was correspondence of a strong nature between him and Mr Mundell in which the latter questioned him on fundamental issues such as Eternal Punishment and the Baptism of the Holy Spirit 'with the Scripture Signal'.[7] The Pentecostal mission in Honan Province, China, was of significant importance to the PMU and for one of its workers to have shown an interest in George Jeffreys and Elim, provoked a reaction.

John McGillivray married Mabel Seagrave in Honan Province. There is virtually no information concerning Mabel, but it seems likely that she was a missionary from another Pentecostal/ Evangelical association already working in Honan Province. Together, the two missionaries performed missionary work of heroic endurance in situations of upheaval and downright terror. 'They cared for the wounded, dying, needy and wretched in a Chino-Tibetan settlement from 1919, bringing spiritual hope and physical comfort to civilian and military Orientals.'[8] Mabel eventually took the two children home whilst John continued to work alone until he met with an accident, contracted an illness and died in 1929. John and Mabel's two children, Ken and Vera went back to China. 'At 21, Ken first joined Elim's marvellous couple in Outer Mongolia, the Paynes, in 1939. When they left, he continued, soon to be harried by the Japanese (who imprisoned him for 4 years) and then by the Communists. Driven out, he landed in Taiwan (formerly known as Formosa) where he remained for the rest of his ministry, building up a fine fellowship of churches.'[9] He returned to Mongolia to work with Pastor and Mrs J Payne before moving to Taiwan. Although an Elim Missionary, John McGillivray linked up with the Pentecostal Assemblies of Canada and most of his financial support came from that quarter. His sister Vera dedicated her missionary career to the Chinese in Hong Kong.

Canty refers to the fact that Principal George Jeffreys, on the death of John McGillivray, 'took a concerned interest in Ken'.[10] Ken was soon to learn, however, that the Principal felt little enthusiasm about Elim workers abroad. 'Consequently Elim people with an urge for overseas work linked with other societies, though supported largely by gifts from Elim either privately or officially.'[11]

Douglas Scott

Douglas Scott was a remarkable man with a clear vision for establishing a Pentecostal work in France. He was an Elim member and came from our Ilford church. He applied to do missionary work in France through Elim but nobody showed an interest. He and his wife set off on their own and 'eventually offered many churches to Elim, but they were not accepted.' Instead, they became the Assemblies of God of France. Donald Gee makes no mention of the Elim connection in his book 'Wind and Flame' but introduces us to this remarkable man who wanted to be an Elim missionary. According to Gee, Scott felt a call to missionary work in Africa and went to stay in Havre to learn French in preparation. 'Mr Scott had been a musician in a jazz orchestra, and had been converted at a Pentecostal open air meeting in the city (London). At a meeting in Sion College one Friday evening all indecision as to a missionary call was swept away through a remarkable word given by the Holy Spirit through means of tongues and interpretation.'[12]

Scott's work in France was phenomenal. After establishing a work in Havre, following a period of hard fighting a flourishing assembly was established in Rouen. Although always conscious of his call to Africa, 'Douglas Scott recognised that the Lord had given them a work to do in France before proceeding elsewhere, and having now become fluent in the language, he commenced a truly apostolic period of ministry.'[13] The Scotts were to proceed to the Belgian Congo, in pursuance of their original call to Africa, and the established work there soon doubled under their ministry. It was my great privilege to have been a pastor to Mrs Scott and her sister during the time of my ministry at the Norwich Elim Church. Mrs Scott had not forgotten her early connections with Elim and took up membership at the Elim Church. She was a most Godly and gracious lady. Her son's mother-in-law, Mrs Sadie Stevenson, the widow of Pastor Tommy Stevenson, a former Elim President, was also a member of the Norwich church at this time. These three ladies were a pleasure to visit, a joy to minister to and a great encouragement to a young pastor and his wife who were anxious to respond in their own way to the call of God upon their lives. The assurance that these fine Christian ladies were praying daily for Ruth and I was a source of great encouragement to us.

Prior to the Second World War, Elim continued to support missionaries who had links with other societies. Jeffreys' acquaintances from the PMU Bible School in Preston, W F P Burton and James Salter, together with E Hodgson had set up the Congo Evangelistic Mission. Elim supplied personnel for the mission. We have already commented on Dr Cyril Taylor, Miss Adelaide Henderson and Miss Elsie Brooks. Right at the beginning of the war, Leslie Wigglesworth, the grandson of Smith Wigglesworth, together with his wife Ruth, the elder daughter of E C W Boulton joined the work in the Congo, but very much as seconded missionaries from Elim.

Missionary work in other fields

Two sisters from Bournemouth came under the ministry and influence of George Jeffreys. They were the Marshall sisters from Springbourne. 'Alice Marshall had a vision of Egypt and a call repeated five years later after the war (World War 1) had ended. She was not disobedient to the heavenly vision, and from 1920 gave herself to the care of children in her Christian orphanage. Her sister Lilian, baptised in the Spirit the same year as Alice, showed similar devotion by her side from 1928. The triumphs of their faith, glorious answers to prayer and the young lives turned from darkness to light were their reward until they had to retire to England.'[14]

Other notable Elim missionaries that established significant works in various parts of the world prior to the outbreak of the Second World War were: Marion Paint, a gentle, but very courageous lady who tackled superstition in India. Joseph and Mina Payne from Hendon Elim Church made the long journey to Outer Mongolia, an inhospitable place where day and night time temperatures were poles apart; extreme heat during the summer days and penetrating cold by night. They encountered devil-worshippers and confronted them with the Gospel.[15]

Thomas and Nora Nosworthy pioneered in Central Africa, eventually concentrating on Tanganyika (now Tanzania). At that time, there were one hundred and thirty-nine different tribes in that country. Writing in the first edition of the Elim Missionary Evangel, he comments:

> We have travelled thousands of miles through tropical Africa in our specially fitted Elim pioneer lorry. Beginning at the Transvaal we travelled through those long and lonely stretches of Rhodesia (Zimbabwe and Malawi) which brought us to the Congo. There it was our great joy to minister to old friends who brought us gifts of all kinds and who pleaded with us to stay amongst them once again. We knelt together amidst the palm trees; we chatted, having met each other in the pathways; we crouched beneath the thatched roofs of their huts; we attended the funerals of those who had died through the indirect attentions of the witch doctors. But still there was a greater call – yes, where there is a greater need, where there are tribes that have never heard the name of Christ Jesus; and so on we went, over the vast Lake Tanganyika into that needy land of the tropics.[16]

Tom and Hilda Johnston from Northern Ireland were accepted as 'honorary missionaries' when they went to Kenya in 1948. Tom went to Kenya as a Civil Servant and in his free time ministered to the Kenyan people. The work that the Johnstons carried out amongst a number of different tribes in Kenya was highly regarded by Elim and they were both granted 'Honorary Missionary' credentials with Elim.

Emmanuel Press

Hubert, the eldest of the three remarkable Phillips brothers (they also had a sister, the wonderful Dorothy Phillips who was one of the pastors of Letchworth Elim Church). All four were to leave their mark on Elim. Frederick Phillips, like his eldest brother, was a printer by trade. He it was who printed the very first edition of the Elim Evangel in December 1919. One of the articles in that first Evangel was a testimony written by Dorothy Phillips of her pursuing a possible missionary call to India. It was not to be, but she most certainly devoted the rest of her life to the Elim cause.

Hubert founded the Emmanuel Mission in the Transvaal. Austin Chawner, supported by the Pentecostal Assemblies of Canada, together with Hubert Phillips began the Emmanuel Press, which although was originally in Elim's hands came under the ownership of another evangelistic agency. H C Phillips married Jean Jones, a member of the Letchworth Elim Church. Both died whilst still working for the Lord, Hubert in 1973 and Joan in 1977. The Emmanuel enterprise provided an outlet for much missionary zeal from 1932 onwards when a member of the Croydon Elim Church, W.H Francis arrived, followed by several couples over the next 40 years. These included the Blythens, Nortons, Gulls and two good friends of mine, David and Maureen Butcher. Others who went to this part of Africa included Ruby Simms, Freda Grossen, Ruby Mapleson, Mrs Hawley, Anne Stephenson and Mrs and Miss Faith Christie.[17]

The decision was taken at the 1944 Conference for Elim to set up its own missionary society. Although there were many recognised as Elim Missionaries and Elim Associate Missionaries, the time had come for Elim to have its own society and open up its own fields. One wonders what would have happened to organisations such as Emanuel Press if that had been opened by the Elim Missionary Society? The Elim Missionary Society began operating on August

1st, 1945. Almost immediately there was a positive response from Elim people. Sunday Schools began collecting for Elim Missionaries. The farthing fund was set in motion. It took 960 farthings to make £1 in those distant pre-decimalisation days, but boys and girls throughout Elim responded magnificently to the challenge. The Elim Sunday School, Englefield Green collected 18,284 farthings in 1946 which amounted to £19 0s.11d. The Pontypridd Sunday School collected 9,600 farthings (£10.0.0) and Ipswich Sunday School collected 4,176 farthings (£4 7s 6d). [18] Three Elim Sunday Schools collected 32,060 farthings in 1946. £33 8s 5d in 1946 had the equivalent purchasing power of £1491 today. That was a remarkable sum of money from three Sunday Schools at a time when the country was on its knees recovering from the huge impact of the war.

George Thomas, the new Missionary Secretary, had a huge task to convince existing Elim Missionaries who were seconded to other Societies to place their trust in this new Society. In one of his early editorials, he emphasised the importance of personal sacrifice when it came to Missionary work. The missionaries themselves would have to sacrifice, but there also had to be sacrificial giving on the part of Elim members and churches.

> Missionaries are not a luxury, nor are they a vent for surplus offerings; they are the evidence of our willingness to sacrifice for the widest interests of the kingdom of our God. If we fail the missionaries, we are failing the Lord who gave the Church, not merely those who have gone abroad, the command to carry His Gospel to the uttermost parts of the earth. Every child of God can join in this enterprise even though not called to cross the seas, for those who do go must be supported: they need our prayers and our money: we can extend the missionary interest among our friends and stimulate others to join this noble work. [19]

Elim people responded magnificently to the challenge of providing money for the Elim Missionary Society. One very important method of raising money was through the old mission boxes. They were reinforced carboard boxes made in the shape of a missionary church. In the third quarter of 1947, the Ilford church collected the magnificent sum of £132 12s 9d. £100 in 1946 would be equivalent to £4462.5 today.

In 1947 Pastor and Mrs Aubrey Hathaway (the son of W G Hathaway) went out to India where they settled in the great city of Bombay (Mumbai). They were joined a year later by David Lewis from Liverpool Elim Church. Elim had a number of missionaries in India at this very tense time as India was granted independence in 1949. Miss M B Ewens from Letchworth Elim Church returned home on furlough after completing an eight-year term in India. After a period home on furlough Pastor and Mrs J Troke and their young daughter, Barbara returned to India on the S.S Franconia on 15th Sept. 1947, bound for Bombay (Mumbai).

G H Thomas, the Elim Missionary Secretary concluded his Notes in the last edition of the Missionary News for 1947 with the following plea:

> *Missionary Income.* We rejoice in God's blessing upon our missionary work, and note with gratitude the continued increase in the missionary income, but with the appointment of new missionaries and the ever-increasing expenses, we are now at a place where the missionary expenditure is higher than the income. This presents a further challenge to our Elim family and friends.[20]

Notes

[1] Jones, Maldwyn, *And they came to Elim, Volume 1*, ibid p190.

[2] James Salter was the co-founder of the Congo Evangelistic Mission alongside Willie Burton.

[3] Peter Wilby, introduction to Taylor, Sir Cyril, *Sir Cyril: My Life as a Social Entrepreneur* (Stroud: Amberley Publishing, 2013) Kindle edition Loc 208.

[4] Canty, George, *History of Elim*, ibid, p159.

[5] Conference Minutes (Representative Session), 1944.

[6] Canty, George, ibid p159

[7] Letter, John McGillivray to Mr Thomas Mundell, August 10th, 1925 (Malvern: Elim Archives).

[8] Canty, George, ibid, p159.

[9] Canty, George, ibid, p159.

[10] Canty, George, ibid, p159.

[11] Canty, George, ibid, p159

[12] Gee, Donald, *Wind and Flame*, ibid, p157.

[13] Gee, Donald, ibid, p158

[14] Canty, George, ibid, p160.

[15] Canty, George, ibid, p160.

[16] *Elim Missionary Evangel, Pastor T A Nosworthy: Pioneering through Central Africa:* Vol 1, No 1, p18.

[17] Canty, George, ibid, p161.

[18] *Elim Missionary Evangel*, April-June 1947, Vol 1, No 2, p19.

[19] Thomas, G H, *Editorial Notes, Elim Missionary Evangel*, July-September 1947, Vol 1, No 3, p1.

[20] *Elim Missionary Evangel*, October-December 1947, Vol 1, No 4, p11.

13
Battered, bruised,
but still alive – just!

The end of the Second World War saw the nations of the world having to get used to new realities. The loathing of fascism gave way to the fear of Communism. The USSR was the new threat to world peace. On the 5th March 1946, Sir Winston Churchill gave his famous 'Iron Curtain speech'.

> From Stettin in the Baltic to Trieste in the Adriatic, an iron curtain has descended across the continent. Behind that line lie all the capitals of the ancient states of Central and Eastern Europe. Warsaw, Berlin, Prague, Vienna, Budapest, Belgrade, Bucharest and Sofia, all of them famous cities and the populations around them lie in what I must call the Soviet sphere, and all are subject in one form or another, not only to Soviet influence but to a very high and, in many cases, increasing measure of control from Moscow...The Russian-dominated Polish government has been encouraged to make enormous and wrongful inroads upon Germany, and mass expulsions of Germans on a scale grievous and undreamed of, are now taking place.[1]

The other post-war grim reality was living under the mushroom-shaped cloud of Atomic warfare. Walter Urch, then pastor of the Elim Church in Exeter, wrote an extremely perceptive article on the Atomic Bomb.[2] The writer was well-enough informed to realise the enormous benefit that splitting the atom could produce for the whole world. 'The right use of the energy imprisoned within this monstrous weapon of destruction ultimately means a higher standard of life for everyone.'[3] Looking to the future benefits of the atomic age, Urch wrote about the benefit of atomic energy to everyday life. But he admits that fear has completely overshadowed the splendid picture of the benefits to mankind from the splitting of the atom. He wrote: 'The first occasion upon which this new and terrible energy was employed was in the form of a weapon of unprecedented destructive power. The way of death opens up to humanity as never before, and the human race has become afraid of its own discoveries.'[4] Urch made the following trumpet call to his readers: 'It is in the face of these perils that the value of the Christian faith and the relevance of the Christian Gospel is fully appreciated. The Atomic Bomb is a stupendous challenge to Evangelism. Civilisation will collapse and we can't prevent it, but, under God, we can do something to save men out of it.'[5]

Elim, like every other Christian denomination, had to face the stark realities of the time. Conscription continued up to the late fifties and that, inevitably had an effect on the churches. Life for the ordinary working person was hard and made harder by the extension of food rationing. The other reality that Elim had to come to terms with was the inevitable change in their evangelistic strategy. They no longer had a dominating, charismatic leader, although P S Brewster was to take up the baton of pioneer evangelistic campaigns.

The glory days of the twenties and thirties were, by the end of the war, a distant memory. Charles Kingston made Elim members face up to the changing strategy on evangelism that had been forced on the Movement by circumstances. In an article with the dubious title 'Crowds not Christ's Way'[6] he advocated that the evangelistic emphasis must be on personal evangelism. What he wrote is perfectly true, but it is almost as if he was saying that evangelistic campaigns would no longer be the main thrust of Elim's evangelistic efforts. Elim had known many large crowds. But times had changed. Kingston's article seemed to express the mood of the Movement at that time. The crowds had dispersed. The vast congregations were greatly reduced. There were no longer opportunities for large campaigns during war-time, so the emphasis was rightly placed on personal evangelism. Elim was blessed with some great exponents of this intimate form of evangelism, chief among them being Joseph Smith. The emphasis of Kingston's article on personal evangelism being the most efficient way of reaching people with the Gospel was not wrong. What was notable in his article, however, is that he almost consigned large evangelistic campaigns to past history.

In his article, he almost condemned ministering to crowds. 'Jesus in His ministry did not seek the crowds, though the crowds sought Him. He went after the individuals. He called the disciples one by one. Nicodemus, the Woman of Samaria, Mary and Martha, they were all won as units. So must His Church be built today – brick by brick. The Church has gone after the crowds and lost the one.'[7] One cannot help but wonder whether this article was a reflection of the need to adjust to new evangelistic realities.

Canty was in no doubt as to the extremely perilous state of Elim immediately after the war. Seeing the situation first hand, Canty came to the conclusion that Elim was virtually left as dead. 'Outside, a rain-washed poster announced a Bright Gospel Service, 6.30pm. Inside, it consisted of a dismally depleted audience and a pastor preaching for converts like casting a net in a wash basin. A "Great Pentecostal Rally" heard the well-known leader talk of the state of things being like Elisha's bones, the prophet dead, his bones left, but "they could still work a miracle"'.[8] A member of the Executive Council admitted to Canty that that there were few who thought that Elim was not dying of her wounds.[9]

Elim had been birthed and grown in a heady revival atmosphere with a charismatic leadership that was its buttress for such a long time. But this had gone. The war had encroached on its dwindling resources. The Sunday evening Gospel services, which was the main service of Elim churches at that time were greatly reduced as an inevitable result of war-time restrictions. Internal disputes which sometimes flared into the public eye convinced many that the death beetle was already gnawing through the newly buried

Elim coffin. The moral state of the country did not give much encouragement to believe that change was on the way. Canty, in his unique style, gives a graphic description of the state of the nation in the immediate post-war period.

> Normal goodness was being despised as Victorianism. Permissiveness overflowed the gutters. Religious interest hardly rose above the question why God allowed the war. National approval of selfishness and covetousness had been given with the legalising of pools and betting shops. Violence, sexual perversion, pornography, crime had begun their ascendancy. Worship took place around the sacred turf of the stadium, trodden only by teams of new gods. Intellectualism knew no more than anybody what Christianity was all about. The raw material for new evangelists was raw heathens, there was little left of the generation schooled in church from which George Jeffreys had drawn.[10]

The 1944 Elim Conference

It is generally accepted by students of Elim's history that the 1944 Conference was pivotal in the restoration of the Movement. Conference minutes state just the plain facts of what was agreed and what was rejected. But an examination of the effects of proposals passed or rejected unfolds the purposes of the stated proposals. There were a number of proposals passed at this Conference that was to prove very beneficial for the Movement in the years that were to follow.

> [1] The first proposal of note does not appear to be of huge consequence, but it proved to be the first faint glimmer of light in the long battle for women to be included at every level of ministry within Elim. The minutes record the following under the item 'Local Preachers': 'The report of the Local Preachers' Committee was presented, After some discussion the Conference adopted the report, it being understood that the term "Applicant" *referred to both men and women*.'[11]

> [2] Foreign Missionary Work. Although Elim had established a missionary department in 1923, most of the missionaries

sent out by Elim worked with other Missionary organisations that were sympathetic to the Pentecostal cause. The 1944 Conference took the huge step to look into commencing an Elim Missionary Society. A committee was set up for the purpose of looking into such a feasibility.[12]

[3] Elim Bible College. The minutes record the following: 'A proposal for the re-opening of the Elim Bible College was presented to the meeting by the Dean, following which, the subject of the Elim Bible College was discussed. It was decided that the Executive Council examine fully the question of the Bible College and Elim Woodlands, and draw up a comprehensive syllabus.' The college had been closed since the resignation of P N Corry as Dean in 1938. Joseph Smith was appointed Dean in place of Corry, but never functioned as such until after the war.[13]

[4] Evangelical Effort: 'It was decided that the Covenant Card entitled 'A resurgence of Faith Crusade' presented to the Conference by W G Hathaway be accepted in principle. The Conference unanimously adopted the motion.'[14]

Why this minute has the title 'Evangelical Effort' assigned to it is difficult to understand in light of a later minute that recorded the decision of the Conference to set up an Evangelical Council, 'with a view for formulating a bold policy for Evangelistic work, particularly in the light of post-war developments.'[15] Canty states that this included a dedication 'to be signed which expressed, viewed by hindsight, a lack of confidence in the commitment to Christ of the average Elim member. Seeing how true and hard-working they proved to be through the years, any such lack of confidence was unnecessary.'[16]

Remaining true to Pentecostal truths

Canty, who was a member of the 1944 Conference wrote out of his personal recollections of that Conference and was of the opinion that there emerged the desire to achieve religious acceptance and respectability. 'The situation was that Evangelical churches seemed to be entered more readily by the public than Elim churches, despite the claim of Pentecostal power. The calm sermons, the composure of the congregations, solid, regular, conventional, "nice" people – was it better after all than tongues and choruses and Hallelujahs?'[17] Something in the nature of his above comment obviously caused him to think that Elim was attempting to achieve acceptance and respectability by other Christian denominations. It is difficult for someone who was not present at the time, indeed who was yet to be born, to disagree with the view of one who was both present and active in the Conference at that time. However, in reading through the Evangels, Executive Council Minutes, Conference reports and minutes during the decade of the forties, I have come to the conclusion that Elim was trying very hard to identify with its Pentecostal roots. Canty referred to the words of the 1947 Elim President, E C W Boulton whilst referring to those willing to extend a hand of fellowship towards Elim for its evangelical keenness, warned of the 'danger of slackening in our testimony to accommodate other fundamental groups who are not in sympathy with the Pentecostal message.'[18]

At the 1947 Conference there was considerable discussion on promoting Pentecostal liberty in church services, particularly at conventions. The following resolution was approved by the Conference:

(a) That a continuous effort be made on the part of ministers to promote and encourage liberty and the blessing of the Holy Spirit at all our convention meetings.

(b) That more opportunity be given to seek the Baptism of the Holy Ghost, and to those who have received this experience be encouraged to seek a refilling of the Spirit.

(c) That more of our convention meetings provide for a time of prayer and worship, not limited to one person leading in prayer.

(d) That the exercise of the Gifts of the Spirit be encouraged in our Convention meetings.

(e) That more of the preaching be along Pentecostal lines: the necessity of being filled with the Spirit, the necessity of being refilled with the Spirit, the necessity of retaining the conscious blessing of the Spirit, and teaching on the Gifts of the Spirit.[19]

That there was some diversity amongst Elim Pastors on the subject of the Baptism in the Holy Spirit and the initial evidence of speaking in other tongues is clearly seen in two Elim Evangel articles that appeared in two editions in 1949. The first was written by E Scrivens the Pastor of the Elim Church in Dudley. He managed to write an article on the Baptism in the Holy Spirit without a single mention of speaking in other tongues. The following lengthy quotation from this article showed what the author believed that the phrase 'baptism in the Spirit' signified.

A study of the Scriptures reveals several facts concerning the relationship between the believer and the Holy Spirit. It is possible to be a believer and yet not have the baptism in the Spirit, e.g., the tarrying disciples in the Upper Room, before the Day of Pentecost: the Samaritan believers: the Ephesian believers, etc. That it is possible as believers to have the Spirit upon us and with us, is revealed by the Old Testament saints, and the fact that Christ had breathed on the disciples the Holy Ghost prior to their Pentecostal experience. That it is possible to yield true and good service to God and not have the baptism is proved by the fact that the disciples were used to heal the sick and preach the Gospel of the Kingdom before the day of Pentecost, and that today God still blesses all types of Christian witness irrespective of creed or denomination. Still further, it is tragically possible for believers to experience this mighty baptism in the Spirit, yet become stagnant in their Christian experience, so that progress is stunted. This latter fact might seem impossible, yet when we look at the Corinthian Church, we are compelled to admit this fact is seen by some of the lives of these baptised believers.

Having established the fact that the Baptism in the Holy Spirit is a distinct experience, and even an elementary one, and that one can miss the great blessing, what is its signification? Simply that, as Christ is the 'Door' into Divine life, so the baptism in the Spirit is the 'Door' into a Spirit-filled life. As the baptism in water is a unique experience denoting the death of the old, and the beginning of a new life, so the Baptism in the Spirit is the beginning, or the initiating experience into the 'Fulness' of the Christian life. One cannot enter into salvation without going through the door, and one cannot experience fully the blessings of a life in the Spirit without the initiating experience of the Baptism.[20]

Whilst Scrivens goes on to give some of the blessings that this experience affords the believer, he remains completely silent about the accompanying initial evidences of the baptism in the Holy Spirit and says nothing on how we can receive this blessing. It could also be claimed that the body of his article could be somewhat insulting to those Christian believers who, though not accepting the Pentecostal truth of Spirit-Baptism, yet display the fruit of the Spirit in the way they live their lives as Christians.

The article written a few weeks earlier by F B Phillips, (the brother of E J and Managing Director of the Elim Publishing Co. Ltd.) was written mainly to refute the counter charge by non-Pentecostal Evangelicals that the baptism in the Holy Spirit was synonymous with conversion. He makes a very interesting point in quoting 1 Corinthians 12:13 'For also in (*en*) one Spirit we are all baptised into (*eis*) one body'.[21] Phillips comments on this verse: 'We are baptised in the Spirit not to put us in the Body, but because we are already in the Body, through the New Birth; we are baptised in the Spirit with a view to the Body.' Referring to the Greek preposition *eis*, Phillips points out that this preposition is translated 'towards' on thirty-two occasions and he is strongly of the opinion that in the light of that fact, 1Corinthians 12:13 teaches that the baptism in the Spirit did not take place at conversion but after. He admits that it should take place immediately after, but nevertheless, it is after.[22]

What is very clear in Phillips' article is that he mentions the accompanying evidence of the baptism in the Spirit in the Book of Acts in which speaking in other tongues is the usual accompaniment of Spirit Baptism. Phillips concludes his article by making reference to the need to be continuously filled with the Holy Spirit. 'Do not get drunk on wine, which leads to debauchery. Instead, be filled with the Spirit. Speak to one another with psalms, hymns and spiritual songs. Sing and make music in your hearts to the Lord, always giving thanks to God the Father for everything, in the name of our Lord Jesus Christ.'[23]

Elim people were encouraged not just to seek the baptism but to be re-filled. A feature at conventions and holiday camps run by the Movement, was the 'waiting meeting'. It was also referred to as the 'receiving' meeting. These meetings were usually held between services at the conventions. There would be a short explanation of what the baptism in the Spirit is and thoughts expressed on how to receive this blessing. Those who had previously received the baptism were invited not just so that they could have a 'spiritual top-up' themselves but to be an encouragement to those seeking the baptism. These meetings diminished along with the conventions. Sadly, nothing seems to have been put in place to replace these meetings. It is my opinion that very few opportunities are given from Elim pulpits these days for people to receive the baptism in the Holy Spirit, and very little teaching is given on the subject of the Baptism in the Holy Spirit.

Notes

[1] Gilbert, Martin, *Churchill: The Power of Words*, (London, Transworld Publishers 2012) pp370-371.

[2] Urch, Walter, *The Atomic Bomb, Elim Evangel*, 12th August 1946, Vol 27, No 32, pp381-383

[3] Urch, Walter, ibid.

[4] Urch, Walter, ibid.

[5] Urch, Walter, ibid.

[6] Kingston, Charles, *Elim Evangel*, 12th June 1944, Vol 25, No 36, p 127.

[7] Kingston, Charles, ibid.

[8] Canty, George, *History of Elim*, ibid, p149

[9] Canty, George, ibid, p 190

[10] Canty, George, ibid, p149

[11] Author's italics

[12] Canty, George, ibid

[13] Canty, George, ibid

[14] Canty, George, ibid

[15] Canty, George, ibid.

[16] Canty, George, ibid, p150.

[17] Canty, George, ibid, p150.

[18] Canty, George, ibid, p150.

[19] Annual Conference 1947, Minutes of the Representative Session.

[20] Scrivens, E, *The Significance of the Phrase – The Baptism in the Holy Ghost, Elim Evangel* 29th August, 1949, Vol 30, No 35, pp410-411.

[21] Authorised Version. The italics in the verse are original inserted by the author of the article.

[22] Phillips, F B, *The Baptism in the Holy Spirit – A Separate and Distinct Experience, Elim Evangel*, 16th May, 1949, Vol 30, No 20, pp234-239.

[23] Ephesians 5:16-20

14
RESURGAM!

Plymouth was one of the most heavily bombed cities during the Second World War. This was due to the Royal Navy Docks in Devonport. It became a target for enemy bombs. The first bombs fell on the city on 6th July 1940, with the heaviest period of bombing occurring in March and April 1941. The following statistics show the devastating impact that enemy bombs had on the City. Between 6th July 1940 and 30th April 1944:

- There were 59 separate raids
- The air raid sirens sounded 602 times
- Two main shopping centres, two guildhalls, a theatre, six hotels and eight cinemas were destroyed
- 26 schools bombed
- 41 churches struck
- 1900 public houses destroyed by bombs or fire
- 3,754 homes were destroyed
- 18,389 homes were in need of major repairs
- 4,448 civilians were injured
- 1,174 civilians were killed[1]

St Charles, one of the oldest church buildings in Plymouth was destroyed and its skeletal remains stands as a memorial to the horrendous blitzing of the city by the enemy. The city's main church, St Andrew's Parish Church was bombed and badly damaged in March 1941. Amidst the smoking ruins, one of the city's headmistresses nailed over the door a wooden sign saying simply

'Resurgam' 'I shall rise again'. This encapsulated the spirit of the citizens of Plymouth. They, like the rest of their fellow countrymen were resilient and not prepared to buckle under the yoke of fascist tyranny. The day after a particularly savage enemy blitz that caused widespread destruction throughout the city, the Prime Minister, Sir Winston Churchill visited the city and was greatly impressed by the spirit of the people. Looking at the devastation and the destruction of homes around him he said 'Your homes are laid low, but your heads are held high.' The city, like the rest of devastated Britain was restored and resurrected.

The same word 'Resurgam' can be used to describe Elim's recovery from a very bleak time in her short history. The Movement was not even twenty-five years old when war broke out. Then, her Founder and charismatic Leader had left and caused a considerable division in the Movement. Also, as has been pointed out in a previous chapter, the leaders had to contend with moral issues of such a nature that at that time could have caused untold damage. Then the Elim leadership was rocked yet again by another resignation of a respected Executive Council member who felt that the level of holiness in the Movement was far from what should be expected of a strong Pentecostal denomination. At the same time, Elim, like every other Christian denomination in the country was having to face the rigour of the war when it became clear that their tried and tested evangelistic strategy of planting new churches by means of evangelistic campaigns was greatly curtailed.

By and large, it was a discouraged band of representatives that gathered in Graham Street Elim Church, Birmingham on Monday, 8th May 1944. The Front-Page heading in an Elim Evangel at that time, summed up the mood of discouragement that had swept through the Movement – 'We are up against it'. An attempt in Parliament sought to prevent all treatment of cancer except by medical people, thus banning Divine healing by law. This failed, but the opposition was revealed.[2] That Elim survived this desperately difficult and traumatic period in its short history was down to Godly national leadership and to pastors who worked extremely hard during the most trying of times. Canty speaks of the mindset of some of the top pastors in Elim at that time.

> The 1944 Conference revealed great heart searching everywhere. Joseph Smith spoke of big assemblies coming down to bedrock. Speaker after speaker sounded the alarm. 'We have sinned and lost power,' said Leon Quest. 'Things must be put right between brethren,' said John Dyke, and the 'danger of losing sight of the most vital things' was expressed by W G Hathaway. 'We must get down to corporate prayer' said V J Walker. It sounded desperate rather than being anticipatory of blessing.[3]

All through this extremely difficult time, the pastors were having to make readjustments. They were having to fit into a new role. Deacons were questioning what was done. Some were capable men, but others quite unused to any kind of responsibility in their jobs were now having to approve new enterprise which the pastor might wish to take and this often proved irksome to a capable minister. Many newly appointed deacons were trade unionists particularly in areas like the East End, South Wales, the industrialised Midlands, the heavily industrialised northern cities. The unions were beginning to make their presence known Some deacons, especially those in the Welsh mining valleys made things very difficult at times for their pastors. They felt that they had a need to keep him to account. To some respect this is true, but it is equally true that some working men in the South Wales mining valleys saw their work as trying to keep the lead on the pastor and to carefully examine his expenditure.

But having gone out such a great distance, the tide began to flow back in. It was slow but steady. Percy Brewster and Charles Hadler had started a work in Aberystwyth in 1941 and Jack Hardman was appointed as the first pastor. This was not a strong work, however and it closed down for a period in the fifties before being opened again, becoming an attractive church to students. The Church in Aberystwyth today is led by a gifted musician and preacher, Joel Pridmore who, along with his wife, is very involved in the life and culture of Aberystwyth. Their determination to learn the Welsh language has been a great help to them in this regard. There is a great need for Elim ministers working in Welsh-speaking areas of Wales to adapt to Welsh culture and learn the language in order to reach first-language Welsh speakers with the Gospel. This first-language Welsh speaker is of the opinion that this ministry would be easier achieved by church leaders and workers learning the Welsh language.

The appointment of an Evangelistic Committee at the 1944 Conference was a declaration of intent. As the war entered its final year, thoughts inevitably turned towards the future. Pioneer evangelism was very much rooted in Elim's core. It was through this means of public mass evangelism that churches, some of them very large ones, had been planted right throughout the United Kingdom. The problem that faced Elim at this time, however, was 'who is going to be the central figure in the Movement's evangelistic drive, now that George Jeffreys was no longer on the scene?' Canty makes the following very apposite comment: 'If Elim was to be reinspired it awaited evangelistic enterprise.'[4]

The answer came in the form of the redoubtable Percy Stanley Brewster. By this time, he had established himself in Cardiff as the pastor to the very large City Temple. Cardiff was one of the few 'super churches' of the nineteen thirties that had come through the ravages of the war and had not been duly affected by Elim's schism. Graham Street, Birmingham was another. But the huge pre-war congregations in cities and conurbations such as Glasgow, Dundee, Carlisle, Nottingham, and East Ham had largely melted away. That Cardiff continued to thrive and grow despite all the odds was down to the gifted leadership of its pastor.

Brewster had been involved in evangelistic campaigns in the late thirties when he pioneered the Elim Church in Neath. He did this whilst he was the pastor of the Swansea Elim church. His evangelistic zeal seemed unbounded. A chapter will be devoted to the story of this remarkable pioneer evangelist, pastor, national leader and statesman later in this book, suffice to say for the present that he was undoubtedly God's man for leading Elim's evangelistic fight-back after so many years in the dreaded doldrums of depressed inactivity.

Brewster was commissioned by the Evangelistic council to spearhead Elim's new Evangelistic strategy. The first and stirring expression of that strategy came in June 1945 on a Sunday evening in Wigan. A marquee was erected on a disused pithead in Crompton Street. The Welsh Presbytery contributed £70 towards the campaign and finance also came in from central funds. Weatherwise, it was an appalling night with heavy rain threatening to stop the campaign before it had begun. That opening night, despite the extreme weather conditions, fifty people made a confession of faith in Jesus Christ. 'In the next few weeks 600 professed Christ, the healing power of Christ was seen and a local businessman summed it up: "The tent has done more good in Wigan than anything I have known. I have seen its good effects in the homes of my tenants."'[5] Brewster had pioneered an Elim work in Aberystwyth in 1941, but the Wigan campaign was a much bigger affair altogether. The war in Europe had ended and it was therefore easier to hold evangelistic campaigns now that many of the war-time restrictions were ended.

The study of Elim history reveals that more often than not, the success of a pioneer evangelistic campaign depended largely on the minister appointed to establish the new church. Elim's Secretary General, E J Phillips described the moment as the turning point in the history of the Movement. Whilst this was true, without the untiring efforts of the Pastor appointed to lead the new church, the Wigan campaign would have amounted to very little. Elfed Francis, known throughout Elim as 'Taffy Francis' was appointed as the first pastor. The opposition that he faced in the town was great. Halls in which to hold church services were closed to him and the response from churches and chapels was very negative. Francis made the following statement: 'I interviewed ministers, businessmen, deacons, trustees, dance hall proprietors, the Fire Brigade Chief, the Mayor, The Education Officer, the Rates

Office…and every estate agent. As soon as I mentioned 'Tent' and that we needed a hall to carry on the meetings, I was politely but firmly told, 'Sorry we can do nothing for you.' One gentleman greeted me affably and asked to which church I had come to minister. When I mentioned the Tent, he didn't speak another word except "Good Morning."'[6]

After a great deal of searching a small hall was hired, but once the congregation of 95 people were seated, they could hardly move as the space was so cramped. Eventually, the Gee School of Dancing was hired which allowed 160 to attend. The Church of Christ allowed their building to be used for a baptismal service that was attended by a congregation of 250. Eventually, the old Methodist Central Hall in the centre of Wigan was bought for £4500. This was a frightening figure at the time, with the only means of repayment being gifts from new converts. For years, the pastor laboured to pay off this debt, contributing large sums himself by selling Christian literature and collecting hundreds of tons of waste paper.[7] The pastor paid the toll for his hard labour and after 14 years at the task, his health suffered. He was ably assisted by his wife who worked equally hard by his side. The Elim Evangel testified as follows: 'Never in the history of Elim have two servants worked harder to establish the work than Elfed and Connie Francis.'[8]

John Woodhead

Whilst Brewster was the prime Elim pioneer evangelist in the post-war years, John Woodhead was also an extremely gifted evangelist who pioneered a number of churches for Elim. Born in Mosborough, Yorkshire, John Woodhead became one of Elim's most fruitful ministers. Married to Alice, they had two daughters, Eileen and Dorothy. Eileen married Pastor Jack Glass. Their son, John, was General Superintendent of Elim from 2000 to 2016. Initially an Assemblies of God pastor, Woodhead joined Elim in 1930 and pastored some of the larger Elim churches including Hull and Bradford. During the war, he led the Carlisle Elim church and as has already been noted, he ministered effectively among the Forces personnel.

In 1946 he held a tent campaign in Plymouth. The city had suffered severe damage from enemy bombing and the tent was erected on the site of a church that had been totally obliterated during the war. The Plymouth church had suffered very badly during the war years. As a result of the bombing of the city, Plymouth Elim Church was forced to use a number of locations to hold meetings, this included Goodbody's café on Mutley Plain. That the congregation could have been housed in such premises shows the disastrous effects that the war had on a church that numbered well over 500 prior to the war.

After successful campaigns in Burnley, Oldham, and Warrington, Woodhead, ably assisted by William Evans, turned his attention to the South West. There were 376 registered decisions for Christ in Warrington and a church was established there, Churches were also planted in Oldham and Burnley. After the moribund years of the war, Evangelism was very much on the Elim agenda in 1946. In August, Woodhead campaigned in Torquay where over three hundred decisions for Christ were recorded.

September 1946 proved to be a 'time of double opportunity, for two campaigns were opened in this month. One in Tonypandy in Wales, where Pastor P S Brewster and party launched a campaign in a marquee erected in the town. At the same time Pastor J Woodhead and party ventured forth in a marquee erected on a bombed site in the centre of Plymouth. The two parties of campaigners experienced trouble through the stormy weather of that month. Both marquees were blown down in the storms. These difficulties were eventually overcome and the campaigns continued. Hundreds of decisions were recorded.'[9]

So successful was the Plymouth campaign that John Woodhead stayed on to be the pastor of the church. With William Evans ministering alongside him, Woodhead was able to leave the church for two major campaigns in Denmark and Sweden in 1947. Towards the end of his time in Plymouth, Woodhead held a pioneer campaign in Newquay where a church was planted with Eldin Corsie, who was to become Principal of Elim Bible College and later, General Superintendent of Elim, as the first pastor. John Woodhead's evangelistic ministry continued in the re-building of the Plymouth Church. Whilst writing this volume, I came into contact with a 96-year-old gentleman who, along with his sister, was converted during this time. He was baptised by John Woodhead.

John Woodhead's work as a pastor-evangelist was recognised by the Movement and in 1960 he became Elim President. This was followed by a two-year stint as a member of the Executive Council. John Woodhead was a great preacher. Wynne Lewis, who, in time was to become John's pastor in York after he retired, penned the following tribute to him:

> John Woodhead, a Yorkshire man from Mosborough who had been wounded on active service during World War 1, began missions in the Docklands in London. He was a strong, brave man. He had been set upon and dragged off the platform by discontents, but refused to be intimidated. George Canty, his pianist on that mission had a wooden mallet by the side of the piano, ready to repel further invasions. He spread into Essex, opening churches in various towns. From here to Southport, Warrington, Burnley, Oldham, Torquay and Plymouth. As a pastor-evangelist, his churches did very well, and grew quite large. His members caught their pastor's enthusiasm for evangelism. John lived for one thing, a compulsion that generated massive enthusiasm to win the lost to Jesus. He loved to preach on the Cross of Christ and when doing so reached heights of passion and eloquence. No-one who heard him preach at the Royal Albert Hall on Easter Monday 1961 will ever forget the experience. Despite the dropped aitches, the audience was spell-bound. George Canty, writing about that occasion reported, 'It was unforgettable to sit and hear him deliver the greatest sermon many thought they had ever heard, on Christ in Gethsemane. He referred to the twelve legions of angels Jesus said He could call to His aid, and

described an angel as a blinding and hypnotic being, awful in intelligence and power, overwhelming to human senses, and then said, " Jesus could 'ave 'ad one 'undred and forty-four thousand of them to 'elp 'im if 'e 'ad asked." The unpoetic literalness and factuality of it seemed to stun the vast audience, more especially because of the preacher's unsophistication. It was communication at its most effective level.'[10]

John Woodhead planted over twenty Elim churches. As well as those already mentioned, he pioneered churches in Leicester, Burton-on-Trent and other places. As well as his campaigns in Denmark and Sweden, he toured extensively in the United States. The General Superintendent of the American Assemblies of God, Thomas Zimmerman, was greatly impressed by John Woodhead's preaching and evangelistic ministry. He said that 'he remembered John with esteem, affection, and Christian love and described the effects of his American campaigning as "a visitation of God."'[11] Canty adds the following comment, 'John Woodhead is a physical part of Elim's history leaving his mark for ever.'[12]

In his first visit to Denmark in the early months of 1947, the Elim Evangel noted that there was a total of 298 conversions. Woodhead and Brewster both emphasised the truth of Divine healing. The Evangel report contains the testimony of one lady, she writes: 'Thanks to the Lord for healing me from ear complaint which I have been suffering from during a long period. On the 4th March I was prayed for, and a lump *and pain disappeared, thanks to Jesus.*'[13]

Evangelism Overflow

The determination of the Elim Evangelistic Committee saw a number of pastors venture out into campaign work. The Field Superintendent, W G Hathaway, reviewing the year 1946 reported the following: 'January began the year with plans being laid for a series of efforts in various towns, which were to result in crowds, converts and cures, and to leave behind a trail of triumph in the cause of Christ. No one but those who have handled the organization of such special efforts can have any idea of the amount of work that has to be done behind the scenes before the opening of a campaign, but it is a labour of love when you know that hundreds will hear the message and numbers respond to the claims of Christ.'[14] Hathaway rightly points to the administration involved in organising the campaigns and in responding to the vision of the Evangelistic Committee.

Two brothers who were active in Evangelistic campaigns at this time were Pastors Cecil and Kenneth Newton. The author readily confesses to the fact that they are not names that were familiar to him in the history of Elim. In 1946, these two brothers held evangelistic campaigns in Holyhead and Beeston. 'They commenced their campaign in the Town Hall and continued there and in the Elim Church for three weeks. At the first meeting five hundred attended. Great interest was aroused and the effort brought another eighty converts to the feet of Christ. One remarkable healing was that of a girl who had been blind in one eye. Her sight was restored.

Evangelism was very much in the mind of the two hundred or so delegates that attended the 1947 Conference in London. Following the Evangelistic Conference Report given by the Field Superintendent, W G Hathaway, there was considerable debate. Details of the campaigns of the previous year were given. The campaigns at Tonypandy by Pastor P S Brewster and Plymouth by Pastor J Woodhead and party were deemed to be 'particularly successful'.[15] 'At Tonypandy a new and flourishing church had been formed, and at Plymouth an existing church had been greatly enlarged. In Nelson, Oldham and Torquay churches have also been established.'[16]

Notes

[1] http//www.plymouth.gov.uk *Plymouth Blitz Remembered*, accessed 1st June 2022.

[2] Canty, George, *A History of Elim*, ibid, p149.

[3] Canty, George, ibid, p150.

4 Canty, George, ibid, p151

5 Canty, George, ibid, p151

6 Canty, George, ibid, p152

7 There were a number of Elim ministers during the second half od the last century who took on second jobs not just to supplement their meagre salaries, but to raise money to pay the mortgage on church buildings or to pay for much needed major repairs.

8 Canty, George, ibid, p152

9 Hathaway, W G, *Crowds, Converts, Cures: Elim Evangel*, 25th December 1946, Vol 27, Nos 51,52, pp652-653.

10 Lewis, Wynne, *A History of Elim*, unpublished, pp 23,24 (Malvern: Elim Archives)

11 Canty, George, ibid, p174.

12 Canty, George, ibid p175.

13 *Elim Evangel, Reports, Danish Campaigns*, 31st March, 1947, Vol 28, No 11, p170

14 Hathaway, W G, *Elim Evangel* 25th December 1946, ibid, p152.

15 Homer, Selwyn, *Day by Day at the Elim Conference*, June 16th-20th, *Elim Evangel*, 14th July 1947, Vol 28, No 26, pp406-413

16 Homer, Selwyn, ibid, p409.

15
Children and Youth

Throughout its history, Elim has placed a strong emphasis on children and young people. From the first Crusader meeting held in the Clapham Elim church in October 1924, right through to the present day where Elim has a full-time National Youth Leader with staff to help him, it can be said that Elim has moved with the times. One could argue that such movement has, at times, been excruciatingly slow, but through its many and varied outreaches for young people, many have been brought into the Kingdom of God through Elim's outreach to children and young people.

Elim Crusaders

The first volume of this history gave a short account of the Elim Crusader Movement.[1] The name of Elim's Youth Movement carried with it the idea of battle. It was not a uniformed organisation, although, in the early days, many young crusaders wore a Crusader sash. On joining a Crusader branch, each member was given a Crusader badge which depicted an open Bible with the inscription 'Elim Crusader' in gilded letters set on a blue background. The badge was made in the shape of a shield.

James McWhirter, one of the earliest members of the Elim Evangelistic Band and a close companion of George Jeffreys was the founder of this work. At the time, he was one of the pastors of the Clapham church and sought a means of consolidating the work amongst the young people of the church. At this time, there were over 200 young people at the weekly youth service. Arthur

Birkenshaw, who was an early Crusader Secretary at Clapham stated that the aim of the Crusaders was 'to bring others into contact with the living Christ.'[2] Soon, many other Elim churches opened Crusader branches. The age group was very wide – between fourteen and thirty-five. It was later decided that the upper age limit be extended to forty!

Issues surrounding worldliness and holiness were a constant theme in the Movement, particularly in the pre-war and immediate post-war years. There was considerable discussion about the Crusader Movement at the first Ministerial and General Conference, 17th – 21st September, 1934. Arthur Longley, suggested that a National Crusader Week be introduced, together with a special Crusader number of the Evangel. P S Brewster called for a Crusader Covenant. Another member made, what would seem to this generation, a very legalistic proposal that those who attended cinemas, etc. should not be allowed to wear Crusader badges.[3] Robert Tweed stated that 'Special Bible studies are an attraction and help to keep them.' The content of these 'special Bible studies' remain a mystery. Mr Ball put forward the quite daring idea that Crusaders should be asked to make suggestions for their meetings. 'Several suggested that Crusader and FGT badges[4] should not be sold at the Crystal Palace[5] meetings as it enables those to obtain them who would not be supplied at their local Church.'

In the pre-war years, the wearing of Crusader sashes was a feature at the large Elim gatherings, especially at the Royal Albert Hall celebrations. It was also customary for the young ladies in the youth choirs to wear white dresses. The subject of sashes and uniforms was discussed at some length at the 1936 Conference. 'Some suggested that the Crusader Sash should be abolished and others that a plebiscite should be taken in all our Crusader branches as to whether they preferred uniform, or white dress, or sash, or no distinguishing mark.'[6]

For a few years, the Representative session of Conference appointed a Crusader President. Those that served in this capacity were J T Bradley, P S Brewster, and J J Morgan. This office was removed in 1946. The following resolution was passed at the 1946 Representative Session of the Elim Conference:

> Crusader President. It was resolved that in view of the appointment of a President of the Alliance from the date of this Conference, no Crusader President be appointed after the term of office of the present President expires, and that thereafter the President of the Alliance be ipso facto Crusader President.

The leadership of the Crusaders, Cadets, Youth work and Sunday Schools came under the overall leadership of the National Youth Secretary. The title was changed at the 1960 Conference to that of National Youth Director.

The first National Youth Secretary was Douglas B Gray who occupied this role from 1928-1952. Gray was an outstanding musician with a background in the Salvation Army as his middle name – Bramwell – clearly testifies. He founded the London Crusader Choir in 1921. The story of this remarkable choir and its many years of Prison ministry will be told in a later chapter. Much of the development of the youth work in Elim was the result of his enthusiastic and visionary leadership. One of the first actions on becoming the Movement's national youth leader was to form an Elim Youth Choir. In 1929 over 2,000 young people sang in this choir at the Royal Albert Hall services on Easter Monday, which meant that the platform had to be extended well into the auditorium.[7]

Douglas Gray is remembered first and foremostly as a musician and conductor of the London Crusader Choir. But his work as the Youth Leader in Elim must not be overlooked, particularly his leadership of the Crusader Movement during the dark and difficult days of the Second World War. His weekly Crusader page in the Elim Evangel was a great help to those service men and women who had left home and church to serve their country. Gray encouraged

Crusader branches to correspond with those who had left their local Crusaders to join His Majesty's Forces.

There was a fear of 'worldly activities' encroaching upon Crusader and youth meetings in the churches. There was something of a schizophrenic approach to youth evangelism in the Movement in the early post-war years. Various government schemes to provide funding for youth clubs were an attractive proposition to churches throughout the nation and many denominations were quick to avail themselves of grants to help them re-establish youth work after the war. However, the fear of allowing 'worldly' activities affecting the spiritual welfare of Elim young people was, at times, like a chain that bound the Movement and prevented Elim churches benefiting from government grants and schemes to help youth work in the country. An example of this myopic approach to youth work was a resolution of the 1945 Elim Conference under the title 'Unauthorised Youth Activities'.

> After some discussion on the subject of unauthorised youth activities in Elim churches, it was resolved: that this Conference is in favour of opportunities to reach youth people being grasped, in an endeavour to influence them to Christ, provided premises used by the Alliance for the worship of God are not used for organised games, gymnasiums or such like activities.[8]

Elim gave the impression that the sanctuary was a holy place in which only 'spiritual' activities such as preaching, prayer, worship and communion services should take place. There was even a decision at an early Conference to recommend that flowers should not be placed on the communion table. Such an attitude stifled many evangelistic enterprises and prevented churches from using their facilities to reach out to people, especially young people. There was no part of the Church building that could be used for 'worldly' activities such as games and indoor football etc. Every room in the building was considered holy and part of 'God's house'.

Concern was expressed by the delegates to the 1944 Conference relating to the youth activities taking place in the Winton Church. The minutes record the following: 'A report was before the meeting concerning certain youth activities in relation to the Boys' club at Winton, Bournemouth. The Conference deputed W G Hathaway, Samuel Gorman and John Dyke to meet the minister and the trustees of the Winton Church relative to these matters.'[9]

It was not until the late eighties that this 'building' concept of the local church was turned around. The Restoration Movement of the seventies and eighties caused us to re-examine the Scriptural teachings on the Church and the Kingdom. We began to see the church not as a building of brick and stone but an edifice where people were the building.

This concept of the local church building being merely a convenient place for the body to meet for worship had a profound effect upon me. Preaching at one of the evening rallies at the 1978 Conference in Clacton, I took for my text the words of Jesus: 'I will build my Church and the gates of Hades shall not prevail against it.'[10] I infuriated quite a few people at that time with my bold declaration that God's people did not go to the Church, they never ceased being the Church.

This new and fresh concept of the Biblical meaning of the nature of the Church began to change people's thinking on the whole concept of fellowship and discipleship. Much more will be written on this in the next volume. But one very practical effect that this change of understanding on the meaning and theology of the Church is that it started to impact on the designs of new buildings in the last twenty years of the last century. New buildings were set up with things other than a sanctuary and a minor hall for prayer meetings and Bible studies. The Irish churches, especially, made major changes in the designs of their buildings. The Ulster Temple in Ravenhill Road, Belfast had an extension built in which twelve Sunday School rooms were built, together with a minor hall that could accommodate approximately 150 people. A large modern kitchen was built. The church already had a large hall to the side of the main building called the Jubilee Hall. This was used for youth activities, Campaigners and other weekly children's meetings.

From this period onwards, the Irish churches certainly set a very high standard when it came to erecting new church buildings. Many of them had gymnasiums built as part of the church complex. Others made changes to their buildings to set up Full Day Nurseries. A prime example of this was the Carryduff Elim Church.

Alongside the Crusader Movement, an organisation was set for those children from eight to thirteen. This was called 'Cadets'. In some churches, it was referred to as 'Sunshine Corner'. This outreach among children was hugely popular. Archie Biddle, the pastor of the Rotherham church ran a very successful Sunshine Corner in that South Yorkshire town. He was granted the use of one of the main parks in Rotherham and had literally thousands of children that attended these meetings in the school holidays. Throughout the country, many Elim churches started Sunshine Corner meetings. Often streams of children would be seen coming out of Elim churches singing on their homeward journeys:

Sunshine Corner it is jolly fine,
it's for children under ninety-nine,
All are welcome, seats are given free,
Elim Sunshine Corner is the place for me.

The subject of age limits came up again at the 1946 Conference and the following proposal was passed: 'It was resolved that the age limits for Crusaders and Cadets referred to in the regulations be considered as recommendations only and not binding, except that the maximum age at which Crusaders be retained on the membership roll should be 40. It was further resolved that the name "Elim Sunshine Corner" be approved as an alternative to "Elim Cadets"'.[11]

Pastor Leslie Green held children's campaigns in various parts of the country at which hundreds of children would gather. The report of the campaign[12] makes note of the difficulties that rationing caused in organising children's activities. The report goes on to state:

Even in these hard times God supplies all our need. A tea was arranged for those who came in the afternoon although there was no water in the building due to the freeze-up we had had.[13] I must explain now that our church was quite badly hit during the blitz, and the lighting system is not of the best. During the Sunday service, the lights failed. The Devil is still working overtime, but God again gave us the victory ten minutes after the starting time of the meeting. With 500 children to keep under control, had the lights not come on, the task would have been too much for the few workers we had. Praise God, they came on, and we were indeed blessed that evening. Even in heavy rain about 500 children came to hear the Word of God.

On the second day, God sent us two cases of apples to add to the ones we already had. Praise the Lord for all His goodness. Result of the campaign! On Sunday twenty new children in the Sunday School! One hundred and seven children attended Sunshine Corner on Wednesday![14]

In addition to the greatly increased numbers attending the Bermondsey Sunday School, they were able also to start a branch of Elim Cadets. As we proceed through our history of Elim, we will discover as we look back on over a century, that quite a few of the churches that started, and some of them in a most healthy manner, eventually closed. What we must never forget, however, when we look back on our history, a work **was** established, a church **was** commenced and many people were reached with the Gospel of Christ. Bermondsey was one of those places where the Elim light shone brightly for a while, then flickered and finally, the flame went out. But there was real kingdom growth that took place in the worship of that church when it was opened. Young children came to hear the message of the Gospel and if nothing else, they had somewhere to go to on those cold winter evenings where for an hour or so, they would be warm.

In his weekly Elim Youth Page, Douglas[15] Gray, would often use the appellation 'Crusaders' in the context of warfare. He made his young readers aware of the fact that they were engaged in deadly combat with the enemy. In one article he reminded Elim youth that: 'For over twenty-one years the Elim Crusader Movement has engaged in a battle for souls, and we cannot dismiss the thought that today finds us facing an adversary with ever-increasing powerful forces at his command, THAT THE BATTLE IS STILL ON,[16] and with a resurgence of fighting faith we must together sound an alarm to Crusaders of Christ everywhere'.[17] Gray, very skilfully, connected each Elim Crusader together so that even if they were members of a very small platoon, they were a part of the regiment. But beyond the regiment, there was the army and Gray reminded the Elim Crusader that there were other crusaders at work for Christ in various parts of the world. Having outlined the symptoms of 'a grave social decline' Gray challenges each Elim Crusader in a soldierly manner:

> What can we do about it? Elim Youth Leaders and Crusaders must feel this dire need, and the call of the hour. The assembling of ourselves together is right and proper, for truly we must worship Him in spirit and truth. Helpful weekly youth activities are necessary, but beyond all this, ATTACK must be our strategy and plan of action. This is no time for procrastination. This is the hour for decision; for taking sides; for engaging in spiritual conflict which is at the heart of human life. WE ARE CALLED – each one of us – to BATTLE FOR SPIRITUAL VALUES; and now is the accepted time.[18]

We can clearly note echoes of Gray's salvationist background in the above quotation and in much of his writing.

Elim and Youth for Christ

In researching material for this book, I discovered that there was a very strong link between Elim and British Youth for Christ in the early days of the latter organisation. British Youth for Christ commenced in 1946 and Gray refers to the meetings in Croydon as though the Elim Crusaders and the new Youth for Christ were in a symbiotic relationship. In his weekly Youth Page, Gray under the heading 'London Programme Continues', referred to the 'Youth for Christ' meetings at Croydon 'which have been well served and supported, and souls have been finding Christ.'[19] In the previous week's edition, the Evangel carried the following report.

> YOUTH FOR CHRIST: This was a new venture during 1946 and has well repaid the effort of those responsible for the arrangement of the programmes. Over one hundred have professed conversion and the meetings Saturday by Saturday have brought inspiration and joy to many young people. The Guest Speakers have included many Elim ministers, beginning with Pastor P S Brewster, so well-known for his evangelistic efforts. Pastors C J E Kingston, Burton-Haynes, J Dyke, S Gorman, J J Morgan, W Bell and J Williams, have all taken part. In addition to our own ministers we have been favoured with the ministry of Major Allister Smith, B.A., of the Salvation Army, and Mr Lindsey Glegg, well known as a champion of evangelism. The 'Youth For Christ' meetings in Croydon have now been taken over by the South London Presbytery and are continuing in the Elim Tabernacle, Stanley Road, Croydon.[20]

On the same Youth Page as above, there is also a report of the 'Pontypridd "Youth For Christ" Week'. This was combined with the Church's fifth Annual Youth Week. The fact that the two events had been augmented into one programme shows the very close links between Elim and Youth for Christ in the early years of British Youth for Christ.

Sunday School and Children's Work

Elim seemed to focus more on Children's work after the war. The leadership of the Movement had come to realise that the days of the great revival campaigns were over and whilst there was a refocussing on evangelism after the war, much time and thought was given to ministering to children and young people.

One cannot write about children's work in Elim post-war without mentioning the indefatigable Sonny Blundell. A short article on her ministry was written for Elim's Centennial Book, an extended extract is included below:

> In the austerity that followed World War 2, 'Sunshine Corner' was an oasis of fun and activity where many children came to faith in Jesus Christ.
>
> Sunny Blundell-Connell was a children's evangelist with the Elim Church. Born in 1904, in Prescot, Lancashire, she was named Ivy until the first day after her conversion when she took the name 'Sunny'. At the time, during the Second World War, she was enlisted in the ATS (Auxiliary Territorial Service, the women's branch of the army). She wrote in a book about her conversion experience of a young Christian woman who worked alongside her in the army and who invited her to church.
>
> Sunny became a member of the Elim Church in Salisbury and entered the Elim ministry in November 1945 leading a number of Elim churches, including a mission hall in Glasgow. She had a great passion for reaching children with the Gospel and developed a highly visual method of communicating through flannel-graphs. This was 'state of the art' in the days when few people had televisions and not all children could afford to go the Saturday matinee at the local pictures.
>
> Her performances were electric and adults as well as children were mesmerised by her infectious humour and natural gift in communicating. Her ministry affected the lives of thousands of children and a number of ministers made their first commitments as Christians in her meetings.[21]

At the 1944 Conference, Joseph Smith introduced the idea of a Sunday School catechism. A Committee was appointed to look into this, but the idea did not come to fruition. However, two important actions were taken: (1) The introduction of Sunday School Examinations. Most Elim churches took this on board and

I can clearly recall sitting probably the last such examination in 1963. (2) The publication of a teachers' hand-book.

Elim's approach to children's and young people's activities certainly changed in the nineteen sixties onwards. Crusader clans gradually declined and eventually ceased. The Movement for a time, encouraged churches to have a uniformed youth organisation. The one that most of the churches who wanted such an activity favoured the Campaigners, a Christian youth organisation, although, in Northern Ireland, some of the churches endorsed the Boys Brigade and Girls Brigade.

Notes

[1] Jones, Maldwyn, *And they came to Elim, Volume 1, 1915-1940*, (Instant Apostle, Rickmansworth 2021) pp216-217

[2] Jones, Maldwyn, ibid, p216.

[3] This concept was very much in vogue within Elim at the time of the Author's conversion. It was not made conditional to being a Crusader member or a Church member, but attendances at Cinemas, football and rugby matches, theatres etc was certainly frowned upon.

[4] Full Gospel Testimony

[5] The Crystal Palace was hired on two occasions by Elim for evangelistic purposes.

[6] 1946 Conference Minutes, Representative Session (Malvern: Elim Archives)

[7] London Crusader Choir, *Golden Jubilee Brochure*, (Grenehurst Press, Cheltenham, 1979)

[8] 1945 Conference Minutes, Representative Session (Malvern: Elim Archives).

[9] 1944 Conference Minutes, Representative Session (Malvern: Elim Archives)

[10] Matthew 16:15, NKJV

[11] 1945 Conference Minutes, Representative Session, (Malvern: Elim Archives).

[12] Sunshine Corner Campaign at Bermondsey, Elim Evangel, 7th April 1947, Vol 28, No 12, p181

[13] The winter of 1947 was one of the severest in the last century. Britain was covered in snow and there was hard-packed snow and ice still on the roads of some of the towns and cities right into April.

[14] Sunshine Corner Campaign at Bermondsey, *Elim Evangel*, ibid.

[15] Referred to by his colleagues and friends throughout Elim as 'Duggie Gray'.

[16] Original capitals.

[17] Gray, Douglas B, *Elim Youth Page, Elim Evangel*, 17th March 1947, Vol 28, No 9, p141.

[18] Gray, Douglas B, *Elim Youth Page*, ibid.

[19] Gray, Douglas B, *Elim Youth Page, Elim Evangel*, 13th Jan 1947, Vol 28 No 2, p30.

[20] Elim Youth Page, *Elim Evangel*, 6th January 1947, Vol 28, No 1, p14.

[21] *Defining Moments – 100 Years of the Elim Pentecostal Church*, (Elim Pentecostal Church 2015) p81. Article written by Maldwyn Jones

16

London Crusader Choir

The London Crusader Choir was formed in 1929 in response to the need of a good singing group at the various evangelistic campaigns, particularly, the revivals that swept London and the Provinces. Apparently, Douglas Gray, who was to be the Choir's conductor for over fifty years, was not given much notice in the formation of a choir. 'On a Monday morning in 1926 Mr Gray received a telephone call from the Secretary-General – E J Phillips, requesting a choir to be present at an evangelistic campaign, on the Wednesday evening. "Sir, it is Monday…." "Well, you have two whole days then", was the reply.' This was the beginning of Douglas Gray's long association with the musical ministry of the Elim Pentecostal Church. The late twenties and early thirties was a time of Revival for Elim. Campaigns were held and churches, some of them very large, were commenced.[1]

An important aspect of the campaigns was the singing. Douglas Gray was very much the man that Elim turned to as far as music programmes for the campaigns were concerned. Following the above request, Gray began to put together singing parties and the basis of a choir. 'In January 1929 in the Elim Tabernacle, Clapham, some fifty Elim Crusaders from the London churches gathered for the inauguration of this combination of consecrated vocalists and instrumentalists.'[2] It was said of these young people that they arrived in trepidation to form the London (Crusader) Harmony Choir. They had no idea what was entailed and was asked what parts they had sung previously. 'One very accommodating gentleman said he would sing whatever part was required!'[3] Those of us who remember the singing of the London Crusader Choir, especially at the Royal Albert Hall Easter gatherings, would find it difficult to imagine that among its early members, the choir was often referred to as 'The London Agony Choir', because initially, the singing, though enthusiastic, left much to be desired.[4] But this was before the masterful hands of the Conductor of this famous Choir was able to bring together this group of young people and form them into a Choir. Mr Gray laid down strong standards of expectation such as punctuality, regular attendance at practice and all engagements. He was able to influence these young singers to the point where the choir became a wonderful avenue of Christian service. 'Gradually, DBG with great patience and perseverance began to weld a good choir and this raw material was moulded and shaped until the singing improved out of all recognition.'[5]

Being Welsh and a lover of choral music and having been a previous member of a very successful young people's choir in the Rhondda, the writer readily testifies to the joy of singing. For the believer, singing is an important part of our worship. At the end of his life, Moses wrote a song and taught it to the Children of Israel.[6] In the Old Testament worship, singing was an expression of joy: 'Then my head will be exalted above the enemies who surround me; at His tabernacle will I sacrifice with shouts of joy; I will sing and make music unto the Lord.'[7] For the believer, singing is a means of testifying to the greatness of God: 'Our mouths were filled with laughter, our tongues with songs of joy. Then it was said among the nations, "The Lord has done great things for them."'[8] Psalms 120-134 are known as the Songs of Ascent. They are the Pilgrim Psalms and were sung by those who journeyed to the temple for the annual feasts. Jerusalem is set on a plateau, therefore the pilgrims from all over Israel would have ascended to the temple. They sang on their way and upon their arrival. The prophet Isaiah wrote these words which reflect the Songs of Ascent: 'And you will sing as on the night you celebrate a holy festival; your hearts will rejoice as when people go up with flutes to the mountain of the Lord, to the Rock of Israel.'[9]

It is clear from the New Testament that singing was prevalent in worship. From the Angelic choir of Bethlehem through to the New Song of Revelation[10], singing is seen to be an important part of Christian worship. Written on the inside cover of the original Redemption Hymnal are the words of Paul: 'Be filled with the Spirit; speaking to yourselves in psalms and hymns and spiritual songs, singing and making melody in your heart to the Lord.'[11] Pentecostal people love singing. But this was not the only motivation for the members of the London Crusader Choir. They loved to sing, that is true, but accompanying that important love of singing the Gospel was the call to service. One of the choristers wrote of the many opportunities provided by the choir which enabled them to serve Christ and His Church.

> To be a member of the Choir has been to be an active participant in a church on the move. The choir not only provided a wonderful avenue of service for the Master, but was also the centre of spiritual growth and development of its members. The Tuesday practices at the Elim Woodlands have always been great times of fellowship and practices always commenced with a time of prayer and devotion.
> The Choir gave great scope for its members to use their talents to the full, with solos, duets, quartets, instrumentalists, and elocutionists, all having their parts to play. Testimonies were often given in fear and trembling. Many a budding preacher has found ample opportunity to preach the Word. You were expected to be an active member of this 'church on the move' but those whose disposition was of a nervous kind would never be forced by DBG to do anything they felt they could not undertake.[12]

Although the Choir had its roots very deeply embedded in the garden that was Elim, its branches soon went over the walled garden and before long, their ministry was being well received in other places and denominations. With his Salvationist background, it is not surprising that Douglas sought and found opportunities for the Choir to minister in various Salvation Army citadels. They often combined this with a prison visit.

The 19th January 1942 edition of the Elim Evangel which celebrated the thirteenth Anniversary of the Choir set out the heavy schedule of the choir members. We must remember that this was during the war years and this added further considerable strain upon the choristers. The Evangel Article details a typical Sunday programme:

> Throughout this period the choir has carried on a regular ministry of soul-saving and soul-inspiring song – a musical crusade that has become nation-wide and knows no limitations in either Christian fellowship or in co-operation with other bodies of believers. In passing, let me quote one of scores of examples, culled from our diary. One Sunday the choir arrives at a provincial prison and conducts the service. At 6.45 they were in the Salvation Army Citadel, and finally, 8:15 in the great Oxford Town Hall, singing at a United Church Service which was supported by most of the clergy of that distinguished city. The speaker was a Canon of a well-known Midlands Cathedral. The Elim singers were welcomed at every place. This is but one page from the choir's chronicle. Self-sacrifice, ofttimes at considerable personal inconvenience and expense, and unswerving loyalty to Christ and Elim – such is a hall-mark of this brand of Youth. One writer says, 'One realises the existence of a loyal and happy spirit of co-operation combined with which is found a no less valuable sense of control to the success which attends the choir's efforts.'[13]

The Man Himself

Douglas Bramwell Gray was born in London's East End of Scottish descent, his grandmother coming from the Orkneys and his father being an Edinburgh man.[14] For thirteen years he was in the Purser's Department of a world-renowned shipping company. Douglas was born into a Salvationist family and from an early age revelled in the musical opportunities this organisation gave him. He played a number of musical instruments as a bandsman and was always to be found both at the indoor meetings and open-air meetings for which the Salvation Army are famous throughout the whole world.

Douglas Gray's long association with Elim began when Stephen and George Jeffreys conducted a revival campaign in his home town of Barking. His fiancé, Eva had a goitre and his mother suffered from suspected tuberculosis. 'She borrowed a wheel chair and had herself taken to the meetings, returning it in the morning knowing she was healed.'[15] Mrs Gray went on to live to the ripe old age of 92. At the same time, Eva's goitre vanished and never returned. This demonstration of Pentecostal power, coupled with the revival atmosphere that was latent throughout the East End saw Douglas lay aside his Salvation Army uniform and joining Elim. He was among the first batch of students that attended the newly-founded Elim Bible College in 1925. Thus began a life-long ministry within the Elim Pentecostal Church.

It was not uncommon in the early years of Elim for people of other church organisations, including evangelical ones, to cause disturbances at Elim meetings. Such an occurrence took place at the Royal Albert Hall in 1926 when the world-famous Evangelist, Aimee Semple-McPherson from Los Angeles, spoke to a packed congregation at the Royal Albert Hall. In one of the high galleries a determined attempt was made to disturb the meeting by a crowd of evangelicals of a West London Church. They made loud noises and caused something of a racket. To drown the opposition, three hundred Elim Crusaders being jammed in one corner of the platform burst into spontaneous song. So was born the first united Elim choir and also the idea that such a feature be continued. The task of organising and forming the choir was passed on to DBG.[16]

On Easter Saturday, 1927, Douglas arrived at his home in Barking at lunch-time to be told there had been a message for him to ring E J Phillips. He was told that he had been chosen to conduct the choir in the Albert Hall at Elim's great Easter Monday celebrations. He was quite taken aback. 'You did say in the Royal Albert Hall?' Back came the reply from Phillips 'Yes. You know the pieces.' The enormity of such a task was not lost on Douglas. He had been present at the celebrations in 1926 and had witnessed at first hand the huge crowds that filled this great hall. 'He listened: Mr Phillips was explaining that there had been a last-minute hitch in arrangements. He (Phillips) was aware that (Gray) had some experience in band and orchestras, that he was the leader of an octet male voice party.[17]

Douglas Gray assured Phillips that he would do his best, all the while wondering whether his best would be good enough. At the time, Douglas was somewhat in awe of E J and was just a little afraid of this man who so calmly, so efficiently, organised religious services for 8,000 people. After a worrying week-end, Easter Monday finally arrived. The following extract from Edward England's book tells something of the story of that memorable day:

> The choir numbered 1,200! It spilled from the platform over into the public seats, and the average age was about 21. He did not need to be told that many could not read music, and although for weeks they had been practising in their individual churches, there had been no previous opportunity to sing together. They looked at him. He was almost their age. He looked at them. If they had been brought up in the Salvation Army, music would have been a part of their inheritance. They looked at the auditorium, with every seat occupied: the atmosphere was overwhelming.
>
> 'I was nervous because of the largeness of the unit. But I was tremendously helped. There was an enthusiasm that created its own momentum, which made it easier for me. From the choir point of view there were no complexes. Simply none at all!'
>
> The day was a triumphant success, and he had taken the first step into a remarkable future. I asked whether he was still nervous before the important occasion?
>
> 'There are some public duties which make me nervous,' he confessed, 'but conducting is no longer one of them. Not even in the Albert Hall. I know the building too well, the layout, the acoustics, where to direct the microphones, and

what to do in an emergency. That's vital. I have a secret code of flashes for the organ, which I operate with my foot.'[18]

The push-button code was arranged between conductor and organist. The organist for most of the time that Douglas Gray conducted the London Crusader Choir and led the Royal Albert Hall Easter Celebrations was Ronald Cooper. He worked alongside the great Conductor for half a century. His playing of the great organ at the Royal Albert Hall was something to behold. He was succeeded by his equally talented son Geoffrey. The rapport between Conductor and Organist was superb, aided, no doubt by the push-button code.

The performance of any choir is dependent not only upon the musical talent available nor to the Conductor's ability, but also to the depth and intensity of regular rehearsals, away from the public eye. The London Crusader Choir, for most of their existence, held their rehearsals at the Woodlands, home of the Elim Bible College that had previously been a Roman Catholic Convent. It was situated in Clapham, London and young men and women from shops and offices met regularly for Mr Gray's gruelling rehearsals.[19]

The work of DBG and the London Crusader choir is nothing short of phenomenal. During its fifty plus years, the Choir conducted over 1,000 prison visits, over 800 visits to churches outside Elim and also in public and concert halls. They fulfilled in excess of 1250 Elim engagements and sang in hospitals, hostels, air-raid shelters and open-air meetings galore. On their travels overseas, they sang in airports, railway stations, on board ship and even on planes. Altogether they carried out approximately 4,000 engagements. Song, testimony and preaching programmes brought people to Christ in all these ways, with some outstanding and moving conversions.

The London Crusader Choir under the leadership of its quite brilliant conductor, helped smooth the ecumenical pathway for Elim. The testimony and the artistry of the Choir, combined with the geniality and East London wit of DBG, reflected the Elim spirit. 'These Elim people know how to do it', said a St Paul's Cathedral dignity. Elim people, as we look back on over a century of our history, have reason to feel proud of the rich and talented musical service and worship of the London Crusader Choir.

The Choir not only found its own funds but also helped with the stipend of its conductor. Following twenty-five years as the National Youth Secretary, DBG became the Musical Secretary. He also served on the Headquarters Office Committee. In addition, he served for a period as a member of the Executive Council. He was elected to the office of President, commencing his year of office in that year's Annual Conference. 'He produced his own hymns, an annual choir songster, many quality recordings and held a notable 160-occasions record for choral conducting in the Royal Albert Hall, including the All-England Massed Male Voice Choirs. Much of Elim's radio broadcasting occupied him along with the general work of equipping Elim for its outreach with the Gospel.'[20]

The Royal Albert Hall and Other Concert Halls

The London Crusader Choir made its debut in the Royal Albert Hall at Easter 1929, and attended every Elim meeting conducted there for the next forty-seven years. Sometimes it involved choir members travelling back to London overnight from various parts of the UK such as Belfast, Glasgow, Cardiff or Plymouth in order to be on duty at this great annual celebration of the Elim Pentecostal Church. The choir had a deep sense of loyalty to Elim and particularly to this Easter Monday celebrations held annually in the nation's premier concert hall. One choir member spoke of the varied service in the choir with no two appointments alike, 'sometimes singing in large auditoriums and sometimes in small mission halls. Once they sang on board ship on the way to Sweden, another occasion flying at 20,000 feet over the Mississippi, the choir's singing being so successful that all available records were sold to the passengers on the plane![21]

The choir sang at various great halls throughout the country such as the Guildhall in Southampton, the Cory Hall, Cardiff, the Kingsway Festival Hall. The Christmas Festivals in the Fairfield Halls, Croydon was an annual event for a number of years in the nineteen sixties. I have clear memories of the Elim Bible College Choir taking part in one of these great Christmas festivals.

Reference was made in the Evangel edition celebrating the thirteenth year of the Choir to 'those Christian brethren serving sentence for conscience's sake, including some of our Elim brethren.' The many visits that the Choir made to Elim Churches throughout Britain remained long in the memories of those who were present. In those first thirteen years the choir made over seventy visits to towns and cities in addition to the London visits which amounted to a total of nearly 800 appointments. Choir members were deeply appreciative of the unstinted kindness and warmth of welcome that was always showered on them by so many friends who had given of their best.

The work of the Choir continued throughout the war years despite the challenges faced by members being called up for war service. The Evangel claimed that since the formation of the choir in 1929 to the time of the writing of the article in January 1942, approximately 100,000 men and women had come under the sound of these gospel messengers, 'and many have found Christ as a result.'[22] A visit to the city that was to become the capital of Wales twenty years later, Cardiff, was made in 1935 and a repeat visit was made for the Easter convention in 1940. In 1937 there was an Easter tour to Northern Ireland. Easter 1938 saw the choir visiting the Elim churches in Scotland. At Easter 1939, it was the turn of the West Country to be thrilled by the singing and ministry of the London Crusader Choir. The choir toured the West of England and Cornwall making Plymouth its crusade centre. 'From all these places, following exceptionally heavy week-ends, and all-night travel each way, the choir was always found in full force and happy to be present at the great London meetings on each Easter Monday.'[23]

Douglas Gray, throughout the course of his long ministry, displayed a scriptural ecumenical spirit. He was happy to work with other Pentecostal and evangelical organisations. It is almost certain that the article celebrating thirteen years of extensive musical evangelism on the part of the London Crusader Choir which appeared in the 19th January 1942 edition of the Elim Evangel was written by the maestro himself. The following lengthy quotation from this article shows the open attitude of Gray and his willingness to co-operate with other Christian bodies.

> Co-operation in evangelism has been a special character of service. The integrity and good name of Elim has been, we venture to declare, lifted high and esteemed, and prejudice has been disposed of as a result of co-operation with other Christian bodies. Whether in State church or humble mission hall, in the largest public buildings in the land or in unseen air-raid shelters, the same spirit and standard of ministry, without compromise, has been evidenced. Co-operation with such bodies as the National Young Life Campaign leaders, the YMCA, the Church Army, the Salvation Army, various missionary and Bible societies, and in churches of all denominations, including our Pentecostal brethren of Assemblies of God, has welded a lasting chain of sincere Christian Fellowship.
>
> Despite war-time conditions the choir is still 'carrying on,' although numerically depleted. (We need help – can you give it?) In addition to church and prison ministry, Evangelism amongst the Forces and Hospitals is now a front-line activity. Visits to Military and Civil hospitals; Church parades of the Brigade of Guards: to RAF Night-fighter depots; to isolated AA gun sites; to other centres as far afield as Salisbury, Southampton, and to other points in the Southern Command. Several of the choir's personnel are serving in the Forces, whilst others who are CO's[24] are regarded with equal respect by all. We deeply cherish the memory of two of its members, Dr F Weston and Sargant D Coveney, who lost their lives in the present conflict.

The above quotation, shows the extraordinary depths of ministry that the London Crusader Choir applied itself to during the extremely difficult and challenging days of the Second World War. Not only did they carry out these many hundreds of appointments whilst the major cities and urban conurbations were for long periods under nightly bombardment by a ruthless enemy, the very places that they chose to sing and minister at, put themselves at even greater risk as such places were often sought out by the enemy for destruction.

In later years, seen sitting in their splendid and oh, so white attire (the ladies), and the gentlemen in their tuxedos, the choir members were looked upon rather critically by some. Being in the centre of the massed choirs, it was almost as if they considered themselves to be the cream. Well, that is precisely what they were. Cream comes from the top layer of milk. The London Crusader Choir in its fifty years of service certainly rose to the top. Having studied their history and read so many reports outlining the practical as well as deeply spiritual ministry of this amazing and dedicated group of godly men and women who wanted to serve God and Elim through song, testimony and preaching, this writer is deeply humbled by the quality of such ministry.

At Large

It had been the established practice of the Choir, prior to the Second World War, to travel to various towns and cities in the UK each Easter week-end. Places such as Cardiff, Exeter, Carlisle and Greenock received ministry from Douglas Gray and the London Crusader Choir during such visits. But the choir always returned to London to sing at the great Easter Monday celebrations at the Royal Albert Hall. After the war, they extended the scope of their ministry to places distant from Great Britain.

The first of these visits occurred in 1947, when on Friday, 23rd May, the London Crusader Choir sailed from Southampton to St Peter Port, Guernsey. This was the Choir's first visit to the Channel

Islands. Such visits were repeated on a number of consequent occasions. Members of the Choir came to refer to Guernsey as 'Our own special island'. The significance of this visit cannot be underestimated. The Channel Islands had suffered five years of Nazi occupation. During that time, the three Elim churches on the Island had no contact with the main-land. So, it was with great excitement that the Guernsey Elim folk under the leadership of the redoubtable Gilbert Dunk, welcomed the Choir to Guernsey. Some members only stayed for the week-end but a large party stayed for well over a week and were engaged in ministry and song throughout the island. A great Festival of Praise was held in the Auditorium of the famous Candie Gardens. This visit was so memorable that a further one was planned for 1948 when the majority of the Choir stayed for two weeks and incorporated services in Jersey during that time.

In June 1949, the Choir visited Switzerland where they ministered at Basle, Zurich, Berne and Geneva. They visited Switzerland again in 1951. In 1953, the Choir went to the Pentecostal churches in Sweden, Norway and Denmark. 1955 saw them taking part at the World Pentecostal Conference held in Sweden. It was in the autumn of 1961 that they went on their first visit to Canada and the United States. It was on an internal flight in the US that the pilot asked them to sing. It was quite an experience singing praises to God at 18,000 feet.

Notes

[1] Jubilee Brochure of London Crusader Choir, (Cheltenham: Grenehurst Press, 1979), p3
[2] The London Crusader Choir, Thirteen years of Extensive Musical Evangelism – 1929-1942, *Elim Evangel*, 19th January, 1942, Vol 23, No 3, pp25-27.
[3] Jubilee Brochure, ibid, p3.
[4] Jubilee Brochure, ibid, p3.
[5] Jubilee Brochure, ibid, p3.
[6] Deuteronomy 31:22. The song itself takes up all fifty-two verses of Deuteronomy 32.
[7] Psalm 27:6.
[8] Psalm 126:2
[9] Isaiah 30:29
[10] Luke 2:13 and Revelation 5:11-14

[11] Ephesians 5:18,19 (AV).

[12] Jubilee Brochure, ibid, p3.

[13] *Elim Evangel*, 19th January 1942, ibid, pp25,26.

[14] England, Edward, *Adventurous Christianity, A journey of discovery*, (London: Victory Press, 1962), p46.

[15] Canty, George, *History of Elim*, ibid, p180.

[16] Canty, George, ibid, p180.

[17] England, Edward, ibid, p48.

[18] England, Edward, ibid pp48,49.

[19] Jubilee Brochure, ibid, p4.

[20] Canty, George, *History of Elim*, ibid, p183.

[21] *The Message through Music*, Jubilee Brochure, ibid p20.

[22] *Elim Evangel*, 19th January 1942, ibid, p26.

[23] *Elim Evangel*, 19th January 1942, ibid, p26.

[24] Conscientious Objectors

17
Prison Ministry

Prison Ministry

The Evangel article outlining the 13th Anniversary of the Choir, while not dismissive of the early days when the Choir's main function was supporting the many revival campaigns up and down the land, but particularly in the London area, was of the opinion that the strenuous efforts of those early days 'were for preparation, test, and experience,' then in answer to prayer the prison ministry commenced. The first prison visit conducted by the Choir was to Wormwood Scrubs prison in June 1933. This was, and remains today, one of the main London prisons. It has a notorious reputation. The Prison was opened in 1875 and is very Victorian in its appearance. It is a Class B Category, Adult Male Prison. One can imagine the fear and slight trepidation that the choir members felt as they were ushered into the large Prison Chapel. Between June 1933 and January 1942, the choir had conducted just short of three hundred prison services in twenty-four of His Majesty's Prisons and Borstal Institutions in England and Wales.[1] A Canon at St Paul's Cathedral, London, who had previously been a senior chaplain at The Scrubs[2] on various occasions expressed deep gratitude for such a ministry. In one of his last letters he said, 'You are doing a great work and God does bless it.'[3]

It appears that the seeds of the Choir's prison ministry were sown during a campaign which was held in Plymouth in 1925, when a young man was converted. This would have been the

Steven Jeffreys campaign in Stonehouse. This young man later joined the Prison Service and became Chief Officer at Wormwood Scrubs. After some years, Chief Officer Pearson met Mr Gray at Kensington Temple and said that he had heard about the London Crusader Choir and was trying to persuade the Governor to invite the Choir there. A date was agreed – 11th June 1933. Mr Gray commented on that momentous occasion: 'I'll never forget it. Though we were a little nervous and unsure at first, we soon realised that the prisoners were just loving our music, and then we became oblivious of our surroundings, and at the end we received a fine ovation. I had felt that we should do more than just sing in churches and halls, and here was the opportunity. We would rather sing to 700 men in prison than to 7,000 in the Royal Albert Hall.' From that point onwards, prison visitation and ministry became a major aspect of the Choir's programme.[4]

Later in the year 1933 at a musical concert attracting a capacity crowd in the Crystal Palace, the band had just started to play Handel's Largo when Douglas Gray felt a tug at his sleeve. He looked round and was rather startled to see that it was his wife. She had stayed at home to await news of her sick father. 'There is nothing to worry about dear' she said reassuringly. 'Just come out quietly.' Mrs Gray explained the reasons for her unexpected arrival. 'We had a phone call from Canon Cottrell at Wormwood Scrubs, a party has let him down, could you take the Choir over to the prison tomorrow afternoon for a concert?' Douglas said that this would be impossible as the Crusaders were scattered all over London and most of them weren't on the phone. But Mrs Gray was prepared: 'It's alright, Willie's outside with his car. He will take us round to see them all tonight.'[5] They set off in an old Austin 7 with solid tyres and an open top. As a result of their late-night efforts a party of 14 choir members arrived at the gates of the Scrubs, so began the successful years of prison ministry.[6]

The Choir was so conscious of the leading of the Holy Spirit, guiding them further in their prison ministry. The assistant Chaplain of the Scrubs was moved to Maidstone Prison, then the

Chief Officer was transferred to Brixton Prison, and so the news spread and at one time, the choir was conducting forty services a year in prisons and borstals throughout the country. These visits had a profound effect on Douglas Gray as it gave him a unique insight into the prison systems of our country. Through his many visits, he found the prisoners quiet, respectful, attentive and he was warmly drawn to his congregation. The choir and Douglas personally, were greatly encouraged by the number of prisoners who were converted as a result of the Choir's visits. Douglas Gray was a man of great compassion and he visited some of these prisoners in their homes after they had been released, he had meals with them and their families, and even received a wedding invitation!

Over a period of forty-five years there were over a thousand visits made to prisons, borstals, young people's detention centres and criminal hospitals such as Broadmoor. They visited forty-six of H M Establishments. In his weekly youth columns in the Elim Evangel, Mr Gray would frequently ask for prayer and would encourage Elim youth to pray for those in prison.

Ministering inside those Prison Walls

What is it like to take a service in prison and to chat with some of the inmates when the service is over? I was a part-time chaplain at Dartmoor Prison for a period of four years in the nineteen eighties and has some understanding of the value of 'outsiders' taking services within prisons. As early as 1935, one prison officer stated in a magazine for prison officers the following: 'In recent years prisons have been favoured by the services of the London Crusader Choir. The warm welcome and kind words of appreciation from Governors, Chaplains, Officers, and ultimately ex-prisoners, is a testimony in itself to the popularity and the good work of this band of Christian youth. Their services are absolutely voluntary and the splendid spirit of sacrifice is a hall-mark of character and goodwill to all.'[7]

The following lengthy excerpt from Edward England will give us some insight into conducting a prison service. In reading this excerpt, the reader must bear in mind that this visit occurred in 1960's and prison conditions have improved from those days. One thing has remained, however, and that is the whole concept of incarceration when the prisoner is deprived his liberty:

We assembled outside the tall, formidable walls, by the great locked gates of the prison. This was to be my first visit inside prison walls, and for some unaccountable reason I was nervous. It was a bitingly cold, February day, the grey clouds heavy with snow, a few flurries of white indicating what was to come. At 2.15 p.m. a door in the massive gate would be unlocked and we would be given a quick, searching glance and allowed to enter. We were going to prison voluntarily, but I could not avoid thinking of thousands of men, from all walks of life, who had entered unwillingly, in anger or anguish, surprised that this was where life had led them. In a prison van, or fast-moving police car, they would pass through to stay for months, or years: to be separated from wife and children, from home and normal routine. Through the same doors men had returned to freedom: to joyous reunion with women that waited: to the old job: and to bitter disillusion, to find the world had changed, that neighbours were no longer friends, that relatives had stopped visiting, that it was advisable to move to a new address.

Huddled together for warmth were members of the London Crusader Choir, some sitting in their cars to shelter from the piercing wind: all having had lunch early so that they could sing in the prion chapel that afternoon. By my side was the Rev. Douglas B Gray, leader and founder of the Choir, he had invited me to accompany the Choir 'inside' – and had promised to bring me out again!

At 2.15, a Warder opened the door and we filed into an arched entrance-way, with offices and noticeboards on either side. We were now neither in nor out. There were vast locks on either side, there being a vast iron gate in front of us.

The second entrance was now opened, and we made our way into the grounds. We were really inside. The lay-out brought to mind an old-fashioned infirmary, with neat areas of grass separating the stone buildings. In a reception room, with a blazing fire, the last-minute instructions were given to the singers. Except for the bars at the windows, there was nothing in there to suggest this was a prison. Slowly we moved to the Chapel. The men were already assembled, in their dark jackets and blue shirts, sitting on long wooden seats. There were about 400 of them in this House of God, with its stoned arches, stained glass windows and no bars, and paintings depicting well-known Bible incidents. There were two bowls of daffodils and narcissi by the altar.

The Choir was introduced by the Anglican Chaplain. Prison visits are by courtesy of the Chaplain, and the Choir members have grown to respect and admire many of these clergymen, engaged in a difficult but noble calling. And many Chaplains have expressed esteem for the Choir.

As we sang the opening hymn, in which congregation and Choir participated, I looked at the rows of men, surprised at how young they seemed, how few old men were there. In the shadows stationed around the Chapel, sat the uniformed Warders. There were some fine, intelligent faces among the men. Why had I imagined that all men 'inside' were thugs, or 'different'? These fellows, in appearance, were as representative of the human race as those one met on the train to business, or saw crowding along Oxford Street. Like you and me![8]

Edward England then goes on to write about the Choir's programme and the appreciative and responsive audience. Each item was received with thundering applause. The Choir's final piece was 'When I survey the Wondrous Cross'. This, unlike the preceding items was received in complete stillness. The Author, having conducted quite a number of services in Dartmoor Prison where he was a part-time Chaplain, can recall how that hymns of this nature had a profound emotional effect on some prisoners. One such hymn that was a great favourite was 'The Old Rugged Cross.'

In writing these two chapters concerning the London Crusader Choir, I have been greatly moved by the willingness of the Choir to take services in forty-six prisons and penal establishments throughout the British Isles. The compassion and dignity that the Choir and its leader showed in over a thousand services is a great credit to them. The choir was able to relate with the prisoners. One prisoner missed the Choir so much when he was released, one Sunday afternoon he rang the bell at the entrance and asked to be allowed in, to hear the choir again! You can imagine the astonishment of the Official on duty! Permission was granted on that occasion.[9] One man, after he left jail wrote: 'I shall try to forget most of my prison memories. But I shall always treasure the happy moments I have spent listening to your singing. When I am free, I shall keep in touch with your activities, and whenever possible come and listen to you again. Your efforts are not in vain. You have clearly helped me to realise that the best things in life are free.'[10] The following tribute entitled 'From a prison chapel bench' shows the powerful impression that the Choir made on the prisoners.

> It is always with eager anticipation that I wait for the visits of the London Crusader Choir. The quality of their music and performance never falls below the high standard set by Douglas Gray, the conductor of this happy unified group. This is in spite of the many and varied problems an amateur choir experiences, and I am impressed by the competent and professional way the difficulties are overcome. The vigorous and unselfish devotion to spreading Christ's message through their music is an inspiration to us all, and for me a comforting and illuminating experience. I find the Crusader Choir unpretentious, their strength lying in their dedication to Christ and the obviously sincere regard for each other in their work.
>
> These are team efforts, coloured by fine soloists where musicianship shows through, and capably led by Mr Gray, a true gentle man![11]

Broadmoor

Douglas Gray and the London Crusader Choir had a special relationship with Broadmoor. This establishment is not a prison, it is a high-security psychiatric hospital in Crowthorne, Berkshire. The hospital was first known as the Broadmoor Criminal Lunatic Asylum. 'The medical Superintendent is assisted by a team of doctors and male and female nurses, and comes under the jurisdiction of the Ministry of Health and Social Security and not the Prison Commissioners.'[12] At the time of the publishing of the Golden Jubilee Brochure (1979) the hospital had between 800 and 900 male and female patients. The hospital is walled and the security measures are very stringent.

It was into this great centre that the choir went on Sunday, 27th March, 1949, and on 19th November 1978, it made it's 67th visit to Broadmoor Hospital. During this long period, the choir members noted many changes as security needed to be enhanced. The comment was made about how very few of the general public knew or even cared about the conditions within the walls. 'Yet these 900 souls have an eternal destiny, and who has offered the hand of friendship, and shown the way to Him, the healer of body and soul?'[13]

At an Elim Royal Albert Hall Easter Monday meeting, a former Broadmoor patient wrote the following to the choir: 'You don't know me, but I am sitting here with you in this hall today. I am here as a result of the faithful ministry of the London Crusader Choir. Only a few years ago I was an inmate of one of Her Majesty's establishments. I was a believing Christian, but until the Choir came within those walls, I, and many others in similar plight could see very little evidence that fellow Christians were concerned. The London Crusader Choir was the direct means of introducing me to the friends who persevered until I was reinstated into ordinary life.'[14]

I will conclude my chapters on the London Crusader Choir with the words of the Inmates of Dartmoor Prison that were written in lovely calligraphy on the back of the Golden Jubilee Brochure

Her Majesty's Prison, Dartmoor,

The Inmates of the above establishment who were fortunate enough to be present in the Prison Chapel today, wish to express their heartfelt thanks and appreciation to

The Crusader Choir

We congratulate them on a wonderful performance that will long be remembered and hope that they will return soon. Sunday, 17th July, 1960

It was signed on behalf of the inmates of Dartmoor by the Prison Chaplain. Prison ministry was very much at the heart of the London Crusader Choir.

Notes

[1] *Elim Evangel*, 19th January 1942, ibid, p26.

[2] Colloquial name for Wormwood Scrubs.

[3] *Elim Evangel*, 19th January 1942, ibid, p26.

[4] Jubilee Brochure, ibid, p9.

[5] Author's note: This may have been a reference to Willie Evans who became Jeffreys' Chauffer for a time. I was a member of the Elim Church, Porth for five years prior to entering Elim Bible College. William Evans was my pastor and informed me that he had been a member of the London Crusader Choir together with his brother Tom who became a missionary to Belgium.

[6] Jubilee Brochure, ibid, p10.

[7] Jubilee Brochure, ibid, p10.

[8] Jubilee Brochure, ibid, pp10,11.

[9] Jubilee Brochure, ibid, p11

[10] Jubilee Brochure, ibid, p11

[11] Jubilee Brochure, ibid, p11.

[12] Jubilee Brochure, ibid, p19. Please note that the Brochure was published in 1979. There have obviously been many changes made since then, but the Hospital has remained under the direction of the Ministry of Health and not the Prison Service.

[13] *Broadmoor: Golden Jubilee Brochure of the Elim Crusader Choir*, p19.

[14] *Broadmoor: Golden Jubilee Brochure of the Elim Crusader Choir*, p19.

18
Times, they are a changing

The end of the Second World War also saw the end of the coalition government and Churchill's premiership. Although he was to return to the office of Prime Minister in 1951 and served in that role until 1955, there can be no doubt that his finest hour had been when Britain stood alone against a ruthless enemy. The result of the 1945 General Election was unexpected. In light of Churchill's leadership and his role in the allied victory, it was inconceivable that he would not continue as Prime Minister

The election was held on 5th July but counting of the votes was delayed until 26th July to provide time for overseas votes to be received and counted. Labour won by a landslide, 393 seats to the Conservatives' total of 197. Labour won on a platform of social reform and nationalisation, of which arguably, the most popular was the establishment of a National Health Service. Although there was a change of government, living conditions were pretty grim for a country that had 'won the war'. Major cities and large conurbations were faced with the huge task of re-building after the devastation caused by enemy bombing. Rationing continued well into the 1950's.

The forces of fascism had been laid low, but fear of another political force gnawed at the minds of Western Europe and the USA – the fear of world communism. This fear intensified when Russia entered the Atomic community. H W Greenway addressed this in his editorial in the Christmas 1948 edition of the Evangel. Referring to Russia and the atom bomb, he compares the situation to circumstances confronting the world at the time of the birth of Christ. 'The first advent of Christ dawned upon a confused world, so confused that scribes who studied the sacred records missed the full import of the prophetic Word, and the wise and noble by-passed the rude manger.'[1] To the casual reader, Greenway's editorial reeks of pessimism but it is clear that he had a grasp on the reality facing the church in general, and Elim in particular. It is one of choice: 'Thus we today are faced with a choice between the sacred and the secular; our faith is either in the kingdom which cannot be moved or the kingdom which shall surely pass away. Christ's coming has divided us into two camps, distinguished by their allegiance.'[2]

The 'baby boomers' generation grew up in the foetid atmosphere of the cold war and had to live with the thought that the world was only seconds away from nuclear annihilation. At no time was this fear felt greater than during the Cuba crisis in 1962. Also known as the October crisis, this was a month-long confrontation between the United States and the Soviet Union which escalated to the point when it seemed that nuclear warfare was almost inevitable. I was just a month away from my fifteenth birthday having made my personal commitment to Christ just three months earlier. I can vividly recall the day when the crisis reached its zenith. On Saturdays and during school holidays I worked on a bread-delivery van. During the course of delivering the bread to our customers, we were made aware of the extreme danger to the whole world and the driver of the van wondered whether we would actually finish the round. He was not a Christian but he asked me to pray that global calamity would be avoided. We were warned by the government that if there was a nuclear attack, we were to find refuge in a room where there were no windows to the outside world and to ensure that we already had bottled water and a small amount of food available. We were told that we would have four minutes to get to a place of relative shelter. In school, the teachers informed us what to do if ever the four-minute alarm was sounded. In reality, we could have done very little if such a warning was ever sounded.

Being faced with such horror certainly galvanised preachers in their evangelistic endeavours. The 'end of the world' was certainly a theme that was often heard from Pentecostal pulpits. Sermons were preached on the subject of the 'end-times' and the return of Christ. Such sermons were all based on the pre-millennial return of Christ and, more often than not, on the futurist interpretation of prophetic Scripture. The satanic number '666' was configured in various ways almost as numerous as the number itself! There was much speculation as to the identity of the Antichrist and the False Prophet.

Post-War Realities

Much has been said and written concerning the advantages that the 'baby-boomers' generation received in comparison with succeeding generations. This generation is usually defined as people born from 1946-1964. The advantages of being one of this generation is that in USA and Europe 'boomers' came of age in a time of increasing affluence. In Britain, in particular, this generation became the 'home-owning' generation. This was epitomised by Margaret Thatcher's policy of allowing Council Hose tenants the right to purchase their homes at a greatly reduced price. This was a major factor in the inevitably huge increases in domestic property in the last quarter of the twentieth century and which has continued into the twenty-first century.[3]

The 'boomer' generation had far greater advantages than those of the previous generation to them. Most of the preceding generation had survived the horrors of the two world wars. They had gone through the hugely challenging economic throes of the twenties and thirties and the financial recessions of those times. Harold Macmillan, in his mind was absolutely convinced of the truth of the words that were certainly questioned by the Labour opposition when he uttered the words that characterised the thinking of many throughout the nineteen sixties: 'You've never had it so good.'[4] This phrase came to embody the social thinking of many people, especially Conservative voters in the nineteen sixties.

Let's be frank about it; most of our people have never had it so good. Go around the country, go to the industrial towns, go to the farms, and you will see a state of prosperity such as we have never had in my lifetime – nor indeed ever in the history of this country. What is worrying some of us 'Is it too good to be true?' or perhaps I should say 'Is it too good to last.'[5]

I would add a third question to the last two mentioned in Macmillan's famous quotation: 'Was it true at all?' For many Britons, the 1950's was an era of austerity. The war had taken the lives of many young men who had children and teenagers growing up in the decade of the fifties. Life was hard for millions of families throughout the British Isles.

One commodity that my generation experienced in abundance as children, is something that, sadly, a huge number of children growing up in the third decade of the twenty-first century, do not experience: I can only refer to it as 'the blessings of a good community.' Feeney expresses it brilliantly in this rather lengthy quotation:

The nation was recovering from the ravages of the Second World War and the camaraderie of wartime was still evident throughout the country. People had great pride in, and loyalty to, their country and seemed to share a common purpose in life. Everyone knew their neighbours and had a sense of belonging. There seemed to be a genuine air of humility among the people and although many found it hard to make ends meet, there was a clear spirit of generosity. People were happy to surround themselves with modest personal belongings, and young couples were content to furnish their homes with post-war utility furniture. It was a time of innocence; children only knew the simple things of life and there were none of the peer pressures that exist today. People were grateful for the comfort of having shoes on their feet and food in their bellies. There was little evidence of jealousy or desire for luxuries. What you didn't have, you didn't miss! People were trusting and they frequently left their

street door on the latch or the door key hanging down behind
the letterbox for their kids to come and go as they pleased.[6]

Whilst the above quote contains much of what was reality for those
of us growing up in the fifties, it only tells one side of the story. At
this time, Britain was still very much a class-based society. Even
within the so-called 'working-class' there were 'upper' and 'lower'
sections and even an 'in-between'. There were those who sat in the
front middle pews of the chapel, and those who sat in the rear side
rows. These were usually decided upon by the prominence of the
family in the town. I was used to sitting in the rear side pew in
chapel. The one factor that is clear from this period is the emphasis
that was laid on education. The South Wales mining valleys were
full of small towns that had their 'Stutes'. These were the Miners
Institutes that were built in order to provide reading rooms and
libraries for the miners. The miners in turn instilled into their
children the importance and value of education.

The social and living changes within the country in the fifties
were reflected in very necessary changes within Elim. The huge
problems caused by the War and internal dissention necessitated
these changes. There was no doubt whatsoever that Elim had to
change. They had to establish a new form of leadership structure.
No longer was one person to be at the head of the Movement. The
Executive Council acted collegially and although, in some respects,
E J Phillips was looked upon as the de facto leader in Place of
Jeffreys, the fact was that he was just one of nine men nominated
and elected by the Conference whose responsibility was to lead and
govern the Movement in between Conferences.

The first governmental changes resulted in all nine members
of the Executive Council being appointed by the Conference.
Prior to 1939, George Jeffreys had the right to appoint three
members of the Executive himself. Both he and E J Phillips were
ex-officio members of the Council so, theoretically, Jeffreys had
the numbers to appoint the majority of the Council himself. E J
Phillips, however, would not assent to this. The right to nominate

members of the Executive Council was given to every member of Conference, providing the nominator had a seconder. When lay representatives were added to the Conference in 1940, they had the right to nominate members of the Executive Council alongside their ministerial colleagues. It was, in fact possible for two lay representatives to nominate a minister for election to the Council.

The other great constitutional change came in the rights given to churches to appoint their own church session members. In Ireland, this involved elders as well as deacons. It was possible for elders to be appointed in churches across the water from Ireland, but at the time, there was no great tradition or much desire to appoint elders. This gave the local church a say in their internal affairs. Each church session had the right to accept or reject a pastor suggested to them by the Executive Council.

Some are of the opinion that the greatest changes in Elim in the forties and fifties was in the area of missions. Both home and overseas, Elim's Missions policy developed and enlarged. In the evangelistic field, pastors were encouraged to develop an evangelistic ministry. A number of pastors put themselves forward to conduct evangelistic campaigns, not just in the place in which they personally ministered, but also to conduct campaigns for other Elim churches. A few Elim ministers conducted large scale campaigns in various parts of the country whilst they continued to lead their local church. The greatest example of this was the tremendous evangelistic ministry of P S Brewster. We will look at his amazing evangelistic legacy to Elim in the next chapter.

Notes

[1] Greenway, H W, Editorial, *Elim Evangel*, 20th December 1948, Vol 29, No 51, p610.

[2] Greenway, H W, ibid.

[3] However, this policy, whilst being very good for those council house tenants who were in a position to buy their homes, it resulted in a huge drop in council provided rental housing.

[4] The phrase was actually mentioned in a speech by Macmillan delivered on 20th July 1957

[5] Harold Macmillan, 20th July 1957, quoted by Stanbrook, Dominic, *Never had it so Good, A History of Britain from Suez to the Beatles* (London: Abacus, 2006)

[6] Feeney, Paul, *A 1950's Childhood, From Tin Baths to Bread and Dripping*, (Cheltenham: The History Press, 2020), p13.

19
Elim's Greatest Evangelist

It is the author's opinion that Percy Stanley Brewster was Elim's greatest evangelist. I can almost hear the protests as I write these words. Surely, Elim's Founder, George Jeffreys must deserve that title? The fact is, Brewster pioneered more churches than did George Jeffreys. It has to be said that the churches George Jeffreys pioneered were considerably larger than those pioneered by Brewster. What must be taken into consideration, however, is the periods in which the two leaders conducted their evangelistic campaigns. George brought forty-seven churches into existence as a result of his evangelistic campaigns between 1915 and 1937. In my first volume I stated that Jeffreys' priorities changed in the mid nineteen-thirties.[1] From that point onwards, he concentrated his efforts on reforming the Movement that he had founded.

The majority of Jeffreys' campaigns were held during a period of time when the nation was more sympathetic to the Christian message than in the post-war period when Brewster conducted most of his evangelistic campaigns. Also, Jeffreys ministered in the long shadow of the Welsh revivals. He campaigned under the 'Revival' banner. He, and his brother Stephen, were considered by many as 'Children of the Revival'. Brewster had no such advantages. The social scene immediately after the Second World War was considerably changed. Gone were the exciting days of Revival. Brewster adapted himself to the culture of the times. In spite of the changing times, Brewster opened over 50 Elim churches. He did this whilst leading Elim's largest post-war Church. He was appointed Pastor of the Cardiff City Temple in 1939, just prior to the commencement of the Second World War. He very successfully merged his pastoral ministry with his evangelistic fervour.

P S Brewster was born on 20th September, 1908 in London's East End. He was converted in 1925 and was a member of the East Ham Elim Church where he became the leader of the Crusaders branch. Most of his family, including his parents were converted under the ministry of the Jeffreys' brothers. The campaigns of George and Stephen Jeffreys in the East End during the years 1925-1927 were phenomenal.[2] 'He was born in Revival. His first introduction to Elim were in those exciting times. He was baptized in the Spirit at meetings in Zion College on the Embankment, (London) under the ministry of Howard Carter.'[3]

Cartwright skilfully outlines the link between Jeffreys and Brewster. Referring to the latter, he writes: 'The major part of his life was spent in Wales, where he served as a minister in Swansea followed by some thirty-five years in Cardiff from 1929 until 1974 when he became Secretary-General of the Elim Pentecostal Church. After his retirement in 1977, he moved back to Cardiff. Though he died in London on 1st July, 1980 following surgery for the removal of a brain tumour, he was buried in Cardiff.'[4]

Cartwright expounds on the reversed geographical areas of ministry of the two Evangelists. 'George Jeffreys, the Welshman, never held a pastorate in Wales and rarely ministered there. From 1922 until his death on 26th January, 1962, he made his home in Clapham, London. He is buried in Streatham Cemetery.'[5] It is fascinating to note the connection between these two great leaders. Brewster was a great admirer of Jeffreys and pressure was put on him to leave Elim and join up with the new Bible Pattern fellowship that was set up by Jeffreys. Referred to throughout Elim by his initials, P S emphasised that evangelism breeds evangelism.[6]

An earlier chapter of this book refers to the post-war recovery of Elim 1945-1955. There was a strong feeling within the Movement that 'the tide had gone out'. This was certainly the opinion of John Dyke who from 1942 until his death in 1960 was the minister of the Graham Street church in Birmingham. He expressed his deep concern in a letter to E J Phillips. Reference has already been made to the 1944 Conference when an Evangelistic Council was formed. John Woodhead and Percy Brewster, Elim's two outstanding post-war evangelists were appointed to this Council. They got to work with a will and ambitious plans were put in place for six pioneer campaigns within a twelve-month period.

Background

Percy Brewster's father was, by profession, a painter and decorator and worked for a firm of shop fitters where he quickly gained promotion. During his time as a member of the East Ham Elim Church, an evangelist by the name of Len Jones from Australia held meetings there and he asked P S to join the evangelistic team that he was forming. Brewster was already conscious of a call to evangelism and according to Cartwright, such an invitation would have impressed the young evangelist.[7] 'He was already engaged to Doris Bracy, and when Len Jones suggested that they get married and accompany him to Australia, he was faced with a tempting choice.'[8] He would have been aware of the strict rules with regard to marriage for ministers and prospective ministers in Elim. 'At first, young men who graduated from the college were not permitted to marry for a year but this was later extended to a total of five years. That rule continued well into the fifties. Percy Brewster and his fiancée were aware of that rule but it was further extended while he was serving his probationary period.'[9]

Brewster spent three months helping out with the meetings in Birmingham in 1931 following Jeffreys' hugely successful campaign in the city the previous year. He was given special responsibility for the work at Winson Green. It was following this short period of ministry that he entered the Elim Bible College on 19th September 1931. After only a few months theological training, he was sent to take charge of the churches at Ashbourne and Tamworth. This would have been quite a daunting mission for him as the two towns are some considerable distance apart from each other. Bearing in mind that he was a city boy, he would not have found it easy in the quiet, rural life of both towns. However, he made his mark and the two churches began to grow. During his time at Ashbourne and Tamworth, Brewster ministered in Sheffield for a three-week period in April 1933. He wrote to the District Superintendent, Robert Tweed and informed him that seventy-two had responded to his evangelistic preaching. Later, whilst ministering in Cardiff for a short period in 1934, he informed Tweed that there were a thousand people at the meeting in Cory Hall and nine had responded to the Gospel invitation. Those were the days when leaders in Elim appeared to be more concerned about pride rather than encouragement. Tweed's reply was somewhat cool to say the least.

> Glad to hear you are having good times. 'Keep low'. Servants of the Lord are never on more dangerous ground than when they are flushed with success from recent victories. I do not say this because I think you are getting exalted, but as a warning, and because I am interested in you.[10]

In 1934, Brewster was appointed to Swansea. Jeffreys had held a very successful campaign in this Welsh town[11] in 1930 and a strong church had been planted there. It was whilst he was in Swansea that Brewster launched the first of his pioneer campaigns. He had no proper team but felt God was leading him to launch a campaign in Neath. He took with him Gwilym Francis who was the Secretary of the Swansea church at that time, Francis was also the church pianist. He wrote to W G Hathaway on 9th February 1935 outlining his proposal regarding a campaign in Neath.

> After much prayer I had a day in Neath and feel it would be a great success to commence a work there…The Gwyn Hall is very central and holds about 400 people. I can hire the hall for 12/5d per night and 17/6d for Sunday evening[12]… Once the work begins, there are plenty of halls we can hire… If you give me sanction, I would like to commence on 18th

March. Please let me know by return as there will be a great deal of preparation.[13]

Hathaway was a cautious man who did everything by the book, yet, remarkably, he gave permission by return of post. Cartwright suggests that Hathaway may well have had a special interest in that area as he had joined the Apostolic Faith work in Swansea in 1910 and, no doubt, he was anxious to see an expansion of the Elim work in Wales.[14]

The campaign commenced on Monday, 18th March, 1934. Such was the response that he sent a telegram to Clapham on the 20th requesting benches to seat 400 people as the place was packed. The following day he sent a request for 1,000 hymn sheets. Some 600 people packed the hall on Thursday, 21st March and there were twenty-three conversions. Hathaway came to visit Neath on Sunday 31st March and decided that Brewster should conduct similar meetings in other places near Swansea. Brewster held meetings in Llanelli, where Stephen Jeffreys had held meetings in 1913 and where he had pastored the Island Place Mission before going to Dowlais. The town had a population of 55,000, but the only suitable place he could find was the Ritz Dance Hall that would accommodate 1,200 people. After some shrewd negotiations, Brewster was able to hire the hall for a two-week period for £30, this included two Sunday and Thursday afternoons. Cartwright reports that there were 700 present at the first Sunday afternoon meeting and the Hall was filled to capacity at night. On the first Tuesday, there were 700 present and eleven recorded decisions for Christ.[15]

Maintaining a work that was established through a pioneer campaign led by a charismatic evangelist posed huge challenges. The numbers attending the meetings in Neath and Llanelli, were not far short of the numbers that Jeffreys had in his campaigns at Cardiff and Swansea. Two large and thriving churches were established in Cardiff and Swansea whereas the churches at Neath and Llanelli which were established after Brewster's campaigns, were nowhere near as strong. Perhaps one of the main reasons for this was that supreme efforts were made to support Jeffreys and the follow-up team in the centres where he campaigned. Other evangelists and campaigns did not have the same support.

Brewster concluded his meetings in Llanelli in October 1935 and returned to his pastoral work in Swansea. During 1936, he held a series of meetings in other parts of Wales including Pontarddulais where a small church was already established. This church was under the leadership of Mr Bell, whose son Llewellyn became well known as a soloist and preacher throughout Elim. The Beulah Mission in this Carmarthenshire town came into Elim following Brewster's meetings. Brewster obtained a marquee that was able to accommodate 600 and held meetings in Port Talbot where another church was established.[16] After this, he was in Aberdare during June and July where Cecil Hadler was the song-leader. The Aberdare campaign also had large attendances but there was considerable difficulty in finding suitable permanent accommodation. A building was eventually found, but the location of the church situated on a steep hill some distance from the town centre was problematic and the church eventually closed just before the turn of the century.

It would appear that Brewster was employed as a full-time evangelist between October 1936 and May 1937. He held meetings in Abertillery, a market-town in Monmouthshire and Pembroke Dock. These were not very successful and no churches were planted there. He campaigned in Worcester, where Edward Jeffreys (Stephen Jeffreys' son) had planted a church that was part of the Bethel Fellowship. The Bethel work had fragmented and whilst Brewster's meetings were fairly successful, many of the people attending the campaign were reluctant to become too closely associated with another group.[17] After the Worcester campaign, Brewster wrote to Elim headquarters requesting that he be appointed to a church and, once more, become a full-time pastor.

Before the war, Elim had a policy of moving pastors on an annual basis. With the changes in May 1937, Brewster went to Guildford in order to establish a new work. Once again, he had a good response and stayed there for a period of three months. From there, he moved to Eastbourne where a strong church had been established following a campaign by George Jeffreys in 1928. 'The church, like the town, was somewhat genteel. Percy Brewster livened things up somewhat, though everything he did was always done with decorum and dignity. He was never shy of publicity. His Scrapbook is filled with cuttings from the local papers. Though he did very well in Eastbourne, he only stayed until May 1939.'[18]

His next appointment was to Cardiff where he was inducted as the pastor of Cardiff City Temple on 6th May, 1939. Brewster's appointment to this prime church would have been controversial. He was only 31 years of age at the time and would have been considered somewhat of a risk because of his youth. He was to remain the Pastor of the City Temple, Cardiff until 1974 when he became Secretary-General of the Elim Pentecostal Church and moved to Cheltenham.

Even at a time when Elim boasted of several churches with Sunday Evening congregations around the thousand, Cardiff City Temple was unique. It was opened as a church in 1934 following George Jeffreys' very successful campaign in Cardiff in the autumn of 1929. An Elim church had been established in the city and only the largest halls and chapels would house the congregation. When the City Temple, situated on Cowbridge Road East, was built a few hundred yards from the City Centre, it was unique. Built more on the lines of a theatre than a church, the interior with its tipping cinema seats with a steep rising terrace had a seating capacity of 1,000, Jeffreys had built a number of churches with the feature of a rising terrace in each of them in order to maximise seating accommodation. The church buildings at Eastbourne, Croydon and Sparkbrook, Birmingham were of this design. But the superb Cardiff City Temple was in a league of its own and was certainly the largest church building that was built according to Jeffreys' specifications. The congregation was regularly around 800 in number. Cartwright informs us that there had been some problems with one of the previous ministers who had left under a cloud. He does not name the minister, but the author is of the opinion that he might have been referring to Arthur Longley. Longley was a popular Elim preacher who specialised on sermons based on the return of Christ. He most certainly would have held a large congregation by the quality of his preaching. One who had heard him felt that his style of preaching was intense. His successor did not have the same appeal and there was a danger of the place declining.

Brewster was ideally suited for Cardiff. The challenge before him was greater than he could have imagined at his induction service. Already, the clouds of war brooded over the nation. After the long years of appeasement and the running down of the nation's armaments, the nation was not in a fit state for devastating warfare, but, four months after Brewster's induction in Cardiff, Britain was at war. Not only that, but, for Elim, there was internal strife also. Just three weeks prior to Brewster's induction, George Jeffreys had preached, together with Lewi Pethrus,[19] in the City Temple. George Jeffreys' first resignation from Elim came at the Conference in November in the same year that Brewster was inducted to Cardiff City Temple.

P S was very close to Jeffreys and a firm admirer of his work. There were similarities between them, the most obvious of which was the evangelistic fervour that gripped both their hearts. Brewster was as equally committed to 'healing evangelism' as was Jeffreys. Throughout his campaigns, P S emphasised the healing work of Christ. He was committed to the Foursquare Gospel. At this time, Brewster was faced with somewhat of a dilemma. Jeffreys wanted him to join his Bible Pattern Church. Cardiff was a 'Jeffreys Church' in so many ways. There was a very serious possibility that the Cardiff Church would be divided and many of the people would follow the Principal when he established his new Movement. A number of people did leave, including some of the more affluent members. However, the main leaders stayed and the work continued to prosper and grow even in the difficult war-time conditions.

Brewster was a genius at turning difficulties into opportunities. On 3rd March, 1940 the Temple was hit by a bomb during an air raid where the enemy was attacking Cardiff Docks. Although the damage was considerable, the main structure remained intact. But it meant that the congregation had to worship elsewhere for a time whilst the Temple was being repaired. Brewster hired the large Park Hall cinema in the city centre for their Sunday evening services. It was very successful and numbers held up. P S was swift to make the most of opportunities whenever they came to his notice. He went in for evangelism among the Forces in a big way. Buses were hired to bring the soldiers from the camps to special meetings. Food would be laid on for them and then a Gospel message followed.

Brewster's thirty-five years as the senior pastor at Cardiff City Temple is impressive to say the least. When one considers that even through the six years of the Second World War, the City Temple was filled every Sunday evening, his ministry there is in quite another dimension in pastoral ministry. Added to this was his role as a member of the Executive Council, his appointment to a number of Conference Committees, his role as District Superintendent of the Welsh Presbytery and his involvement in the leadership of the World Pentecostal Conference. Through all these years, he was also Elim's leading evangelist. This aspect of his ministry will be considered in the next chapter.

Notes

[1] Jones, Maldwyn, *And they came to Elim, Volume 1*, ibid, p351.

[2] Jones, Maldwyn, ibid, chapters 18, 19.

[3] Cartwright, Desmond, *Some Evangelists, the life and ministry of George Jeffreys and PS Brewster in the formation of the Elim Pentecostal Church.* (MA Dissertation, Sheffield University) p34.

[4] Cartwright, Desmond, *Some Evangelists*, ibid, p1.

[5] Cartwright, Desmond, *Some Evangelists*, ibid, p1.

[6] Canty, George, *History of Elim*, ibid, p167

[7] Cartwright, Desmond, *Some Evangelists*, ibid, p34.

[8] Cartwright, Desmond, *Some Evangelists*, ibid, p34.

[9] Cartwright, Desmond, *Some Evangelists*, ibid, p34.

[10] Robert Tweed was Brewster's pastor in East Ham, so he obviously took an interest in him. In 1975, Pastor and Mrs Brewster stayed with us for a weekend's meetings in Beeston. Robert and Alice Tweed were in the congregation that Saturday evening. We invited them to join us for supper. It was the first time that Pastor and Mrs Tweed had met the Brewsters since 1940.

[11] On 3rd July, 1969 Prince Charles, during a tour of Wales to celebrate his investiture year, made the announcement that the town of Swansea was to become a city.

[12] 62.5 pence and 82.5pence.

[13] Letter: Brewster/Hathaway, 9th Feb 1934, (Malvern: Elim Archives).

[14] Cartwright, Desmond, *Some Evangelists,* ibid, pp35,36.

[15] Cartwright, Desmond, *Some Evangelists,* ibid, p36

[16] This church was small and eventually closed. George Canty held a campaign in the town in 1967 and an Elim church was once again established in Port Talbot.

[17] Twenty years later, Ken Mathew, a leading Elim evangelist would have a very successful mission there. He was greatly encouraged by Brewster at the time. Mathew stayed on to pastor the church.

[18] Cartwright, Desmond, *Some Evangelists,* ibid, p38.

[19] Lewi Pethrus was the leader and founder of the Swedish Pentecostal Churches. A former Baptist pastor, he was firmly of the opinion that each local church should be independent. He was a strong advocate of local church government and had no time for centralisation. He was greatly admired by Jeffreys who looked to him as his guide and example on matters of church government.

20
The Leader

We continue to explore the extraordinary ministry of P S Brewster. His impact upon the Elim Movement is, in the opinion of many, on a parallel with that of George Jeffreys, the founder of Elim. There are comparisons and differences between the two men. Jeffreys was a Welsh speaking Welshman who spent most of his ministerial life in London. Brewster was a Londoner who spent the greater part of his pastoral years in South Wales. Jeffreys was foremost an evangelist, Brewster was a pastor and evangelist. Jeffreys spent almost all his years in the Christian ministry as a denominational leader. Brewster became the leader of the Elim Pentecostal Church in the latter years of his ministry. One major factor in both their lives was their evangelistic zeal and their commitment to propagating the Gospel.

Despite the difficulties which affected all aspects of life in Britain during the Second World War, Brewster continued his evangelistic work. Apart from his work amongst the members of the Forces, he sought opportunities to open up into new areas. In 1941, he conducted a campaign in Aberystwyth with Ken Mathew and Douglas B Gray on his team. The Pontypridd Church which had been opened in 1928 joined Elim in 1941. Churches in Barry and Newport were opened as a result of Brewster's campaigns in those town in 1942 and 1943.

One of the major decisions of the 1944 Conference was to set up an Evangelistic Council to initiate a bold policy for evangelistic work.[1] Just as the nation had received fresh hope after the dark years of the war with the combined allied fleet assaulting the beaches of Normandy on D-Day and landing large battalions to aid the liberation of France, so too, Elim was determined to set up a spiritual beachhead against the enemy. The one chosen to lead this evangelistic forward movement was Percy Brewster. The Wigan campaign triumphed in spite of the odds against it.

Elim's Elisha

For almost twenty-five years of its existence, Elim had an undisputed leader, George Jeffreys. Whilst E J Phillips, admirably led from behind the scenes, as it were, there was no dynamic, charismatic personality to lead from the front. Canty was strongly of the opinion that Percy Brewster was a more-than-capable substitute to fill the chasm left by Jeffreys' departure. The following lengthy quotation by Canty reveals the depth of appreciation felt by those who had been inspired by Brewster to launch into evangelism themselves.

> Percy Brewster had typical East London verve, free of any inferiority complex. Not an intellectual, he possessed what some brainy men lack – ideas, initiative and the optimism to see that a thing could be done. He could, however, get through to the core of a situation, which made his opinion respected. In much committee work, especially when he acted as chairman, discussions tended to end when he felt he knew what was wanted, his colleagues commenting, 'It seemed good to the Holy Ghost and P S!' His steady, irrepressible confidence and unswerving evangelistic aims made him a figure in the world Pentecostal landscape…When George Jeffreys receded from prominence, a cry for a leader was often expressed. Nobody else could be a founder-father, but Percy Brewster's extensive pioneering of new churches thrust him forward as a possible substitute. To some degree the Elisha to George Jeffreys as Elijah. Those before him in the work and themselves possessed of leadership qualities did not see him in that role. He was not a careerist determined to dominate the

scene, either. Ultimately, his great value as a man that others would follow became evident. His appointment as Secretary-General meant something of sacrifice for him, but in that office, he exercised a powerful driving effect which touched the whole Movement.[2]

As early as 1939, whilst the Movement was embroiled in governmental disputes, Brewster showed that he was clearly capable of filling a major part of the chasm that would be created by the resignation of George Jeffreys. He conducted a major evangelistic campaign in the city of Hull. The meetings were held in the Regal Cinema where congregations in excess of 2000 gathered to hear him. 'The Year was 1939, and to the Regal cinema and to the City Temple in Hull came a revival party, as they were known then. The leader was P S Brewster. As a teenager then, the impression made upon me and my contemporaries was enormous. The dynamic of the preaching and the concerned fervency of the prayer for the sick left an indelible mark for good and for God.'[3]

Following the Wigan campaign, Brewster concentrated his evangelistic campaigns in Wales. Jeffreys held two campaigns in Wales, Cardiff and Swansea. These were hugely successful and two strong churches were established. By 1948, Brewster had already held campaigns in Neath, Llanelli, Aberystwyth, Barry and Newport with churches being established in these five towns.

In the same year, Brewster turned his attention to the most famous of the South Wales mining valleys, the Rhondda. A campaign was held in Tonypandy. This was the town that was made famous for its riots in 1910 and 1911. These were a series of confrontations between the striking miners and the police at various locations in the Rhondda. As a result of the confrontation between the miners and the police in Tonypandy Square on 8th November 1910, The Chief Constable of Glamorganshire requested military support from the War Office. The Home Secretary, Winston Churchill did not send in troops but instead despatched Metropolitan Police officers, both on foot and mounted. He did, however sent some cavalry troops to Cardiff.

It is clear that Churchill did not want to send in the troops to Tonypandy but his hand was forced by local magistrates and troops were deployed. The people of the Rhondda in general, and Tonypandy in particular, were very slow to forgive Churchill for sending in the troops.

So, it was to this valley, and to this town that Brewster brought the message of the Foursquare Gospel. A marquee was erected in an area near the town centre. The campaign was a great success. He was ably supported by his song leader and soloist, William Plowright. Bill Plowright campaigned with Brewster for many years. A former Welsh chapel was purchased in the nearby town of Trealaw. The church commenced with a considerable number but, over the years, the congregation declined and the chapel became unusable. The small congregation struggled until it was finally closed in 2021.

In 1948, Brewster held a pioneer campaign in Mountain Ash, a mining town in the Cynon Valley, South Wales. Following the campaign, a former Welsh chapel was purchased and a strong Elim Church was founded. Brewster campaigned in Lancashire also in 1948 and a church was established in Bolton. The Bolton campaign lasted for seven weeks. It was a difficult campaign, but Brewster continued campaigning until a church was established.

Caerphilly, is a large town some eight miles north of Cardiff. Famous for its cheese and castle with its leaning tower, welcomed Brewster and his campaign party in 1949. The campaign was a great success and a strong church was established and Ron Jones, who was from and Assemblies of God background, was appointed the first pastor. In the same year, Brewster held a campaign in Camberwell, Surrey and re-established an Elim church there. Bill Plowright, Brewster's song-leader and soloist in most of his pioneer campaigns was appointed as pastor. Canty's reporting of this campaign is worthy of inclusion:

> In that spiritual Sahara of South East London, in a tent pitched
> on ground cleared by Hitler's bombs at Camberwell, for two
> months he persisted against incredible public apathy until

hundreds had professed Christ and meetings were transferred to an immense old chapel. Big enough to be a film setting for Fingal's Cave, it became a spot of Pentecostal warmth in one of the coldest places on earth for religion.[4]

In 1950, Brewster conducted a pioneer campaign in Porth in the Rhondda. The name of the town signified its importance to the two Rhondda Valleys. It is a Welsh name which means 'entrance way' or 'gateway'. The town itself is situated at the confluence of the two main rivers - Rhondda Fawr, the larger of the two valleys and Rhondda Fach, its smaller sibling. Again, the campaign was held in a marquee and a former Welsh Methodist Chapel called Ebenezer Chapel was purchased. The first pastor of the church was William Evans, a Yorkshire man who was, for a short period, Brewster's assistant in Cardiff. He was married to Mary whose father, Alderman George Williams, was Lord Mayor of Cardiff in 1950/51. Porth is my home church and I take this opportunity to pay tribute to a very fine pastor and father in the faith. He and Mrs Evans, served not only the members of the Elim Church in Porth, but countless others. They encouraged myself and others as we tremblingly made our first faltering steps in the Christian ministry. Together, they led the Porth Elim Church for almost 35 years. William Evans was my pastor and throughout the many years, whenever we met, I always called him 'Pastor Evans'.

There was no let-up as far as pioneer campaigns were concerned. P S was determined to hold as many campaigns as possible whilst also pastoring the Cardiff City Temple. In 1951, he held campaigns in the small mining town of Pontlottyn and also in the border city of Hereford. Another couple of Elim churches were planted. In 1952, it was the South Wales market town of Brecon that became the focal point of Brewster's campaigning. Three hundred farmers and their families gathered from the countryside and the majority of them responded to the Gospel.[5]

The Derby pioneer campaign in 1960 saw the establishment of one of Elim's largest churches with Wynne Lewis as its first and very successful pastor. Wynne had previously pastored the new

Bridgend church which had also been launched as a result of a Brewster pioneer campaign.

Arguably, the greatest campaign led by P S was held in Bristol in the holiday month of August, 1952. This was the year that he was inducted as Elim's President for the first time.[6] H W Greenway, Editor of the Elim Evangel at the time refers to the Bristol campaign in his editorial entitled 'Evangelical Drive':

> The President's address at the ordination service in the Bloomsbury Central Baptist Church and the evangelistic report given at the Conference the next morning have both added encouragement to the soul-saving enterprise of the Elim Movement. Pastor P S Brewster, the new Elim President, is able to speak from experience on this important subject, having conducted campaigns in many parts of the country, the last of which, in the beautiful Colston Hall, Bristol, was the most powerful of his career.[7]

When Brewster enquired about booking the Colston Hall in Bristol for his campaign during the month of August, he was told that it would be sheer madness to do so because it was the holiday month and virtually no-one would come. No-one would book the Colston Hall, with its 2,000 seats, for any event during the month of August. 'The manager openly stated that he considered anyone who attempted it was crazy.'[8] 'Encouraged by his Elder, Mr Chivers, and joined in the ministry by Willard Cantelon, P S Brewster and his team of workers took over that very hall during the month of August 1952, and so the Elim Pentecostal Church in Bristol was born.'[9] P S Brewster was a visionary, furthermore, he was not afraid to take risks when it came to evangelistic enterprise. 'He loved spiritual adventure.'[10] But always, he combined in a very rare manner, the joint gifts of Pastor and Evangelist. His campaigns were, in the main, held for the purpose of establishing a new church. In this respect, he was single-minded.

The author was a member of the 1974 Elim Conference and can vividly recall the shock of reading the Conference agenda and discovering the name of P S Brewster being nominated for the office of Secretary-General. This was a huge surprise. The men who had previously filled this position had been appointed for their administrative gifting. John Smyth made the following comment: 'P S Brewster was the first Elim Secretary-General to take office straight from a church situation. His coming to office had something of the effect of a whirlwind on the administration.'[11] His great love for people and his overwhelming passion to see them won for Christ, and his evangelistic fervour was soon felt at Elim Headquarters in Cheltenham. 'To him everything had to serve the one cause of telling others about the Lord Jesus and his saving power.'[12] He was a great initiator. Whilst many can keep something going when it is started, it takes a very special person to successfully change a whole Movement's cause. P S did just that. In his thinking, everything had to serve the one cause of telling others about the Lord Jesus and his saving power. He turned the Movement's policy in a different direction and changed the course of the Movement's history back to its original values.[13] It has to be said that there had not been an abandonment of the prime purpose of Elim's existence. Elim was born in evangelism. It was, and is, a Missional Movement. Evangelism has, throughout its history, been Elim's passion. Brewster led the Movement in such a way that evangelism became the all-consuming goal.

In recording the momentous decision of the 1974 Elim Conference to appoint Brewster as the leader of the Movement, it is right to honour the Executive Council of the day who made the nomination. The members of the Executive that made this decision were: A A Biddle, J T Bradley, P S Brewster, R B Chapman, G W Gilpin, W R Jones, J Lancaster, J C Smyth, A B Tee and T W Walker. Of those, only four were perceived to be evangelists, they were A A Biddle, Brewster, Jones and Tee. It must be noted that Chapman conducted a number of evangelistic campaigns during his years of pastoral ministry. One can only speculate as to the discussion around the table when a successor to the retiring Secretary-General, J T Bradley, was nominated.

At the time, the practice was that each member of the Executive Council would write a name for the position in secret and the suggested name(s) were handed to the President who was the chairman. The person who received the most nominations would be asked to leave the room and the rest of the members would discuss the nomination. Also present at the meeting in which the nomination of Brewster as Secretary-General was made, was H W Greenway who had served as Elim's Secretary General for thirteen years. He succeeded the great E J Phillips. Greenway was an emeritus member of the Executive Council by virtue of having been a member for over 25 years. He would not have had a vote at the meeting, but would have been free to express an opinion. He was a close friend of Brewster and the author has no doubt that Greenway would have spoken strongly in favour of the nomination.[14]

In his three years leading the Movement, Brewster initiated a fresh evangelistic policy that resulted in the creation of a full-time post of Evangelistic Secretary. The first appointed to this office was Alex Tee. Brewster also encouraged the release of full-time evangelists, although there was no national budget for their salaries. George Canty became Elim's first unsalaried 'on-faith' itinerant evangelist since the war and he continued to hold evangelistic campaigns and rallies until he was over 90 years of age. Also, Mark Drew who had been mentored by Canty, was another full-time Elim evangelist.

Percy Brewster was not only Elim's Secretary-General; he was also Secretary of the Advisory Committee of the World Pentecostal Conference. It was during the World Pentecostal Conference held in Helsinki that he was elected to the Advisory Committee, a position he held until his death. In the Conference held at Dallas in 1970 he was appointed Secretary to the Advisory Committee. In addition to these appointments, when it was decided at the Dallas Conference to republish the World Pentecost magazine, Brewster was invited to become the Editor. 'During these years he travelled the world in the interest of Pentecostal unity and global evangelism. He was esteemed by leaders, ministers and members involved in the World Pentecostal Conference. His evangelistic enthusiasm, Pentecostal fervour, and balanced judgement made him a statesman in international affairs.'[15] Thomas Zimmerman, a former General Secretary of the Assemblies of God, U S A, in his tribute to Brewster said of him: 'He exemplified the compassion of Christ that compels men to fulfil God's purpose in seeking the lost and bringing them to Christ. No one of his generation was responsible for the opening of more Pentecostal churches.'[16]

In the course of a person's ministry, one's family can often feel the strain of that. Brewster was often away from home either conducting evangelistic campaigns in this country or travelling the world in his role as a member of the World Pentecostal presidium. His own dedication to evangelism was matched by that of his wife, Doris, who accepted the sacrifice of often being alone to look after their four children, Ruth, Allan, Anne and Linda. In conversing with George Canty, he especially wished it to be recorded that, 'My wife has been a tower of strength behind me in all my campaigns. Never once has she complained about my going away for so long. In many ways she has sacrificed so much.'[17]

In concluding these two chapters on the contribution of P S Brewster to the Elim Movement, it is fitting that I include, as part of his legacy, his training and encouragement of other, younger evangelists to carry on the baton. A good leader always ensures that, as far as possible, there is no gap left when that leader moves on. Brewster was a firm believer in the fact that evangelism and the passion to reach people with the Gospel could be caught from successful evangelists.

> My relationship with George Jeffreys were very close and I admired and loved him very much. He was a man who led thousands to Christ and gave many men the opportunity to enter the full-time ministry. It was the brothers Jeffreys who inspired me to commence evangelism, but it was not

entirely them. It does seem that evangelism can be caught from successful men.[18]

P S gave very clear proof of his judgement in the number of men who followed him in the very needed ministry of evangelism. He never campaigned alone, but had those with supporting ministries to his own. In the Bristol campaign, he involved a Canadian evangelist by the name of Willard Cantelon. He shared some of the preaching, but as a gifted artist, most nights he would paint pictures while the service proceeded. These were usually given away to the person that had brought the most people with them to the campaign.

He had on his teams, gifted musicians, singers and song leaders. Some of these worked with him for many years such as Billy Plowright. In his first campaign in Neath, he took with him Gwilym Francis, who went on to become a fine evangelist himself in the Bible Pattern Movement. When he held the Aberystwyth campaign, he had in his team Cyril Hadler. In later campaigns, Ken Matthew worked alongside him and became a notable evangelist within Elim. Alex Tee, perhaps Elim's greatest pioneer evangelist after Brewster, learned much whilst working alongside P S. Others followed each having been touched by Brewster's evangelistic fervour. George Canty himself, Ron Jones, Alan Caple, Wynne Lewis, Brian Edwards, David Woodfield, Paul Epton and Mark Drew, all of these were to some extent or other influenced, helped and encouraged in their evangelistic endeavour by the resolute, determined and gifted master-evangelist, P S Brewster.

A final note, P S made a request, carried out at his funeral for a Gospel call to be given. The preacher on that momentous occasion was Eldin Corsie. He took as his text Joshua 24:39, *'Joshua died... and they buried him in the land of his inheritance.'* Eldin made the following comment: 'It is fitting that P S Brewster should be laid to rest in Wales. He was a Londoner by birth, but Wales became the land of his inheritance.' Following the sermon, as requested by Mr Brewster and impressed upon by Mrs Brewster, an appeal for salvation was made. There is a difference between Canty's recorded decisions and Cartwright's. In his account of the Thanksgiving Service for the life of Percy Brewster, he states that 'about six hands were raised'.[19] Canty states the following: 'Her husband's irrepressible assurance was reflected in Mrs Doris Brewster. Despite her tremendous loss, her comment about it all (the Thanksgiving Service) will be ever remembered: "Wasn't it a wonderful service, and twelve people getting saved."'[20]

Notes

[1] 1944 Conference Minutes.

[2] Canty, George, *History of Elim*, ibid p167

[3] Walker, Tom W, *A burning and shining light, Elim Evangel*, 16th August 1980, p12

[4] Canty, George, ibid, p168.

[5] Canty, George, ibid, p169.

[6] He was one of four men to have been elected President on two occasions, the others being E C W Boulton, Joseph Smith and W R Jones.

[7] Greenway, H W, *Elim Evangel*, 15th September, 1952, p578.

[8] Jones, Ron, *P S Brewster – Elim's great leader, Elim Evangel*, (P S Brewster Memorial Issue) 16th August, 1980 pp7-8.

[9] Jones, Ron, *P S Brewster*, ibid.

[10] Jones, Ron, *P S Brewster*, ibid.

[11] Smyth, John, *'P S kept Movement on right course', Elim Evangel*, ibid p8.

[12] Smyth, John, *'P S kept Movement on right course'*, ibid.

[13] Smyth, John, *'P S kept Movement on right course'*, ibid.

[14] This is supposition, not fact, but it is supposition based on conversations between the author and Greenway's son Michael and his wife Peggy, on the many occasions we were together at the Elim Archives in Malvern under the direction of the Archivist, Philip Thompsett and his wife Sally.

[15] Dando, Eric, *'A Prince in Pentecost', Elim Evangel*, ibid, p10.

[16] Zimmerman, Thomas F, *A tremendous loss, Elim Evangel*, ibid, p12.

[17] Canty, George, ibid, p168.

[18] P S Brewster, quoted by Canty, George, *History of Elim*, ibid, p168.

[19] Cartwright, Desmond, *Elim Evangel*, 16th August 1980, ibid, p12.

[20] Canty, George, ibid, p170.

Alex Tee, National Youth Director, Evangelistic Director, President 1969-1970

David Ayling, International Missions Director. President 1977-1978

David Ayling presenting Sandy Wilson with the Presidential Bible, Conference 1978

Elim Bible College Students 1968

Two former National Youth Directors, Eldin Corsie and Jack Hywel Davies.
Eldin Corsie was President 1980-1981 and General Superintendent.

George Wesley Gilpin, Principal
of Elim Bible College 1958-1980,
President 1965-1966

George Canty, President 1973-1974,
preaching at the Royal Albert Hall

Mrs Chapman singing at the Memorial Service of the Elim Missionaries and their children who were martyred in the Vumba 23rd June, 1978

Ron Chapman, Field Superintendent, President 1966-1967, dedicating the Memorial Plaque at Elim International Offices, Cheltenham for martyred Elim Missionaries

Left: Tom Walker, President 1972-1973 and 1988-1989, Field Superintendent and General Superintendent
Above: Jack Osman, President 1979-1980 with Maldwyn Jones

Elim Easter Celebrations at the Royal Albert Hall, Circa 1975

Ron Jones, President 1970-1971 and 1982-1983

Executive Council, 1975. Left to right: H W Greenway, D J Ayling, J T Bradley, G W Gilpin, J C Smyth, T W Walker, J MacInnes, P S Brewster, W R Jones, A B Tee, A A Biddle, John Lancaster

21
Ethical Issues

The changes in society and moral values after the Second World War brought its challenges to the Elim Movement. Britain's position in the world changed. The era of Empire was gone. For almost three centuries, India had been looked upon as the glistening jewel in the empirical crown. Years of nonviolent resistance to British rule led by Mohandas Gandhi and Jawaharial Nehru, eventually resulted in Indian independence in 1947. The 1947 Independence Act saw the partition of British India into the two new independent countries of India and Pakistan.

Britain was forced to leave India for purely financial reasons. Following on from the war, Britain left not only India but nearly all its other colonies and protectorates. This included Jordan (1946), Palestine (1947), Ceylon (1948), Egypt (1952), Malaysia (1957). British rule in Singapore ended on 16th September 1963 when it became a state of Malaysia after one hundred and forty-four years as a British colony. Singapore separated from Malaysia to become an independent sovereign state on 9th August 1965. The 1950's and 1960's saw most African and Caribbean countries gain their independence from Britain.

The gaining of independence by many of its colonies had a major impact on life in the UK. Following the granting of independence, Commonwealth citizens were given the right to live, work and settle in the UK without any restrictions. But there was a racist backlash against Black and Asian immigration that led to the Commonwealth Immigrations Act 1962, which was intended to stem the flow of immigrants from Commonwealth countries. However, the flow of people from former Commonwealth countries changed the composition of British society. Immigration has enriched British society. The ship 'HMT Empire Windrush' arrived at Tilbury from the Caribbean on 22nd June, 1948. Britain, with its new reforming Labour government was short of workers. Men and women were needed to rebuild an economy ruined by the ravages of World War II.

It has to be said that these citizens from our colonies were not well received at first. In the immediate post-war years, the government had recruited white Europeans displaced during the war to fill labour vacancies rather than look to the Empire. It must be remembered that at this time, Britain's Caribbean colonies were still under British control. Those who came to Britain from her colonies were invited to come by the British government. The labour vacancies in the country were added to by the emigration of large numbers of white British people to Australia, New Zealand and Canada.

The church in the UK had to adapt to this changing society. Most of the Caribbean and African people came from countries where Christianity was the major religion. In the case of Caribbeans, many of them were Pentecostal. Elim, slowly but surely, began to reach out to the ethnic population and many of our churches, especially in the large cities, experienced considerable growth as a result of Caribbean and African people coming into membership. It took quite some time for people from the Commonwealth countries to be accepted. The scandal of the Windrush generation where many hundreds came from the Caribbean to what was then viewed by some to be the mother country and settled in this country thinking that they were full citizens of the UK, discovered that they had no papers, even though they have lived in this country for well over 60 years, has only recently surfaced. The immigration of people from Commonwealth countries has contributed immeasurably to the economic and social conditions in Britain today. It is true, there are problems involved with illegal immigration, but Enoch Powell's infamous 'Rivers of blood' speech delivered on 20th April, 1968 strained race relations almost to a breaking point. The speech was made on a Saturday at a gathering of Conservatives in Birmingham. Enoch Powell was at the time a member of Parliament for Wolverhampton South West, the seat he took at the 1950 General Election. The imagery contained within the speech had a profound effect on the country and certainly heightened racial tensions to a point where it had never been before in this country.

Powell was renowned for his oratorical skills and his maverick behaviour. This became clear in his 'rivers of blood speech'. He declared to his audience what he believed would be the consequences of continued unchecked mass immigration from the Commonwealth to the UK. 'Above all it is an allusion to the Roman poet Virgil towards the end of the speech which has been remembered, giving the speech its colloquial name'.[1] A portion of the speech is included here in order to show the possibilities within it to cause a disturbance of the peace:

> As I look ahead, I am filled with foreboding. Like the Roman, I seem to see 'the River Tiber foaming with much blood'. This tragic and intractable phenomenon which we watch with horror on the other side of the Atlantic but which there is interwoven with the history and existence of the States itself, is coming here by our own volition and our own neglect. Indeed, it has all but come. In numerical terms, it will be of American proportions long before the end of the 20th Century. Only resolute and urgent action will avert it even now. Whether there will be the public will to demand and obtain that action, I do not know. All I know is that to see, and not to speak, would be the great betrayal.[2]

Powell's speech found favour with a large section of the British electorate and this included part of the Christian community. Those members of the Windrush generation and beyond testified to not being welcomed into Pentecostal churches, including Elim. It is to their immense credit that many of the West Indian and African people who came to Britain at that time persevered and became valued members of our churches. Eventually, to a greater or lesser degree, British society and British churches came to terms with the changing dynamics to the population caused by large-scale immigration from the Commonwealth. Many new churches were opened and existing churches were numerically strengthened as a result of Caribbean, African and Asian people from the Commonwealth attending our churches.

There were other issues at play that were to have an effect on church life in the 60's and 70's. British and Western society itself changed out of all recognition in the three decades after the war. As rationing eased and wages rose, people began to feel good about themselves. In spite of the fears of jobs being taken by immigrants, there was plenty of work. Unemployment had started to rise in the nineteen seventies. Margaret Thatcher, who had been elected leader of the Conservative and Unionist Party three years earlier, attacked the Labour Party and its 'Winter of Discontent'. The Conservative Party campaign employed the advertising agency Saatchi and Saatchi, and pledged to control inflation as well as curbing the power of the trade unions. They also ran their campaign on the theme that 'Labour isn't working' (unemployment reached a 40 year high of 1.5million during 1978). In actual fact, it was to reach much higher rates under the new Conservative Government.

There can be no denying that the Thatcher years (1979-1991) was a time of political polarisation in our country. A great many people loved her and a great many people disliked her intensely. Suddenly, politics began to be discussed among Elim people as it had never been done before.

Then there was the 'spirit of the age'. Increasingly, Britain and its Western allies have become a more hedonistic society. Alcohol, drugs and sex seemed to have entered the mindset, particularly young people, to a degree that had not been known prior to the 1960's.[3] Furthermore, the family unit was affected in a number of ways. Divorce had increased phenomenally after the war. The sixties and seventies also saw the phenomenon of the one-parent family. By 2021, there were 3 million lone parent families, which accounted for 15.4% of families in the UK; the proportions ranged from 13.1% in the South East of England to 17.8% in the North East of England.

To many church people, it would seem as though the very foundations of our nation were crumbling. Accepted moral standards were breaking down before our eyes. The family unit, which for hundreds of years had been the bedrock of our society was no longer looked upon as such. Marriages were breaking down, divorce rates going through the roof. Added to this, in more recent days have been discordant voices on sexuality, homosexuality, lesbianism, and trans-gender issues. These are issues that are very much a centre-point in society at present and it is something that the church cannot ignore. Elim, like every other religious organisations will continue to be challenged.

It may come as a surprise to some readers, but even in the early days of its formation, Elim was not afraid to confront some moral issues within society. Indeed, the pre-war Conferences, in some cases, appeared to be more progressive in their thinking on some of these issues than their immediate post-war gatherings. They discussed subjects such as fornication, birth control, annulment and divorce. As far as the subject of birth control, it has to be said that although it was on the agenda, they decided to pass on to the next item with the intention of it appearing on the following year's agenda, which it never did. The point I wish to make is that even before the last world war, the Conference was fairly broad in its lines of discussion. I would go so far as to say that it was progressive both in the debating quality of its speakers and in the items that appeared on its agenda. It is the author's opinion that the Conference in its current state is far less progressive nor is it as capable in debate as its predecessors of years gone by.

Matters relating to Ministers

The early conferences are important because they laid down the basic rules governing the lifestyle of the minister. The First

Conference was held in Glossop in October 1932. This was not a full Conference as it only included ministers of the Northern Division.[4] The very first matter of consequence to pastors and churches that was discussed was that of Harvest Thanksgiving Services. The argument against holding such services was that it was a doubtful practice and likely to cause jealousy regarding the distribution of the produce. The argument in favour was that such services drew crowds. The following comment appeared in the minutes: 'The majority were certainly against Harvest Thanksgivings, and the few who were for it, were against the practice of selling produce afterwards. It was suggested that no Harvest Thanksgivings should be reported in the Evangel.'[5]

Elim has, throughout its history, placed some stringent rules as to its ministers' interaction with the opposite sex. The Constitution requires that a minister informs the General Superintendent of the commencement of a courtship. In the early days, the breaking of an engagement was a disciplinary matter. Under the heading 'Breaking off Courtship', the following appears in the 1932 Conference minutes: 'All looked upon this as a serious matter, and it was suggested that a suitable punishment would be to extend the minimum period before marriage by two years. It was generally felt that our younger workers should have special instruction on the subjects of courtship, engagement, etc.'

The early Conferences revealed a strong suspicion of sports activities of any kind and the employment of any sporting games were to be discouraged among Elim youth. The Christian's attitude to sports etc. was discussed at the 1935 Conference. The following statement appears in the minutes:

> Several spoke on the need for recreation for young people, and others on the dangers. It was generally agreed that the dangers to be guarded against in connection with any form of games or sport were (i) Time being used which could be more profitably spent. (ii) A keen interest in the game leading to attending matches in order to improve one's playing. (iii) Taking part in games with unbelievers. The

dangers of organised sport in connection with Churches were emphasised and the declension which so often has followed in its wake was pointed out. The subject of mixed bathing in connection with Crusader outings, holiday homes, etc. was also discussed. The following resolution was carried unanimously: "That this Conference expresses its disapproval of regular organised sport and games and also of mixed bathing in connection with our movement."[6]

This would have been in keeping with the then traditional Pentecostal views of sanctification. Worldly pursuits must be eschewed. Separation from the world, its customs and pleasures, was a standard of Pentecostal teaching. Attitudes regards this changed with the ending of hostilities and the Movement encouraged the setting up of youth camps where it was inevitable that games and outdoor activities would be prominent

The 1936 Conference debated the question of fornication and adultery. There is little doubt that when the subject of fornication was discussed, the Conference had in mind pre-marital sexual intercourse. There appears to have been a degree of double-mindedness amongst some of the Conference members. They differentiated with those who had engaged in sexual intercourse before marriage, but there was no resultant pregnancy and those cases where children were born outside of marriage. The Conference minutes use the very old-fashioned expression 'issue' in addressing such a situation. Of course, the only way that an act of fornication without children resulting from such a union, could be known, would be by confession. In the case of a child being born as a result of pre-marital sexual intercourse, if the parties confessed, why should they be treated any differently? The full script of the notes on the debate that were entered into the Conference minutes is included as follows:

> The matter of how to deal with fornication and adultery among church members was discussed at length. Several expressed the view that there should be no suspension from membership (which would include from communion service

and taking part in meetings) unless there was issue. But it was generally agreed that there must be punishment to show we do not countenance sin, and that those concerned should be suspended whether there is issue or not. In the latter case, every endeavour should be made to keep the suspension and the cause of it private. In the case of a courting or engaged couple, Pastor Mercer said his practice was to suspend until after marriage and birth of the child, and then for them to come back as backsliders, but he kept it as far as possible from L.C.O.'s. (Local Church Officers). In the case of an L.C.O., he should be asked to resign.

In the case of a Minister, we were reminded that two years ago the Conference agreed to a suspension for fornication for 12 months, the Council to decide the case after that time.[7] It was generally accepted that all cases must be treated alike, whether there is a scandal or not. Dismissal should always be the punishment for adultery.

It was agreed that fornication between courting or engaged couples should be dealt with in exactly the same way as between others.

A request that the subject of Birth Control from the standpoint of the Scriptures be discussed at the next Conference was acceded to.[8]

The above minutes show the enlightenment of the Conference in discussing such matters in their ministerial sessions. It must be noted that there were women ministers as well as ministers' wives who would have been present when the above discussion took place.

Total Abstinence

The subject of ministers and church officers partaking alcoholic beverages has, historically, been a thorny issue in Elim. It appeared on the Conference agenda in 1944. At a later Conference, it was linked with smoking. The participation of either of these was considered unacceptable as far as Elim ministers were concerned. The minutes of the 1944 Conference on the subject of consuming alcohol: 'The Conference resolved that no Minister or Office

Bearer in Elim be appointed to any position of authority unless he declares himself to be a total abstainer.' The resolution is somewhat ambiguous because it does not state whether the said Office Bearer is someone who occupies a national or local position.

The subject of total abstinence became a subject of considerable debate in the Conferences in the 1970's. The matter was debated at the 1972 Conference with a view of strengthening the Movement's position on the subject. I was a probationary minister at the time. I asked for permission to speak on the subject but the President, Tom Walker felt that my speaking on the subject whilst a very new and young minister might be harmful to me and so he suggested that the Conference denied me the opportunity to speak, such denial was granted.[9] The minutes simply state 'Example', the Conference rejected. The matter was brought to the following year's Conference when the Church Session of the Greenock church called for the constitutional position on total abstinence be strengthened. The minutes read as follows:

> Example. After discussing a proposal that the word 'demands' be inserted in place of the word 'expects' in Working Arrangements, Section B, IV, 6 and Section C, III, 5, the Conference passed to the next business.[10]

It had become clear that by the end of the decade (70's) the total abstinence position was not being strictly adhered to by all Elim ministers and local church officers. Under the heading, 'Suggestion Time', the General Superintendent made the following statement relative to the Executive Council's interpretation of the above-mentioned Working Arrangements:

> The clauses referred to above were proposed by the Progress Committee when the Elim Constitution was considerably revised. The intention of the Committee was that they should be interpreted as a prohibition of both smoking and partaking of alcohol. Conference approved the insertion of this clause. An interpretation of the word that would allow a relaxation of

224

this standard for the total abstinence section would also be a relaxation of the standard for non-smoking.

Conference is aware of the fact that all applicants for the Elim ministry are asked to complete a questionnaire which deals with matters relative to doctrine, character, ministry and constitutional requirements. Numbered among the questions are the following: 'Are you a non-smoker? Are you a total abstainer? Do you promise to uphold these standards. Should the question be left unanswered or should the answers be 'no', the Field Superintendent is instructed by the Executive Council to take up the matter immediately with the person concerned, and a clear undertaking must then be given by the applicant that the standard of total abstinence will be upheld before the application is considered further.

Since this is the action taken by the Executive Council relative to all applicants whether they be direct from our own College or elsewhere, it would lead to problems and apparent double standards if when the same people go out into the work, they were to find that there are ministers who do not uphold these particular standards.

Because of the foregoing, the Executive Council feel that it owes it to the Conference to make its interpretation clear – namely that it believes these clauses constitute a prohibition as far as ministers and church officers, including deacons and elders are concerned from smoking or partaking of alcohol.[11]

The above statement was not worth the paper that it was written on. Within a few short years of this statement, there were some members of the Executive Council who did not abide by the sentiments that were expressed in the said statement. The fact is, views on total abstinence have changed considerably within Elim.[12]

Notes

[1] www.en.wikipedia.org Enoch Powell, accessed 17th September 2022.

[2] www.telegraph.co.uk *Enoch Powell's 'River of Blood' speech.* The Telegraph, 12 June 2020, accessed September 17th, 2022.

[3]

[4] North from Birmingham to Scotland. It did not include Ireland or Wales.

5 Northern Division Conference Minutes, 24th – 26th October, 1939, (Malvern: Elim Archives)

6 1935 Conference Minutes

7 There is no record of such a decision in the minutes of any of the three previous Conferences to this matter.

8 It did not happen. There was no such discussion.

9 In applying for ordination, the probationary minister was required to fill in a questionnaire. One of the questions was 'Are you a total abstainer?' I left that question blank. A few days later, I received a phone call from the Field Superintendent, R B Chapman. He informed me that I had not answered all the questions. I feigned surprise. He proceeded to ask me if I was a total abstainer. I replied, 'By practice, yes, by conscience no.' 'That will do, came the reply, 'I am not interested in your conscience, just your practice.'

10 Elim Conference 1973, Minutes, (Malvern: Elim Archives).

11 Elim Conference 1980, Minutes, (Malvern: Elim Archives).

12 It is my personal opinion that we have become a little too relaxed on the issue of consumption of alcohol especially by church leaders.

22
An Ending and a Beginning

I am writing this chapter on 20th September, 2022, the day after the funeral of Her Majesty, Queen Elizabeth II. Born in 1947 under the reign of a king, I shall doubtless die under the reign of another king. King George VI died on 6th February 1952. The BBC made the following announcement: 'On Wednesday, 6th February 1952, His Majesty, King George VI passed peacefully away in his sleep at Sandringham.' It came as a profound shock to the country. Following the abdication of his brother, Edward VIII in December 1936, his brother Albert, Duke of York, became King and assumed the name and title of King George VI. As the film 'The King's Speech' reveals, the Duke of York had a stammer and he engaged the speech therapist Lionel Logue to treat the stammer. The lessons with Logue obviously helped and he was able, to a large extent to overcome the stammer.

The Abdication Crisis

King George was never intended to ascend the throne. His brother, the charismatic David, Prince of Wales, was the successor to the British throne. The Prince of Wales was very popular in the mining communities of South Wales, but in reality, his younger brother was more concerned with the working conditions of the British people than the heir to the Throne. Prince Albert married Lady Elizabeth Bowes-Lyon on 26th April 1923. They had two children, Elizabeth who was born in 1926 and Margaret who was born in 1930.

Because of his stammer, the Duke of York dreaded public speaking. Following sessions with Logue an Australian-born speech therapist and the patient help of the Duchess, his delivery improved, but he remained, as far as the public were concerned, very much in the shadow of his elder brother.

In 1936, the country was in turmoil as a result of the abdication crisis caused by Edward's involvement with Wallis Simpson, who was divorced from her first husband and divorcing her second. Edward had been advised by the British Prime Minister Stanley Baldwin that he could not remain king and marry a divorced woman. Although Edward, the Prince of Wales, was the next in line to the throne, his father, King George V expressed his deep concern as to the suitability of his first-born son to be King.

Albert, Duke of York, had no desire to be King, neither did his wife. When Edward VIII abdicated in December 1936. Albert succeeded him, taking the regal name of George VI, no doubt, in honour of his father. George VI was a man of deep faith. He was confirmed in the church at Sandringham on Easter Sunday, 1912.

> He had learned a simple, deep faith in God from his grandmother, Queen Alexandra, which was always to be of great importance to him. Although no great reader, one book on the historical truth of the Resurrection, *The Empty Tomb*, made a great impression on him and he frequently referred to it. His confirmation, signifying that he had entered into full membership of the Church of England and could now take Holy Communion, meant a good deal to him.[1]

In her Christmas broadcasts, Queen Elizabeth II made many references to her faith and her personal relationship with Jesus Christ. She also spoke of her father's faith and influence on her life. George VI was, to a large extent, unprepared to wear the Crown and be head of state for the United Kingdom and her Empire. He was, after all, the second son and Edward had received the training for such a high position. Prince Albert would have had some training because of the possibility of his elder brother dying before him without a legitimate heir. But the focus was very much on Edward.

King Edward VIII abdicated the throne on 11th December 1936. There had been growing concern within the Government and in the dominions concerning the King's determination to marry Mrs Wallis Simpson. There had been suggestions by the King's supporters of a morganatic marriage in which Edward and Mrs Simpson marry, she not become Queen, instead receiving some courtesy title. There were some very influential political figures who supported this and were very much behind Edward. The Prime Minister, Stanley Baldwin was utterly opposed as were the Prime ministers of the Dominion nations.[2]

George VI was certainly less outgoing and dashing than his elder brother who had undoubtedly won the hearts of the vast majority of the British public. There were serious doubts among some of his subjects, including those close to the throne and the British monarchy. King George had suffered a number of illnesses whilst young and was considered by many to be in delicate health. His stammer was a concern to many and although he had on-going sessions with Lionel Logue over a number of years, public speaking was always something of a trial for him. However, the new King had one great advantage, both he and his wife, Queen Elizabeth, were convinced that they had come to the throne in the will and purpose of God.

> The Coronation is the single most significant ceremony of a sovereign's life, transforming him or her from an ordinary mortal to a powerful symbol, half-man, half-priest, in a solemn ritual whose history goes back over a thousand years and whose significance is far older. No man or woman could fail to be affected by it; for George VI in particular, whose interest in ritual and sense of history was very strong, it was to have an extraordinarily strengthening, confidence-giving effect. For both him and the Queen the religious significance

of the ceremony in which they were to dedicate themselves before God to the service of their people was very strong.[3]

Cosmo Lang, the Archbishop of Canterbury held a private meeting with the King and Queen at Buckingham Palace on the evening of the Sunday before Coronation Day, at which the three of them knelt in prayer:

> I prayed for them and for their realm and Empire, and I gave them my personal blessing. I was much moved and so were they. Indeed there were tears in their eyes when we rose from our knees. From that moment I knew what would be in their minds and hearts when they came to their anointing and crowning.[4]

The Death of the King

Throughout the reign of King George VI, prayer and the reading of Scripture was a daily practice within the Royal family. The following testimonies that appeared on the front page of the Pattern Magazine in February 1942, bear witness to the strong Christian faith of both the King and Queen:

> **A ROYAL MESSAGE:** The King having heard of the illness of Mr G. Goodman, who for several years edited the Scripture Union Notes, sent him a message of sympathy, in which he said that his wife and daughters read his notes from the Scripture Portions daily, and found great help from doing so.
>
> *ROYAL TESTIMONIES:* On June 9th, 1939, Chief Whitefeather was summoned by the Indian Bureau to sing for the King and Queen of England, who were at that time in Washington D.C. He sang 'Rule Britannia' and 'God Save the King' and 'I'd rather have Jesus than Silver and Gold.' Then he said, knowing that Queen Elizabeth was a religious woman, 'Your Majesty, I would like to ask you, do you know Jesus as your personal Saviour? She looked on him and said, 'Some people know about God, some know about Christ, but the Lord Jesus is the Possessor of my heart. My husband is

also a believer.' Then with a smile on his face, the King of England said, 'I'd rather have Jesus too.'[5]

The reign of George VI was a happy and successful one. He had endeared himself to the hearts of the British people and his subjects in the Empire[6], in his leadership of the nation and Empire during the terrible struggles of the Second World War. His unexpected death, therefore, at the young age of 56 was a great blow to the country. George VI died on the 6th February 1952 at his Sandringham Estate. His daughter, the Princess Elizabeth was in Kenya at the time of her father's death and the news of his passing was given to her in private by her husband, HRH Prince Philip, Duke of Edinburgh. She returned home immediately and was met at the airport by the Prime Minister, Sir Winston Churchill. She was officially crowned Queen Elizabeth II on 2nd June 1953 at Westminster Abbey.

Elim acknowledged the great services of the king to his subjects in a special editorial in the Evangel. Under the title of **The Passing of the King**, the tribute paid on behalf of the Movement is printed in full:

> The announcement by the BBC on Wednesday, 6th February, that His Majesty King George VI had passed peacefully away in his sleep at Sandringham, came as a profound shock to the nation. It had been obvious from recent photos the King felt severely the strain of the operation performed a short time ago, but no one seems to have anticipated this dramatic turn of events. The sympathies and prayers of all our members and readers are offered at this hour of bereavement, that Her Majesty the Queen, the Queen Mother, and members of the Royal Household will be sustained and blessed.
>
> King George VI has reigned through critical periods in our history, having taken the throne following the abdication crisis. His integrity has been an example to the people, and he has maintained always the high traditions which

have made the British Throne a bulwark of strength amid failing empires.

The last war was a severe trial, and the King shared the sufferings of his people in that his own home was bombed in the London raids. It was this fellowship among his people that caused him to be so dearly loved. Thus he fulfilled the promise made in the radio speech on May 12th, 1937, the day of the coronation: 'I will only say this; If, in the coming years I can show my gratitude in service to you, that is the way above all others that I should choose… We will, God helping us, faithfully discharge our trust.'

Royal interest in the religious life of the country was always deeply appreciated, and we remember the message sent to the World's Evangelical Alliance Exhibition, part of which read: 'I can truly say that the King and I long to see the Bible back where it ought to be, as a guide and comfort in the homes and lives of our people. From our own experience, we know what the Bible can mean for personal life.'

The following telegram has been sent on behalf of the Elim Churches:

HER MAJESTY THE QUEEN,
BUCKINGHAM PALACE.

MINISTERS AND MEMBERS OF THE ELIM CHURCHES THROUGHOUT BRITAIN AND THE WORLD EXPRESS LOVING SYMPATHY IN THIS HOUR OF BEREAVEMENT TO YOUR MAJESTY AND THE MEMBERS OF THE ROYAL FAMILY.

E C W BOULTON,
PRESIDENT

May God bless and give wisdom to our new Queen in the great task which lies before her.[7]

Boulton, Elim's President, wrote a moving article in honour of the late King.[8] He made some very moving and beautiful references in his article. He used expressions such as 'A great and much beloved monarch has been suddenly and unexpectedly taken from us.' 'A nation has been plunged into mourning over the loss of one who has won their love and esteem.' 'His throne was in the hearts of his people.' 'He was Sovereign by right of a nation's love as well as by the Constitution of the land over which he ruled.' Boulton was clear in his opinion that the strength of George's reign was spiritual as well as temporal. He referred to the fact that 'The reign of King George VI covered a dark and tragic period in the life of this nation, a time of terrible world upheaval and ordeal, when Britain passed through her baptism of blood and tears, and agony which our Beloved Sovereign shared with His people.'[9]

Although he was clearly in awe of the magisterial splendour of the late King and an avowed Royalist, Boulton did acknowledge the 'intensely human' side of the king. He was described by Boulton as 'A lover of the countryside, and often found enjoying the open-air life.' I note, however, that he failed to mention that a vital part of his open-air activities included hunting.

Boulton was clearly convinced of the King's strong faith and his love of God's Word:

King George VI will be remembered as a ruler inspired by the highest Christian ideals, one who honoured God, and loved His Word, and in whose heart lived a deep and vital interest in spiritual and eternal realities. To the cause of the Christian Church, he gave his support, and sought by his example and influence to live by its principles and further its aims. In his personal life, and his own family life there were the unmistakable marks of true godliness...What stirring memories we have of those great and beautiful words which he quoted (in one of his Christmas broadcasts) 'I said to the man who stood at the gate of the year: "Give me a light that I may tread safely into the unknown." And he replied: "Go out into the darkness and put your hand into the hand of God. That shall be to you better then light, and safer than a known way." So I went forth, and finding the hand of God trod gladly into the night, and He led me towards the hills and the breaking of the day in the lone East.'[10]

A New Age

The late Queen came to the throne at a bleak time in the history of our country. Britain had emerged from the ravages of the Second World War very badly bruised. Yes, Britain, against all odds, triumphed but her economy was ruined. With the granting of Indian independence in 1947, Britain lost her Empire. The Suez Crisis was to further undermine Britain's position as the third leading power in the world.

In spite of this, however, the Coronation of Her Majesty, Queen Elizabeth II in June 1953, brought hopes of a national renewal. The impact that the coronation had upon the nation was huge. Although televisions were the exception rather than the rule in British homes, there were enough of them for millions of people to cram into hundreds of thousands of parlours throughout the land to witness the crowning of Her Majesty. Children throughout the land were given commemoration mugs, plates, New Testaments and Bibles. Street parties were held or villagers came together in school canteens to provide a sumptuous feast for all.

Elim was determined to latch on to the renewal of hope. As has been noted in earlier chapters, Elim's history was a microcosm of the nation's history. She too, like the nation, had lost a leader of charism, charm and eloquence. Elim had also, with the nation had gone through six years of horrendous warfare. Just as the nation, Elim had to encourage and lead its shattered membership and rebuild those edifices that had been destroyed by enemy action. Here, the corollary breaks down, however. Because whilst in the Constitutional Government of the United Kingdom of Great Britain and Northern Ireland, there is a line of succession that brings with it its own sense of continuity and stability, the same was not the case with the Elim family.

There was undoubtedly a renewed enthusiasm within Elim that coincided with the beginning of the Age of the Second Queen Elizabeth. Eight new churches were accepted into Elim by the 1952 Conference and a further five in 1953. Evangelistic campaigns were being encouraged in local churches and there was a new enthusiasm within the churches. The emphasis was on salvation and divine healing.

In the same edition of the Evangel in which Boulton wrote the article on the King's death, there is an account of the conclusion of the Mansfield campaign conducted by Ken Matthew. The report claims that there were over 400 decisions for Christ and 150 membership cards taken. On the last Sunday of the campaign: 'Pastor Ken Matthew gave the right hand of fellowship to 100 of these people.'[11] A similar number of people attended the morning communion service the previous Sunday. There were a number of cases of healing that were testified to during the campaign: 'A brother given up by doctors, healed of cancer; sister healed of involuntary jerkings: three deaf people had their hearing restored: a paralysis victim unable to walk was healed: a boy with a terrible stammer instantly delivered.'[12] The many reports of the Mansfield campaign clearly shows that there was an immediate increase in the congregation of a church that had declined numerically over the years of its existence. A considerable number of people were added to the church as the above report shows. The tragedy is that these numbers declined over the years and the church was closed some ten years ago. Sadly, there were a number of churches that were born from evangelistic campaigns that started very well but, over the years, the numbers declined and the churches closed. Tonypandy (Trealaw), Bolton, Burnley, Truro, Bodmin, Kirkintilloch, Treharris, Abercynon, Lydney, South Shields were some of the churches that were commenced through very successful evangelistic campaigns but, over the years declined and were finally closed. This, in no way detracts from the success of the original pioneer crusade and neither is it a comment on the pastoral quality of the majority of ministers who were appointed to these churches, although, in a few cases this was a factor.[13]

It is clear from historical records that the flame of pioneer evangelism was re-ignited within the Elim Movement during the decade of the fifties in the twentieth century. This continued into the nineteen sixties; the decade that was to be the most successful one in Elim's history as far as growth in the number of churches is concerned. Those ministers who had a clear evangelistic edge to their ministry were encouraged to launch out into campaigns. Despite the lack of sufficient money, many new churches were established and not only survived, but thrived.

Notes

[1] Bradford, Sarah, *George VI, the Dutiful King*, (London: Penguin Books, 1989) Kindle, Loc 1358

[2] These were: Canada, Australia, New Zealand and South Africa.

[3] Bradford, Sarah, ibid, Loc 5226

[4] Bradford, Sarah, ibid, Loc 5228

[5] Extracts from 'Living Links', *The Pattern, Vol 3, No3, February 1942*, Front Page Lead.

[6] The British Empire as such existed until Indian independence was granted in 1947, thereafter the Empire morphed into the British Commonwealth. Today, it is referred to as the 'Commonwealth of Nations'.

[7] The Passing of the King, *Elim Evangel*, 18th Feb. 1952, Vol 33, No 7, p98

[8] Boulton, E C W, *A Manly King – A Kingly Man, Elim Evangel*, 23rd Feb. 1952, Vol 33, No 8, pp115-117

[9] Boulton, E C W, *A Manly King – A Kingly Man*, ibid.

[10] Boulton, E C W, *A Manly King – A Kingly Man*, ibid. The Quotation is from a poem written by Minnie Louise Haskins: 'God Knows'. The popular name for the poem is: 'I stand at the Gate of the Year.'

[11] 'Mansfield Campaign Concludes' *Elim Evangel*, 25th Feb. 1952, Vol 33, No 8, pp118,119.

[12] 'Mansfield Campaign Concludes' ibid.

[13] An Elim Church has been re-established in Bodmin through the vision and ministry of John Berryman who has also established an Elim Church in Launceston. There was an Elim Church in this Cornish Town that was closed in 1940.

23
New Zealand

The Elim Pentecostal Church has had a presence in New Zealand officially since 1939. This followed a visit to New Zealand by James McWhirter and his wife in 1938. On 18th December of that year, McWhirter met with the leaders of the first Pentecostal Movement in New Zealand – the Pentecostal Church of New Zealand.[1] The PCNZ was a small Movement but it was the oldest Pentecostal Movement in New Zealand and it had grown out of the Smith Wigglesworth revival in 1922. In her very impressive doctorate, Linda Flett sets out the establishment and growth of Elim New Zealand in a couple of paragraphs:

> In Scripture, Elim is the name of an oasis, a place of refreshing for those who enter its sphere. The denomination known as Elim sought to emulate this reality. As a branch of classical Pentecostalism, it was (and continues to be) committed to championing personal spiritual renewal through baptism in the Holy Spirit and motivated to move beyond its borders by the urgent task of mission.[2]
>
> Elim's growth is significant in that it spans the nearly 100 years of 'Classical Pentecostal History', is rooted in revival, yet suffered many setbacks. By today's standards, it should have closed on many occasions. Nevertheless, Elim repeatedly rose from the ashes of major setbacks, re-focussed their energies on mission and embraced the task of re-expansion with an extraordinary tenacity that is only possible when a Movement believes it is called for a purpose and has a message worth proclaiming. In its own time and season, that determination

bore fruit. Whereas major Pentecostal denominations such as the Assemblies of God and New Life expanded exponentially in the 1960's, Elim's term awaited the 1980's following the peak of the Charismatic Renewal and after growth in other Pentecostal streams had begun to slow.[3]

It was at this time that the Elim Pentecostal Church in the UK reconnected in a very meaningful way with our New Zealand churches. But there was a distinct difference. The UK Elim had always been looked upon as the 'mother church'. We were the ones that sent out Gilbert Dunk and his family to New Zealand in 1952 and for a while supported him financially in New Zealand. It is the personal opinion of the author that we could have, and should have done much more to have helped in the growth and development of the oldest Pentecostal denomination in the 'land of the long white cloud'. Since the time of Gilbert Dunk, Elim New Zealand has consistently valued its connection with Elim UK.

It was in 1953 that three congregations in Auckland, Wellington and Blenheim, changed their name to Elim. This was the fruition of the PCNZ's application in 1939 to link up with the Elim Foursquare Gospel Alliance. This was to prove to be a very successful union. A sceptical view of the three New Zealand churches uniting with Elim was that the PCNZ had declined to a very small number of churches. The arrival of Gilbert Dunk, a seasoned Elim veteran, undoubtedly contributed to the stability and growth of the Elim churches in New Zealand. We must not, however, view this union as being one-sided. The contribution of New Zealand Elim leaders has had a substantial impact on the Elim Movement in the UK.

Although Elim had accepted the invitation to link with PCNZ in 1939, it was not until 1949 that positive action was taken to progress in establishing Elim in New Zealand. It is important to understand that Elim built on an already established work in New Zealand. Flett has clearly established in her PhD thesis that Elim was invited to link with an existing historic Pentecostal work in New Zealand, and although the work was small, it had a clear

238

Pentecostal foundation that those sent from the home country could build upon. The PCNZ asked EFGA if they would recommend pastors for the assemblies at Auckland and Wellington. The Elim Executive Council agreed to do so and in the ministerial circular of 21 March 1950, details of the link between the two Movements were given and a request made for two ministers and their families to consider moving to New Zealand to 'strengthen the work in New Zealand'.[4]

The response from Elim pastors was very positive. A total of 18 ministers expressed an interest in moving to New Zealand, although some of these were on a short-term basis. Those expressing an interest included Gerald Ladlow, Leslie Reeves and R Knox. Even the Field Superintendent of the day, W G Hathaway, offered his services for a year to help with organisational matters.

G W Gilpin

This section deals only with Gilpin's application to link up with PCNZ and commence an Elim work in New Zealand. Having received 11 applications (the others came when a second appeal for workers to New Zealand was made), the Executive Council accepted the application of George Wesley Gilpin and his wife Marguerite to go to New Zealand. 'Gilpin expressed interest in the work in Wellington and in the possibility for starting a Bible school given that he was currently working toward the completion of a BD degree.'[5] Gilpin was an experienced pastor who had spent his entire ministry up to this point in Northern Ireland, which like New Zealand, was more of a rural community. He had pastored Elim's largest church in Northern Ireland – The Ulster Temple in Belfast.[6] At the time of his application, he was pastor of the Elim Church in Bangor, a large town on the coast of Co. Down. He was also a member of the Irish Executive Council and a member of the Missionary Board.[7] Being the experienced leader that he was, Gilpin was soon asking strategic questions regarding the relationship between the assembly at Wellington and the PCNZ. He also queried the ecclesiastical position of PCNZ.[8]

Wesley Gilpin was a man who was very perceptive in his judgements. He was quick to assess weaknesses whilst being very generous in his overall assessments of people and organisations. More will be said of this in a later chapter. Suffice to note that Gilpin was not one who would make huge decisions such as moving to the other side of the world without making his own enquiries. Flett outlines the cautious steps taken by PCNZ before fully committing themselves to a link-up with Elim.[9] The 1950 circular sent out to Elim ministers inviting them to apply to go to New Zealand had stated that there were four assemblies operating under the PCNZ banner. In January 1951, Gilpin wrote to E J Phillips[10], expressing his doubts about the state of the work of PCNZ, claiming that of the five churches originally referred to, only two were still in existence. In what can only be interpreted as providence as far as EFGA is concerned, Gilpin withdrew his acceptance of the position in New Zealand. Seven years later, he was appointed Principal of the Elim Bible College.

Philip Dunk, in his biography of his father, gives a different reason for turning down the invitation to go to New Zealand. The arrangements were at an advanced stage for the positioning of Gilpin who was set to leave for New Zealand in August 1951. Dunk states that the reason for Gilpin's withdrawal was that of family considerations. 'His elderly, widowed mother's health had taken a serious turn for the worse and, as the only son able to provide assistance and accommodation, he did not believe it honourable to leave her alone in England in that condition.[11] He felt it incumbent upon him to stay behind to enable him and his wife to take on his mother's care.'[12]

The Executive Council then invited Gilbert Dunk, the pastor of Eldad Elim Church, Guernsey. Dunk's heroic leadership of the three Elim churches in Guernsey during the Second World War had been greatly admired throughout the Elim Movement. His outstanding leadership and quiet determination, coupled with what can only be described as obdurate perseverance, made him an ideal candidate for the task of establishing Elim in New Zealand. Also in his favour was the fact that he had been instrumental in pioneering an Elim Church on the largest of the Channel Islands, Jersey in 1948. Gilbert Dunk was the epitome of a fine, upstanding Englishman. He was more often seen in a suit and tie, regardless of the weather. What is more important, however, is that he was a family man. He married Irene in 1937 and they had two boys, Michael and Philip. Irene was very much involved in her husband's work, especially during the very difficult years of occupation. Together, they cared for three Elim congregations on the Island of Guernsey. In so doing, they earned the huge respect and love of the people on that beautiful island. It is not an overstatement to say that the whole Elim Movement was somewhat in awe of their hugely sacrificial work in Guernsey.

It is interesting to note that all three ministers of our churches in Guernsey responded to the invitation extended by the Executive Council to go to New Zealand. The pastor at Vazon, the oldest of the three Elim churches on the island was Gerald Ladlow. The pastor at Delancey was Les Reeves. Both of them were married men. But, after Gilpin withdrew, the Executive Council turned to Dunk. 'Adopting "plan B", the Executive immediately contacted the second of their list of prospective pioneers, asking Dunk to pray about accepting the challenge. Dunk agreed to seek God's guidance in the matter. A letter of recommendation from Sam Gorman (Field Supt) read, in part:

> We are sorry to inform you that Pastor Gilpin has now decided that he cannot undertake the ministry in New Zealand. (We) have, therefore, got in touch with one of our Senior Ministers, Pastor Gilbert Dunk, who has been our District Superintendent in the Channel Islands for about fourteen years, this including the period of the German occupation.
> He is a splendid man in every way and, if he finally decides to undertake this ministry, (we are) sure he will be blessed of God to you. He is married and has two children. He has

practically, but not finally agreed to go to New Zealand –
he is waiting on definite confirmation from the Lord about
the matter.[13]

The financial situation relative to the Wellington assembly had
changed considerably due to a substantial legacy left to the church
by three sisters who had died within four months of each other.
This included a sum of £5000 plus three two-storey properties in
the heart of the city.[14] Flett makes the following statement: 'After
a short period of discernment, the Dunks accepted the invitation to
New Zealand and sailed from Guernsey in March, 1952.[15] From
Philip Dunk's account, it would seem that his parents took two
months praying about the situation.

> Throughout this month and into November Gilbert and
> Irene spent much time in prayer regarding this life-changing
> call which would surely turn their own world upside down,
> literally and metaphorically, as they considered the move
> 'down-under'. The pull of family, friends and their beloved
> Eldad congregation made it a difficult enough choice but
> when added to the fact that their boys would likely grow up
> on the far side of the globe without extended family, the load
> seemed immense...But God is gracious and soon Gilbert
> and Irene's hearts knew a serene peace and some excitement
> towards the adventure in faith. By early December, the 'die
> was cast' and Gilbert sent word to headquarters who cabled
> the news on to New Zealand. The Dunk Family's answer
> was 'YES!'[16]

On arrival in New Zealand, they were warmly welcomed by PCNZ
leaders who looked forward to a new era, bolstered by the belief
that "from this time on the church would prosper in the hands of
the Lord".[17] This signalled the commencement of the affiliation
of PCNZ with the Elim Movement. The New Zealand churches
became part of Elim Church Incorporated. The following report
appeared in the Elim Evangel under the heading 'Family Affairs':
'A letter from Pastor G Dunk tells of a wonderful reception in New

Zealand. Representatives of the various Pentecostal bodies met the Dunk family at the quayside and gave them a wonderful welcome. Mr Dunk feels that he has a good opportunity to establish a splendid work, and looks to us in prayer on his behalf, that God will give enablement and guidance.'[18]

On Sunday, 9th March 1952, Gilbert Dunk preached at his home church in Brighton. His parents and many who knew him from his earlier years in the Essex and Sussex areas went to hear him. It must have been a poignant occasion as far as Gilbert and Irene were concerned. Ahead of them was the exciting challenge of forging a new Elim work in New Zealand, but they were leaving aged parents and close family. Of equal sadness to them and the boys was the fact that they had left their 'church family' on the island of Guernsey. They had forged life-long friendships with church members that had been tried and strengthened during the long years of occupation.

Dunk's first challenge of establishing Elim, drawing up a constitution and reorganizing PCNZ into the Elim Church of New Zealand was considerably easier than that of expansion by opening new churches. This was evident in an article that he wrote for the Evangel:

Three years have passed since we left England for this distant land of New Zealand, though it seems little more than months. During those years we have been very much aware of the good hand of our God in all His dealings with us. We are very comfortably settled in New Zealand's capital city, with a fine body of saints in our Church – New Zealand's first Elim Church – who stand by us with a steadfastness which leaves little to be desired by a pastor. The work was very small when we arrived and though not large now, it has shown steady growth in numbers and strength. After settling down to our new surroundings and conditions, we had to tackle many things associated with the change-over from what was the Pentecostal Church of New Zealand to the Elim Church of New Zealand. A new Constitution had to be drawn up, transfers of property had to be effected and many incidental matters called for attention. Now all these have been straightened out and we are ready to go ahead as the Elim Church of New Zealand, Incorporated.[19]

Dunk goes on to set out his plans for the erection of a new church building in Wellington with an office attached which would serve as a headquarters. This might have appeared as a somewhat grandiose title for what was at the time consisting of only two or three churches. What comes across in his article, however, was Dunk's vision and determination to establish an Elim Movement in New Zealand and also to provide training facilities whereby Elim New Zealand could provide from its own ranks pastors that would lead newly established Elim churches right across the islands.

Notes

[1] Flett, Linda Mary, *A Search for Resonance: A History of the Elim Churches in New Zealand 1922-2000*: PhD Dissertation, Otago University 1921.

[2] Ever since the early eighties when the Elim New Zealand Movement began a period of unparalleled growth, it has had a profound impact upon its parent body in the UK. The author would go so far as to say that within the last 40 years, the growth of Elim in New Zealand has surpassed that of its sister denomination in the UK.

[3] Flett, Linda Mary, ibid, p1

[4] Flett, Linda Mary, ibid, p108.

[5] Flett, Linda Mary, ibid, p109

[6] The author was the pastor of this fine Elim Church from 1986-1988.

[7] From 1940 through until 2000, much of the Elim Movement's work was carried out by Conference Committees. These consisted of one or two ex-officio appointees, 2 or more Executive Council appointees and two or more Conference appointees. Gilpin was one of the ex-officio appointees to the Missions Board by virtue of the fact that he was the Secretary of the Northern Ireland International Missions Committee. The International Missions Board was one of the most powerful of Elim's Conference Committees.

[8] Flett, Linda Mary, ibid, p110.

[9] Flett, Linda Mary, ibid, p110.

[10] Flett refers to E J P as Elim's 'the incoming EFGA Superintendent'. The actuality is that Phillips had been Elim's Secretary-General since 1935.

[11] There is an obvious mistake here. At the time, Pastor Gilpin was leading the Elim Church in Bangor, Northern Ireland. It was to be another seven years before he moved to England when he was appointed Principal of Elim Bible College.

[12] Dunk, Philip, *Occupation Pastor: The Early life and times of Gilbert T S Dunk:* Copyright, Philip M Dunk, 2012, P190

[13] Letter from S Gorman to Harry V Roberts, General Supt on PCNZ, quoted by Philip Dunk in *Occupation Pastor:* ibid, p191.

[14] Dunk, Philip, ibid, p192.

[15] They did not sail direct to New Zealand but visited family and friends in England first. They also made a visit to Elim Headquarters in Clapham.

[16] Dunk, Philip, ibid p192.

[17] PCNZ "Exec. Min. Bk", 2nd May, 1952, quoted from Linda Flett, ibid, footnote 254, p112.

[18] Family Affairs: *Elim Evangel*: 15th Sept 1952: Vol 33, No 37, p580.

[19] Elim in New Zealand, *Elim Evangel*: 13th August, 1955, Vol 36m No 31, pp362,363

24

Prominent Personalities in the Fifties and Sixties

We have already noted that evangelism was a major thrust within Elim in the early fifties. Coupled with this evangelistic thrust was the erection of new buildings. In 1953, there were 23 new buildings erected. Most of these were as a result of the settlement of Government grants to replace buildings that had been destroyed or very badly damaged during the war. A committee was appointed by the Executive Council to negotiate with the appropriate Government Department regarding adequate reparation for church buildings and manses that had been destroyed or badly damaged by enemy bombing. The committee had two lay representatives appointed to it; they were Don House, an Estate Agent in Bournemouth and lay representative for the Winton Elim Church, also appointed was Mr Arthur Selleck, the lay representative for the Plymouth Elim Church.

The Executive Council had changed very little in the first seven years after the war. The only changes had been in the early forties when H W Greenway was elected following the forced resignation of P N Corry in 1941. Following the resignation of F Cloke in 1944, J J Morgan took his place on the Executive Council. There were two changes to the Executive Council in the early fifties.

Charles Kingston

Charles Kingston, who had been a member of the Council since 1937 resigned his membership of the Council in 1951. This was due in no small measure to the death of his father. Some of his father's business responsibilities fell on the shoulders of Charles and so he gave up his position on the Council. He continued in the Elim ministry and was the pastor of the Croydon church for many years. He served as Elim President in 1964-1965. He was the Conference Chairman from 1940-1946. His work in this capacity must not be under-estimated. He had to guide the Conference in the years immediately following the schism with George Jeffreys and the Bible Pattern. Those Conferences in the early forties were taken up with rules and regulations needed to secure the Movement. Added to these internal matters were the huge difficulties caused by the war. The Movement had a steady hand in control of the day-to-day administration of the Movement in the form of the redoubtable E J Phillips. Phillips, however, realised that he needed to be free of the Chairman's duties so that he could take part in the many Conference debates that were made necessary due to the difficulties caused by the schism and the war.

Kingston proved to be an excellent Chairman. His business acumen was such that he was able to guide the Conference in its many debates. Kingston was not afraid to express his views on the subject of mass evangelism. He expressed doubts about the methods used in campaigns in which people were asked to raise their hands in acknowledgement of their intention to follow Christ. In an Elim Evangel article he starts by making what some saw as a very poor illustration: 'When they were trying to instil a few words of French into my obstinate English pate the French master used to discourage the raising of our hands by a phrase, rapped out in French, "put down your paws!"' For some Elim evangelists, such an introduction to an article with the title 'False and True forces in effective evangelism' would have been considered offensive. The next statement in the article would have annoyed them even further: 'There seems to me to be something strangely reminiscent of school-days and schoolroom psychology in the oft-repeated request by preachers to their unconverted hearers to raise their hands if they wish to accept Christ.' Kingston was not afraid to make statements that were guaranteed to cause controversy or even contention. He expressed a genuine concern that hands raised in response to a Gospel appeal were often reported as conversions. His alternative suggestion, however, seems to me to cause as many problems as that of hand-raising:

> Lest it should be thought that this criticism of hand-raising in evangelistic appeals leaves no possible means of bringing a congregation to a point of decision, it is suggested that at the end of the address there be given a brief explanation of the way of salvation, and during a time of silent prayer the unconverted be invited to accept Christ by a conscious act of the will and in silent prayer to God. After such an appeal an opportunity should always be given for personal conversation with any who have accepted Christ in the meeting or with any others who have honest difficulties. Such conversations may be secured by offering helpful and attractive literature suited to beginners in the Christian life.[1]

His article brought a swift, stirring and lengthy reply from P S Brewster, Elim's leading evangelist. He suggested that Mr Kingston's article was unfortunate. Kingston's article and Brewster's reply show the depth of thought and maturity in the Movement. Brewster did not give an inch of ground in his stirring response. He makes his position very clear in his opening paragraph:

> I think Mr Kingston's article is unfortunate. It is not my nature to enter into controversy, but I feel that the illustration which opens the article, and which associates the raising of hands for conversion, the greatest act in the world with such a term as 'Put down your paws' is unfortunate. Then he states he does not like to hear the preacher keep asking the unconverted to raise their hands for salvation. The commission given to the Church is to preach the Gospel, heal the sick, teach and baptise. How can this be done if men and women are not brought to a decision? No balanced evangelist claims that those who raise their hands are converted, but rather that it is the first decision towards a move to God. I heartily commend

that more and more we urge men and women to make a decision back to God.[2]

Both these men were members of the Evangelistic Committee. Kingston had been the Conference Chairman for six successive years and a member of the Executive Council until his personal withdrawal the previous year. One can imagine that there would have been quite a debate on the subject at the next Evangelistic Committee meeting!

Although a member of the Evangelistic Committee, Kingston was more of a teacher than he was an evangelist. He was a lecturer at the Elim Bible College for over thirty years. He was renowned for his sane, classical Pentecostal view on the Gifts of the Holy Spirit. His book 'Fulness of Power', was first published in 1939 and was reprinted several times. This book is a true Pentecostal classic in which Kingston produces clear historical proof of the use of the Gifts of the Spirit throughout the ages. To my knowledge, there has been no book written on the Gifts of the Spirit by Elim writers since this one by Charles Kingston. In 'Fulness of Power', Kingston gives a Biblical exposition of all nine Gifts of the Holy Spirit as delineated in 1 Corinthians 12 and 14. He does, however, spend far more time on two of the Gifts than he does on the others. He devotes six chapters to the Gift of prophecy and seven on the Gift of tongues.

The initial evidence of the Baptism in the Holy Spirit has been argued over by Pentecostals since the beginning of the modern Pentecostal Movement in 1906. Most Pentecostal denominations, especially those in the USA express the view that speaking in other tongues as inspired by the Holy Spirit is the first or initial evidence of the baptism in the Holy Spirit. This is the stance taken by the Assemblies of God in the United Kingdom. It was also the prevailing view within Elim until the nineteen seventies.[3] Elim's earliest constitutions stated that the baptism in the Holy Spirit was evidenced in the first place by speaking in tongues.[4] Whilst taking a generally classic Pentecostal approach to tongues being the initial evidence of Spirit baptism, Kingston admits to the possibility of some other evidence such as prophesying.[5] He comments thus: 'Does this instance show us that, while the speaking in tongues is in the pattern of Pentecost, God is still sovereign, in His dealings with man, and refuses even His own pattern to bind Him?'[6]

Charles Kingston's legacy to Elim lies in his careful and yet firm chairmanship of the Conferences from 1940-1946. His fourteen years of service on the Executive Council covered a period of great uncertainty for Elim. Added to his spiritual leadership, he had a keen business knowledge which was a benefit to the Executive Council in their deliberations on expenditure and building works.

John Dyke

John Dyke was a Welshman who was brought up in the Assemblies of God in the Monmouthshire valleys. As such, he would have come into contact with the three leading Assemblies in that region, Risca, Cross Keys and Newbridge. A leading figure amongst the AOG in that region was Tom Mercy. South-East Wales was an AOG stronghold. The first and most prominent assembly was that in Crosskeys that was founded by Sidney Mercy and whose son, Tom took over the leadership of the assembly from his father. Through the influence of the Crosskeys assembly, a number of other Pentecostal centres were pioneered in the region. A significant emphasis was placed on divine healing at the Crosskeys assembly.[7] Mercy states that the Pentecostal centre which grew in Llantwit, Rhydfelin, Pontyclun, Peterstone, Machen, Bedwas, Aberbargoed, Thomastown, Caerphilly and Newport came into being as a direct result of healing miracles.'[8] Crosskeys was one of the original assemblies that became part of the Assemblies of God in Great Britain and Northern Ireland which was established in 1924. Tom Hicks from the Crosskeys assembly was one of the seven members of the first Executive Council of that denomination. The Crosskeys assembly had a great influence on other developing Pentecostal centres in Monmouthshire, particularly Risca, Newbridge and

Pontllanffraith – all of them mining communities. It is quite remarkable to note that Tom Mercy, the first official pastor of the Crosskeys assembly remained a working miner all his life and was the union representative for his local coal-mine. This example was taken by other Assemblies of God fellowships throughout South Wales, the other notable example being that of Eli Sibley, the founding pastor of the Tonyrefail assembly.

It was against this background that the early ministry of John Dyke was forged. The circumstances of his joining Elim are unclear, but one thing is evident, his theological background, especially his views on the baptism in the Holy Spirit, was greatly influenced by his up-bringing in the Pentecostal fellowships of South-East Wales. It would appear that his views on the initial evidence of the baptism in the Holy Spirit had altered slightly from the AOG view that speaking in other tongues is the initial evidence of the baptism in the Holy Spirit. In an article titled 'The Baptism in the Holy Spirit', Dyke explains his views concerning the evidence of Spirit baptism:

> The actual reception of the Spirit[9] will be accompanied by miraculous 'signs following.' This is confirmed by the five records in the Acts, of believers receiving the Baptism. While our Fundamental does not attempt to define these, it is the writer's personal experience, an opinion confirmed by almost thirty years of seeing people baptised in the Holy Ghost, that the sign of the Spirit's incoming is the supernatural speaking with tongues, accompanied sometimes with prophecy.[10]

In the same article, Dyke shares what he considers as the many and varied results of the coming of the Spirit. The first is boldness and power to witness for Christ.[11] The second result that he gives is that the experience leads to a deeper and fuller intimacy with God, through faith in Jesus Christ. Thirdly, Dyke suggests that the baptism in the Holy Spirit introduces the Christian to an extraordinary and supernatural life.[12] Dyke seems to go into a blessed digression at this point when he writes:

251

Happy is he if he can join himself to a company of people with a like experience. He will discover heights and depths of congregational worship undreamed of hitherto: seasons when the services are swept by the Spirit of God, as a master sweeps the harp springs: rare times, blessed with the exquisite and haunting cadences of the singing in the Spirit.[13] The writer thinks of one great visitation along this line. The whole assembly was gripped by the Holy Spirit and all hearts were filled with adoration and praise. Spontaneously the heavenly anthem began and soon the entire company was singing in the Spirit. The singing rose and fell like the waves of the sea, now sinking to the softest whisper and then rising in thunderous crescendo, striking lost chords again and again and filling hearts with exquisite ecstasy. The unsaved thronged the street without and when eventually the anthem subsided, rushed to the church door to enquire where they could obtain the music of that wonderful song![14]

The final result that Dyke gives of the baptism in the Holy Spirit is quite an unusual view-point on this subject. He puts forward the suggestion that the baptism in the Spirit leads to the quickening of a believer's intellectual powers. 'Abiding under the anointing, he becomes "of quick understanding of the fear of the Lord" as he is led by the Spirit into all truth.'

John Dyke was very much a pastor-teacher-preacher. As is often the case with Welsh preachers, he was inspirational in his style of preaching. At the same time, however, he was a capable Pentecostal theologian as his writings clearly show. He was in great demand as a convention speaker and was highly regarded throughout the Movement. He was pastor of the East Ham church and the District Superintendent of the North London Presbytery. He was appointed pastor of Graham Street Elim Church (Now Birmingham City Church) which was the mother church of the Birmingham Elim churches in 1946. His predecessor was Samuel Gorman, a man who was greatly loved and esteemed throughout Elim. The Graham Street church had well over 600 in attendance at their Sunday evening services. Gorman was renowned for his teaching and devotional preaching. So, it was no easy task for Dyke to lead such a large congregation and follow such a renowned pastor as Samuel Gorman. The fact that he remained as the pastor until his untimely death in 1960 and that the church flourished during his ministry is clear evidence that he was the right man in the right place at the right time.

John Dyke was a caring and compassionate pastor. The writer was the pastor of the Selly Oak Elim church in Birmingham from 1991-2012. During the course of his ministry there, he was regaled with accounts of various people who had been blessed and helped by John Dyke when they were members of Graham Street. One lady spoke of the great kindness shown to her by John Dyke and his wife. She had become an outcast from her family due to her life-style. She received love and acceptance from this godly pastor and through his non-judgemental dealings with her, she recommitted her life to Christ and became a valued member of our church. Another couple spoke of Pastor Dyke's great kindness to them during a very harsh winter. He made sure that they had enough provisions and heat in the home.

Dyke was a formidable debater on the Conference floor. But it appears that E J Phillips was his nemesis. Time and again, despite his eloquent speeches, E J usually got the last word and won the argument. One year, having been defeated again in a debate where E J opposed him, Dyke in sheer exasperation pointed his finger at the Secretary-General and vowed, 'I'll get you yet, Mr Phillips'. He never did, because shortly after that he became President and joined the Executive Council and remained until his death.

John Dyke's preaching and teaching skills were very evident and he was in demand throughout the Movement to preach at rallies and conventions. His teaching ministry was comprehensive as he sought to teach the whole counsel of God. But there was one subject that was close to his heart and that was teaching on the personality and works of the Holy Spirit. He was inducted as President of Elim in September 1954 at the Movement's annual Conference in London. The title of his message to the Conference on the occasion of his induction was 'The Mechanics of the Holy Ghost.' Basing his remarks on the account of Peter's visit to the house of Cornelius he gave a truly Pentecostal message that was evidently anointed by the Holy Spirit. He emphasised the need for another outpouring of the Holy Spirit.[15]

Wherever he went in the course of his Presidential tour, John Dyke led hundreds of people into the baptism in the Holy Spirit. Joseph Smith, the Irish Superintendent wrote an account of John Dyke's Presidential visit to the six counties:

> It is with great pleasure that we report on one of the most successful and blessed tours ever carried out by any visiting speaker of our churches in Ireland. For although frost and snow ruled the atmosphere without for a great part of the time Mr Dyke was with us, yet the fire of God ruled within.
> Mr Dyke's teaching was sound, logical and Scriptural, and his words of counsel to those who were recently filled with the Holy Spirit were both timely and good.
> A number professed salvation during his visit, and the number of those who were filled with the Spirit was between sixty and seventy. Whilst we may have some idea of the number who were baptised with the Holy Ghost, yet we have no idea of the number who were refilled with the Spirit – but we know they were very many.[16]

Among those who received the baptism in the Holy Spirit during the Presidential visit of John Dyke to Belfast was a young man of fourteen years of age who is now a very well loved and respected retired minister, Pastor Norman Christie.

John Dyke was from a working-class background. He never tried to hide that fact but neither did he glory in it. The following account is anecdotal as I have not found an actual archival record, but this was told to me by a former member of the Executive Council who was present when this incident occurred. Apparently, Dyke was nominated by the Council to the position of Field Superintendent. According to what was told to me, Ken Matthew, one of Elim's leading evangelists, opposed Dyke's nomination to such a high position in the Movement. He considered Dyke to be unsuited for the role because 'he did not look the part'. Matthew criticised Dyke's lack of sartorial elegance and said that the position required someone who dressed to a certain standard, a standard Dyke did not attain. As can be imagined, such an attack devastated Dyke and he withdrew his name. There is no record of this in the Conference minutes. I would suggest that the situation occurred at the 1953 Conference. The following statement appeared in the minutes of the 1953 Conference: 'After prolonged discussion, the following appointments were made.' The person that was appointed to the office of Field Superintendent was H W Greenway. Up to that time, Greenway had been Editor of the Elim Evangel, a position that he was eminently suited for and one that he greatly enjoyed. It is fairly obvious to a student of Elim history with a knowledge of Conference procedures that the 'prolonged discussion' would have taken place due to a change in the Executive Council's original nominations. The writer would suggest that this would have been the time when Dyke's nomination to the position of Field Superintendent would have taken place. He had just been elected vice-president earlier in the Conference and had, by this time, been a member of the Executive Council for two years having filled the vacancy caused by the decision of Charles Kingston not to stand for re-election. Dyke was very popular among his fellow ministers and, obviously, his colleagues on the Executive Council thought him to be suitable for the position.

Dyke was deeply hurt by the comments of Matthew and withdrew his name from the list. Although greatly loved and admired throughout Elim, especially in his beloved city of Birmingham, Dyke was a humble and unpretentious man. He remained pastor of Graham Street Elim Church much to the joy of the large congregation there who loved and admired their pastor. One member of his congregation wrote: 'John Dyke was a man well beloved by his congregation. He was a real "man of God" in every sense of the word. His Bible teaching was inspirational and he conducted powerful prayer meetings (sometimes all night). He also had a real pastor's heart, visiting his congregation on a bike.'[17] He was also renowned for his open-air meetings that he held in Birmingham's Bull Ring every Monday lunch-time.

Dyke was nominated to the position of Principal of the Elim Bible College in 1957 (to be voted on at the 1958 Conference), but after returning home to Birmingham, he wrote to the Council withdrawing his name.[18] The reason he gave was that his wife did not wish to leave Birmingham to go to London. Could it be that the events of the 1953 Conference affected this decision?

Notes

[1] Kingston, Charles J E, *Elim Evangel: False and True Forces in Effective Evangelism*: 10th Dec 1951, Vol 32: No 50, pp 594-597

[2] Brewster, P S, *Elim Evangel: I Commend Evangelism*: 14th Jan 1952, Vol 33, No 2, pp 24-28.

[3] Four of Elim's General Superintendents believed that the baptism in the Holy Spirit was accompanied by the gift of tongues. Interestingly they followed each other in tenure of office. The four were: P S Brewster, W R Jones, T W Walker and E R Corsie.

[4] The first Elim Constitution was published in 1922 and tongues was stated to be the evidence of such a baptism. The Constitution was updated in 1925 and 1927. There was a change made in the 1927 Constitution when, at the bidding of George Jeffreys, speaking in other tongues as the first evidence of the baptism in the Holy Spirit was removed and the words 'with signs following' put in its place.

[5] Acts 19:6

[6] Kingston, Charles J E, *Fullness of Power, Talks on the gifts of the Holy Spirit*: (London: Elim Publishing House, 1965), p141.

[7] Palmer, Chris, *The Emergence of Pentecostalism in Wales: A historical, theological evaluation of the early development of the Assemblies of God denomination in South East Wales with special reference to Crosskeys and Newbridge*: (London: Apostolos Publishing Ltd, 2016), p184.

[8] Mercy, Paul, *Redemption Tidings*, Nov 1985, quoted by Palmer, Chris, ibid, p185.

[9] The word 'reception' here is somewhat misleading from a Pentecostal point of view. The classic Pentecostal position is that the Holy Spirit enters the life of the believer at conversion, but there is a subsequent baptism in the Holy Spirit which is granted the believer on the basis of faith and it is an enduement of power to witness and to evangelise. The context of the phrase within the article clearly shows that in using the word 'reception' here Dyke was referring to the baptism in the Holy Spirit.

[10] Dyke, John, *Elim Evangel*: 27th Oct 1952, Vol 33, No 43, pp680-682.

[11] Acts 15: 29-32.

[12] Mark 10:15-18; 1Cor 12:7-11

[13] 1 Cor 14:15; Eph. 5:19

[14] Dyke, John, ibid, p682

[15] Reed, Ronald, *Presidential Induction and Ordination of Ministers, Elim Evangel*: 18th Sept 1954, Vol 35, No 38, p449.

16 Smith, Joseph, *Elim Evangel*: 12th Feb 1955, Vol 36, No 7, p74

17 Vi Heslington, 6th Nov 2022.

18 Letter John Dyke to EJ Phillips: 14th July 1957, (Malvern: Elim Archives).

25
Elim Presidents

Following the resignation of George Jeffreys, it was decided not to appoint a permanent President. The office of President was made an annual appointment and authority was given to the Conference to elect the President. This became a means of honouring those pastors that had served the Movement faithfully down through the years. At first, those elected were members of the Executive Council. It was the 1945 Representative Session of Conference that made the decision to appoint a President who would remain in office for one year or, as in the case of E J Phillips, from one Annual Conference to the next.[1] As has already been referred to in this book, Ernest Charles William Boulton was the Movement's first President under the new rules. He was elected as vice-President again in 1951, taking office in 1952.

Boulton was succeeded as President by Samuel Gorman (1947-48). Hathaway was the next President (1948-49), followed by Joseph Smith (1949-50) and J T Bradley (1950-51). Following Boulton's second term in office, P S Brewster was appointed and served as President (1951-52.) Although by the time he was appointed President, Morgan had served as a member of the Executive Council for eight years, he was, to some extent an 'outsider' in that all his fellow Executive Council members had served from 1940, the year that Elim parted company with George Jeffreys. Boulton, Gorman, Hathaway, Kingston, Phillips and Smith had all served as members of the Executive Council prior to 1940. H W Greenway was elected to the Executive in succession to Percy Corry in 1940, the same year that J T Bradley replaced Robert Mercer who, although having been elected to the Council as Conference appointee, left Elim and joined with Jeffreys and the Bible Pattern Movement. The biggest, and in many respect, the most challenging change to the established order came with the appointment of P S Brewster. If Morgan was something of an 'outsider', Brewster was even more so in that at the time he was elected vice-President, he was not a member of the Executive Council. Morgan's departure from the Executive Council was for a two-year period. He was re-elected to the Council in 1954 when Boulton informed the Conference of his decision not to stand for re-election.

Election of members of the Executive Council were by postal ballot following a nomination and a seconder who were members of the Conference. The announcements of the results of the election of the Council members were usually very early on in the Conference business Agenda, following which the election of the vice-President usually took place. Following the appointment of Brewster to the Executive Council in place of Morgan, the Conference appointed Morgan as Brewster's successor to be President.

James J Morgan

'J J' as he was referred to throughout the Elim Movement was an Ulsterman with Welsh ancestry, hence the surname. Morgan was, from the earliest days an active member of the Conference. His name first appears in the Conference minutes of the 1933 Conference in the debate involving the Stationing of Ministers. At the time, it was the accepted rule that ministers were appointed on an annual basis. 'It was generally agreed that senior ministers would be asked whether they want to move after their first year. This would include changes at other times than the annual change. Headquarters could not always agree to meet the Minister's request. Ministers should not be consulted as to where they should go. The maximum stay of a minister in any church should be 3 years, except in exceptional circumstances. The meeting was entirely against church members having any voice as to the retention of a minister after the first year.'[2]

The Conference minutes records that three suggestions were made for easing the situation at the annual change. The suggestion from Robert Mercer leads to the conclusion that Headquarters' decisions were sacrosanct. His suggestion was that the minister should 'tell the church when he announces the change that he regards the decision as from the Lord, and he has decided to do as headquarters directs, and it will not matter however many petitions may be signed as he has decided to go.[3]' Morgan's suggestion was much less abrasive. His suggestion was as follows: 'A circular letter be read to the churches advising the dates and changes being decided, asking the members to pray, and not to bring pressure to bear on headquarters.' This prayerful attitude of Morgan was typical of the man who was endearingly referred to by his colleagues as 'Jimmy' or 'Jim' Morgan.

It is evident from reading the Conference minutes that Morgan was not afraid to make suggestions nor to ask difficult questions. An example of this is a request made by him at the tension-riven 1937 Conference. In a session conducted by George Jeffreys as to the invitation for suggestions from ministers with regards to the future policy of the Movement with the local government and central government churches uniting, Morgan shrewdly requested a 'full statement of debts and liabilities'.[4] Morgan's increasing influence upon the Conference is noted by his appointment to an influential Committee that was appointed by the 1942 Conference to negotiate the amalgamation of the Essex Churches fully into the Alliance.[5]

Jimmy Morgan was the pastor of the Glasgow Elim Church in 1939. The Glasgow City Temple was one of George Jeffreys' churches and he was one of two trustees for the building. Morgan made it clear that his loyalties were with Elim, whereas the majority of the deacons and membership of the church supported Jeffreys. A section of the Glasgow church left and joined Morgan in setting up a new Elim Church in Glasgow. He remained there for two years before moving to the 'city of jam, jute and journalism,' Dundee.[6] Morgan was fierce in his defence of Elim and there was regular correspondence between himself and Phillips in which he informed the Secretary-General of the situation in Glasgow.

Morgan was elected to the Executive Council at the 1944 Conference and filled the vacancy caused by the resignation of Fred Cloke. He served on the Executive Council for a period of 23 years. Although he lost his place in the most surreal manner as noted above and was off the Executive for a period of two years, one of those years he was President and therefore, chairman of the Executive Council. James Morgan was a popular member of the Executive Council and was appointed to the office of Field Superintendent in 1960 and served in that capacity for six years. Those pastors who knew him and served under him whilst he was Field Superintendent spoke of his understanding and kindness. Apart from Glasgow and Dundee, Morgan led three other large Elim churches: Bradford, Birmingham Sparkbrook and Clapham.

James Morgan was a fine preacher. I had the privilege of being present at the Clapham Elim Church when Morgan preached his last sermon. It was shortly after the Conference of 1968. I was in my first year at Bible College at the time. Mr Gilpin, the Principal received a request at short-notice for a couple of students to go to Clapham to assist Pastor Morgan in the evening service. Under normal circumstances, such an appointment would have been put to second year students, but most of them were engaged in ministry at other locations. Mr Gilpin asked Mike Sherwood[7] and myself to go to Clapham. Mike convened the service and I sang a couple of solos. I can, to this day recall J J's sermon. He preached on the subject of church membership. He mentioned first the importance of becoming a member of the universal Church through salvation and the new birth. He then spoke of the privileges, responsibilities and duties of believers as members of a local church. He ended his sermon with a two-fold appeal aimed at convincing those who were not yet Christians to give their lives to Christ and then for members of the church to commit themselves to fulfilling their roles in the assembly as members.

When he had finished, he knelt in front of his chair and prayed the message home. His sermon, the passion with which he preached it, left a lasting impression on me. It showed me the importance of praying after I had preached, as well as praying beforehand. When the service was over, he took us into his vestry where he had sandwiches, cake and tea prepared for us before we returned to the College. Although he was desperately ill (he died a few weeks later), he stayed and talked to two raw young men who were getting ready to serve God and the Movement that he so loved. James J Morgan was, to the very core of his being and calling, a wonderful pastor. The Conference minutes record the following tribute to him:

> Prior to the Conference, Pastor J J Morgan had intimated his intention to relinquish his position as an Executive Council member because of ill health. The Secretary-General paid a warm tribute to Mr Morgan for his loyal and faithful services to Elim as an Executive Council member for twenty-two years.[8] The Conference applauded the suggestion that its appreciation should go on record. News of a serious deterioration in Mr Morgan's condition having been reported, the President adjourned the Conference for a season of prayer.[9]

James Craig Kennedy

Kennedy was elected vice-President at the 1956 Conference and served as President in 1957-58. His election was unusual in that prior to his serving as President, he did not feature on a national scale within Elim. He was not the first non-Executive Council member to serve as President, P S Brewster had that honour. The difference, however, is that Brewster had a much higher profile within the Movement. There is no record of his being appointed as a Conference appointee to any committee. However, he was the Executive Council appointee to the Evangelistic committee.

Whatever the circumstances of his election, it is clear that Kennedy was popular with his ministerial colleagues.

A Ballymena man, Kennedy entered the Elim ministry in the late twenties. He, like most of his Executive colleagues at the time, had gone through the trauma of the division in Elim. For an Ulsterman, coming from the province where Elim had been established, the decision to have to choose between George Jeffreys and Elim could not have been an easy one. There were five Irishmen on Elim's first Executive Council. Three of them were appointed by Jeffreys (Ernest Darragh, Robert Tweed and James McWhirter), two were elected by the Conference (Joseph Smith and Samuel Gorman). The three Jeffreys' appointees left Elim and remained loyal to Jeffreys. Smith and Gorman stayed with Elim. To have to take one side or another in a major dispute would have caused great pain to many of our pastors and church members. The fracturing of friendship and fellowship had a profound effect on many. For the Irish pastors, the pain of breaking fellowship with those who had led them into the blessings of salvation and the Pentecostal blessing must have been heart-breaking.

J C Kennedy was looked upon first and foremost as a pastor. He was a fine preacher and soon became a popular convention speaker. James Kennedy was the second Elim President to have been appointed from outside the Executive Council, the first being John Dyke. It was fitting that it was Joseph Smith, who had just completed his second term as President, should have handed the Presidential Bible to Kennedy at the 1957 Conference held in Bournemouth. Kennedy was an excellent pastor and led some of Elim's most significant churches, including Plymouth and Clapham. His last pastorate before retiring was Southampton. Pastor and Mrs Kennedy had one daughter, Vivien who was married to Eldin Corsie, one of Elim's General Superintendents and a former Principal of the Movement's Bible College. Kennedy was a straight-speaking Ulsterman who endeared himself to his congregation.

Harold Burton-Haynes

Burton-Haynes[10] was a lecturer at the Elim Bible College and was a Conference appointee to the Bible College Synod. His lectures entitled 'From Egypt to Canaan' traced the wanderings of the Children of Israel from their captivity in Egypt, through the wilderness and on to the Promised Land. Whilst lacking a certain academic rigour, his lectures provided young and inexperienced pastors with a great deal of material for sermons and Bible studies.

Bournemouth (Springbourne) and Clacton were two of the churches that Burton-Haynes pastored. He was a dignified, but never aloof, gentleman who was greatly respected throughout the Movement. He was inducted to the office of President at the 1959 Conference which was held in the North Wales seaside resort of Llandudno. He was elected to the Executive Council in 1960 where he replaced John Dyke who had died earlier in that year.

Tommy H Stevenson

Stevenson commenced his ministry in Ireland where he met his wife, Sadie. He was a member of the Greenock Elim Church. He was one of eight children brought up in a working-class town, Greenock in Renfrewshire. His father was well-known and respected throughout the town. The family were greatly impacted by George Jeffreys' revival campaign which was held in the town in 1929. The whole family attended the church. The youngest son made his mark in politics and served as a councillor for over forty years. His name was Simpson and he was knighted. 'Sir Simpson Stevenson was a Greenock-born politician and businessman who became a highly influential chairman of Greater Glasgow Health Board. Sir Simpson (1921-2015) was always proud of his working-class roots as a member of a hard-working and loving family, he was forever providing tales of overcoming hardship. His father was a highly respected shipyard worker. He joined the Labour Party, becoming a local councillor in 1949, he was to be involved in local politics until the age of 78. In 1962 he was appointed Provost of Greenock then in 1984 served as Provost of Inverclyde. In 1976 he was appointed to a Royal Commission to the National Health Service and was knighted by the Queen the same year.[11] The same newspaper report states that he was a member of Greenock Elim Church for 70 years, and was a regular attender at Greenock Baptist Church for the last 12 years.'

Another brother to Tommy Stevenson was Danny. Danny Stevenson was a loyal member of Greenock Elim and served as a deacon and elder for many years. He was also the lay representative for the church and attended the Conference annually for a large number of years. Danny was a debater and was never reticent to make his views known on a number of subjects. He is best known for his fiery speeches on the total abstention clause that related to pastors and members of the local church session. Danny was a lifelong teetotaller and he believed strongly that ministers and church leaders should not partake of alcoholic beverage. Like many of us who have strong opinions on one subject or another, Danny often allowed his passion to boil over as he expressed his opinions on the Conference floor. Having clashed with him on more than one occasion, I have to say that whilst we were miles apart on some subjects and attacked each other's views strongly, once the debate was over, appreciation and friendship became the order of the day. I disagreed with him strongly on a number of issues, but I retain a great respect for Danny Stevenson and the role he played within Elim on a national as well as local platform.

Tommy's upbringing influenced him in many ways. He was proud of his family connections and had no difficulty in looking upon himself as a working-class man. He was a very able pastor, teacher and writer. He led a number of Elim's larger churches including Ilford. He was elected President-Elect at the Harrogate Conference and served the Movement as President in 1961-62. Stevenson was an acknowledged writer within Elim and regularly wrote a page in the Evangel entitled 'From my Diary'. These were a collection of matters that had grabbed his attention from time to time. His Labour-Party upbringing can be discernibly noticed in some of his writings. The following is an example of this:

> And while in this land millions, 'never had it so good.' In many lands others could hardly have it worse. The chairman of a leading British bank has said: 'The growing disparity in living standards between peoples of the highly industrialised nations and those inhabiting the rest of the world poses perhaps the greatest problem that has ever encountered the human race.' President Eisenhower has declared that the first of four freedoms – freedom from want – is denied to one billion seven hundred million. In 1958-9 the total of Britain's aid to meet such needs amounted to one half of one per cent of the gross natural produce, according to a parliamentary reply to Mr Jo Grimond. And before me I read an item appearing in the press stating that we as a nation spend on alcohol at a rate of £1,774 a minute; on tobacco at £181; and £181 a minute to the cinema box office – a grand total of £2,582,000,000 in a year. In neither respect is it a proud national record.[12]

In the same year that he was elected President-Elect, Stevenson's name was put before Conference for the position of Editor of the Elim Evangel. For some unknown reason, the name was withdrawn. Whether the Executive Council withdrew the name, or whether Stevenson had a last-minute change of mind is unclear. The minutes simply state: 'A D Hathaway was appointed Editor of the Elim Evangel after the name of T H Stevenson had been withdrawn.' Stevenson resumed his pastoral ministry and carried out his Presidential role in an exemplary manner.

One further thing which needs to be said concerning Tommy Stevenson whilst he was the pastor of the Ilford church is that he opened himself up to other ministers and churches outside the Elim family who were seeking to come into the fulness of the Holy Spirit. George Canty writes about the changes within Elim towards reaching out to other groups seeking to adopt a free style of worship and the speakers were men from bodies previously noted for their opposition to Elim.[13] Stevenson was looked upon as being a traditionalist, but he had a high view of the baptism in the Holy Spirit, speaking in tongues and exercising the gifts of the Holy Spirit. He encouraged his congregation to be free in their worship. More will be said in the third volume concerning the renewal and restoration groups that both challenged Elim, but at the same time threw a lifeline out to us that made us look again at our founding beliefs. Many Elim pastors, including and especially this author changed their thinking on the Pentecostal message and were challenged to bring it out in to the open. The Elim Constitution at one time stated that the gifts of the Spirit were not be exercised in the evening Gospel service for fear of people getting confused if the Gifts were exercised when there were unbelievers present. It caused great heart search within the Movement of which more will be said later. It was a big deal for someone of the stature of Tommy Stevens, a former Elim President who was widely respected throughout the Movement to make approaches to other denominations and to share the blessings of Pentecost with them.

Notes

[1] E J was appointed President-elect at the 1957 Conference. This was the year that he retired having served as Secretary General for 34 years. He became President in October 1958. The following year, the date of the Annual Conference was changed from October to May. So, E J Phillips, the longest serving Chief Secretary of the Movement became the shortest serving President in Elim's history serving in that capacity for only eight months.

[2] Ministerial Conference 18th-22nd September 1933, *Conference Minutes*: Author's copy, now at Malvern: Elim Archives.

[3] Ministerial Conference 1933, ibid, James Morgan

[4] Annual Ministerial and General Conferences, 13th-17th September 1937, *Conference Minutes,* Thursday Morning, Ministerial Conference.

[5] The Essex churches were officially named 'Elim Pentecostal church'. They were a group of up to 18 churches in Essex and the wider East Anglian area that were a part of Elim but were not in the Alliance. The ministers of the churches were allowed to attend ministers meetings and Representative Sessions of Conference, but could not vote and could only speak by permission of the Conference. It was to be a further 22 years before the Essex churches were finally amalgamated into the Alliance.

[6] Dundee became known as the city of jam, jute and journalism because these were the three major industries in the city in Victorian times. The city was known particularly for its marmalade production. It was also the city made famous for the printing of comics such as D C Thompson's the Beano and the Dandy. The 'Sunday Post' and the 'People's Friend'

were also published here. Jute was used in the city's sail-making industries. It was then used for the making of ropes.

[7] Mike Sherwood is a well-known and respected retired Elim minister. He led some of our larger churches including Ilford, Cardiff and Chelmsford. He was a member of the NLT for over ten years and also served as a Regional Superintendent He has been a close friend of the author since our college years and was the best man at our wedding.

[8] As mentioned above, James Morgan served 23 years on the Council not 22. The reason is that the chronicler had not included his year as President when he served as chairman of the Executive Council and Conference.

[9] Conference Minutes 1968, p2.

[10] He was the only minister elected to the Executive Council that had a double-barrelled surname.

[11] www.heraldscotland.com: *Sir Simpson Stevenson*: 8th May 2015, accessed 3rd Dec 2022.

[12] Stevenson, T H, *From my Diary, Elim Evangel*, 12th March 1960, Vol 51, No 11, p 165.

[13] Canty, George, *History of Elim*, ibid, p207.

26
Ron Jones

W Ronald Jones was one of Elim's great leaders. Like the redoubtable P S Brewster, Ron Jones transitioned from Pastor/Evangelist to the office of General Superintendent. He was gifted in so many areas. He was undoubtedly one of Elim's greatest preachers. He had a most unique style of preaching. Those not fully acquainted with the manner and styles of the old Welsh preachers would have said that Ron preached with 'hwyl'.[1] Ron was not a Welsh speaker and this rules him out as an exponent of the 'hwyl'. But Ron adopted a style similar to the old Welsh preachers and it became a unique feature of his preaching. He would hold out certain words that he wished to emphasise. This would be done to such an extent that the word took on a musical quality. He would also raise his voice at the last word of a phrase or sentence. I remember him preaching on the subject of Esau devaluing his birth-right. 'And Esau sooooooold his birth-right for a bowl of lentil sooooup.' The word 'soup' was at a much higher note than the rest of the phrase.

The quite amazing fact is that this very Welsh style of preaching was well received wherever Ron preached. He refused to change his style of preaching and it worked. It is my firm belief that he developed this style. In conversation and Conference debate, he never once went into his preaching style. Some would say that it was because he preached under 'the anointing' of the Holy Spirit. However, the point I would make is that Ron preached like this in every sermon. As much as preachers crave for a constant anointing of the Holy Spirit upon every word of every sermon they preach, it just does not happen. But this was the style of preaching that Ron Jones adopted and it was very well received and very successful.

W R Jones was born at 61 Norfolk Street, Mount Pleasant, Swansea on 12th July 1915. He was born into a typical Welsh working-class family. It would appear that Ron was an only child as there is no mention of any siblings in his biography. The family attended the Methodist Central Hall. Music was an important feature in Ron's life and his love and knowledge of music was a great feature of his Gospel meetings and evangelistic campaigns. He was particularly fond of Welsh male voice choirs.

> Male-voice choir singing is the heart-warming genre of music that traditionally flourished in Wales, the 'Land of Song'. It has always been in essence a 'home-grown' or church-grown' commodity. 'Calls to worship' nearly always meant the local congregations joining together in singing the Gospel. Musical accompaniment was generally quite simple. Down-to-earth sincerity and heartfelt identification with the sentiments of the songs from the singers filled the heart of the listener with genuine emotion. Over the decades of the last century, I thrilled often to the rich, melodic message of the Gospel presented by the wonderful Welsh choirs and discovered even as a youth, genuine inspiration and peaceful consolation in the music of the Gospel.[2]

In his biography, Ron does not refer directly to his conversion, but it would appear that he committed his life to Christ under the ministry of Watkin Williams his pastor at the Methodist Central Hall. Shortly after the death of Williams, Jones found a new spiritual home in the Full Gospel Church in Swansea. This was an Assemblies of God church led by Arthur Boston a young minister with whom he established a strong friendship. Being conscious of the call of God upon his life, Ron entered the Hampstead Bible College in London. He was only in the College for two months when he was appointed Pastor of Ball Green Pentecostal Church. The congregation numbered less than a dozen but it had a house and Ron's widowed mother moved from nightly-bombed Swansea and lived with Ron in the church manse. After 18 months in Ball Green, Ron took over the pastorate of South Kirkby Assemblies of God church. It was a larger and more stable work and was able to pay him a salary. His next appointment was to be his last with Assemblies of God. This was Fleetwood in north-west Lancashire. It was there that he met his wife, Kathleen Gillingham. It was also in Fleetwood that his dear mother died. Ron fulfilled his mother's wishes by making it possible for her to be buried with his father at Swansea. Nine months after the death of his mother, Ron moved not only to another church, but to another denomination. He was appointed Pastor of Hull, Mason Street. He returned to Fleetwood where he was married to Kathleen on 20th April 1948, the service being conducted by his old friend and pastor Arthur Boston.

Ron and Kathleen were only in Hull for six months when they were asked to lead the new Elim Church in Caerphilly, South Wales. The church had been established as a result of a very successful evangelistic campaign under the leadership of P S Brewster. It is obvious that Brewster saw in Jones a kindred spirit. They were both pastor/evangelists. Brewster's campaign in Caerphilly was very successful. The campaign tent was set up in the castle grounds. Caerphilly castle is one of the largest fortresses in the United Kingdom and has a leaning tower. The town is also famous for its cheese. Ron comments on those early days in Caerphilly:

> We had no church building of our own in Caerphilly, so we were grateful to be able to hold most of our services in the quaint old Welsh Twyn Chapel. Their service in Welsh was at 6.00 pm on Sunday evening and so we were able to have our service at 7.30 pm. There was a really good organ but the pews were quite hard and rather uncomfortable.
>
> Those were the days of open-air meetings, cinema rallies and street marches of witness. Every Sunday evening we packed the chapel with some two hundred people. There were many who came to faith in Christ and now hold positions of leadership in church life.[3]

In 1951 a new church building was erected and the Caerphilly Elim church soon became one of the leading Pentecostal fellowships in South Wales. It was whilst he was in Caerphilly that Ron had his first experience of preaching in the Royal Albert Hall. Willard Cantelon a well-known American preacher who had conducted campaigns with Brewster was due to preach at Elim's Easter celebrations but had to cancel. Ron Jones was asked to preach at the world-famous venue in Cantelon's place. This was quite an accolade for a young minister who had only been with Elim for three years.

Bristol

Reference has already been made to the quite astonishing evangelistic campaign held in the Colston Hall in Bristol during the summer of 1952. Ron Jones was approached three times by the Executive Council to go to Bristol. It was very unusual in those days for the Executive Council to approach a pastor a second time to ask him to go to a certain church, it was unheard for them to give an invitation a third time. One can understand Jones' reluctance to go to Bristol. Having led the Caerphilly church through the difficulties that arose in having no building of their own and having had to negotiate and plan for a building of their own, Ron was asked to do this again but on a larger scale. It was with some reluctance that he finally agreed to go to Bristol. His wife challenged him to find out what God wanted them to do. Like Gideon of old they put out a 'fleece'. They had said 'no' twice. They prayed and asked God that if it was His will for them to go to Bristol, they would be approached a third time. Less than a week later they received a letter from Elim headquarters asking them once more to go to Bristol.

> It was as simple as that. I must confess I was not in love with the idea. Caerphilly was a lovely small Welsh town where an impact could be made through the preaching of the Gospel. Bristol held many negatives. Firstly, it was a vast major city

with thousands and thousands of people. Secondly, there was no accommodation for the Jones family. Thirdly, there was no church building and not even a building site.

I had no enthusiasm for searching through a large city for a site on which to build another church. We would have to hold our meetings in any hall that we could rent in the city. That prospect did not appeal to me either. I was also well aware of the fact that it would be very difficult to raise the money necessary for building a church. It was one of the most difficult decisions Kath and I ever had to make. Paradoxically, at the same time we felt sure that it was God's plan for us to move to Bristol. Consequently, on 31st August 1952 I was conducting my first service in the rather dirty Shepherd's Hall in Old Market, Bristol.

Ron Jones was not only a brilliant preacher and a superb pastor he was also a first-class leader with planning and administrative skills. It was these qualities that led the Elim Movement to appoint him as General Superintendent following the tenure of his mentor P S Brewster. Jones was a superb negotiator and had the skills needed to speak to the right people at the right time. Eventually a parcel of land came available in Jamaica Street but on its own, it was not large enough for building a church complex to seat in excess of five hundred people. However, other small plots adjoining the site offered to Elim came available and Jones negotiated the purchase and building of a church in Jamaica Street. A minor hall was erected first where the church held their morning services. The evening services were held in the Bristol Corn Exchange.

The building of the new main church, named the City Temple was completed. The date for the opening was settled for a Saturday in October 1954. The one factor that was not settled was how many of the folk who faithfully attended meetings in a public hall would now attend a church? It was crunch time. We were leaving a familiar environment to go into completely different surroundings; from a public hall to a church with a denominational tag. The big day arrived. I need not have worried. It was impossible to accommodate the large crowd in the new City Temple. There had to be an overflow relay in the minor hall. From that moment on, the City Temple was packed almost every Sunday evening. People were weekly coming to faith in Jesus Christ. Many were being healed in answer to prayer and there were those who were filled with the Holy Spirit as on the day of Pentecost. There was a marked spiritual progress in the lives of many of the new converts.[4]

The building of the City Temple in Jamaica Street, Bristol was quite an astonishing feat given the immense challenges of leading a congregation of largely new converts and having to hire a number of different halls. To maintain such a growing congregation with all the challenges that brought with it and then to negotiate for land and oversee a major building project was a phenomenal achievement. The new church building was packed from day one! Ron advertised his Sunday evening Gospel service as 'the best Sunday night in town'. The 'Church Full' signs regularly appeared at the door of the church on a Sunday evening. Some people arrived at the church at 5.00 pm for the Gospel Service that commenced at 6.30.

Within a couple of years of the opening of their building, Ron Jones realised that he would have to enlarge the building. The problem they faced was that the plot on which the City Temple stood was surrounded by properties that had a number of owners and they were most unlikely to sell them. Ron and Kath were faced with a further dilemma when in 1962 they were invited to take over the pastorate of Clapham which at the time was Elim's central church in London. It seemed as though the invitation to London had come just at the right time for the Joneses. Someone had been appointed to take over Bristol and humanly speaking it seemed the right thing for Jones, Bristol and Clapham. Pastor and Mrs Jones travelled to Clapham to view the manse. Whilst they were taking measurements, the phone rang and they were called to a meeting of the Executive Council. E J Phillips, who was chairman at the time, informed them that the move to Clapham was off. Apparently, the church officers at Bristol had phoned Elim Headquarters and in no uncertain words had made it very clearly that they wanted their minister back. This was unheard of in those days. When a minister had agreed to leave a church and move to another and it had been agreed upon by the church to which the minister was appointed, nothing could stop it. The Bristol church session must have presented a cast-iron case for them to retain their pastor. 'It had been announced in Bristol that we would be leaving. But we were back in the City Temple on the Sunday.'[5] Over the next few years, various properties surrounding the church came available and altogether, the church made 28 transactions to get the plot of land they needed. A new complex was built including residential accommodation for twenty residents. It was a magnificent structure and was brought into being due largely to Ron Jones' vision and indefatigable negotiation and sheer hard work. The new complex was opened on 20th April 1974.

The Evangelist

With regards to his evangelistic ministry, Ron Jones was greatly influenced by P S Brewster, who was in many respects his mentor. Brewster formed evangelistic teams and conducted many evangelistic campaigns throughout the country. Most of these were pioneer campaigns. Ron Jones determined to spend some of his time each year holding evangelistic campaigns in various parts of the country. At first, he concentrated his efforts near to Bristol. The first pioneer effort was in Keynsham, a town some eight miles to the east of Bristol. A Methodist church was purchased for the sum of £1000 and Des Morton agreed to be the bi-vocational pastor. Des Morton did a magnificent work for God in Keynsham and the church is still flourishing. Campaigns that resulted in new Elim churches being established under Ron Jones' ministry included Bridgewater, Weston-Super-Mare, Clevedon and Carrickfergus.

Ron Jones loved music, although by his own confession he 'didn't understand a note of music.[6] He formed a youth choir in Bristol and named it 'New Creation Singers'. The group consisted of between seventy and eighty enthusiastic young people who made up their own harmonies as they went along.'⁷ Ron Jones used them in his campaign services and also in the Royal Albert Hall on Easter Mondays. When Douglas Gray retired, Ron Jones was asked if he would take over leading the massed youth choirs. This was some challenge. Douglas Gray was a masterful musician and a great conductor. Ron Jones was no musician as such as he himself readily confessed; but he had a superb gift in leading sung worship.

General Superintendent

Ron Jones was one of a small number of men who were elected by the Annual Elim Conference to be the Movement's President on two occasions. He was elected vice-president of the Movement in 1970 and served as President in 1970-71. His second term of office was 1982-83. He was elected to the Executive Council in 1971 and served as an elected member for eleven years.

When the Executive Council nominated P S Brewster to be General Superintendent which was verified by the Conference, it came as a huge surprise to the delegates. The Executive and Conference appointed an out-and-out evangelist to be its leader. There had been a subtle but definite change in the spiritual giftings and ministries of the members of the Council. In the 30 years following the resignation of George Jeffreys, the men who were appointed to the Executive were in the main, administrators and pastors. We should not be swift in deriding the thought of leadership being expressed in terms of administration. Certainly, in the leadership of E J Phillips, his administrative, organisational and constitutional genius was precisely what the Movement needed at a time of great crisis. When Brewster was elected to the Executive Council in 1952, he was the first man appointed who was looked upon as an evangelist. The nineteen seventies saw the balance of pastors and evangelists become more even. Ron Jones, Alex Tee and Archie Biddle were elected to the Executive between 1971 and 1974. George Canty, another evangelist, served as

President in 1974-1975. These men had an expansive vision as far as opening new churches and encouraging evangelistic endeavour throughout the Movement. Although he only served as General Superintendent for three years, Brewster most certainly impacted the Movement and changed the strategy of Elim from slow but steady growth to a more dynamic and expansionist vision.

When Brewster retired from office in 1977, the Executive Council deemed it right to appoint another in Brewster's evangelistic mould. That man was Ron Jones. He was not overwhelmingly endorsed by Conference and only narrowly achieved the required two-thirds percentage of votes required for a HQ officer; 185 votes for and 77 against. Two years later, it was a different situation, he polled 243 with only 31 against. Brewster and Jones were both in their sixties when appointed to the office of General Superintendent. It is obvious that the nineteen seventies Conference delegates were not put off by the age of the men nominated to the highest position in the Movement. Another feature of this period in Elim's history is that the Executive Council and the Conference were not against short-term leadership. J.T Bradley served four years, Brewster three years and Jones four years in the role of General Superintendent. The writer would support the argument for short-term periods of office when there is an obvious need. It is significant that the first two Secretary-Generals (General Superintendent) served for a period of 48 years.[8] From 1970-1981 there were four General Superintendents appointed.[9]

Ron Jones took office as General Superintendent at a critical time in Elim's history. The Charismatic Renewal and the Restoration churches saw a tremendous growth in the nineteen seventies. Their services were marked by freedom of worship on a scale that Elim had not experienced for many years. Bible weeks were organised and held in various parts of England and Wales that proved to be exceedingly attractive to many Elim People. The Dales, Downs and West of England Bible weeks saw a large number of Elim pastors in attendance. Space does not allow me to go into more detail and this subject will be dealt with in my third volume (1980-2020) where the early chapters will deal with the Southport Conferences (1981 and 1984) and the impact on the Movement.

It was not just the worship that impacted the Pentecostal churches in the UK. The teaching given at the Bible weeks was fresh, radical, dynamic and, more importantly, Biblical. It is true to say that some aspects of the teaching of some of the speakers at the Bible Weeks went to somewhat uncomfortable areas. Elim people heard sermons on discipleship, accountability, apostolic leadership, spiritual covering and the five-fold gift ministries that they had not previously heard. I should say that they had not heard these things taught in a systematic manner and in language and terms that they fully understood. It is the writer's personal opinion that by 1980 Elim was in a more critical position than at any time in her history. As it was, Elim lost four congregations and six pastors; two of these congregations were large.

In his final report as General Superintendent, Ron Jones addressed the issues that were facing the Movement. It was his report to the 1981 Conference, his last as General Superintendent, that prompted the Ministerial Session of Conference to call for the ministers to adjourn and meet again at a date and place to be decided. The Conference minute is included here:

> Secretary-General's Report. A question was raised relative to the Secretary-General's Report and following discussion it was resolved that the Ministerial Session of the Conference be adjourned to a date and place to be announced for a discussion lasting for at least two days on the role of the ministry and to formulate a report of proposals to be referred to the Representative Session of the Conference as necessary.[10]

Jones had grasped the seriousness of the situation that faced the Movement and in his last report as Secretary-General he was determined that the Movement should look closely at itself in the light of the Charismatic and Restoration Movements. Elim needed to change and it was Ron Jones' report to the 1981 Conference that was the catalyst for Southport. I was very involved in the Southport

Conference and was a member of the Steering Committee that was appointed to prepare the sessions and subjects to be discussed at the Conference. This will be expanded upon in the third volume on Elim History.

In reporting on the ministry of Ron Jones, it is important to include a note of his Radio ministry. It was in 1962 that Jones was approached by Frank Topping to record five three-minute sessions to be broadcast as 'Thoughts for the Day' on BBC Radio Bristol. Following this, he recorded five sessions on a tour of the Holy Land. These also were broadcast on Radio Bristol and these five-minute talks were also broadcast on BBC radio 2. Ron's radio ministry made way for some television appearances and due largely to his influence, the Conference communion service (1981) was broadcast.

Notes

[1] This was a style of preaching that was uniquely Welsh. For a preacher to be accolated with the word 'hwyl', he would have had to preach in Welsh. The preacher would start his sermon in the usual manner but, as he progressed, would experience an anointing of the Holy Spirit and would then almost sing his sermon. This would be punctuated with cries of the elders and deacons with 'Diolch iddo' (Thank Him), 'Ie wir' (Truth indeed). The greatest exponent of this style of preaching was Christmas Evans. The last true exponent of 'preaching with the hwyl' was Jubilee Young.

[2] Jones, Ron, *Then Something Remarkable Happened, the Autobiography of Ron Jones* (with Paul Davis), (Bromsgrove: Crossbridge Books, 2005), p9.

[3] Jones, Ron, ibid, p52.

[4] Jones, Ron, ibid, p75.

[5] Jones, Ron: ibid, p83.

[6] Jones, Ron: ibid, p101.

[7] Jones, Ron: ibid, p101.

[8] It has to be noted that E J Phillips served for 16 years under the leadership of George Jeffreys.

[9] T W Walker was appointed General Superintendent at the 1981 Conference and served in that office for a period of seven years.

[10] Minutes of the Ministerial Session of Conference 1981, Item 6, Secretary General's Report.

27
The Evangelists

Throughout her history, it is clear that Elim has been a strongly evangelistic Movement. In its earlier days, Elim was very much a revivalist Movement. Campaigns were held, the Gospel preached, sick people were healed and churches were opened. The methodology of planting new churches has changed somewhat over the years, but Elim is still committed to a programme of evangelism and the establishment of new churches throughout the British Isles and in various countries world-wide where the Movement is represented. An examination of Elim's history clearly reveals that evangelism and church-planting is firmly embedded in Elim's DNA. This is how we came into existence; this is how we will grow.

Societal changes over the years have undoubtedly impacted evangelistic outreach within Elim. Until the early nineteen nineties, the largest attended of the Sunday services in most Elim churches was the evening service. There was a clear intended difference between the two main Sunday services. The morning service was looked upon as 'the believers meeting', also referred to as 'the breaking-of-bread service' because communion was served in those meetings. A characteristic of those services was that people were encouraged to bring prayers of thanksgiving to the Lord for His grace, mercy and, above all, His salvation. It was not unusual for people to sing a devotional chorus or hymn, which would then be taken up by the congregation. At the age of 75, it is too much of a temptation for the writer to look back with heavily-tinted golden spectacles and wistfully long for a return to such services.

I have to remind myself of the dreadful drivel, the violation of musical rhythm and the total inability to hit the right note that often occurred. This, coupled by endless repetition, deathly silences between each contribution, repetition of the same three-phrase message in tongues, often by the same person week in, week out: a sacramental approach to the Communion Service, so that if the minister did not very carefully replace the communion cloth over the trays containing the bread and wine immediately after communion had been served it would be commented on at the next church session meeting. We were as bound by our traditions as any other Christian denomination. But there were aspects of the Pentecostal communion service of yester-year that stand out clearly in the writer's mind as being very precious. Whilst some very inappropriate choruses were sung in some communion services, many hymns and choruses beautifully expressed our thanks to our precious Lord for his sacrificial and atoning death for us. Some, were very simple and lacked theological fulness but managed to express our appreciation for Christ's sacrifice on our behalf. One such chorus that comes immediately to my mind is a very simple one: 'Still it flows, still it flows, still it flows as fresh as ever, from the Saviour's wounded side.' The reference is to the Roman spear that was thrust into the side of Christ to make certain that he was dead. 'But one of the soldiers pierced his side with a spear, and at once there came out blood and water.'[1] The thought behind the words of this simple chorus is that the blood of Christ is still flowing with cleansing power to a sin-stricken world.

The Sunday evening service in Elim churches was meant to be different from the morning service. It was in the evening that the Gospel was preached. This was the service that we invited, expected, hoped for, longed for non-Christians to come in so that they could be presented with the Gospel. It was forbidden for the gifts of the Spirit, especially tongues and interpretation, to be used in a Gospel service. The truth is that the Sunday evening service referred to as the Gospel service, was little different from a service in an evangelical church. In many Elim churches at the time, there were hardly any 'outsiders' or 'unsaved' people that attended the Gospel service. Yet we persisted in the practice of not allowing supernatural manifestations in our evening 'Gospel' presentations. Back in the sixties and seventies, even praying for those who were in need of healing was confined to the morning communion service. One thing is certain however, evangelism has always featured prominently in Elim's history.

Following the departure of George Jeffreys and the outbreak of the Second World War, evangelistic campaigns came to a halt. As has been shown in this book, the on-going work of evangelism within the churches continued, particularly in the ministry of local churches to the armed forces. Following the war, Brewster and Woodhead renewed pioneer evangelism. There were others that followed the example of these two. This chapter and the next gives an account of Elim's other gifted evangelists.

Ken Matthew

Ken Matthew entered the Elim ministry in 1939 after spending some time as a student at Elim Bible College. He was ordained in 1942. He became the pastor of the Elim Church in Pontypridd in 1941 and stayed there until 1954. It was whilst he was in Pontypridd that he developed his evangelistic skills being mentored by Brewster. He was a member of Brewster's campaign team in the early years.

His first major pioneer crusade was in the then small town of Kidderminster about 15 miles west of Birmingham. 'Evangelist-pastor Ken Matthew eyed it, coveted it for God, and taking one or two young Elim probationer ministers – hardly out of their adolescence – he entered the town unknown. Not an Elim member was known to live there.'[2] The odds against him making an impact for Christ in this town were very negligible. The lack of premises was an obvious problem. He was able to hire the spacious Town Hall to begin with where a good crowd gathered and a number of decisions for Christ were made. But the Town Hall was not available permanently, so other premises had to be found to house the considerable crowd that had now formed themselves into some sort of congregation. Canty made the important comment that these people were not gathered from the various churches in Kidderminster, 'they were mostly with little or no previous religious background.'[3]

Matthew's first pioneer campaign was in Salford, Lancashire. It's worth noting that the campaign was conducted by a 'new' evangelist and the first pastor of the church was a seasoned campaigner – John Woodhead. This campaign was held in July 1950. Pastor Matthew was elected to the Evangelistic Committee in the same year. In 1954, he campaigned in Worcester where the Elim church there had declined considerably. Following the campaign, Matthew was appointed the pastor. He had been in Pontypridd, for over twelve years and his evangelistic ministry had resulted in a strong church being established in this South Wales town. A successful campaign was conducted by Matthew in Mansfield.

His last Elim campaign, was one of the best that Matthew conducted, this was in Norwich in 1958. Sadly, he was disciplined by the Executive Council and this led to his resignation from Elim. The Christian Gospel is a message of grace as well as forgiveness, hope and salvation. Ken Matthew was restored to Christian ministry and was, some years later, ordained as a minister in the Church of England.

George Canty

George Canty (1911-2010) was probably the most gifted minister in Elim's history. This is quite a bold statement to make, but one that the writer believes to be factual. Canty was a pastor, evangelist, musician, artist, theologian, historian, writer and a brilliant communicator. His was a unique ministry because of his many talents. Canty came from the East Riding city of Kingston-Upon-Hull. Adrian Hawkes was a member of Sparkbrook Elim Church, Birmingham where he was greatly impacted by Canty's ministry. From a personal point of view, having heard Canty preach on many occasions and having been in Bible College with Adrian, the writer can understand the connection between them. The following is Adrian's personal tribute to George Canty.

> Misunderstood, misplaced, somewhat eccentric. My personal point of view is that the misunderstood eccentrics are the people we need to treasure. Such people often 'think outside the box'. They do not fit into establishment shoes, nor do they keep their noses clean. They are the people that create ideas, get things done and change culture – as we should do. George Canty was one of those.
>
> Originally from Hull, he told me that he lived in a 'drain-side house'. He wanted me to understand that 'Pentecostals generally came from such working-class roots as he did. It was not a case of the middle-class denominations reaching down, but the working class stretching up.[4] George Canty was a prolific writer, my favourites being 'In my Father's House' and 'Jack Yorkshire's Weekend Book'. The latter was sold at railway station newsagents. He sometimes used pseudonyms when writing and this puzzled me. One day, I read an article in the Elim Evangel with the name George Pulford assigned to it. I knew Mr Canty well, and Mr Pulford's writing read very much like Mr Canty's. I took the article to him and asked 'Mr Canty, did you write this?' 'That's not my name', he replied. 'Yes! said I, 'but it's very much like your style of writing. 'But it is not my name', he retorted. He then explained that 'some would reject my writing because they think my views are out of sync with conventional opinion. So, sometimes I will use pseudonyms'.[5]

It is interesting to note that when asked to write a short biography of Canty, the first thoughts that Hawkes commented on in relationship to his pastor and mentor, was not his evangelistic prowess, but of his radical thinking when it came to all things to do with church and mission. This brilliant man was, at times, uncomfortable to be with and listen to. Constantly he challenged one's thinking and preconceived ideas. I first encountered him at my home church in Porth, he was one of the convention speakers. In the course of his ministry that evening, he paid glowing tribute to my pastor William Evans. George had had an encounter with God that completely changed his future ministry. By his own admission, there were aspects of the Gospel that he preached, but did not fully believe. Facing his questions squarely, he set aside time to pray and seek God for answers. Whether or not he received all the answers to his questions and assurances to all his doubts, I cannot say. It is clear, however, that as a result of this encounter, George Canty's ministry was radically changed. Having been an Elim minister for fifty-five years, I can testify to the average Elim pastor's reluctance to change, especially if it is radical.[6] He paid a warm tribute to Pastor Evans for being bold enough to invite him for a campaign when others were hesitant to invite him.

George Canty shared his spiritual change with other pastors, especially his new thoughts on divine healing. Some of his colleagues were uncomfortable with George's new evangelistic approach. George Canty had been converted during George Jeffreys' revival campaign in Hull. He had witnessed the miraculous at first hand. He came to the conclusion that whenever the Gospel is preached, it should be accompanied by the supernatural. Hawkes refers to this change in Canty:

> What was he really like? Well, he will be missed, but from my perspective again, he was awkward, sometimes difficult to work with, highly intelligent, a man who when I first met him as a youngster was already ahead of his time, thinking in new ways, understanding where others did not, not willing to be boxed in by the past and unwilling to fit in to the establishment and their expectations. As usual, people like George fall foul of the establishment who, of course, want them to conform and become establishment figures.[7]

Hawkes makes too much of Canty's radicalism. In some respects, Canty was very conventional. He was a passionate music lover, but his musical tastes were considerably more advanced than most of the people to whom he ministered. His reflections on the evening service at the Easter Monday meetings at the Royal Albert

Hall in 1952 reflect his musical understanding and also his wit. He reminds his readers of his presence in the first of the Easter conventions in the RAH:

> I had travelled from the north and sat, with a splitting headache and a longing for a cup of tea, right up against the loudest organ pipes. The seat was a narrow form and the raised decorations of the wall stuck into my back. My knees, small as they were, pressed into somebody else's back. I tried to listen to a sermon on 'The Old Man'. My friend remarked, 'By gum, there'd be a big 'ole in this roof if the Lord came!' I sang, and sang, and sang, and left London at midnight to endure hour upon hour of travel sickness, and – the following year I was on a London bus again asking for the Albert Hall. No wonder the conductor replied 'Elbert 'Ole? We call it Kainsington Lunatic Asylum on Easter Mondye.' Obviously, we were healthy enough then, And now - ?
> They are still coming in thousands, coachloads of them facing the loss of two nights' sleep and physical exhaustion as not too dear a payment. Do you remember how we used to wave our hymn-sheets and thunder back a mighty Hallelujah when asked to respond by the leader? Well, we still do, for despite the disillusionments that time always brings, we have deeper reason than ever for our enthusiasm. True we did not sing, and sing, and sing, and instead of us all roaring, 'Just the same, God is just the same today', the London Crusader Choir, 50 strong, gave a well-nigh perfect rendering of 'I know that my Redeemer liveth' from Handel's Messiah. I fancy we did not have such an item in the early days because there was not a body of singers in Elim capable of it. And we did sing shortened versions of four hymns and three choruses, including, 'Christ the Lord is Risen today'.[8]

At this point in the article, Canty shows his knowledge of music when he states that 'the new hymn-book[9] pitches that song in C instead of D. We must have a top F when we sing these electric words – I could get top B I do declare, when I sing this thrilling song with that organ and so many to help me up, always providing we do not get swept along at the tongue-twisting speed that seems the fashion in London these days.'

Notwithstanding his acerbic wit, Canty puts forward the following assessment of the Movement at that time: 'But the pulse rate of Elim is steady and firm – the throbbing of immortal life, and the temperature is still that of the Holy Ghost fire. Congregations still climb into the balcony and cram arena, stalls and boxes to make Britain's greatest Pentecostal meetings.'[10]

In the next section of the article, Canty makes reference to the ministry of Willard Cantelon. He was an American evangelist from Washington who was a cousin of Walt Disney. Cantelon would paint a picture whilst speaking to the congregation. This had a profound impact on Canty who added the ability to paint pictures to his already wide portfolio of gifts. In typical Canty fashion, he dismisses details of the service to get to that which impressed him:

> I have not mentioned the details of the service – they can be found from the posters. When Willard Cantelon stood before his easel he painted two pictures, and the better was not on canvas, but was his own personal appearance – his grace and charm and Christian radiance, while with wonderful deftness he put an eastern scene of trees and hills and sky in vivid reds and greens on a large canvas, with the stark blackness of three crosses stabbed into the centre, but an empty tomb in the foreground. It needed no interpreting, but the picture-sermon was raised to real power by the music rendered during its production, chiefly by Mrs Cantelon, who put her lips to a trumpet to render 'Open the Gates of the Temple', and, 'the Old Rugged Cross', with amazing breath-control. The massed choirs and Pastor Plowright also sang out the message being painted. I must say too it was a joy to hear a speaker so fluent and so ready in Scripture quotation as Mr Cantelon, and his address on the Christ for soul and body brought spontaneous hallelujahs to our lips.[11]

I have majored on this article by Canty because it is an accurate summary of his views as an evangelist and preacher. He referred to the sartorial elegance of Willard Cantelon. George Canty never appeared on a platform without being 'correctly dressed' as he saw it. It is also clear that Cantelon impressed him greatly with his artistic skills and, it would appear, George was influenced by Cantelon to develop his own skills in this respect. Those of us who can remember George's painting and preaching gift and who have also seen Cantelon's paintings can readily see where George got his inspiration and style from.

The conclusion to Canty's article on this momentous evening service from the Albert Hall, Easter 1952, puts into perspective the evangelistic style and ministry that he was to adopt whilst conducting his evangelistic campaigns. He pays tribute, not only to the gifted Evangelist but to the 'unknown folk' who played their part in this momentous service:

> The service was in the hands of Pastor Brewster who gave a short Gospel exhortation on the Axe that Cuts, the Fan that Divides, and the Fire that Burns. The scene of converts walking from all parts of the great building down to the platform would be reward enough, I am sure for all Pastor Brewster's labours in the great evening service. And not only for his. During the service I made a note to remember the cores of Crusaders who had worked on their songs and parts. Behind me were rows of contraltos, each individual probably feeling she was making such a small contribution to that volume of harmony, yet faithfully sticking to the part. As Mr Cantelon said, 'God will one day spotlight these unknown folk and great will be their reward.'[12]

George Canty never lost 'the common touch'. He was always in tune with those who worked with him and with his congregation. He inspired young people to take up the mantle of evangelism. In 1967 he conducted a major pioneer campaign in the South Wales town of Port Talbot. He took with him two young men from his congregation in Sparkbrook and infused into them a passion to evangelise. The two young men were Adrian Hawkes and Mark Drew. Hawkes saw Canty very much as his mentor. He was not afraid to go out on a limb. More will be said on his radical evangelism and the sad parting of the way with Elim in the third volume. Drew was also inspired by Canty to take up the mantle of evangelism and, following Brewster's restructure of Elim's evangelistic ministry was launched into full-time evangelism within the Movement.

I will conclude this chapter with Hawkes' comment: 'George Canty would paint an oil painting in each session and then present it to the person who brought the most friends to the meeting. I told him that some people called it a gimmick. His answer was that 'one person's gimmick is another person's excellent idea.' George Canty was endowed with many ideas and the gifting to put those ideas into practice.

The Elim Conference honoured Canty by electing him President (1973-74).

Notes

1 John 19:34

2 Canty, George, *History of Elim, 1915-1983,* ibid, p186.

3 Canty, George, ibid, p186.

4 George Canty lectured on Church History' at Elim Bible because they think my views are out of sync. His lectures were incisive, challenging and illuminating. He made the claim that Elim was the first Christian Movement in the UK that was working class. British Pentecostalism, according to Canty, was birthed in the working-class conurbations of British society.

5 Hawkes, Adrian, *George Canty, October 5, 1911-31 December 2010 (Aged 99).* Elim President 1974-75. Article sent to the Author, Nov. 2022 with permission to include it in this book.

6 The Author experienced a radical change as regards to the leading of the Holy Spirit in his own life and ministry. Being conservative and traditional in his views on the Pentecostal Movement, he was greatly disturbed by the charismatic renewal. There came a point in my life and ministry where I realised that my traditionalism was restricting my ministry. I had just moved to a new church and my predecessor had booked a speaker that I would not have invited. His name was David Woodfield. God spoke to me and gently encouraged me to let the speaker have total freedom. I obeyed and the course of my ministry changed from that point onwards.

7 Hawkes, Adrian, *A Pioneer Dies: George Canty 1911-2021*: ASSIST News Service, 3rd January 2011.

8 Canty, George, *General Reflections on the Evening Meeting: Elim Evangel,* 5th May, 1952, Vol 33, No 18, pp282-283.

9 The Redemption Hymnal had been published a few months earlier

10 Canty, George, *General reflections on the Evening Meeting*: ibid.

Canty, George, *General Reflections on the Evening Meeting*: ibid.

12 Canty, George, *General Reflections on the Evening Meeting*: ibid.

28

Committee on Progress

As has been shown in previous chapters, Elim's main strategy for planting new churches was through the means of evangelistic campaigns. This was certainly the strategy almost to the end of the twentieth century. As has been noted, the Sunday evening service in most Elim churches was referred to as the 'Gospel Service'. Each local church pastor was encouraged to major on evangelism. Pioneer evangelism was a major tool in Elim's survival and expansion following the split with Jeffreys. A study of Elim's history will show how that the method of evangelistic campaigns so miraculously and brilliantly modelled by Jeffreys was revived after the Second World War. It has to be said that the post-war campaigns lacked the impact of Jeffreys' campaigns, but this is explainable by the radical change in British society following the war. Jeffreys himself, found mass evangelism post-1945 a completely different proposition to the twenties and thirties. In those halcyon pre-war years, Jeffreys ministered very much in a revival atmosphere. His emphasis on divine healing had a great attraction to countless thousands of people who had to pay for medical treatment. Furthermore, the change in people's income and the burgeoning leisure industry affected attendances at campaign rallies.

The fact that Elim stabilised and expanded as it did from 1945 onwards is a tribute to the leadership of the Movement and the support of the Conference in the on-going evangelistic programme as emphasised by the 1944 Conference.[1] It is clear that the number of Elim churches more than doubled in the years

1945-1990.[2] Approximately half the number of churches accepted by the Conference between 1950 and 1959 were as a result of pioneering evangelism. It has to be said, however, that a number of such churches that were opened by this method were closed a few years later. However, the same is true of those churches that were commenced as a result of church planting by local churches.

Between the years 1942 and 1979, there were a total of one hundred and thirty-five churches opened and accepted by the Elim Conference. Some of these closed within two or three years of their establishment. The number of churches reported to the Conference as having been closed during this period was twenty-nine. It follows, therefore that during this period, the number of Elim churches had grown by an overall number of one hundred and six. It is very difficult to establish the exact number of Elim churches following the outbreak of the Second World War and the internal difficulties within the Movement. The writer, however, has established that by 1942, the number of Elim churches was at its lowest ebb with just one hundred and ninety-one churches.[3]

Presbyteries

By 1970, the number of Elim churches was 324. This was certainly steady, if not spectacular growth. Of the 135 churches added to Elim's list of churches over this period, forty-two came into being as a result of pioneer campaigns. Some of the others came into being through the efforts of the various Presbyteries. The 1940 Conference approved the setting up of a Presbytery system throughout the country. The presbyteries were formed on a geographical basis. The Conference minutes record the following:

> That District Presbyteries shall be set up with an equal representation of Ministers and Laymen on the lines of the Annual Conference. Probationers of three years standing shall be considered as ministers for this purpose. Laymen and Ministers to have the same qualifications as for those on the Annual Conference. There shall be quarterly meetings of the

District Presbytery. A District Committee shall also be set up. The Minister who is District Superintendent to be elected annually by the District Presbytery. A District Committee shall also be set up in each District, composed of two Ministers and two Laymen with the District Superintendent as Chairman: their main function shall be to extend the work in their District.[4]

It was clearly intended that the Presbyteries should exercise an evangelistic ministry and see to establish new churches within its boundaries. Some Presbyteries were excellent at this, whilst others, due to the geographical size and the scattered churches within found it difficult. The Devon and Cornwall Presbytery, for example, covered a huge geographic distance and journeys between towns and cities that had Elim churches were long. The two main churches in this Presbytery were Plymouth and Exeter. There is a distance of 46 miles between Devon's main cities. Penzance, which has the most westerly Elim church in England, is a further 75 miles from Plymouth. The Welsh Presbytery went from Holyhead in the North-West of Wales to Newport in the South-East, about 170 miles apart. The situation in Scotland was even worse. It extended from Whitehaven in Cumberland to Aberdeen in the North-East of Scotland, a road distance of 267 miles. When churches were opened in Fort William and Wick it added to the huge problems of churches within such large areas coming together to evangelise other towns with the view of planting new Elim churches.

The Birmingham Presbytery was probably the most successful presbytery in establishing evangelistic campaigns and also in opening churches within its boundaries. The following churches were opened and established as the result of the evangelistic policy of the Birmingham Presbytery: Banbury, Great Barr, Yardley, Weoley Castle, Kitts Green, Hanley, Halesowen, Redditch, Wednesbury, Madeley (Telford) and Stirchley. This is not to say that all these churches were formed through the efforts of the Birmingham Presbytery, but a combination of the vision of a local pastor/evangelist and the decision of the Presbytery resulted in these churches being opened. Sometimes, it was the vision and determination of an individual, supported by a local church that resulted in a new church being planted. Such an example was the establishment of the Halesowen Church which is now one of the largest Elim churches in the Midlands.

Brian Cole was the eldest son of Edward Cole, who was one of Elim's leading pastors. Brian was an elder at Birmingham Christian Centre, a church that his father had led for over ten years. Brian was a manager of the Britannia Building Society in Halesowen. Brian, together with a group of friends had a vision for starting a church in Halesowen. The group met regularly for prayer and eventually, a former Congregational church called 'Zion' became available. This was purchased and an Elim church was formed in the town. Eventually, much larger premises became available in the Cornbow district of the town. It was formerly the Webb-Ivory Greeting card building.

The Birmingham Presbytery hired the Town Hall on a number of occasions to hold city-wide crusades. Alex Tee and also the Dutch Evangelist, Hans Koonstra held Evangelistic campaigns in the city that were very successful. On a couple of occasions, Elim linked up with the Assemblies of God and other Pentecostal bodies in the city to present city-wide Full Gospel campaigns. As far as Elim people were concerned, Birmingham was an exciting place to be in the seventies and eighties.

Over the years, however, Presbyteries became less centred on Evangelism and became a centre for fellowship for pastors and laymen. They continued to have a purpose and would meet quarterly. They were often full-day events. There would be prayer fellowship in the morning with an invited speaker. The business would be discussed in the afternoon with a Presbytery Rally in the evening. Over the years, the meetings tended to become stale and pretty sterile. The evangelistic purpose retracted over time until in most presbyteries, it disappeared altogether. Presbyteries were disbanded in the first decade of this century. It was felt that they had served their purpose and a major restructure of the Movement resulted in the setting up of Regions with full-time Superintendents. This will be covered in the third and final volume.

The Progress Committee

It is my opinion that throughout its existence, Elim has always tried to remain true to its 'raison d'etre'. In the inaugural meeting of what was to become 'The Elim Evangelistic Band', held in Knox Temperance Hotel in Monaghan, Ireland, a group of eight young men met for prayer and discussion. One of them, George Jeffreys, was invited to take up permanent evangelistic work in Ireland. The Minute Book records that 'they came together for the purpose of discussing the best means of reaching Ireland with the full Gospel on Pentecostal lines.'[5] Although methods and means of evangelism in general have changed considerably over the years, it is truer today than at any time in the Church's two thousand plus year history that the Christian Church exists for mission. This is the reason that we exist. Elim has always taken this view of mission very seriously. Conference after Conference has emphasised the need to reach the lost with the saving Gospel of Jesus Christ. In addition to the Annual General Conference, other gatherings have been held in which the sole topic was evangelism. Such a Conference was held in Birmingham in October 1973 where three whole days were given to discussing evangelistic themes and ideas.[6]

The 1964 Conference, being aware of Elim's history and the importance of evangelism to the Movement passed a resolution to set up a Committee on Progress. The minute reads as follows:

> The Conference adopted in principle a proposal: That a Committee be set up to examine every department of the Elim work, to make recommendations if desirable for any changes in the Constitution, and outline our policy for future advancement. The Conference also approved that the Committee consist of three Executive Council appointees, three ministers appointed by the Conference, and three laymen appointed by the Conference.[7]

The idea behind the formation of a Progress Committee was an excellent one. There was a strong desire within the Conference, if not to completely overhaul the Constitution, to at least make substantial changes that would result in the Constitution being more readily understood and become a progressive legislative document that made provision for easier changes to it. The fact that the format of the Constitution remains unchanged from its last major revision (1942), some would argue, speaks to the brilliance of the original, whilst others (the author included) is very much of the opinion that the Deed Poll which was legalised in 1934 and revised in 1942 should have been completely re-written years ago. The NLT on the recommendation of the General Superintendent, Chris Cartwright, have made strong efforts to address this matter and, at last, the Deed Poll, General Rules and Working Arrangements, (together with the many Standing Orders passed by Conference over the years, but not included within the wording of the Constitution) and major changes to the 'blessed Constitution' are afoot!

The Progress Committee was, in many ways, ahead of its time. Some notable recommendation of the Committee did not see the light of the debating chamber for many years, but eventually came into being. The committee was in trouble almost from before it held its first meeting. The Conference resolution was quite clear as to the composition of the committee, three Executive Council appointees, three ministers appointed by the Conference and three lay members also appointed by the Conference. There is no record whatsoever in the Minutes of the Representative Session of Conference of the ballot nor the names of those appointed. One presbytery wrote to the Committee expressing its disapproval as to how the members were appointed. The presbytery did not say so, but implied that the voting had been somehow 'rigged'.

Indeed, it was not until the 1971 report to the Conference (which was its last) were the names of the Committee members revealed. The Constitution allowed for the Secretary-General (General Superintendent) to be a member of every Conference committee. It also allowed for the President to be a member during the year in which he served. This resulted in eleven, not nine members as originally intended by the 1964 Conference resolution. As it turned out, all eight members of the Committee were either already members of the Executive Council or were elected to the said Council in years to come. The following were Executive Council members, J T Bradley, H W Greenway, P S Brewster, T W Walker, D B Gray; two other members were appointed to the Executive Council in 1971 (J Lancaster and J C Smyth), the other minister on the committee was L P Cowdery who was elected to the Executive Council in 1981. So, it could be argued (and it was) that the Committee did not have a fair representation of non-Executive members.

The three laymen appointed were: Charles Pendrill (Ilford), Fred Croker, (Romford) and Leslie Northcote (Hove). These three men were qualified in their respective fields of employment. Over the years, Elim has been blessed highly by the quality of the lay representatives that have been members of the Conference and taken an active role within its business. The quality of the reports submitted to the Progress Committee and sub-committees by these men show their abilities to understand the Constitution and to make recommendations for change. Charles Pendrill was appointed the Secretary of the Committee.

Having gone through the very thick file on the 'Committee on Progress', it is evident that the Committee got bogged down on Constitutional matters and lost sight of the little phrase within the original Conference proposal: *'and outline our policy for future advancement'.*[8]

The Interim Report of the Committee on Progress was submitted to the 1965 Conference. The Committee's terms of reference were noted as being threefold:

[1] To examine every department of the Elim Work.

[2] To make recommendations, if desirable, for any changes in the Constitution.

[3] To outline our policy for future advancement.

The report concluded that 'Despite the fact that Pioneer work has become more difficult in recent years, the Committee is convinced that in the interests of the Kingdom of God, and the progress of our Elim Movement, Pioneer Campaigns are essential.'[9] The report went on to suggest that there should be fewer such campaigns but that each campaign should last longer and 'each should be more thoroughly carried out.'[10] One interesting recommendation within the report concerning pioneer evangelistic campaigns was that 'An experienced Minister be appointed Campaign Manager in the early stages of arrangements to organise the distribution of Campaign literature two weeks before the Campaign is due to commence. The manager to work under the jurisdiction of the Campaigner.'[11]

The Evangelistic Committee met with the Executive Council in March 1965 and they discussed the proposals made by the Committee on Progress. The Field Superintendent, Jimmy Morgan wrote to the Committee on behalf of the Evangelistic Committee, he made the following observation and suggestion:

> The purpose of the meeting was to discuss with the Evangelistic Committee the whole policy of Evangelism and (the) Council first considered the recommendations of the Committee on progress which were approved in principle with the proviso that under item 17 – 'Appointment of Full-time Evangelist' the next Council consider the suggestion of the Birmingham Presbytery to set up a Department of Evangelism. It was also agreed to give more time to building up smaller churches by arranging a major campaign where this is felt to be practicable. A 16-point policy for pioneer crusades submitted by A. Tee was approved following certain amendments.[12]

In the same letter, Morgan also drew the Committee's attention to the fact that since the beginning of January, 1965 seven full-time ordained ministers had left Elim. He was deeply concerned about this: 'This is a serious blow to any forward move and we feel the Conference should be informed of this situation and plans made to build up the ministry as a whole, so that we may thrust forward in Evangelism, with ministers available for new churches.'[13]

Members of Conference were invited to submit suggestions and ideas to the Committee for their consideration. A number did so including Frank Lavender and George Canty. Frank Lavender was a senior Elim pastor who was respected throughout the Movement. He became Elim's prayer organiser and was involved in praying for Members of Parliament. In retirement, he took on the task of praying for pastors' children. He took time and made the effort to remember the names of the children and would assure the parents of his prayers for their children. In this respect, he made a huge contribution to the life of the Movement.

Lavender wrote a paper titled 'Headquarters Re-organisation'. He presented this to the Committee. He stated that two years previously, he had proposed resolutions to Conference in which he called for the establishing of departments of Evangelism and propaganda. George Canty was not impressed by the proposals because in typical Canty fashion he argued that 'Evangelism ought not to be just another department, added to those already existing.'[14] Canty visualised evangelism as a spirit permeating the whole work, or the blood reaching every organ within the body. Don House, the lay representative from Winton, Bournemouth objected to the concept on the ground that 'our Headquarters establishment was already unwieldy as a result of a multiplicity of departments and committees.'

Lavender, in his very full submissions to the Committee came forward with some radical suggestions.

[1] To completely reconstruct Headquarters organisation.

[2] Combine all departments into two with two committees.

[3] The appointment of a General Overseer or Superintendent.[15]

[4] The two departments would be Administration and Evangelism.

[5] To combine Home Missions and Foreign Missions under one Evangelistic Department.

Lavender was realistic enough to be aware that although there would be just two departments with two main committees, there would have to be sub-committees of three or four persons so that the load would be more evenly shared and meetings would be more easily arranged. He further suggested that no person should serve on more than one main Committee with the exception of the General Superintendent. 'Further, Committee work must not be treated as of secondary priority: the future of our work is so vital that Committee appointments must be regarded as of fundamental importance and not as prestige positions.'[16]

Lavender's proposals did not see light of day and the Committee, after seven years of meetings, reports and suggestions was allowed to quietly die. I will end this chapter by quoting in full, Lavender's closing paragraph:

> I believe in Elim! I believe that God has raised us up for a purpose and that, no matter how wonderful the early days may have been, God's best for us – and for our world through us – is still in the future. We, who are the heirs of revival, shall see a mightier work of God than our spiritual fathers ever knew. Some who have gone from us because they thought Elim was a sinking ship and that our day was over, will wish with all their hearts to be back among us. Young men, lift your hearts and take courage; you will live to bless God that He gave to you the privilege of serving Him in this Fellowship. I know very well that there can never be any substitute for prayer, faith and hard work if we are to fulfil the purpose for which God has brought us into being. Yet, I believe that an efficient organisation will make a good foundation for the work to be done and will help to ensure that hard work has its reward in the conserving of the gains made.

Notes

[1] Whilst writing this chapter and examining Elim's evangelistic policy throughout it's history, the writer is unable to evaluate the present approach to opening new churches and compare it with the policy of pioneer campaigns. This will be assessed more fully in my third volume.

[2] Exact figures will be presented in the third volume.

[3] From a limited number of year books at the Archives in Malvern, the author saw the figures for 1948 which showed 219 churches. Going through the Conference minutes and

viewing the recording of new churches and the closure of any current church, the author was able to deduce that the number of churches in 1942 was 191 and 28 churches had been added between 1942 and 1948.

4 Minutes of Elim Conference, May 1940, Item 2, p2;

5 Elim Evangelistic Band Minute Book, kept in the office of the General Superintendent of Elim, Elim International offices, West Malvern, Worcs. See Also: Jones, Maldwyn, *And they came to Elim*: ibid, Chapter 7, The Birth of Elim.

6 The author attended this Conference and can testify to its success. It was there that I arranged to meet up with the young lady who was to be my wife.

7 Minutes of the 1964 Representative Session of the Annual Conference.

8 Author's italics.

9 Interim Report of Committee on Progress: Malvern: Elim Archives.

10 Interim Report: ibid.

11 Interim Report: ibid.

12 Letter, James J Morgan to Committee on Progress, 17th March 1965.

13 Letter, James J Morgan, ibid.

14 Lavender, Frank, *Headquarters Re-organisation*, Committee on Progress file, (Malvern: Elim Archives).

15 Lavender maintained that the General Overseer would be the Chief Executive Officer and would co-ordinate the work of the two departments. Evidently, he will be a man of spiritual wisdom and business acumen, able to judge the health of the Movement and to guide its affairs.

16 Lavender, Frank, ibid.

29
Alexander Tee

Whilst Elim has always recognised the five-fold gift ministries of Ephesians 4:11,[1] in church life, it seems that we only train pastors. Certainly, from the time when I was in Bible College, it was only the pastoral role that was open to us. The fact that Elim has, over the years of its history, produced very capable and anointed evangelists is down to the grace of God rather than training. Despite that, however, Elim has produced some outstanding evangelists.

Alexander Tee

Alex Tee was one of Elim's greatest evangelists. He was born in Kilsyth, Scotland on 25th June, 1925. He was raised in a Christian home and he testified to the fact that he received Christ as his personal Saviour. 'It was at my mother's knee in November 1931 where I knelt down and received Jesus Christ as my personal Saviour.'[2] Not only was he brought up in a Christian home, Alex was raised in a Pentecostal home.

Kilsyth was a small mining town some 15 miles north-east of Glasgow. Although a village, it had a number of very well-attended churches within its boundaries. The village was well-known within the early British Pentecostal Movement. John Glass, Elim's General Superintendent (2000-2016) was the pastor of Kilsyth Church of God for seven years prior to his election as General Superintendent of Elim. He says of Kilsyth: 'There must be very few places on earth that have experienced as many significant moves of God as have occurred in Kilsyth.'[3] Glass outlines three specific revivals that occurred within Kilsyth. The third was the Revival of 1908. A new fellowship had commenced in the town in 1902 and a committee of four elders and four deacons was appointed and was called 'The Church of God, Kilsyth.'

When revival fell in A A Boddy's church in Sunderland in 1908, one of the people who flocked to witness the Pentecostal outpouring was Bill Hutchinson, an elder of the Kilsyth Church. This visit, together with the fact that Boddy made a timely visit to Scotland, generated a hunger in the hearts of a number of the Church of God leaders for an outpouring of God's Spirit. On 1st February 1908, the fire fell.

Between thirty and forty people were prostrated on the floor under the power of the Holy Spirit. Crowds flocked to the hall to see what was happening and those who could not get inside climbed up to the windows. In the weeks that followed two hundred people were baptised in the Spirit. Meetings were conducted every night of the week for four months. On a Sunday on which Cecil Polhill, one of the 'Cambridge Seven' who served with Hudson Taylor as part of the China Inland Mission, preached, twenty-eight young people offered themselves for missionary service. The Church of God, Kilsyth, became Scotland's first Pentecostal congregation.[4]

It was into a Pentecostal family that Alex Tee was born. He testifies to being 'gloriously baptised in the Holy Spirit', on 2nd January 1940. 'For almost one hour I spoke aloud in other tongues, hence I would never doubt that this experience is the inheritance of every born-again believer.'[5] Tee goes on to state that three months later, his father baptised him in water. Harry Tee was a presiding elder in the Kilsyth Church of God and he was a great hymnist. One of his hymns became the stirring cry and song from thousands of British Pentecostal throats:

They were gathered in an Upper Chamber,
as commanded by the Risen Lord,
And the Promise of the Father,
there they sought with one accord,
When the Holy Ghost from heav'n descended
like a rushing wind and tongues of fire:
So dear Lord we seek Thy blessing,
with glory now our hearts inspire

Chorus:
Let the fire fall, let the fire fall, Let the fire from heaven fall:
We are waiting and expecting, Now in faith, dear Lord, we call:
Let the fire fall, Let the fire fall, On Thy promise we depend:
From the glory of Thy Presence let the Pentecostal fire descend.[6]

Both the words and the tune were written by Harry Tee. His parents' influence radiated through Alex's life and ministry. He was very much a classic Pentecostal when it came to the doctrine of the baptism in the Holy Spirit. He, like Brewster, his mentor, held strongly to the view that speaking in other tongues is the initial evidence of the Baptism in the Holy Spirit. But throughout the course of his ministry, Tee did not dwell long on the subject of the initial evidence, he emphasised the purpose of the baptism in the Holy Spirit, and that was an enduement with power to proclaim the Gospel. He interpreted Acts 1:8 in a singular fashion: always the soul-winner and born evangelist, Tee would proclaim that the power to witness came on the Spirit-baptised believer as they witnessed. In other words, one only received this blessing as one proclaimed the glorious good news of salvation! Where this places his view on the initial evidence is unclear. What is clear, however, is that Alexander Tee boldly proclaimed the Foursquare Gospel.

Alex Tee was a bold, forthright and inspired preacher. He also inherited some of his father's musical talent. It is evident that from a young age, Alex was conscious of the call of God in his life to preach the Gospel. He left school at the age of fifteen and worked for a railway company in Glasgow. Being a conscientious objector, Alex opted to fulfil his National Service requirements by working in the coal mines where he served three and a half years working underground at Dumbreck Colliery, some three miles east of Kilsyth. Alex's heart was very much in line with becoming a preacher. He and a friend preached regularly in the nearby village of Queenzieburn. In a letter to P S Brewster, Alex added a postscript. 'If ever you need a pianist for your crusades, I would be willing to help you.'[7] This was to lead to a life-long association between these two evangelists.

He applied to be released from the coal mine in Dumbreck. This and his subsequent appeal was dismissed. He then applied to the Minister of Labour, Ernest Bevin. Although sympathetic to Alex, his appeal was turned down. Alex got injured whilst working in the colliery and was signed off work for a month. At the end of the month, he received a letter from the Ministry of Labour informing him that his case had been reconsidered and he was free to take up the appointment of assistant pastor at the City Temple, Cardiff. He commenced his ministry on the first Sunday in January 1947, without any Bible College training.

Tee's first evangelistic campaign was alongside Brewster at a campaign in the Monmouthshire mining town of Pontlottyn. A good church was planted there and it is still functioning as an Elim Church. This campaign, together with the mentorship of P S Brewster set him firmly on the road as one of Elim's three greatest pioneer evangelists. Add to that the large number of church campaigns that he conducted, it is clear that Tee's exemplary evangelistic ministry contributed hugely to Elim's stability and steady growth from the fifties onwards.

Alex Tee was a Scotsman. Almost every word he spoke bore a tartan hue! He never tried to hide his accent, yet, at all times his diction was excellent so although he had a strong mid-Scots accent, one could understand every word he spoke. The passion and power of his preaching made him popular to his Celtic cousins in Wales and Ireland and he was to conduct great campaigns in these two countries. But it was, naturally, Scotland where he conducted his most effective campaigns. He took his first pioneer campaign in Scotland in the town of Kirkintilloch, some six miles from his home town of Kilsyth. This was in 1950 and was a successful campaign. The young pastor appointed to follow on as leader of the new church that was commenced was a young Welshman who was years later to become Elim's General Superintendent. His name was Wynne Lewis. I have just realised that whilst writing this chapter, I have referred to three of the four most prolific evangelists in Elim's post-Jeffreys' history. Percy Brewster, Alex Tee, Ron Jones and Wynne Lewis conducted hundreds of evangelistic campaigns throughout the British Isles. All four of them were not only great evangelists, they were also thoroughly Pentecostal in their ministry. Add to this the following names, Sandy Wilson, George Canty and David Woodfield, we can see how vital the ministry of evangelism was to Elim in the years 1950-1980.

His second, and some would view it, his greatest Scottish campaign was held in the town of Motherwell, Motherwell is a large town situated twelve miles south-east of Glasgow. It was at one time the centre of Scotland's steel production. It is a North Lanarkshire town with a current population of just over 32,000 . The town houses the offices of the North Lanarkshire Council.

It was to this town that Alex turned his attention to in 1952. He formed a close relationship with his cousin Joe Grey and together, they sought out places to launch pioneer campaigns. They commenced campaigning in the spring of 1952. The first meeting was held on 26th April. They held regular services in the Orange Hall in the town every night of the week except Friday. They then hired the Motherwell Town Hall for after-church rallies on Sundays and two hundred and fifty people attended the first rally. In August, they erected a marquee in Mary Street, Motherwell where many people came to faith in Christ. Alex Tee and Joe Grey had a broad approach to the hire of buildings. In this respect, Tee was obviously influenced by his mentor in Cardiff. Brewster used any large hall that he could hire for Evangelistic outreach. He hired cinemas, St David's Hall, the old Sofia Gardens pavilion, amongst many. Tee, taking his cue from Brewster, held several rallies in the Gaumont and Odeon cinemas in the town where congregations in excess of a thousand were sometimes present. The following account appeared in the Evangel when the campaign had finished.

> The pioneer Campaign at Motherwell is now over, but many joyous memories of God's blessing remain with us. As usual in Scotland, the people were very cautious at first but it was remarkable to see how the reserve barriers were broken down and how the tide of enthusiasm rose night after night. We praise God that over 100 decisions were made for Christ.
> At the close of the campaign a great baptismal service was held...A fleet of special buses was chartered to convey the people to the service in Westport Hall, Kilsyth. The building was packed to capacity and after a powerful service a further ten men and women surrendered to the Saviour. It is a long time since we have experienced such a move of God's power in Scotland, and we rejoice that another new church has been opened as a result of the 'Foursquare Gospel.'[8]

It was whilst he was in Motherwell that Alex met Winifred who was a nurse in Edinburgh. They were married in the Town Hall in Motherwell and about nine hundred people were there to witness the marriage.[9]

Not only was Alex Tee a great evangelist, he was also a superb pastor. He stayed and looked after the new church in Motherwell for eight years. The church was given a piece of water-logged land in Airbles Road and after much prayer and sacrifice by the members, a fine building was erected. In Alex's own words:

> After long and difficult negotiations we were given a site in Airbles Road to build our church. It was mainly under water from a spring at its northern end. The church stands today, an imposing fine brick building which cost us £11,750 in all. This was a large sum in those days.[10]

In 1959, after a hugely successful period of ministry in Motherwell, Alex moved his centre of operations to Paisley where he conducted a pioneer campaign with the opening service being held in the Town Hall on 8th September, 1959. Sunday services were held in the Paisley YMCA. Once again Pastor Tee had the arduous task of leading a new congregation of mainly new converts. Such a task was not without its challenges and sacrifice. Initially, he and his wife lived in a caravan in Renfrew. After a while, a three-bedroom house was bought for £2,150 that served as the church manse. Somewhat miraculously, a site on the main road was bought to build a church. It was land that was owned by the Post Office and after demolition of a couple of houses, a smart, purpose-build building was erected for the incredibly low sum of £8000.

Whilst in Paisley, Tee held a number of pioneer campaigns including Clydebank, Coatbridge and Govan. He had a real heart for Scotland. It was at this point that Alex Tee experienced his greatest disappointment and, according to some of the Elim pastors of those days, Elim lost a major opportunity to develop an evangelistic strategy that would have blazed through Scotland.[11]

Following the death of George Jeffreys, the City Temple in Glasgow reverted to the ownership of Elim. It was a huge and impressive church building right in the centre of Scotland's largest city. Alex held a very good campaign in the Woodside Halls in Glasgow:

> I had hoped that when the Glasgow City Temple reverted to Elim, I might be able to take this over and make it a centre of evangelism for the West of Scotland. To my bitter disappointment, the Executive Council sold the building to the proprietors of a dance hall for some £15,000. They, in turn, sold it to a property developer within a year and the building was demolished. This grieved me very much. My mission for a mother church in Glasgow similar to that in Cardiff was dashed for ever.[12]

There are almost always, another side to an account such as this. Whilst indeed, it was the decision of the Executive Council on the advice of Elim Headquarters to sell the building, there were obvious reasons for their decision. At the time, in the early sixties, £15000 was a considerable sum of money. The City Temple, though a beautiful and large building would have been very costly to maintain. The decision to sell it would have had its attractions to the Executive Council. What the money acquired by the sale of the City Temple was used for is unclear. At the time, Elim had a policy that if a church building was closed and sold, the money from the sale, after fees taken or mortgage or any debt cleared, the money was left in trust for the area in which the building was so that it could be used for the opening of a new church at a later date.

Hindsight is a luxury that we cannot afford to indulge in too often. The 'What ifs?' of past decisions can create a frustration that cannot be solved. As great as that disappointment was to Alex Tee, it did not deter him in his evangelistic ministry. Neither was this the end story of Elim in Glasgow. Through the ministry of a succession of good pastors, the Elim Church in Glasgow today is flourishing. A new building was erected and enlarged and the Glasgow Elim Church is flourishing and growing. The current pastor, Fraser Donaldson, is building on the very firm foundations laid down by his predecessors James Glass, Simon Foster, Kevin Peat and Stephen Hilliard.[13]

Following his disappointment regarding Glasgow, Alex Tee was presented with a very different challenge. In 1962 he was appointed as Elim's National Youth Director, a position that he occupied with distinction for a period of ten years. After fourteen years of ministry and evangelistic campaigns in Scotland, it was a case of 'London Calling'. In 1967, Elim Headquarters were moved from Clapham to Cheltenham. As National Youth Director, Alex Tee and his family moved to Cheltenham.

During his time as National Youth Director, the number of scholars in Elim Sunday Schools rose to over 15,000. Evangelism was still the compelling feature in Alex Tee's heart. The number of evangelistic campaigns that he conducted during this ten-year period is quite astonishing. Four of them were pioneer campaigns. Strong churches were established in Northampton, Sunderland

and South Shields.[14] The fourth campaign was in Leamington Spa, but no church was formed as a result of this campaign. He held campaigns involving a number of churches in a number of the country's largest cities including Birmingham and Belfast.

He was appointed Elim's President and served as such from 1969-70. In 1973 he was elected as a member of the Executive Council in which he served for ten years. He served as a full-time evangelist for a short period after leaving Southport where he had been the pastor. He was then appointed to the role of Evangelistic Director, but shortly before he assumed that office, he was asked if he would go as the senior minister to Cardiff at the request of the Church Session of the Cardiff City Temple.

Space does not permit me to cover the many campaigns led by Alex Tee. His name is entered into the annals of Elim's history as one of her greatest evangelists. He was fiery in the pulpit, passionate in his Conference speeches but, in my opinion, he was by nature a little shy, but every inch a gentleman. It is difficult to give the exact number of Elim churches that he pioneered, but it is very clear that only his mentor, the indomitable P S Brewster opened more churches through pioneer evangelistic campaigns than did Alex Tee.

Notes

1 The Author's personal view is that this is a four-fold gift ministry as he is of the opinion that the gift of 'teacher' is linked up with that of 'pastor'.

2 Tee, Alexander, *Handwritten autobiography*, texted to the author by Ian Jones, husband of Sharon, daughter of Alexander and Winnifred Tee.

3 Glass, John, *The Best is Yet to Come*, (Kindle edition, Life Publications 2017), p139.

4 Glass, John, ibid, pp143-144.

5 Tee, Alexander, ibid

6 Tee, Harry, *Redemption Hymnal*: (Eastbourne: Elim Publishing House, 1966), Hymn No 249

7 Tee, Alexander, ibid.

8 Gray, Joe, *Revival blessing at Motherwell, Elim Evangel*, 21st July, 1952, Vol 33, No 29, pp457,458.

9 Tee, Alexander, ibid.

10 Tee, Alexander, ibid.

[11] Wynne Lewis, who was to become Elim's General Superintendent, in a conversation with the author, spoke of how this incredible opportunity to open Scotland for Elim was lost and also of the devastating disappointment this was to Alex.

[12] Tee, Alexander, ibid.

[13] Whilst mentioning the four ministers who were so instrumental in the success of the Glasgow church, it is important to note that there was one member of the congregation who served as a deacon and elder in the ministry of all five pastors of the Glasgow church over the past sixty years and his faithfulness and ministry has been a constant feature in the growth of the church. I refer to Jackie Clark. Such men and women who have stayed and laboured for many years and remained faithful to the cause whilst pastors have come and gone, are often a vital factor in the stability and growth of such churches. There are hundreds of them in churches and fellowships throughout the land, I salute them and thank God for their work and ministry.

[14] Sadly, the South Shields church was closed at the turn of the century, but it was a strong church in its early years.

30
Some Evangelists

Throughout Elim's history, evangelism was expected to be high on the agenda of every local church. Churches, however small, were encouraged to hold evangelistic campaigns. In the 1970's, the Executive Council, in conjunction with the Evangelistic Committee chose a number of Elim churches in towns throughout the country in which to hold evangelistic crusades. Firstly, ten churches were chosen and the 'Ten Towns' evangelism was launched. A campaigner was chosen by the Evangelistic Committee and a grant was provided to the chosen church to enable an evangelistic campaign to be held. This project was considered to be moderately successful and the policy was used again, but this time the number of churches was doubled to twenty, hence they were called 'Twenty Town Crusades'. Evangelistic conferences were held and pastors who felt they had an evangelistic gifting were chosen to lead these crusades.

As a historian, and being the age that I am, it is important that the names of those who carried an 'evangelist' label on them be remembered. Some of the names that I shall now name come out of memory rather than from searches in the archives or from thousands of Evangels. The problem with memory is that it can be selective. But from memory, the following is a list of Elim ministers who displayed a distinct evangelistic as well as pastoral ministry and who were used to conduct evangelistic campaigns.

Willie (William) George was of Welsh origin and he served Elim largely in the South of England. He conducted a number of campaigns including Plymouth and Wembury in the early fifties.

Ronald B Chapman was Elim's Field Superintendent from 1969-1974. He was a pastor with a very keen evangelistic edge. He was a great exponent of open-air evangelism and he was in his element when he was preaching in the open-air. A feature of his evangelism was the training, mentoring and practice of encouraging young people to go with him on evangelistic campaigns. He conducted a campaign in Jersey in the mid-fifties and he took a team of young men with him from the Sheffield church, where he was pastoring at the time. More will be said concerning his work as Field Superintendent and also his missionary service in a later chapter.

Richard Lighton was pastor of City Church Birmingham (then known as Birmingham Christian Centre) for many years. Richard had received a remarkable healing from cancer and this was a factor in his evangelistic ministry. He conducted a number of evangelistic campaigns in various parts of the country.

Archie Biddle was renowned for his children's evangelism in Rotherham where he held Sunshine Corner meetings in the city parks (with permission) where he ministered to literally thousands of children. He had a remarkable evangelistic ministry and was in demand when it came to holding church campaigns.

Alfred Chuter was a native of Eastbourne. He was a popular pastor and evangelist in the fifties and sixties. He was treated with a certain degree of suspicion by some Elim pastors because of his 'deliverance' emphasis. When praying for people, he sometimes felt that there was some degree of demonic activity in the person being prayed for and he would address that demonic influence and rebuke it. Time and space does not permit me to go into great detail on this subject.[1]

Evangelism was the great cry that reverberated throughout Elim in those difficult post-war years. The heart-rendering realities expressed in the 1944 Conference were still fresh in the minds of those who were present. Pastors were discouraged, almost devastated by the state of Elim at that time. They set to pray, and they prayed for a purpose. The delegates to that Conference realised

312

that evangelism was the life-blood of the church and not the sole gift of one man. In God's providence, another man came to the fore, and we have spoken at length about him. But Percy Brewster was not only a superb and outstanding evangelist, he was also a mentor and encouragement to many others. Pioneer evangelism was still the favoured approach to opening new churches and I have named four of the outstanding Pioneer evangelists that rose to prominence within Elim. There are three others who were in great demand as evangelistic campaigners.

Sandy Wilson

Sandy Wilson was an Ulsterman with a great love for his province. He entered the Elim ministry in the late 1940's and was an outstanding pastor/evangelist. He conducted hundreds of campaigns throughout Ireland and quite a few across the Irish Sea. His preaching was clear, forthright and inspired. He developed a musical band who would go with him to the campaigns.

He first came to the attention of Elim Evangel readers when Joseph Smith, the Irish Superintendent and a well loved and respected senior minister in Elim wrote a glowing account of what appears to be Sandy's first major Campaign. Joseph Smith was a long-serving member of the Executive Council and was twice honoured by being elected President by the Elim Conference. Smith was intrigued, to say the least, concerning Sandy Wilson's decision to hold a campaign in the church where he pastored. He was pastor of Saunders Street, later to be rebuilt and situated on the Lower Newtownards Road, East Belfast. Smith pastored the Ulster Temple on the Ravenhill Road, Belfast some one and a half miles away from Saunders Street. I include a large part of Smith's article on Wilson's 'home-made-campaign'.

> When I heard that Pastor Wilson was going to conduct a campaign in his own church my faith did not raise too high. He told me that he was having the help of an orchestral band drawn from various Pentecostal assemblies. That was some

encouragement. But I was not expecting anything like the results which followed. The campaign finished with a total of 172 decisions. There were also testimonies of God's healing power. A woman suffering from rheumatoid arthritis in her hands testified the following week that she was able to do things she had not been able to do for years. Another man suffering headaches for years was instantly healed. A woman suffering from inflammation of the chest and abscess was made completely well, and has been attending the meetings ever since.[2]

Commenting on the great amount of preparation that went into the campaigns, Joseph Smith was deeply impressed by the levels of prayer that went into the preparation for the campaign. Smith himself was a great man of prayer. He commented:

I have never known any band take a campaign on their hearts as these young men did. They fasted and prayed for the success of the meetings. Mr Wilson announced one night that there would be a prayer meeting at 10.00 pm. When I had finished our own prayer meeting, I went along to Saunders Street for this time of prayer. It was a joy to see those young men lay aside the musical instruments, and get down on their knees in real earnest, prevailing prayer.[3]

Following this hugely successful 'home-brewed' evangelistic campaign, Sandy Wilson held a baptismal service in the Ulster Temple, where Joseph Smith was the Pastor. According to Smith, thirty-one 'passed through the waters of baptism. Twenty more intimated their desire to be baptised at the next opportunity. About 800 were present at this service, and seven more were added to those who had already professed salvation.'[4] This report not only speaks of the evangelistic drive and a willingness to take risks by the young evangelist, it is also a great reflection on the generous and encouraging spirit of the Irish Superintendent. The Ulster Temple is a magnificent building, erected on the Ravenhill Road, overlooking Ormeau Park, East Belfast. It was considered to be the centre of Elim in Northern Ireland. Joseph Smith not only pastored this church but was also the Irish Superintendent. The fact that, having concluded his own prayer meeting, he went to Saunders Street to join in their prayer meeting speaks of the encouraging and prayerful nature of the man. Despite the close proximity of the two churches, there was no hint of envy in Joseph Smith at the great success of a young minister so near him. There is a lesson for all pastors here. When you hear of great blessing being poured out on a church near to where yours is situated, rejoice with them and encourage them.

In August of the same year, Wilson conducted a major campaign in Lurgan when, for the first week they hired the Town Hall which was filled to capacity. One hundred and fourteen decision for Christ were registered during that first week. The campaign continued in the church building when a further one hundred and sixteen decisions were recorded. A baptismal service was conducted in the church on the last Saturday night of the campaign when thirty-four converts were baptised in water by Joseph Smith, the Irish Superintendent.[5] A campaign was held in Portadown the following year by Sandy Wilson and team with similar results.

In the summer of 1954, Sandy was invited to England where he conducted a tent campaign in the city of Hull, East Yorkshire. The campaign lasted for three weeks. 'The campaign started with an After-Church rally at 8 o'clock, and at 7.30 you could hear chorus singing right across the Anlaby Road.'[6] Sandy also conducted a short campaign in Rotherham just after the Hull campaign.

Sandy Wilson played a huge role in the growth and development of the Elim work in Northern Ireland. He was, for a number of years, the Irish Superintendent and was a mentor to many of the young pastors. I include the following tribute from one of our retired pastors, Billy McCandless:

> I remember first hearing Pastor Sandy Wilson preach when I was a teenager in my home church, Apsley Street Elim, Belfast and being enthralled with his passionate preaching of the Gospel. Little did I realise then that not many years

later he would become my Superintendent and colleague in the ministry. That change in relationship did nothing but heighten the awe I felt for him then and continue to feel for his memory now. As a young pastor he treated me generously, as an equal and gave me so many opportunities for ministry outside my own church. He was an example of hard work and dedication – pastoring a church, caring for his own family and at the same time dealing with the administrative affairs and giving spiritual leadership to the Elim Church in Ireland as well as being much in demand as a preacher inside and outside Elim.

Pastor Wilson was a gifted evangelist, holding Gospel Crusades in churches, town halls, marquees across the Province. He was always a great encourager of people inspiring many a Pastor to have confidence in God and in themselves when faced with problems in their church. His eye was always on the future of the work in particular on expansion in the South as well as the Northern Ireland and on encouraging the young people of the Movement. It was his inspiring leadership that released funds for expansion into Co Mayo and the opening of the first Elim Youth Centre in Co Down, not to mention his own physical contribution to its renovation and maintenance.

Among my last memories are of him preaching with an obviously weak body and almost sightless eyes. Unable to read the Bible or notes or to see the faces of the congregation, he nevertheless preached with his usual fervour, quoting the Scriptures with accuracy, punctuating his serious message with flashes of humour and completely captivating his audience.

It was an honour to know him, to travel with him, to learn from him and to serve alongside him.[7]

The above warm tribute shows the great respect that those who worked alongside him in Northern Ireland had for him. Sandy's influence went beyond the shores of Ireland, however. His prayers and support were felt on the mission field. His colleagues throughout the whole of the Elim Movement honoured him by appointing him Elim's President in 1978-79.

David Woodfield

David Woodfield was converted through the witness of the Apostolic Church in Shrewsbury. He trained as a nurse and became a RSN before responding to the call of God and entering the Elim Bible College in the early sixties. David is a gifted musician and he became a member of the 'Gospel Evangelaires', the College male singing group.

David was very much a pastor-evangelist. He was an assistant pastor to Ron Jones in Bristol and soon became involved in some of Ron's campaigns. He was pastor of the Newcastle Elim church before being appointed to Selly Oak Elim church, Birmingham. Throughout his ministry, David has tried to be open to the leading of the Holy Spirit. He was never afraid to innovate. Whilst leading the church in Selly Oak, he invited a missionary who was based in Argentina to speak at the church. The name of the man was Ed Miller. There was a remarkable outpouring of the Holy Spirit and expressions of worship started taking place in the church that was quite unusual as far as Elim churches were concerned. There was a sense of unbridled joy and worship in the meetings. People praised the Lord with an abandonment that was frowned upon by some Elim ministers, including myself. As for people dancing before the Lord in the services, well....enough said!

David's evangelistic gifting was evidenced and he conducted a number of evangelistic campaigns throughout the country. David exercised a definite prophetic ministry and frequently gave words of knowledge inspired by the Holy Spirit when he preached. He had a profound effect on me. He was invited by a predecessor to preach at an Easter convention at one of the churches I pastored. This arrangement was in situ when I arrived and I was not too pleased about it. David Woodfield was far too radical for this Welsh traditional Pentecostal. Whilst praying about David's visit, I became conscious of God speaking to me and the gist of His message to me was that I must allow the speaker total freedom. This I did, and it had a profound impact upon my future ministry.

The Stirchley Elim church was birthed from Selly Oak and Woodfield gave considerable encouragement to the establishment of this new church plant. He was involved in the pioneering of the Redditch church which today is flourishing under the ministry of Robin Baker. David conducted a city campaign in Norwich when I was the minister there. We booked and filled the St Andrew's Hall for four nights before continuing the campaign back in the church. A number of people came to faith in Christ during that campaign and were added to the church.

David was appointed Elim's Director of Evangelism in 1980. Woodfield had given full proof of his evangelistic credentials and he fitted perfectly into the new evangelistic strategy of the Movement. He succeeded his friend Wynne Lewis who was the Evangelistic Director prior to his move to Kensington Temple, London. After about one year in the office, David resigned as Evangelistic Director. He spent a short time in the USA before returning to Britain and took up the position of Pastor of the newly established Christian Life Centre in Selly Oak. The church at the time was not linked to Elim, so his Elim credential was withdrawn.

The Christian Life Centre became part of the Elim Church Incorporated. [8] Woodfield gained a credential as an ECI minister. Some years later he moved to Birmingham City Church (then named Birmingham Christian Centre) to work alongside Richard Lighton, the senior pastor. He regained his credential as an Alliance[9] minister. Woodfield became a Regional Superintendent and became a member of the National Leadership team. He was also involved in teaching at Regents Theological College in Nantwich. True to his evangelistic zeal, he became involved in the small campus church and it grew considerably. It is now a healthy fellowship under the leadership of Michelle Nunn, Elim's first female NLT member.

Wynne Lewis

Idris Wynne Lewis was a native of Carmarthenshire and was born in the village of Llannon on 7th July, 1932. Wynne was to become the senior pastor of Kensington Temple and General Superintendent of Elim. There will be more written concerning his last twenty years before retirement in the third volume.

Wynne was a gifted evangelist. He was also a caring and faithful pastor.[10] He was a proud Welshman and a first language Welsh speaker like myself.[11] Wynne entered Elim Bible College in 1950 and was appointed the pastor of the new Elim Church in Kirkintilloch, Scotland. It was the first church pioneered by Alex Tee. In his long years as a pastor, Wynne led just six churches; four of them were new churches: Kirkintilloch, Bridgend, Derby and Luton. 'He was a popular preacher and was frequently asked to speak at churches and meetings around the country and it was in 1955 whilst preaching in Wales, that he met Carol his wife, for the first time.'[12]

In 1976, Wynne Lewis was appointed Evangelistic Director of Elim, during which time he was responsible for the planting and support of a number of churches. Wynne was a man of keen vision. He was also prepared to try innovative means of evangelism. This sometimes got him into difficulties with the leaders of the Movement, but Wynne's set purpose in life was to evangelise and this he did throughout his life.

Notes

[1] To the age-old controversy within Pentecostal circles as to whether or not a Christian can be possessed by demons, the writer is of the clear opinion that a Christian – one who has given his life to Christ – cannot be demon possessed. However, a believer can sometimes provide a platform for demonic activity to influence the Christian to such a degree that the person concerned can become bound by demonic activity from the outside. In such a situation, the believer needs to be delivered and this can be done if the believer wants to be delivered. This is a very profound subject and I only mention it here because the ministry of Deliverance did become a feature of evangelistic meetings from the seventies onward.

[2] Smith, Joseph, *Revival in Belfast: Elim Evangel* 3rd March 1932, Vol 33 No 9, p139

[3] Smith, Joseph, ibid.

[4] Smith, Joseph, ibid.

[5] Sewell, S, *Elim Evangel*: 13th March 1943, Vol 35, No 11, p123.

[6] Conversions in the Big Tent at Hull: Elim Evangel, 11th Sept 1954, Vol 35, No 47, p 424

[7] Pastor William McCandless, tribute sent to the Author, 22nd Dec 2022.

8 ECI is a fellowship of churches both in the UK and internationally that are in fellowship with Elim, accept Elim's statement of faith and to a certain degree accept the leadership and discipline of the Elim Movement. Churches coming into ECI are now encouraged to become full members of the Alliance.

9 This refers to the Elim Foursquare Gospel Alliance which is the official name of Elim.

10 When I set out to write the history of Elim, I thought it would be easier for me to write about my contemporary colleagues and those a few years ahead of me than it was writing about those whom I did not know for historical reasons. It has turned out to be the other way around. Wynne Lewis was a friend. He encouraged and helped me through the course of my ministry. I consider David Woodfield a personal friend. I first met David sixty years ago at the Elim Youth Camp in Cornwall. Both these men have impacted my life. It is difficult writing about them from a historical point of view because they were and still are a part of my personal story.

11 This was a source of mischief-making between the two of us. I was born in North Wales and speak North Wales Welsh. Although it is the same language, the dialects are different. I, of course, proclaimed loud and clear that North Wales Welsh is superior to that spoken by our southern neighbours. Wynne always rose to that challenge!

12 *A Celebratory Tribute to Rev Wynne Lewis*, p5.

31
The Missionaries

At the 1945 Conference, Elim took the huge decision to set up its own Missionary department to send out and support missionaries under the Elim banner. Up to this time, Elim had seconded missionaries to work in various Missionary organisations such as the 'Congo Evangelistic Mission'. 'After some discussion on the missionary work it was decided that a committee be set up to investigate fully the position of Elim Missionaries and Elim Associate Missionaries in their relation to other Missionary Societies with a view to commencing an Elim Foreign Missionary Society.'[1] This was a momentous decision and it was met with overwhelming support throughout the Elim family.

From that point onwards, there was certainly an increased interest in Elim missions work overseas and there was an up-turn in candidates applying to serve as Elim missionaries. It is not possible for me to write an account of all Elim missionaries between 1940 and 1980. I will write short accounts of what I would term 'pioneer' missionaries.[2]

John and Gladys MacInnes

John MacInnes was a Scot from the west Scotland industrial town of Greenock. He was converted through the ministry of Samuel Gorman, the first pastor of the Greenock Elim Church following the hugely successful pioneer campaign in 1929. John responded to the call of God on his life, entered Elim Bible College and was appointed to Armagh. He was a natural evangelist and was involved in campaign work in Northern Ireland. He later became pastor of the Neath Elim Church where he met his wife, Gladys. John was aware that his main calling was to be a missionary. At first he had China on his heart, but this became impossible because of the governmental restrictions in China. Africa was another field that the Elim Missions Board suggested to MacInnes. Ultimately, British Guiana became the country that both the missionary and the board agreed would be the right place for John and Gladys MacInnes to go to. After farewelling from Greenock on the 22nd March 1949 where there were 600 people present at the Elim church there, Pastor and Mrs Mac, as they became fondly called by their new congregation(s) in British Guiana[3] arrived in Georgetown in May 1949.

From the very beginning of his ministry in this, the only British colony in South America, John MacInnes set out an aggressive programme of evangelism involving himself in a wide area of church work which took him to countless open-air meetings, hospitals, prisons and even to a leper colony. John and Gladys were terrific workers and soon, out of virtually nothing, Elim established a mission in Guyana which today, has 30 plus churches.

Most of the population of Guyana live around the coastal area of the country. The interior was sparsely populated by the native Indian tribes. Guyana is bisected by two huge rivers, the Essequibo and the Demerara. Quite early on, Pastor Mac crossed the Demerara River which was two miles wide at the point of crossing. He went on an ancient ferry to visit the only TB hospital in the country. There he found hundreds of patients from all over the colony and among them were Indians from the interior. He visited all the wards giving out Gospel leaflets and chatting with the patients and shared the good news of Christ and His saving grace with them.[4]

Pastor Mac loved going into the interior. In his letters and reports to Headquarters he frequently mentioned his trips. During visits to the lumberjacks and the Amerindians he led many to Christ. 'The journey was made by steamer, train, motor-launch, canoe, motor-truck and on foot, with the missionary sleeping in all kinds of places and under varying conditions.'[5] The following is an account given by McInnes himself:

> Journeying up the Essequibo in the 40-foot motor-launch the river seemed just like a long wide lake, and we were 100 miles inland from the sea. On both banks the jungle comes right down to the river. One of the passengers had a mandolin, and as I sang choruses, he soon picked up the tunes and the others picked up the words. They listened well to the Gospel and accepted and read the tracts handed to them. Mile after mile and hour after hour we moved along without seeing another boat or human being…At night we tied up to the bank as there were rapids ahead which could not be negotiated at night, even in the light of the glorious tropical moon. Immediately after sunrise we launched out into the deep. We passed through two series of rapids, the Trickery and Crab Falls. The skill of the man in charge of the boat was amazing. The water rushed past at a tremendous speed as he steered the launch between the rocks with his paddle fixed to the stern. One false move and a hole would have been ripped in the launch.[6]

Through John's long ministry in Guyana, thousands of people came to know Christ and many Elim churches were established. His son Ian and his wife Valerie, joined his father and mother in Guyana and stayed for a while after his parents had retired. Later on, Bill and Ethel West went out on a number of occasions to Guyana to teach and help the churches in any way they could. Bill was past retiring age when he and Ethel went to Guyana for the first time.

The one area of John MacInnes' remarkable ministry in Guyana was his ministry in the leper colony twenty-two miles away from Georgetown. On any given Sunday, John would conduct a bible class, preach in two Elim churches in Georgetown in the morning. He would then cycle the twenty-two miles to the colony, minister to the lepers and then cycle back to Georgetown in time to take an evening Gospel Service. He did this in the scorching tropical heat of Guyana. Executive Council members who visited Guyana during John's ministry were astounded at his work, his compassion and his love.

The Elim Evangels informed the readers of the activities of missionaries. The missionaries themselves would write letters and reports that were published in the Evangel. John MacInnes was a frequent Evangel contributor. He sometimes wrote under the heading of 'A day in the life of a Missionary'. His report in the 16th January, 1954 Evangel shows the Sunday routine of the MacInnes family who had two sons. His day commenced with a prison service at 7.30 a.m.

> In the cool of the morning, I cycled to the prison and at 7.30 we commenced our service. It is a pity a pit to see the young black men and East Indians (first timers) mingled with the old hardened criminals. They do enjoy the singing, especially the black men, and soon they were singing on top of their voices, the old hymn: 'There is life for a look at the crucified One.' The singing could be heard all over the prison and even outside the walls. We ministered the word of life to a large and attentive congregation.

The missionary then wrote of the rest of his day's activities that Sunday. There was a Sunday School at 9.30 a.m. at which 96 were present. At 11.00 a.m. communion was celebrated in the morning service. In the afternoon heat he cycled to a town called Ruimveldt to conduct another Sunday School. From there he proceeded to Georgetown for the Gospel Service at 7.00 p.m. There were 92 present and John was encouraged to see the number of men in the meeting. A normal Sunday, one would think. John went on to write the following:

> At 9.00 p.m. quite a number of our people gathered at the quay, not for a meeting this time, but for a parting. They had walked the two miles from Georgetown to wish our boy Ian, God-speed as he embarked for Scotland for his education. Among those gathered were a number of black boys from the

Sunday School and who had been Ian's playmates. They were crying at the thought of parting. During the prayer meeting on the quay, one brother of African descent prayed "God bless our little brother who is leaving us.' In the cabin we knelt and prayed together and committed Ian – who is 13 years of age – to the Lord's keeping, for he was travelling alone, yet not alone. It was hard to look on at the parting of Ian and Philip (the younger brother). They hugged and kissed each other and wept. The ship's gramophone was playing, 'It is time to say good-bye'. At 11.00 p.m. we saw the 'Amakura' cast off her last moorings, and with three blasts of her siren, slip out into the river, then out into the Atlantic to be smothered up by the darkness. In 16 to 18 days, it will arrive in Liverpool. We turned homeward with the thought, 'There will be no parting there, in my Father's House.'

The above lengthy report reveals the huge family sacrifices that missionaries have made over the years. This pattern was repeated many times and the heartache of separation between parents and missionaries when children left and returned to the home country to pursue their education. In 1967, Pastor and Mrs P S Brewster visited Guyana. 'What they saw and heard astounded and humbled them as they considered the dedication that had brought the work into being.'[7] In a report published in the Evangel, Brewster wrote of what he had seen in Guyana, highlighting the MacInnes' work among the lepers.

Our missionaries, John and Gladys MacInnes have laboured for God in South America for eighteen years…They are tireless and versatile in their dedication and have early morning prayer meetings at 6 o'clock. How they love these people; and nothing seems too much trouble for them to do for the aged members of the assembly.

When Pastor and Mrs MacInnes obeyed the urge to Guyana eighteen years ago, they virtually started their pioneer missionary work from nothing. A few children gathered in their home, they preached in the open-air, and eventually won a few precious converts for the Lord. Thus, Elim was born in

Guyana. Today, they have a beautiful church, a home and several outstations run by the local men. They have a regular ministry in the local prison and a tremendous ministry in the leper colony. The church is very well attended and their thriving Sunday school fills the church to overflowing.

Over 300 lepers, men, women and children, most of them in the advanced stage of this dreadful disease, will ever bless the day that Pastor and Mrs MacInnes came to Georgetown. I personally spoke to almost forty lepers who could all testify to their personal salvation, and so many have been led to Christ through the ministry of our Elim missionary. How these unfortunate lepers love this compassionate man of God. He prays for them, lays hands upon them, takes them in his car and has absolutely no fear of the disease at all. Some had no eyes, no hands, no legs. Others had shapeless bodies. Some lay on the floor. Others hid behind curtains to hide their dreadful condition. In spite of all this, those who were saved were full of the joy of the Lord and thanking Him for His goodness in saving them.[8]

The above report serves as a glowing tribute to a man, together with his wife and two sons who served and laboured so sacrificially, and established a work, almost out of nothing, that is still active and growing. John MacInnes, upon his retirement, became pastor of the Elim church in Armagh for a three-year period. He was the only Missionary who was elected President of Elim (1976).

George Thomas

George Henry Thomas (1892-1970) was a Welshman from Dowlais, South Wales. He, and his wife Maud were married in 1917 and worshipped in an Anglican (Church in Wales) church. The Church in Wales was disestablished in 1915, but its liturgy was Anglican with a strong sacramental approach to worship. The arrival of George Jeffreys to Dowlais in 1920 impacted this young couple greatly. They witnessed the many miracles of healings that took place in Dowlais when George and Stephen

Jeffreys campaigned in this heavily industrialised town adjoining Merthyr Tydfil. A former Welsh Methodist chapel was bought and such were the miracles that took place in the early years of its existence that crutches, walking sticks, spinal supports and all manner of instruments used to support broken or paralysed limbs were festooned around the building. I remember as a young man attending a meeting in the old church and seeing these implements tied on to pillars. It was a visual reminder of what God had done in the past.

The Dowlais Elim church had a strong Spanish connection. Merthyr was very much a coal, steel and iron Town. The Cyfarthfa steel works employed thousands of workers. They came from all parts of the country and from outside the U.K to work in the steelworks of Merthyr and Dowlais. Among the workers from the European mainland was a group of Spanish steel workers. By 1911 there were 264 Spaniards living in the borough of Merthyr Tydfil. A number of these Spanish workers were converted and became members of the new Elim Church in Dowlais. George and Maud soon became involved with the 'Spanish' work of the church and they both learned to speak the Spanish language. With their hearts on fire for God and a love of the Spanish language, it is not surprising that they felt a call to serve God further afield than Dowlais and Merthyr. They were among the first to enrol in the Elim Bible College when it opened in 1925. A year later, they set off for Mexico and associated with a few American missionaries there. Their intention was to set up an Elim work in Mexico. They faced enormous difficulties in Mexico and they moved to San Diego, just across the U.S.A border in California. There they set up a Bible School for Mexican Bible students and stayed there until 1932. They moved to the town of Ronda in Spain in 1933 and spent their time on literature distribution and evangelism and a church was planted in Ronda.[9] The Spanish Civil war, followed closely by the Second World War resulted in the Thomas' moving back to Britain.

It is George Thomas' role as Elim's Missionary Secretary that is worthy of consideration when it comes to mentioning key Elim missionaries. He was appointed to the position by the 1944 Elim Conference on the recommendation of the Executive Council. 1944 was a key Conference for Elim as has been mentioned in an earlier chapter. The Conference minute reads as follows:

> After some discussion on the missionary work, it was decided that a committee be set up to investigate fully the position of Elim Missionaries and Elim Associate missionaries in their relation to other Missionary Societies. It was also decided that members of the Elim Foreign Missionary Council be appointed annually by the Conference and that the number of members be 9, Elim Missionaries on furlough being invited as a usual practice to sit on the Missionary Council, such Council to have power to co-opt a representative from the Elim Pentecostal Churches (previously known as the Essex Elim Churches).[10]

The recommendations of the 1944 Conference were instituted and the Elim Missionary Department (now known as Elim International Missions Department) came into being. George Thomas was appointed as the Missionary Secretary in 1944 and served in that position until 1958. During this time he also pastored the Thornton Heath Elim Church and was a frequent speaker at Rye Park Elim Church also.

Leslie Wigglesworth

Leslie was the Grandson of Smith Wigglesworth.[11] Leslie went to the Congo in 1933 in response to the call of God. He went to work with the Congo Evangelistic Mission which was established by William Burton and James Salter. He returned to the U.K. and married Ruth Boulton, the daughter of E C W. Boulton and they both returned to the Congo, but this time under the auspices of Elim. They left shortly after the Second World War commenced. Ruth was a trained nurse and her contribution to the ministry in the Congo was to prove significant. Leslie and Ruth were based at Katenta a province that took six days to cross from north to south.

One of the challenges regularly put to Leslie by the natives while on trek was the question why the missionaries would always keep to set paths when in the bush, there were thousands who had never ever heard the Name of Jesus. Eventually, after all possible sorts of delays, Leslie managed to reach such an area and found great acceptance of the message, with requests for a soon return. Despite much prayer, there was always official restrictions on sending native evangelists into those areas but, just about one week before he was due to leave on furlough, permission was granted and the work opened up.[12]

The story of the Congo (Zaire) Evangelistic Mission is truly inspiring. Elim's involvement in that Mission was significant. Peter Smith gives a full and inspiring account of Elim's significant contribution to this work, in his book 'Global Mission'. My main reason for writing about Leslie and Ruth Wigglesworth is that after fifteen years working in the Congo, they returned with their family to England in 1953. Leslie was appointed Missionary Secretary in 1964 and served in this role for 14 years until his retirement in 1978.

I have chosen to highlight the work of these three Elim missionaries because one of them, John MacInnes opened up an entirely new mission field for Elim and established a strong work in Guyana. Thomas and Wigglesworth, having both served for many years as missionaries, were appointed to head up the department of International Missions for Elim. Wigglesworth was succeeded by David Ayling who was appointed International Missions Director in 1978.

Notes

1 Minutes of the Representative Session of Conference, 1944.

2 Peter Smith has written an anecdotal account of the history of the work of Elim Missionaries (1919-1989) titled: Global Warming, (Antrim Printers, 2006)

3 The country changed its name to 'Guyana' on gaining independence from Britain.

4 Smith, Peter, *Global Warming, an anecdotal history of the work of Elim Missions 1919-1989* (Antrim: Antrim Press, 2006).

5 *Elim Evangel,* 13th May, 1950: Vol 31, No 20, pp250,251.

6 *Elim Evangel,* ibid.

7 Smith, Peter, ibid, 218.

8 Brewster, P S, *Elim Evangel,* Vol 48, No 39, p620,621

9 Smith, Peter, ibid, p79.

10 Minutes of the Representative Session of Conference 1944, Malvern: Elim Archives.

11 Smith Wigglesworth is a household name in Pentecostal circles not just in the U.K. but world-wide. He exercised an incredible healing ministry, but was somewhat eccentric in the way that he sometimes prayed for people. Towards the end of his life, he attended the Elim Church in Bradford together with his son-in-law James Salter.

12 Smith, Peter, ibid, p90.

32
Presidents

The office of President was instituted in 1946 when E C W. Boulton was elected as Elim's first president following the departure of George Jeffreys. This role was largely an honorary one and was granted to those ministers who had played significant roles within the Movement. Most of the Presidents appointed from 1946 until 1990 when the office was discontinued, were members of the Executive Council (NLT). This chapter will highlight those ministers who were not members of the Executive Council but were honoured by their colleagues to serve as President.

William John Hilliard (1907-1974)

William Hilliard was elected vice-President at the 1962 Conference and was inducted to the office of President by his predecessor Douglas Gray. I am indebted to his son, Stephen a retired Elim minister himself, for details of his father's ministry. Stephen's account is worth quoting because he shows the opposition that early Pentecostals received from the evangelical community.

> William was born in Glasgow on 13th August 1907, into a Baptist family, and accepted Christ as Saviour when aged about twelve. In his teens he began preaching in churches and mission halls around the city, whilst working in a wholesale warehouse. At the same time, he studied part-time in a local Bible College, with a view of entering the Baptist ministry. During this period, he experienced, in the privacy of his own room, what he later recognised to have been the

Baptism in the Holy Spirit. Not understanding what had happened, but feeling sure it was of God, he told no-one what had taken place. In early 1927, he attended George Jeffreys' pioneer campaign in Glasgow and immediately knew where he belonged. He left the Baptist church where his father was a deacon, in May 1927, and joined the City Temple. He was quite shaken by the sharp rebuke of the Baptist pastor at his decision to join the 'tongues people', probably his first experience of the odium in which Pentecostals were held by many evangelicals, but he knew he had taken the right step. Soon his parents and sisters followed him into Elim.[1]

Following the evening service at the City Temple on Sunday 29th July 1928, William Hilliard was approached by the pastor, Joseph Smith who was also Irish Superintendent at the same time, if he would accept a pastoral appointment in Ireland. Having prayed over the request and accepted the appointment the following day he was inducted as pastor of Moneyslane and Rathfriland Elim churches on the 12th August. The following August he was moved to Lurgan where he stayed for another year and shared accommodation with Edward Cole, the pastor at Annaghanoon. He served as pastor of Melbourne Street, Belfast from May 1930-August 1931. Whilst there, he undertook evangelistic campaigns with Edward Cole in Ballymena, Portadown, Banbridge and Annaghanoon. It was in Melbourne Street that he met his wife-to-be, Anna Fleming. His courtship with a church member resulted him being moved from Northern Ireland. He was obviously very well regarded as a pastor and preacher in that he was appointed to large churches on the mainland whilst still a young man. He served as pastor of Southport Elim church (1931-1934) and was ordained at Kensington Temple on 16th December 1932. He then moved to Bath and spent a few weeks looking after the Nottingham City Temple following the sudden resignation of W G Channon.

William and Anna were married in Melbourne Street on 7th July 1935 and their first church as newlyweds was Aberdeen. Together they served in Sheffield, Swansea, Bradford, York, Springbourne in Bournemouth and Greenock. After serving the Movement as President, he and Anna moved to Halifax and then to his last church before he retired – Ipswich. He retired in 1972. William was the second non-Executive Council pastor to be appointed President, the first being T.H Stevenson. William Hilliard was a quiet, thoughtful man. He was a fine pastor and was loved and respected by people throughout the Elim family.

Leslie W Green

Leslie Green served as Elim President in 1968-1969. He was inducted as President at the Conference held at Pontin's Holiday Camp, Blackpool by his immediate predecessor Ron Chapman. Leslie Green was short in stature but high in personality. As a preacher, he was in high demand throughout the Movement. He got quite excited when preaching and was full of life when he preached. He displayed nature and character when he preached and could cause a reaction from his listeners. He could get gales of laughter from the congregation and, in the same sermon would cause tears to flow as he wept whilst preaching.

Leslie Green was one of the first Elim preachers I heard. He was the pastor of Caerphilly Elim church at the time. I was fascinated and spell-bound by his preaching. He was a superb orator and would quote Scriptures, hymns and poems with great feeling and pathos. He was in great demand as a convention speaker and had a proven ministry of leading people into the baptism in the Holy Spirit.

Pastor Green was an outstanding children's evangelist as well as being a fine pastor. He was an excellent theologian and served on the Bible College synod for a number of years. He was approached by the Executive Council to be principal of the Elim Bible College in succession to James Bradley but did not accept the invitation. He was very popular and much loved in Wales. He was the pastor of three Elim churches in Wales, Pontypridd, Swansea and Caerphilly. He had an excellent understanding of the Welsh temperament. His last pastorate before his retirement was Paisley in Scotland. He and his wife had one son, Derek who followed his father into the Elim ministry and became Youth Director and was for many years a member of the Executive Council.

Jack Osman

Jack Osman was a Welshman from Swansea. He was a prominent member of the Swansea church and served as a deacon. He and his wife May were tireless workers in the Swansea Elim church, especially during the ministry of H W Greenway. May wrote a glowing, personal tribute to 'her pastor' in the Evangel following Pastor Greenway's death. I mention this because, in my opinion, the best pastors are those who were always supportive of their own pastors whilst they were local church members. Jack Osman was a fine pastor.

He was one of the few post-war pastors who did not go into Bible College before entering the Elim ministry. He served in a bi-vocational capacity in Aberdare. His first full-time appointment was in Selly Oak, Birmingham. He was the pastor of that church for eight years and the church grew considerably through his ministry. From Selly Oak, Jack hopped across the city to become the Pastor of Sparkbrook Elim church. From Birmingham, he moved to Springbourne Elim church in Bournemouth where he led the church there until his retirement.

Jack Osman was a great pastor, a sound Bible-teacher and a good evangelist. He was one of two Welsh preachers at the Trafalgar Square open-air meeting on Easter Monday 1960, the other being Wynne Lewis. In reporting the meeting in the Evangel, the writer was obviously impressed by Osman's preaching

> Rev. J. Osman, minister of Selly Oak Elim Church, was introduced. He spoke with directness and firmness. We were conscious right from the commencement of his message that God was speaking through him. This was the needed finale under God to convince the unsaved and bring them to Christ. He considered it a privilege to preach from the plinth

334

of Nelson's column, but reminded us that we were celebrating a greater victory than any Nelson had ever known, for our conqueror (unlike Nelson) 'is not dead, but He is alive.' 'What is news?' he asked, 'Is it the Aldermaston march, the royal wedding or the slaughter on the roads? No! It is that Jesus is alive. The resurrection,' declared Mr. Osman, 'sets the seal of authenticity on every promise in the book'.[2]

Jack Osman was gifted in leading Christians into being baptised in the Holy Spirit. Not long after moving to Plymouth to pastor the Elim church, I felt the need to invite someone who was gifted at leading people into the baptism in the Holy Spirit. I recommended that we should invite Jack Osman. Through his anointed ministry in the week that he was with us in Plymouth, some sixty people testified to being baptised in the Holy Spirit.

Jack was a great encourager to young pastors starting out on their ministry. He was my District Superintendent when I was a very young and raw pastor at Eastleigh. Although there was quite a difference in our ages, we struck up a friendship and I was honoured to be asked to speak at his funeral service. Jack Osman was the Elim President 1979-1980

Gerald Ladlow

Gerald Ladlow was a native of the city of Sheffield in South Yorkshire. Together with Margaret his wife, they made a considerable contribution to the Elim work both here in the UK and overseas, especially Ghana. Gerald was ordained prior to the Second World War. He exercised a strong evangelistic ministry during his early years with Elim. In this historical account, Gerald Ladlow's prominence was first witnessed during the unpleasant situation in Portsmouth where he accompanied Phillips, Smith and a private detective when Elim made it clear that they were going to repossess the church building. Gerald Ladlow was installed as the new Elim Pastor.

Ladlow pastored a number of Elim churches including Motherwell. He and Margaret had long felt a call to be more involved in International missions. He was a member of the International Missions Board. He also served as Secretary of the Elim Evangelistic Band for a number of years.[3]

Gerald Ladlow held successful pastorates within Elim. He led a total of twelve churches in Elim, but it must be borne in mind that four of these were only one-year appointments because pre-1939, Elim would move ministers once they had been in a church for twelve months.[4] Ladlow entered Elim Bible College in 1933 and did a year's course. Between 1934 and 1938 he was the pastor at Preston Park (Brighton), Llanelli, Thornton Heath and Dundee. He was at Hendon (1938-1941) where he would have led his congregation through the trauma of the blitz. Then followed the appointment to Portsmouth where he stayed for four years and made a huge contribution in re-establishing the Elim church there. The next move was to Glasgow where he stayed for six years. He and the family then moved to Vazon, Guernsey (1951-1955) Then followed the Ladlows' longest period of ministry, this was in the Ulster Temple, Belfast (1955-1964) The family then moved to Motherwell (1969)[5]

David and Margaret Mills went as missionaries to Ghana in 1966 and linked in with five churches that had been established by a Ghanaian citizen, Rev Tonbi. A situation arose that threatened the stability of the work, and at an early stage in the work, Ladlow was asked to visit Ghana to help sort out the difficulty. Gerald felt that his input had been unacceptable, but that was not the case. He and Margaret went out to Ghana for a year after leaving Motherwell. Their ministry was greatly appreciated. Margaret Ladlow was a very warm and kind lady. She came across as being everyone's mum. She was a good preacher and spoke at many women's rallies and conventions in the U.K. They returned to the UK and were appointed to the Elim church in Salisbury (1970-1974) Following their time in Salisbury, they made the huge decision to go to Ghana as full-time missionaries. In the meanwhile, Elim had linked up with the Church of Pentecost. The Executive of the Church of Pentecost asked Gerald Ladlow to take over the organisation of setting up a radio programme. This went out regularly on a Monday at 9.45 p.m. Gerald became the Radio Pastor and had responsibility for answering the letters and enquiries that arrived from all over the country.[6] The association between Church of Pentecost and Elim remains strong to this day. There is no doubt that the immense work put in by David and Margaret Mills, Gerald and Margaret Ladlow, and Lionel and Ruth Currie[7] played a huge role in creating and maintaining this close link between the two Movements.

Gerald Ladlow was honoured by Elim and was appointed President (1980-81) Although he had reached retirement age, they continued in active ministry after Gerald's term of office as President. He became the pastor of the new Elim church in Southey Green, Sheffield and during his five years there, established a small but stable church.

Below is a table with the names of all the Presidents that were elected to serve in that capacity by the Elim Conference. Those Presidents who served also as Executive Council members are indicated with an asterisk. Five men were elected to serve the Movement as President on two occasions: they were E C W Boulton, Joseph Smith, P S Brewster, W Ronald Jones and T W Walker.

Elim Presidents 1946-1988	
1946-1947	Ernest C W Boulton*
1947-1948	Samuel Gorman*
1948-1949	William G Hathaway*
1949-1950	Joseph Smith*
1950-1951	James T Bradley*
1951-1952	Ernest C W Boulton*
1952-1953	Percy S Brewster*
1953-1954	James J Morgan*

1954-1955	John Dyke*
1955-1956	Henry W Greenway*
1956-1957	James Craig Kennedy*
1957-1958	Joseph Smith*
1958-1959	Ernest John Phillips*
1959-1960	Harold Burton-Haynes*
1960-1961	John Woodhead*
1961-1962	Thomas J Stevenson
1962-1963	Douglas B Gray*
1963-1964	William J Hilliard
1964-1965	Charles J E Kingston*
1965-1966	Percy S Brewster*
1966-1967	George Wesley Gilpin*
1967-1968	Leslie W Green
1968-1969	Alexander B Tee.*
1969-1970	W Ronald Jones*
1970-1971	Ronald B Chapman*
1971-1972	Archie A Biddle*
1972-1973	Tom W Walker*
1973-1974	John Lancaster*
1974-1975	George Canty
1975-1976	Leslie Wigglesworth
1976-1977	John H MacInnes
1977-1978	David J Ayling*
1978-1979	Alexander (Sandy) Wilson
1979-1980	Jack Osman
1980-1981	Eldin R Corsie*
1981-1982	Gerald L Ladlow

1982-1983	W Ronald Jones*
1983-1984	John C Smyth*
1984-1985	Leonard P Cowdery*
1985-1986	Idris Wynne Lewis*
1986-1987	Brian G Edwards*
1987-1988	Eric McComb*
1988-1989	Tom Walker*

Notes

[1] Hilliard, Stephen, *William John Hilliard*, document sent to the Author by email, 8th Dec 2022.

[2] Sainsbury, John, *Trafalgar Square, 1960, Elim Evangel*, 21st Vol 51, No 21, pp326,327.

[3] The original Elim Evangelistic Band was in existence from 1915-1925 and the commencement of the Elim Bible College. After the war, the idea of reviving the Evangelistic Band by concentrating on lay students was tried and Ladlow was appointed Secretary. The idea behind the band was to get a group of people throughout the country who would develop open-air meetings and personal evangelism.

[4] There were some notable exceptions to this rule: Brewster, Greenway, Kingston, Tweed to name a few.

[5] This information was passed on to me by Carl Seppsy who is now an Assemblies of God Regional Leader in Australia. Carl was my assistant in Selly Oak for a period of five years when he went to Southey Green Elim church (Sheffield).

[6] Smith, Peter, *Global Warming*, ibid, p117.

[7] Lionel and Ruth spent 10 years in Ghana where Lionel was the Principal of the Church of Pentecost Bible College.

33

The Administration

The Elim Foursquare Gospel Alliance was registered as the official name of the Elim Pentecostal Church in 1934. This was the year that the Deed Poll came into being. Prior to this, Elim had a written Constitution which was changed five times by the founder of Elim between 1921 and 1929. E J Phillips, in close consultation with George Jeffreys drew up a Deed Poll which was agreed to by the 1934 Elim Conference.[1] In 1942, the Deed Poll went through a major revision in that it catered for lay representatives from the churches. It also contained the provision for an Irish Conference and Constitution.[2]

When George Jeffreys presented his eight points for change within Elim to the 1939 Conference, all but one of them were accepted by the Ministers and lay representatives who gathered for the 1940 Conference. This entailed a major change in the Deed Poll that came into being in 1934. The changes came into being by a Deed of Variation which was accepted and signed in 1942.

The Deed of Variation resulted in two sessions of Conference; the Ministerial and the Representative sessions. It was the latter that became the governing body of the Alliance. Each Elim church was given the authority to appoint a lay representative. He had the right to attend the Annual Conference and could speak and vote in the Representative Session. George had strongly advocated for this change. It is likely that one of his main reasons for wanting this change was that he thought it would strengthen his cause for the reformation of Elim's government.

Broadly speaking, Elim is a centrally governed Movement. In its earlier days, this form of church government meant that ministers were moved from church to church at frequent intervals. At one time, ministers were moved on an annual basis. As Elim grew, difficulties arose due to the types of churches involved in the Elim Church Incorporated. The majority of the churches were centrally governed but there was a section of churches that were locally governed as well as others, such as the Essex Elim churches, that had their own trust and were outside the Alliance but were in fellowship with Elim.[3] 'There were churches under direct government, churches that had greater local freedom to determine their local policies and some churches that were under the jurisdiction of the minister.'[4]

Following the secession of George Jeffreys, most of the churches that remained under Elim's banner were EFGA[5] churches. The property connected to these churches was owned by the Elim Trust Corporation. This is still the case today. Although local church properties are paid for by the local church, the properties are held in trust by the fore-mentioned Corporation. 'George Jeffreys himself had argued strongly for central government and he had written all the early books of rules and regulations. His experience on the continent in 1935 and again in 1939, led him to advocate local government.'[6] The Conferences of 1939 and 1940 overwhelmingly rejected the method of local church government advocated by George Jeffreys. 'Elim now vests its final authority in the General Conference composed of an equal number of ministers and laymen.'[7] George Canty was of the opinion that whilst the Movement was centrally administered, 'no local church is subject to interference with its internal affairs, but the Elim system ensures that a church is the concern of the Movement and not left to fend for itself if it suffers reverses.'[8] Canty was adamant that Elim is centrally administered and not centrally governed:

> The military-sounding Elim Headquarters is no more than the central administrative office, dealing with general matters of tax, insurance, legal matters, capital and property, pensions,

national insurance, youth direction, publishing, records and so on. The Executive Council have no governing power, but are responsible for carrying out the wishes of Conference between Conferences. Elim has no central government, but only a central administration.[9]

Canty, in his summation of Elim being a centrally administered organisation as opposed to being centrally governed, ignored the fact that no local Elim church can own property in its own name. He also ignored the fact that every Elim minister is subject to the Movement's Constitution and discipline. It is disingenuous to state that the National Leadership Team (formerly the Executive Council) has no governing power. The Constitution lists the functions and powers of the NLT. Under the heading 'Function and Powers', the Constitution sets out the functions of the NLT which are to

(i) Provide spiritual leadership to the Alliance as it seeks to fulfil the objects set out in the Deed Poll, and

(ii) To have the general control and management of the administration of the Alliance.[10]

Whilst the Constitution grants the local Elim church the right to determine its own procedures and to pursue its local vision, this right is subject to the will of the Conference under the supervision of the NLT. The NLT is duty-bound to ensure that each Elim church operates within the parameters of the Objects of the Alliance.

Post-1940, the recognised leader of the Movement was the Secretary-General (General Superintendent). He had a spiritual as well as an administrative responsibility. Until the turn of the century, there were a number of Headquarters officers, nominated by the Executive Council and appointed by the Conference. In 1972, there were seven such officers appointed.[11] Two of these office positions were closely linked: Secretary-General and Field Superintendent. Percy Brewster was elected Secretary-General in 1974 and he served for three years. He instituted a number

342

of changes as regards evangelism. When he retired in 1977, Ron Jones was nominated in his place and the office was changed to that of General Superintendent.

By 1972, only J T Bradley remained on the Executive Council from the members elected in 1940. He had succeeded H W Greenway as Secretary General in 1970. Greenway had retired having reached his 65th birthday, yet the Council, in their collective wisdom elected a man to lead them who was, in fact, three months older than Greenway. He served as Secretary-General for four years.

Field Superintendent

The role of Field Superintendent was an interesting and varied one. His first responsibility was that of a supervisory role over the ministers in the field. Of particular concern to him would have been the Probationary ministers. In the first instance, the probationers would have come under the supervision of their District Superintendent to whom he had to submit a form outlining his activities as a minister, once a month, He would also have been required to submit a copy to the Field Superintendent. Repeated failure to send your probationary form in on time usually resulted in a phone call, or in a few cases, a visit from the Field Superintendent. From memory, the form would require information on (1) The number of visits made to members. (2) The number of visits to non-members. (3) How many decisions for salvation were recorded in your church during the past month? (4) How many were baptised in water? (5) How many were baptised in the Holy Spirit? The supervision of probationary ministers was considered very important although, a lot depended on the relationship between the probationer and his District Superintendent. Occasionally, if the District Superintendent was situated a long way from the probationer, a senior minister nearer to him was appointed to keep an eye on him.[12]

If there was a problem in a church, the Field Superintendent, together with the District Superintendent would visit the church and work together with the minister and the church session to try to solve the issue. The Field Superintendent was also an ex-officio member of the evangelistic committee and would be involved in formatting evangelistic policy throughout the Movement.

Secretary-General

The position of Secretary-General was the highest administrative office in Elim. This title was changed in 1982 when it became 'General Superintendent'. The office of Secretary-General had been greatly enhanced by the ministry of the first, and longest serving, of Elim's Secretary-Generals/General Superintendents. The person holding this office was regarded as Elim's leader. The role of the President tended to obscure the leadership position of the Secretary-General somewhat. This was because the President was ipso-facto chairman of the Conference in the year that he served, he also chaired the Executive Council meetings during his tenure. For this reason, many people in Elim looked upon the President as Elim's leader. Among the members of the Executive Council, however, the Secretary-General was considered to be 'chief among equals.'

The chief role of the Secretary-General seemed to have been that of carrying out the decisions of the Executive Council. He would, of course, have had a voice and influence in the formatting of the Council's policy. He would, of necessity, have to possess detailed knowledge of the Constitution. In Conference debates, whenever there was clarification on aspects of the Constitution, in the early days especially, it would be the Secretary-General who provided such clarification. This aspect of the role changed to some degree in the early seventies with the increasing influence of the Administrative Secretary. This was a headquarters office that was created with one man clearly in mind – John C Smyth.

List of Secretary-Generals and General Superintendents

The office of Secretary-General was created in 1923 and at the time, it was not considered to be the leading office in the Movement. George Jeffreys was, without doubt, the leader of Elim until his resignation in 1939-1940. E J Phillips' role was very much an administrative one in the first ten years. From 1933 to 1940, his work was mainly constitutional. Following the departure of George Jeffreys, Phillips in an unobtrusive manner took hold of the reins of leadership within Elim. The list of Elim's 'Generals' are:

E J Phillips	1923-1957
H W Greenway	1957-1970
J T Bradley	1970-1974
P S Brewster	1974-1977
W R Jones	1977-1981
T W Walker	1981-1988
E R Corsie	1988-1990
I W Lewis	1990-2000
John Glass	2000-2016
C Cartwright	2016-

Those who served as Field Superintendents during the period to 2002 were: S Gorman, W G Hathaway, H W Greenway, James Morgan, R B Chapman, T W Walker, J C Smyth, T G Hills.

Two men, Greenway and Walker served both as General Superintendent and Field Superintendent. John Smyth served as Administrative Secretary and Field Superintendent. He was nominated for the position of General Superintendent in 1980 but failed to get the required majority by just one vote.

A profile on J T Bradley has already been given and much has been written concerning E J Phillips in both volumes. A full profile of the work and ministry of H W Greenway was included in the first volume. Chapters have been written in this volume on P S

Brewster and W R Jones. Full profiles on E R Corsie, I W Lewis and John Glass will be included in the third volume.

T W Walker

Tom Walker and Harry Greenway were unique amongst Elim office holders as having occupied what was considered at the time, the three main offices within Elim. They both served as General Superintendent, Field Superintendent and Director of Publications. Between them they served on the Executive Council for over 56 years, Greenway 39 years and Walker 26 years. Both men carried with them a sense of stability which made it easy for the ministers to trust their actions. At the same time, neither men were afraid to advocate and support change when needed.

Tom Walker was born in the East Riding city of Hull on 27th March 1924. As has been noted, he served the highest office in the Movement and served in almost every capacity. 'Dates and facts can only hint at the huge contribution he has made to the life and development of Elim over the past 60 years.'[13] It is not easy to estimate the huge contribution that he made to the life and development of Elim.

> Tom committed his life to Jesus Christ at the young age of six years old when Principal George Jeffreys conducted a Campaign on Walton Street Fairground, close to West Park, Hull in 1933 which resulted in the formation of the City Temple, Hull. His parents joined the church under the ministry of the first pastor, F G Cloke. H W Fardell became pastor in 1934. Later, Tom was baptised in water as a teenager by another pastor of Hull City temple, Jack Tetchner.[14]

Tom Walker applied to enter the Elim Bible College in 1942 and he was accepted as a theology student. In actual fact, at this period of time, the Bible College was closed. This closure was due, not only to the war, but also due to serious challenges within the Movement. Cartwright refers to this in his tribute to Tom Walker:

Tom entered the Elim Bible College, Clapham, on May 16, 1943 at the age of 19. At the time Elim faced the challenges of the Second World War – as well as significant internal challenges. Originating from our Hull church, Tom had already served in ministry posts prior to attending Bible College, as minister at Bradford Elim. He also served in a number of our churches in London, including Sydenham, Croydon, Barking, Finsbury Park, Woolwich and Ealing.[15]

Trevor Harris throws some needed light on Mr Walker's Bible College training. 'He was accepted as a theology student in 1942 but the College was closed due to war restrictions and he was sent instead to Bradford as an assistant to Pastor W J Hilliard. He eventually entered Elim Woodlands Bible College on 16th May 1943 at the young age of 19 years old.'[16]

Although Mr Walker spent some 26 years at Elim Headquarters, he had proved himself to be an excellent and well-loved pastor. He first came to Elim Headquarters' attention in 1945 when he was a student at the Missionary School of Medicine, Great Ormond Street, London. He applied to be accepted as an Elim Missionary with a view to serving in the Belgian Congo. 'You will be interested to know that at a recent meeting of the Missionary Council your application was considered and it was agreed that you be accepted as a prospective missionary subject to a satisfactory medical examination and your attaining language proficiency, this in your case will mean proficiency in French, should your field be the Belgian Congo.'[17] The same letter issued him with a request to be present at the Royal Albert Hall on Easter Monday afternoon to 'speak for a few minutes along with other missionary candidates.' Tom Walker did not become a missionary, although he and his wife Ruth, maintained a keen interest in the work of Elim missionaries throughout their lives.

Tom Walker met his wife Ruth at an Elim Youth Camp in Rye Park, Hoddesdon which was organised and led by Leon Quest.[18] They were married on 3rd August 1945 and went on to have five children. 'Tom entered into Elim royalty when he married Ruth

Hathaway.'[19] Over the next sixty and more years they served God and Elim in a remarkable partnership. Ruth Walker was a remarkable lady. She was appointed leader of the Elim Women's Missionary Auxiliary. In the many years of her leadership, EWMA later to become known as Life-Link, raised hundreds of thousands of pounds for various missionary projects in the many mission fields that Elim had in various parts of the world. Cars, trucks, land rovers, bicycles by the hundreds were purchased and distributed to grateful missionaries. Ruth Walker was an excellent leader in her own right. In any tribute paid to her husband, it is only right to highlight the incredible and efficient work of Ruth Walker.

After periods of ministry in Bolton, Pontypridd, Scarborough and Ealing, Mr Walker was appointed to Clapham which at that time was considered Elim's central church. He was very popular with the young people and took a great interest in the outreach ministry of the youth singing groups and would accompany them to the various cafes and dingy halls where they set out to evangelise and witness for Christ. One member of the group told me how that Tom would pray for them and made sure they were safe, in her words, 'He was a great and caring pastor.'[20]

In 1966 Walker was elected as Elim's Field Superintendent, a full-time role based at Elim Headquarters which was then still in Clapham.[21] He carried broad responsibility for our members and churches. He was only in that role for two years. Tom Walker was a man of great honour and impeccable standards. Due to a situation that arose within his family, Tom resigned as Field Superintendent against the advice of his colleagues. Let me emphasise this point very clearly here, Mr Walker upheld the very highest standards of spiritual honour and integrity, he was never more honourable than when he resigned as Field Superintendent. He remained on the Executive Council and pastored the Elim Church in Salisbury for a short period. He moved to Elim's new offices in Cheltenham in 1970 to become National Communications Director, where amongst other duties, he edited the Elim Evangel.[22]

He resumed his former role of Field Superintendent in 1974 and remained in that office until 1981. In 1981, Elim changed the name and role of the Secretary-General, and Tom Walker became the Movement's first General Superintendent. He remained in this office for a period of seven years before retiring in 1988.

> In preaching, writing and lecturing, Tom excelled. In each of these fields one would recognise that his material was well researched, prayed over, exegetically sound and clearly delivered. He was a great leader and an efficient administrator. Tom Walker was a man who loved God. He believed that what was needed in ministry was 'a real love for God, an absolute burning love for God, a real personal love for God.' He was a good man. A godly man. He was a man of great character who believed that having surrendered your life to Christ means God is in control. His legacy to us as a Movement is that we take note and follow his example.[23]

John C Smyth

This is of necessity a brief summary of the ministry of John Smyth and the huge contribution he made to the Elim Movement. The main aspects of his work especially as Field Superintendent will be elaborated on in the third volume. John Smyth was born in Belfast in 1935. Converted under the ministry of Joseph Smith, he was a member of the Ulster Temple. Brought up in a working-class area of Belfast, he entered the Elim ministry at the young age of 18 years. John's first appointment was to Penzance and then Camborne in Cornwall. Some 40 years later, his son, David was to follow in his father's footsteps when he became the pastor of Camborne Elim church. His next appointment was Weoley Castle, Birmingham where he came under the supervision of John Dyke, the redoubtable pastor of Graham Street Elim. An important part of any probationary minister's training in the Birmingham Presbytery was a Monday noon appointment at the Bull Ring in the centre of the city where John Dyke conducted his weekly open-air meetings. His next appointment was to the City Temple in Bristol as assistant to Ron Jones. It was there that he met his wife Mary, they went on to have two sons, David and Jonathon.

John had some training in the field of accounts and his administrative skills brought him to the attention of Headquarters. He worked for a period of time with E J Phillips. John considered E J as his mentor and worked closely with him for a few years until ill-health caused the great man to retire from his administrative duties. The position of Administrative Secretary was created for him a post which later became a Headquarters office in its own right.

He was elected to the Executive Council in 1971 where he replaced a fellow Ulsterman, James Kennedy. At the age of 36, John was a very young member of the Executive. He remained a member of the Council for thirty years. To the great surprise of many of his colleagues, he was elected as Field Superintendent in 1981. This was a time of considerable challenge to Elim. Traditions and values had been challenged by the impact of the charismatic renewal. Many Elim people attended the various Bible Weeks held in Harrogate, Shepton Mallett and the Downs in Sussex. Elim found herself at a cross-roads and John's Key Note address to the Southport Conference held just five months after he became Field Superintendent was a huge factor in preserving the unity of the Movement and of changing the structures within the Movement that allowed for more flexibility in all aspects. A comprehensive account of this will be given in the first few chapters of the third volume.

Notes

[1] At this time, the Elim Conference was a Pastors' Conference only. Lay representatives were admitted to the Conference in 1941.

[2] The Deed Poll gave the Irish churches the right to hold their own Conference and certain items within the main Constitution are delegated to the Irish Conference. This would include stationing of ministers within Ireland, the allocation of the 10% and International Missions. The Irish churches still come under the main Constitution and Deed Poll. Changes to this policy can only be made by a 75% of both the General Conference and the Irish Conference, in two successive years.

[3] Jones, Maldwyn, *And they came to Elim*, ibid, p356.

[4] Lewis, Wynne, unpublished account of Elim History, (Malvern: Elim Archives), p15

[5] Elim Foursquare Gospel Alliance.

[6] Cartwright, Desmond, *Elim Evangel*, 11th Oct 1980, p11.

[7] Canty, George, *History of Elim 1915-1983*, ibid, p141.

[8] Canty, George, ibid, p141.

[9] Canty, George, ibid, p141.

[10] The Constitution of the Elim Foursquare Gospel Alliance, 2012 Edition, General Rules, Part 1, National Leadership Team and subsidiary Bodies, sub-section Functions and Powers, 15, pp15,16.

[11] Secretary-General, Field Supt, Director of Publications, Principal of the Bible College, National Youth Director, Missionary Secretary (International Missions Director), Administrative Secretary. In 1978, an additional Headquarters Office was created, that of Evangelistic Director with Alex Tee being appointed.

[12] I was appointed to my first church in Kirkintilloch, just outside Glasgow. My DS at the time was Frank Frost who was the pastor of the Carlisle church, some 85 miles away. He asked Fred Jones, the pastor of the Motherwell church if he would keep an eye on me. He and his wife were extremely kind to me and had me stay in their home quite a few times. Without their help and encouragement, I would not have survived in the ministry in those early days.

[13] Cartwright, Chris, *Tribute, Direction,* January 2016.

[14] Harris, Trevor, *Profile on T W Walker,* Facebook, Elim History Page, 25th August 2022.

[15] Cartwright, Chris, *Tribute*, ibid.

[16] Harris, Trevor, *Profile on T W Walker*, ibid.

[17] Letter, George H Thomas, Missionary Secretary, Elim Foursquare Gospel Alliance, 27th Feb 1945. (Copy of letter sent to the author by Philip Walker, 16th Jan 2023.

[18] Harris, Trevor, *Profile on T W Walker*, ibid.

[19] Cartwright, Chris, *Tribute*, ibid.

[20] Conversation with Peggy and Michael Greenway, Regents Theological College, Friday 20th Jan, 2022.

[21] Elim moved its Headquarters Offices to Cheltenham in 1966.

[22] Cartwright, Chris, *Tribute*, ibid.

[23] Smyth, John *Tributes to a man of many gifts, Direction,*

34
Executive Council Members

This chapter will contain potted histories of those members of the Executive Council who were appointed in the sixties and seventies who have not been addressed previously. The decade of the sixties saw the retirement of most of the members of the first Executive Council appointed after the resignation of George Jeffreys. E C W Boulton retired in the early fifties and George Kingston resigned from the Council in 1954 due to business commitments. Sam Gorman, W G Hathaway and E J Phillips resigned due to age and ill-health. Joseph Smith failed to get the required number of votes in 1960. John Dyke died in 1960 and Jimmy Morgan in 1967. H W Greenway failed to get the required number of votes in 1973 and J T Bradley retired as Secretary-General and a member of the Executive Council in 1974.

Prior to 2000, the Conference had the right to nominate members for election to the Executive Council. The Conference minutes show the various factors that propelled an Elim minister to the Executive Council. The most common feature seems to have been by membership of a Conference committee. Pre-1970, the most advantageous of these committees was the Evangelistic Committee. Brewster, Tee, Jones, Chapman and later, Lewis and Woodfield were all members of this committee. Membership of the International Missions Board was also seen as an advantage for those seeking to be appointed to the Executive Council. Gilpin, Ayling and later, Edwards all benefitted from their membership of the IMB. Towards the end of the century, membership of the

Youth Committee seemed to heighten one's Executive Council ambitions. G Feasey, G H Neale, B Killick and M Sherwood were all members of the Youth Committee and each of them was elected to the Executive Council.

John Lancaster

John Lancaster was the exception to the above notion in that he did not serve on any of the above-name committees before he was elected to the Executive Council. Granted, he was a member of the Bible College Synod which carried a fair amount of influence. John's pastoral and theological qualities shone and sparkled throughout his remarkable ministry. It was this that caught the attention of his colleagues in ministry and thrust him toward a position of leadership and influence within Elim. Many years after his retirement he was still in great demand as a preacher and lecturer. At the age of 92, he was the guest speaker at the Donald Gee Lecture in Mattersey. John was loved and admired throughout the Elim Movement, having influenced countless lives for Christ during his 97 years. John died in November 2022 having served the Elim Movement for 74 years.

> John Lancaster was one of those ministers whose reach and influence carried way beyond Elim. His classic book 'The Spirit-Filled Church' contains recommendations from no less than Michael Green, David Pawson and Reinhard Bonkke. That remarkable shortlist alone, from across the spectrum of the Christian Church, reveals so much about the respect in which he was held as a pastor, preacher, teacher and author. He was regarded as a leader who seemed to always balance the passion of Pentecost with the strength and security of Scripture.[1]

John came from the small town of Petersfield in Hampshire. It was there that he first came to faith. As a young Christian during World War II, he served in the Royal Air Force and was stationed for a period in St Athan in South Wales. During this time, he attended the City Temple in Cardiff. P S Brewster, the senior pastor at the City Temple was struck by John Lancaster's strong and active faith. Brewster encouraged him to play an active part in the life of the church. This he did, including leading a young men's Bible class. Years later, John would serve alongside the legendary P S and they became firm friends.[23] John Lancaster was to become one of Brewster's successors as pastor of the City Temple.

There was a deep Christian quality in John Lancaster's life and demeanour that drew people's attention. He carried with him a quiet authority that was notable. 'As a strong Christian, his character and love for Christ was such that he was a great example, keen to strengthen and encourage others. Those qualities would never leave him.' [4] Those of us who had the privilege of working under his guidance and tutelage, even for a short time, became the beneficiaries of his gracious and wise counsel. 'He was arguably Elim's greatest theologian and lectured on Systematic Theology at our Bible College for over 30 years.'[5]

In 1946, he entered the Elim Bible College in Clapham. After graduating the following summer, he was appointed to Letchworth where he assisted Samuel Gorman during his Presidential year. A strong bond of friendship developed between these two great Bible teachers that was to last a lifetime. He was ordained in 1951, the same year he married Dorothy Davies, the daughter of one of our pastors, and they began 63 years of married life together. He was appointed to the Elim church then meeting in Bayswater and Holland Park. This fellowship, which had its origins in the Kensington Temple was commenced by those members who wished to remain with Elim. One of the pastors, Percy LeTissier, left and became the pastor of this new fellowship. LeTissier was re-admitted into the ranks of Elim Pastors. He died in 1951. Later, during the ministry of John's successor, Eldin Corsie, this fellowship moved back into Kensington Temple in 1964 as Elim re-acquired the building following the death of George Jeffreys.

In 1957, Lancaster moved to the Elim church in Eastbourne where he enjoyed his longest period of pastoral ministry. The Eastbourne Elim church flourished under his ministry and John was highly respected by his fellow ministers in this East Sussex coastal town. It was during this time that he began to play a growing part in the wider Elim Movement. He was appointed to the Executive Council in 1969 and served on it for 23 years. John Lancaster was a prolific writer, contributing regular articles for the Elim Evangel. He wrote the last article in every Direction magazine under the title 'And Finally'. His last article appeared in the copy of Direction which contained a report of his funeral service in Leeds. He wrote the article a month before his death.

Although a gifted writer, John loved nothing more than pastoring the local church. He moved to Leeds in 1977 and saw substantial growth under his ministry there. His colleagues on the Executive Council had long expressed their desire that he become Editor of the Elim Evangel. Eventually, after five years in Leeds, John relented and he became the fulltime National Communications Director. But he greatly missed pastoral life and became pastor of Northampton Elim church in 1984, although he continued as editor of the Evangel for 18 months alongside pastoring the church.

His last pastorate was to the church that he had attended as a young RAF serviceman, Cardiff City Temple. Eric Gaudion, who in my opinion is of the same mould as John Lancaster, worked alongside John 'during a time of considerable change and in a season of renewal across the wider church. He challenged the church to be open again to the fresh wind of the Holy Spirit.'[6] Mr Lancaster was an outstanding theologian and his theological convictions led him to believe God for a fresh and dynamic move of the Holy Spirit in this generation. He was thoroughly Pentecostal and was able to bring together Biblical balance alongside spiritual fervour. He was an example to his peers and colleagues and a superb mentor to many young ministers. Many years after his official retirement, he was in great demand as a preacher.

John Lancaster carried a distinct prophetic touch in his preaching. There were also a few times when he exercised the gift of prophecy in Elim's national celebrations. One such occasion was at the 1986

Elim Conference. In the 70's and 80's there was much talk about God restoring His church along Kingdom lines. It was a time of challenge for Elim. It was a time of reflection and change. The 1981 and 1984 Southport Conferences (which will be covered in the third volume) resulted in a time of transition. John Lancaster's prophetic word to the 1986 Conference was very much a word from God to Elim. In this prophecy, he touched on the burning issues of the time. 'The Kingdom of God is not in word but in power.' One sentence stands out: 'God is calling those who are leaders in his church to recognise that the reign of God cannot come in the church until it comes in the lives of those who are its leaders.'

The prophecy went on to touch on the vexed issue of authority: 'Authority is not a matter of public projection, of personal statement – Authority comes to those who have learned to bow the knee to Jesus Christ in the intimate details of their own personal life.' The prophecy ended with a yearning that God's servants would 'Repent, turn, yield, submit.'

I was present when this powerful prophetic word was given, it had a profound effect upon all the delegates present. We were left in no doubt that God had spoken to us through his prophet. John Lancaster was a godly, humble and courageous leader. He was a superb pastor, an outstanding theologian, a brilliant preacher and a gifted writer.

R B Chapman

Ron Chapman was Field Superintendent of Elim from 1968-1974. His appointment to that office was unusual because in some respects, he was an 'outsider'. By that I refer to the fact that apart from the honorary position of President, he had not served in any other national office. Ronald Bryan Chapman was born on the 2nd October 1914 to a middle-class family in Beverley, in the East Riding of Yorkshire. 'Ron's religious background in his early years was strictly high Anglican with his parents regularly attending Beverley Minister where Ron became the Sunday School Superintendent and later at St Mary's Church of England.'[7]

His attention to detail and administrative gift was noted whilst attending Riley High School, Hull. After leaving school he joined the Prudential Assurance Company as a trainee Underwriter, an apprenticeship he served for five years until 1936.[8]

The whole course of his life was changed when one night in 1933 he attended the Hull City Temple. It was there that he heard James McWhirter preach the Foursquare Gospel message during a healing and revival campaign that was being conducted in the city. At the age of 19, Ron Chapman surrendered his life to Christ and experienced a definite conversion. The many articles written by Mr Chapman and featured in many weekly editions of the Evangel revealed his passion for open-air preaching and ministry. In each church that he pastored, open-air meetings were high on the agenda.

> Such was the spiritual fire which had entered his life that night that almost immediately Ron passionately thrust himself into the work of God, often cycling nine miles to attend meetings in the City Temple and to assist in weekly open-air meetings under the leadership of T W Walker's father (also named Tom), where a continued lifetime friendship was nurtured with T W Walker with Ron thereafter regularly going to T W's parents, Tom and Annie Walker's home for Sunday lunch. As someone gifted with a clear and powerful voice these early open-air meetings with the Walker family proved to be a good grounding for Ron's continued open-air work in several of the churches he would later pastor.[9]

Responding to a clear call of God on his life, Ron Chapman wrote to George Jeffreys describing to him the deep desire to serve the Lord in Elim. The Field Superintendent, W G Hathaway contacted him and Chapman was sent to Northern Ireland in May 1936 as a student probationer to work in a tent campaign under the direction of Robert Tweed. Two years later he went to Hayes, Middlesex where he assisted Ken Matthew in an evangelistic campaign. He went to Glasgow and then Dundee in the role of Assistant Pastor.

It was while he ministered in Dundee that he met his wife Janet, always known as 'Nettie' and they were married in the Dundee church with Pastor James Morgan officiating. They went on to have two daughters, Sheena and Kathryn.

Mrs Chapman had a beautiful singing voice and had won a number of awards at various Scottish singing competitions and later was a Gospel recording artist for Sharon records. She was often the soloist at services and campaigns conducted by her husband, but she also appeared on national platforms such as the Elim Easter celebrations in the Royal Albert Hall.

Ron Chapman ministered in some of Elim's larger churches including, Southampton, Rowley Regis (Blackheath), York, Springbourne (Bournemouth), Sheffield, Paisley and Ilford. He served as District Superintendent to three presbyteries. He served on the Elim Missions Board from 1959-1974. Following his Presidential year of office, he was elected to the Executive Council in 1968 and took over the role of Field Superintendent upon the death of his close friend James Morgan.

He appeared somewhat stern to us young probationary ministers and we had to ensure that our monthly reports were on time and that our annual thesis was completed to the satisfaction of the Principal of the Bible College. He was very helpful and supportive of those ministers in his care. He had a good sense of humour and was very quick in his replies.

Ron Chapman was a good and caring Field Superintendent. Upon retiring from this office in 1974 he and Mrs Chapman went to Southern Africa where he served as Field Superintendent Overseer of the Elim Mission in Southern Rhodesia and South Africa.

David Ayling

David Ayling was destined to be involved with Ron Chapman in the aftermath of the horrendous massacre of thirteen Elim missionaries and children in Rhodesia (Zimbabwe) in 1978. David had been appointed to the role of International Missions Director in succession to Leslie Wigglesworth in the month prior to the killings in the Vumba.

David Ayling came from Ealing, London. His parents were long-standing, committed members of the Elim Church in this West London borough. His father was a deacon and member of the church session at Ealing for a number of years.

David entered Bible College in 1949 and unusually at the time, did a two-year course where he graduated with Distinction. In the course of its almost 100 year history, certain intakes of students have left quite an impression due to the number of students who went on to hold high office in Elim and other Christian organisations. The intake of 1967 and 1968 saw a number of students become members of Elim's National Leadership Team with one of that number (John Glass) being appointed as General Superintendent of the Elim Pentecostal Church. The intake of students to the Elim Bible College in 1949-1951 produced an equally glittering roll of ministers who were to serve in the highest positions in Elim. Eldin Corsie, Wynne Lewis, John Smyth, Desmond Cartwright, David Ayling and Richard Lighton were all students at Elim Bible College during these three years. Two of that number became General Superintendents (Corsie and Lewis), Corsie was also to become Principal of Elim Bible College.

David Ayling responded to the call of God to enter the Christian ministry at a young age. He served in a number of our churches including Motherwell where he assisted Alex Tee the pioneer pastor of this fine Scottish Elim church. His first church as sole pastor was Llanelli, South Wales. Whilst there, he was appointed Youth Commissioner for the Welsh presbytery. He obviously caught the eye of the District Superintendent, P S Brewster. Brewster conducted a major pioneer campaign in the north-east city of Newcastle-upon-Tyne. Typically, he hired a cinema as well as the largest halls in the city to hold his meetings. David Ayling was a member of the team and was appointed pastor of the new Elim church that was founded following the campaign.

After five successful years in Newcastle where he helped establish a fine church in the east end of the city, David, his wife Doreen and children moved to Brighton. George Jeffreys held a major campaign in Brighton in 1927 and Elim were able to purchase the Glyn Vivian Hall in the Lanes. The hall was historic and somewhat dilapidated in appearance. The congregation had also diminished considerably since those halcyon days of revival. The task of leading a smallish congregation in a large, draughty and dishevelled building was a huge challenge for the pastor. Slowly, the church began to grow.

David Ayling's next appointment was the Ulster Temple, Belfast. This was a large building situated on the Lower Ravenhill Road facing the Ormeau Park in East Belfast. Built in 1926, the building was designed with the object of holding large Elim rallies. Although there was a healthy congregation in the Ulster Temple during the early sixties, a Sunday evening congregation of some 200 still left huge gaps of empty seats. David and Doreen Ayling fitted into the Ulster Temple extremely well. With a fine assistant in the person of Graham Wylie, the Temple 'took off'. The congregation more than doubled. During his time in Belfast, David Ayling made an impression on the 'Voice of Protestantism', none other than Dr Ian Paisley. He did this by visiting Dr Paisley whilst he was imprisoned in Crumlin Road Prison. He was one of the very few clergymen who did this and Paisley never forgot it.

Ayling was elected to the Executive Council in 1974 and was President in 1977-78. He was also the Irish representative on the International Missions Board and a member of the Elim Bible College Synod. In May 1978, just a month prior to the martyrdom of our missionaries in Rhodesia (Zimbabwe) he was elected Director of International Missions.

David Ayling suffered a heart-attack which resulted in him passing into the presence of his Saviour at the young age of 51. His loss was a great blow to Elim.

Eldin Corsie

Eldin Corsie followed John Lancaster as pastor of the Elim Church in Penzance Street, Holland Park. One could imagine the shock that this young minister received one morning in 1965 when his telephone rang and the caller asked, 'Eldin, how would you like to take your congregation to the Kensington Temple?' The caller was a member of the Executive Council of the Elim Pentecostal Church calling from the headquarters in Clapham (It was almost certainly H W Greenway, the Movement's Secretary-General).

Kensington Temple in 1965 was a shell of what it had been and certainly, nowhere near to the beautiful fully attended building that it is today. The building had come back into Elim's ownership when the last living trustee, James McWhirter had, following the death of George Jeffreys, negotiated the sale of his trusteeship to Elim. According to Eldin's great friend Jack Hywel-Davies, when asked what his thoughts were when he took over the imposing Kensington Temple without any financial backing, stated that he usually replied with just one word 'despair!'[10]

Eldin's parents became Christians in 1930 during the great Birmingham campaign conducted by George Jeffreys that culminated in the last two weeks of the campaign being held in the huge Bingley Hall. Whilst Eldin's father had a Salvation Army background his mother, in Eldin's words 'was perfectly godless – she had no background in the Christian faith at all.' She found herself one evening in 1930 in the Bingley Hall, Birmingham listening to George Jeffreys preach. She went in for ten minutes and stayed for the whole service. She responded to the Gospel appeal and went to the front and 'prayed the sinner's prayer'. She then persuaded her husband to attend the meetings and he too became a Christian. As regards his own commitment of faith Eldin took his stance for Christ in a very courageous manner.

> It was during my period in the army that I was challenged to dedicate my life to the Lord. I was in a queue in the NAAFI canteen waiting for a cup of tea when a young man

came along the line giving out gospel tracts. He seemed a nice fellow so I ordered an extra cup of tea for him, and we sat down at the same table. The remarkable thing is that he talked to me as if I was a heathen! He didn't know anything about my background. I wasn't offended, in fact I was so impressed by his clear stand for the Lord that when he invited me to kneel with him there in the NAFFI, and in front of my mates, I did.[11]

Eldin Corsie was an excellent musician and this came to the attention of John Woodhead who called on him to play the organ at a campaign in East London. Eldin left the army in 1949 and entered Elim Bible College. His first appointment as a young minister was to Burton-on-Trent where he was involved in the pioneer campaign held in that famous Brewery town by John Woodhead. Eldin stayed on to be the first pastor of the new church there.[12]

His next appointment was as the founding pastor of yet another campaign conducted by John Woodhead, it was the Cornish sea-side town of Newquay. It was whilst pastoring this new Elim church that he met Vivien, the daughter of James and Babs Kennedy. Pastor Kennedy was the District Superintendent of Devon and Cornwall, based in Plymouth. Eldin and his young bride moved to Holland Park and then to Kensington Temple. The huge challenge was a daunting one. One of the first things he did was to purchase a second-hand Hammond organ. Then he found a good organist – John Evans who travelled from Clapham.[13] Eldin persevered and the church grew from 60 to over 600 by the time he succeeded Wesley Gilpin as Principal of Elim Bible College in 1980. He had been elected to the Executive Council two years earlier. Eldin Corsie had a wonderful combination of ministry gifts. He was a great pastor, a fine preacher, a very able expositor of Scripture. His evangelistic credentials were clearly seen in the large number of conversions that occurred under his ministry. Eldin was also deeply Pentecostal in his convictions and ministry. He frequently exercised the gift of prophecy and in a televised Sunday morning service from our

Conference in 1981, he gave the interpretation to an expression of the gift of tongues that occurred during the service.

Eldin Corsie was a spiritual giant. He carried with him the presence of Christ.[14] He was very suited to the office of Principal. He had excellent connections throughout the British evangelical scene. He and Vivien brought their own distinct leadership to the College and were greatly appreciated and loved by the students.

In 1988, Eldin was elected General Superintendent. It was a popular appointment and Eldin was well received by the Conference. In his Executive Council vote in 1984, he received the highest number of votes of 303. His confirmatory vote for Principal at the 1984 Conference was 303 in favour and only 16 against. He was well respected and loved. He only remained in the office of General Superintendent for a period of two years. He resigned his position in 1990. The circumstances surrounding Eldin's resignation left many unanswered questions in the minds of most of the delegates. His resignation was made in a dignified and non-combative manner which was so typical of the man that he was. He returned to pastoral life going to Coventry and then to St Helens. In his retirement he pioneered a new Elim Church in Widnes. He contracted Parkinson's Disease which quieted that fine, powerful preaching voice to a soft whisper. He went to be with his Lord in 2016. As it was said of Barnabas, it could be said of Eldin Corsie: 'He was a good man and full of the Holy Ghost and of faith: and much people was added unto the Lord.'[15]

Notes

[1] Cartwright, Chris, *John ran a great race and he finished well*, *Direction*, Dec 2022/Jan 2023, Issue 243, pp20,21.

[2] Cartwright, Chris, ibid.

[3] Cartwright, Chris, ibid.

[4] Cartwright, Chris, ibid.

[5] Jones, Maldwyn, *Our greatest theologian*, *Direction*, ibid, p21.

[6] Cartwright, Chris, ibid.

[7] Harris, Trevor, *Elim Lives Remembered – Pastor R B Chapman*, Facebook, Elim History Page, 31st Oct 2022.

[8] Harris, Trevor, ibid.

[9] Harris, Trevor, ibid.

[10] Hywel-Davies, Jack, *The Kensington Temple Story* (Crowborough: Monarch Books, 1998) p47.

[11] Eldin Corsie, quoted by Hywel-Davies, Jack, *The Kensington Temple Story*, ibid, p45.

[12] Hywel-Davies, Jack, ibid, p46.

[13] John is a great musician and a superb organist and pianist. I have known him for over fifty years and value his and Ruth's friendship.

[14] This is, of course, my personal impression. There have been a number of ministers that I have known personally that I can only use the words 'deeply spiritual' to describe them. They have been those men and women of whom to be in their company, immediately brought Jesus into one's thoughts. They were not uncomfortable to be with, quite the opposite in fact. It is always a danger to categorise in areas such as this, but Sam Gorman, Eldin Corsie and John Lancaster were of that calibre.

[15] Acts 12:24 (AV)

35
Elim Bible College

The Early Days

For the first twenty years of its existence from its inception in 1925, the sole purpose of the Elim Bible College was to train its students in basic pastoral theology and prepare them for becoming ministers of the Alliance. E J Phillips who, at the time served as both the Secretary-General of Elim and Editor of the Movement's weekly magazine, the Elim Evangel, was appointed the first Dean of the Elim Bible College. George Jeffreys had taken on the title of Principal and therefore the head of the Bible College was given the title of Dean. It soon became clear that Phillips could not hold all three positions and his administrative genius was required to arrange campaigns, purchase buildings and houses and also working on the constitutional and legal requirements of a new denomination.

The College course began in April 1925 and was housed in the minor hall in the Clapham church. Later that same year, the Alliance bought a former Convent in Clapham and this became the first site of four in the history of the Bible College to date. Elim Woodlands was just that. The College was bordered by large trees. It became the home of Elim Bible College for the next 40 years. In 1927, George Jeffreys appointed Percy Corry a retired major in the British army in India to the position of Dean. They had been fellow students at Thomas Myerscough's Bible school in Preston under the auspices of the Pentecostal Missionary Union. Corry proved to be competent and the student intake grew year on year.. 'He was an able, all-round Bible expositor with special expertise in Romans and Ephesians.'[1]   Corry was not in favour of allowing unmarried female students to become students at the Elim Bible College and in 1936 the college suspended the admission of female students. This was certainly a retrograde step. In the early days of its existence, women had the freedom to minister in various capacities. George Jeffreys regularly invited Mrs Crisp who ran a Bible School for women in London, to speak at his many conventions in Northern Ireland. Margaret Streight, was a founder member of the Elim Evangelistic Band. Adelaide Henderson, a former missionary to the Congo, was appointed Missionary Secretary. A meeting was held in 1928 to consider whether women could be ordained. There were three women present at the Committee meeting to consider the ordination of women. They were Adelaide Henderson, Nan Kennedy and Mrs Charles Kingston.[2] Corry, who was the chairman of the committee was strongly opposed to the ordination of women and the male members of the committee followed suit and it was to be another 50 years before the next tentative steps were taken to allow women the same Biblical right to preach and minister as their male counterparts.

The College governing council of the day did not seem it prudent to take a different line towards women in ministry to that of Percy Corry, but they, and the rest of Elim were pleased enough to receive healthy financial contributions for the purchase and upkeep of the College from those whom they deemed unsuitable simply on the grounds of gender. 'A benefactor and the first Matron was Miss M F Barbour, whose aristocratic bearing combined with her Christian grace fitted her in a special way to 'mother' and advise the successive waves of enthusiastic but often raw recruits for the ministry. Successors were Mrs C Taylor, Miss A Kennedy, Miss L Gammans and Miss O Mogford.'[3]   Marjorie Taylor was the widow of Cyril Taylor, Elim's first missionary who died in 1935 in Switzerland whilst taking his first furlough having gone to the Belgian Congo to work alongside Willie Burton and James Salter.

The College became much more than a building to teach and train students for the Elim ministry.

> 'Elim Woodlands', the umbrella name for the wider uses of the new property, became the centre for conferences, open-air baptismal ceremonies in the grounds, and Saturday gardening parties culminating in services. To this restful place returned missionaries and evangelists. It became the rendezvous for Pentecostal leaders from all over the world and, with the new administration building built next door (no.20), the 'Woodlands' (no. 30), became the hub of a movement that was growing fast, as the tide of Pentecostal blessing came in all over the country.
>
> George Jeffreys himself was regarded as the Principal and not a few of the young men who came there for training from 1926 onwards were fired and directed by the magnetic personality of this pioneer of Pentecostalism in Great Britain.[4]

The War Years and After

Percy Corry resigned as Dean of the Elim Bible College in 1938 so that he could spend time on itinerary work preaching and teaching through the country. Joseph Smith was appointed as Dean in his place. 'Joseph Smith brought to the task the dedication of a real man of God and the inspiration of a keen personal soul-winner, to say nothing of the fire and fighting qualities of an Irishman.'[5] Joe Smith was a Pentecostal phenomenon. With his bushy grey eyebrows, steely eyes and white hair, he had the appearance of an Old Testament prophet. And, he most certainly prophesied. Often, when preaching, he would soar into the realms of what I can only describe as 'prophetic preaching.' He was as near as Elim ever came to having a national prophet. He was an old man, well into his eighties, when I first heard him preach, but there was a fire in his soul that was utterly compelling.

The war seriously curtailed the activities of the College as an institution of theological studies and ultimately resulted in it being closed for these purposes for a temporary period. It is clear that there was some acceptance of students for the Elim ministry and a degree of supervision from the College during this period.

Although lectures and curriculum activities ceased for most of the war years, the college was certainly occupied in other areas for the benefit of Elim. It became a place of residence for some Elim people and a comfortable lodging place for some military personnel as they passed through the capital. 'Miraculously, the building was preserved from the fate that became the lot of so many fine buildings during war-time.'[6] It also became the centre from which Joseph Smith organised and trained the team of workers to visit the various refuges set up throughout London to provide safety for the people during the bombing raids on the capital by enemy aircraft. The team were covered with prayer by a number of people gathered at Woodlands. Joseph Smith and his team became widely known in that part of London for their 'shelter evangelism'.

The College was the place where the London Crusader Choir met for their weekly rehearsals for much of their history. This was invaluable to the choir especially during the dark years of the war. The Executive Council also used the College premises for their meetings. These were conducted in what was known as the 'Evangelists room'. Other committees also used this room for their meetings. 'Here, plans were laid, momentous decisions were taken and from time to time new personalities took the place of retired or deceased brethren who had held seats on the various councils of the movement at the will of Conference.'[7]

The College Re-opens

Following the end of the war, there was a regrouping of college activities and new plans were put forward for the work of the college to recommence in earnest in 1946. The irrepressible Joseph Smith with the full support of his wife Cynthia, set the standard and pace for a new phase in the history of the Bible College. In his letter to applicants seeking to be accepted as students at the Bible

College, Joseph Smith made the following interesting comment that reflected a major change in the objects of the College:

> The College is now being opened on a wider basis than in pre-war days. Hitherto it has been our usual practice to accept students into the College for training for our own work and an application for admission to the College was virtually regarded as an application to enter the Elim ministry. We have now decided to disassociate these two, and students may return to their homes after completing their course of training, or to any other field of service as they feel led. The design of the College is simply to fit men and women for the work of the Lord.[8]

The length of the College course was set at one year with the three months covering the summer vacation being allotted for students to 'assist in the work of the Lord wherever there is an opportunity. Along with the letter, there was included a set of rules which students were expected to obey. They reflect the culture of the day and some would be considered astonishing in today's society. It is clear that the College Synod had the reputation of the College and the Movement very much in mind. Here are some of the rules:

> Students are reminded that before their acceptance as students they have signed an application form in which they have bound themselves to obey conscientiously the rules of the College. The College Synod therefore expect that this promise will be kept and that students will bear in mind that these rules are not framed to curtail their liberties, but for the smooth running of the College as a whole.

> It is expected that all students will be loyal to the Elim Bible College and be conscientious in obeying these rules, regarding the interests of the College as their own, and co-operating to promote a happy spirit and a true respect for each other and for those in authority. Students should consider the comfort and happiness of their fellow-students, even if it means the loss of some personal gratification and pleasure.

> All students must be present at morning and evening prayers unless prevented by sickness or other legitimate cause.

The bedroom of any person of the opposite sex is strictly out of bounds for students.

Radio sets may not be brought into the College by students.

Courting or keeping company by students is prohibited during College terms.

Cleanliness and personal tidiness are expected of all students.

Students are expected to help in the washing of dishes after each meal.

Practical jokes are not permitted.[9]

There was a total of 24 rules which students were expected to observe. Such rules could have been repressive and would have been more suitable for those occupying the building in its former state.[10]

Rules apart, the re-opening of the College to train students for the ministry was a positive forward-step for the College and the Movement. E C W Boulton took over the role of Dean in succession to Joseph Smith in 1947. Boulton was almost a 'mystic' within Elim circles. A member of the Executive Council from its inception and Elim's first President after the break with George Jeffreys, Boulton was a theologian, poet and hymnist who 'brought qualities to the college that were different.' Boulton was loved by the students who often sought his counsel. He was affectionately known as 'Pa'. Whilst it was necessary for students to have someone to whom they could go to for advice, prayer and personal guidance, surely this was not the prime work of the principal of the College.

A New Era

J T Bradley

Some writers of Elim history would have seen the dawn of the new era as far as the College was concerned, with the arrival of G Wesley Gilpin. I believe that this new era actually commenced with the appointment of James T Bradley as Dean of the Bible College. J T reorganised student life and, with the college council, re-fashioned the curriculum, raised the standard of tuition, and established a sense of discipline as being integral and important to training for the ministry. He was a man of great experience having been a member of the Executive Council for most of his 34 years as an Elim minister. A distinct theological approach was introduced to the curriculum under Bradley's leadership. His administrative skills, combined with his theological rigour, enabled him to leave a mark on the college for many years to come.[11] The curriculum was completely overhauled and the theological input improved. The output of students between 1950 and 1959 brought into Elim a cadre of ministers who were to become leaders in the Movement.

George Wesley Gilpin

The appointment of Wesley Gilpin as principal of the Bible College was certainly a totally unexpected one. The position was first offered to John Dyke who accepted the nomination when offered around the Executive table but withdrew after discussing it with his wife on his return to Birmingham. Two other ministers were approached, but neither was willing to accept. The main reason for nominating Gilpin seems to have been the fact that he was undergoing Bachelor of Divinity studies at the time. Another factor in his favour was that he and his wife had owned a Christian hotel in Bangor, Northern Ireland. This gave them experience of catering for a large group of people.

Whatever the reasons that eventually led the Executive Council to nominate Wesley and the Conference voting to accept the nomination, it proved to be a stroke of genius. One of the first things that Gilpin did was to extend the College course to a two year period. He encouraged students to consider doing a third year with a view of obtaining a degree in theological studies. This was unheard of in a British Pentecostal seminary. The study of English grammar was included on the curriculum and those students who had not achieved a G C E 'O' level pass were given extra tuition to help them achieve this. New Testament Greek was added to the curriculum.

Wesley Gilpin was the Principal of Elim Bible College for a period of twenty-two years. His influence on the lives of his students cannot be over-estimated. Almost 200 Elim ministers came under his tutelage and training. He was an outstanding leader of men and women. He had a great understanding of human nature and he knew his students. He knew when to encourage them and when to take steps to ensure that they were not getting too full of themselves.

I was privileged to have been a student under Wesley Gilpin 1967-1969. His influence on my life and preaching was enormous. I learned from him the importance of application when it comes to preaching. It was a lesson that he imprinted on me in Sermon Class. I had been determined to preach a perfect sermon, one that my colleagues would not dare rip apart. The day arrived and I delivered what I, in my youthful arrogance thought was the perfect sermon. I had prepared well and made sure that my three points all began with the same letter. I sat down to whispers of congratulation from my fellow students. I thought that none of them would criticise me, and they didn't. As I revelled in the adulation of my fellow students, Mr Gilpin rose to his feet and added his congratulations. 'A fair effort Maldwyn', he said. He then went on to complement the composition of the sermon. As I was revelling in all this, he dealt a killer blow to my ego. 'It is what I would call a glass-case sermon. It looks beautiful on the shelf, okay to polish so that it gleams and then goes back on the shelf. A lovely presentation, but of no practical value whatsoever.' He then went on to emphasise the importance of application in preaching. It was the greatest homiletic lesson that I ever learned. Some twenty years later, I reminded him of the event. He was shocked. 'I didn't say that to you, did I?' 'Yes you did' I replied with a smile. From that time onwards, I always made sure that whenever I preached and whatever the subject, it would have a practical and spiritual application in it that would benefit the listeners. Lionel Currie was a fellow-student with me, he was privileged to give the address at Mr Galpin's funeral service. He has written the following tribute:

> Rev G W Gilpin was known to a generation of Elim ministers (1958-1980 as 'Mr Gilpin', and in later years and affectionately as 'Wesley'. His influence on my life, and that of many now retired ministers, was probably greater than we realised at the time. Whether at Woodlands or the Capel campus he was our 'Principal' during our period of study and training at Elim Bible College.
>
> A favourite and well-quoted verse of Wesley's during our college time was 2 Timothy 3v10 – in the KJV of course – '...thou hast fully known my doctrine and manner of life...' Doctrine and manner of life were indivisible for Wesley. What you believed and how you lived it out were inseparable. Wesley believed that personally, pastorally and publicly the Bible must so shape our understanding of God Himself and His purposes in our world, that we allowed it to affect every aspect of our everyday living for Him. 'Doctrine and manner of life' still echoes within me to this day because of Wesley's influence.
>
> Committed to Elim as much as anyone, he was also a man committed to God's Kingdom purposes in the wider church. During the late 60's he hosted a Conference in the grounds of our Capel college campus out of which came the House Church movement, thus showing us the need to be magnanimous and open to all that the Holy Spirit was doing in and through His Church.[12]

Mr Gilpin was humorously referred to by his students as the 'Apostle of balance'. Balance was a word he frequently used in his lectures. There could be no denying his Pentecostal convictions and practice, but he saw the dangers of excess. He believed that Word and Spirit should flow together. Wesley Gilpin exercised the gift of prophecy and not always in the conventional manner. At the end of one of our Conferences where there had been serious debate about the Movement's willingness to allow the Holy Spirit to lead us into new areas in the realm of worship, Wesley was asked to close the last session of the Conference in prayer. It is the most singular example of a prophetic prayer that I have ever heard. In praying for Elim he used a flow of language that I can only describe as 'prophetic praying'. It had a huge impact on the Conference.

Marguerite Gilpin worked alongside her husband and was very involved in many aspects of College life. She gave lectures and individual lessons on public speaking. Another development with which Mrs Gilpin was involved with was the establishment of a curriculum to teach English to students from various parts of Europe. 'Elim Bible College for many years had close connections with Christian groups in Europe. Some members of these groups wished to take up theology courses offered by the College but were unable to do so because of a lack in the knowledge of English. J T Bradley had endeavoured to meet this by the commencement of English language classes for overseas people. In 1964 Mrs Gilpin with qualifications under the Academy of Music (in spoken English) and some teaching experience formed an English class with some Scandinavian and Swiss students.'[13] This was the beginning of the Elim Bible College English Language course for overseas students.

Wesley Gilpin oversaw the huge step of moving the College from Clapham to Capel. This was a huge step for the College. It was in 1963 that Wandsworth Borough Council first made an approach for the four and a half acre plot on which the College was situated. Finally, the Council put a Compulsory Purchase order on much of the Woodlands property and grounds. The College Synod and the Executive Council scoured the country for alternative premises. Their search took them to York, Bradford, Nuneaton and to the counties of Buckinghamshire and Kent. Finally, a 120 year old Mock Tudor Mansion, previously owned by a Greek shipping magnate and situated in the village of Capel became available. Situated on the Surrey/Sussex border, halfway between Dorking and Horsham, on the main road from London to Worthing, this property was considered to be ideal. In July 1964 a public auction was held in Horsham at which the property was on sale. After seeking the Lord's guidance, the Executive Council made a successful bid of £32,250. More money was spent on renovations and furnishings and in January 1965, the Elim Bible College moved from Clapham to this wonderful building set in beautiful grounds.

Wesley Gilpin made strategic appointments to the College faculty. He added considerable depth to the educational and theological prospectus of the college by bringing on staff who were well qualified and capable. Wesley did not just look for academic qualifications in adding to the faculty. He gave former students opportunities to lecture at the College. One of his earliest appointments was that of Christopher Gornold-Smith, the son of Joseph Smith. Wesley later brought former students such as Keith Warrington, Malcolm Hathaway and Peter Davies. He also brought onto the faculty, two former London Bible College students, Neil Hudson and Julian Ward. At the time, Julian was not an Elim minister but Wesley was convinced that Julian's academic prowess, great theological understanding and deep spirituality would be invaluable for the progress of the College. He was right. Julian Ward became an Elim minister and has contributed widely to theological rigour not just in the College, but in the Movement as a whole.

Wesley Gilpin became a member of the Executive Council in 1960 and was Elim President 1965-1966. Through his leadership, Elim Bible College became more than a denominational theological training establishment. Students came from a variety of Christian denominational backgrounds. Wesley made provision for students to study for University degrees and the academic standards of the College improved greatly.

Wesley retired as Principal in 1980 after 22 years. Those of us who were privileged to have trained under his leadership will never under-estimate his impact on our lives and ministry.

Notes

[1] *The Elim Bible College, 1925-1975*, Booklet produced on the occasion of the Bible College Golden Jubilee, 1957.

[2] Jones, Maldwyn, *And they Came to Elim, Vol 1*, ibid, The role of women, Chapter 25, pp296-230

[3] *The Elim Bible College 1925-1975*, ibid, p5.

[4] *The Elim Bible College 1925-1975*, ibid, p5. The writer who may have been an Ulsterman himself, left out the province that was the birth-place of Elim and which at the time of the writing on this brochure housed over thirty Elim churches. Today, there are over 80 Elim churches in Ireland, most of them in Northern Ireland.

[5] *The Elim Bible College 1925-1975*, ibid, p6.

[6] *The Elim Bible College 1925-1975*, ibid, p7

[7] *The Elim Bible College 1925-1875*, ibid, p7.

[8] Letter from Joseph Smith on behalf of the Elim Bible College, undated but informing applicants of the re-opening of the College on 7th January 1947.

[9] Elim Bible College, *Rules for Students 1947*, Malvern: Elim Archives

[10] When it was a convent.

[11] *Elim Bible College 1925-1975*, ibid, p8

[12] Lionel Currie, Tribute, sent by email, 10th January 1922

[13] *Elim Bible College 1925-1975*, ibid pp10,11.

36
Sparkling like Diamonds

Southern Africa is renowned for its mineral deposits, among these are goldfields and diamond mines. The Marange diamond fields are an area of widespread small-scale diamond production in Chiadzwa, Mutare District, Zimbabwe. The quality of the riches in these mines are not measured by their quantity but by their value. Their value is in their carats. In a cemetery in the town of Mutare are buried nine missionaries together with four of their children. They were a group of extremely talented people whose Christian love, service and sacrifice sparkled more brightly than any of those diamonds from the nearby Chiadzwa mines.

The events of Friday night, 23rd June 1978 will be remembered as one of the darkest period of hours in Elim's history. It was the night when armed men crossed the Mozambique border and descended on the Elim school and mission station, newly located from Inyanga North to the Vumba mountains in Southern Rhodesia (Zimbabwe) and brutally murdered eight missionaries and four of their children. One critically ill survivor died several days later. The news of the atrocities was conveyed to Peter and Brenda Griffiths who, together with their sons Stephen and Paul were visiting the Elim Bible College where Peter was to be the guest preacher at the Graduation service in a large marquee in the college grounds. The Griffiths family were on furlough from the Elim mission and Peter used a great deal of that furlough completing his degree programme.

Elim in Zimbabwe

The Elim mission in Zimbabwe had commenced in 1949 when Pastor and Mrs Jesse Williams and their seven-year old son set sail from England to take up missionary work in Southern Rhodesia and Portuguese East Africa (Mozambique). They based themselves in Penhalonga, a gold mining town in the Eastern Highlands of Zimbabwe, some five miles from the country's border with Mozambique. There were a large number of mines and plantation workers and their families in the many camps that were set up in the area. The new Elim missionaries soon set up a church and a school in the area. Within 18 months, there was a congregation of about 120 meeting regularly and eventually a church building with a capacity to hold 200 people was bult. This was achieved despite the new building being destroyed shortly after it was opened due to flooding. The destruction of the building was a huge set-back for the work, but Jesse Williams and his wife continued with their mission of reaching the people of the area with the message of the Gospel.[1]

The Doctors

The Elim work in Southern Rhodesia was greatly enhanced by the arrival of two doctors, Cecil and Mary Brien. Although Jesse Williams and his wife were the first Elim missionaries in Southern Rhodesia, the Doctors Brien will be forever linked with the Elim story in this part of Africa. Dr Cecil was a pharmacist and a surgeon, and his wife. Mary, was a physician and an anaesthetist. The doctors had been working in Africa for two years before they linked up with Elim, but both of them had previous connections with the denomination. Mrs Brien was in touch with Elim in Belfast and had taken part in open-air meetings organised by Apsley Street (now South Belfast) Elim church. They also had contact with P S Brewster in Wigan whilst the pioneer campaign was in process in that industrial Lancastrian town. Cecil Brien was a doctor in the town at the time. They had also been in close contact with Leslie Green when he was the pastor of the Swansea church. 'They had read in the Elim Evangel of the coming of Jesse Williams to Africa and the Lord had stirred their hearts towards joining up with him, but they had hesitated to make any move until they were sure it was the Lord's will. The confirmation of a letter from Leslie Green that suggested that they go, was taken as a sure sign that they should go.'[2]

Cecil Brien was an Ulsterman, born in Enniskillen in Co Fermanagh in 1905. He trained as a pharmacist before entering medical school at Queen's University, Belfast. He was an intense, fiery man with a deep evangelical faith. He got in trouble with his fellow medics when he persisted in open-air preaching, particularly during his time spent in the Rhondda valleys of South Wales. It was whilst he was at Queens that Cecil met Mary Campbell Chambers, a doctor's daughter from Natal, South Africa. They married in 1936 and then went to the Bible College of Wales where they came under the influence of Rees Howells who was known for his prayer life.

They went out to Rhodesia and worked under the covering of the Evangelical Alliance Mission. After working under the auspices of the Alliance for two years, the Briens became increasingly frustrated at the anti-Pentecostal views they encountered and linked up with Elim. At the beginning of his ministry in Africa, Jesse Williams had visited the un-evangelised area of Inyanga. It was this very area that had been laid on the hearts of the Drs Brien. Eventually, a hospital was built, with Cecil laying many of the bricks himself. Meanwhile, in Penhalonga, Jesse Williams had established a school which by 1952 had 200 pupils.

There were appeals made for workers to join the Elim mission in Rhodesia. Among those that responded were Archie Nicholson who was a member of the Greenock Elim church and Alan and Anne Renshaw. Alan and Anne worked for a year in Rhodesia before going to Tanzania for three years. They returned to Zimbabwe in

1964. This was the same year that Elim was granted permission to open a Secondary School in Inyanga North.

Peter and Brenda Griffiths

Brenda Hurrell and Peter Griffiths both went as missionaries to Rhodesia. Both had responded to the appeal made by Cecil and Mary Brien. Brenda was a member of the first Elim Church founded in England, in Leigh-on-Sea, Essex. Brenda joined thousands of others at the great Elim Easter Monday rallies in the Royal Albert Hall in 1956. She had read of the activities of the Briens and their appeal for teachers to assist the missions work in Rhodesia. Brenda had no thought of responding to the appeal made by Cecil Brien for teachers and was somewhat alarmed when a friend caught her arm and introduced her to the missionary doctor. 'Sensing Brenda's reluctance to discuss service abroad, with uncharacteristic gentleness Cecil said, "I'm not going to ask you to come to Rhodesia, God will have to ask you because the work is hard."'[3] This encounter made a deep impression on Brenda and some weeks later she met up again with the Briens and this led to her applying to the Elim Missionary Society with a view of becoming a teacher in Rhodesia after consulting with her local pastor. The reply came as a shock to her. She was the wrong gender. It was not women they wanted in Rhodesia, but men. This reprieve allowed her to make her own plans, but the sense of God's call for her to go to Rhodesia was not easily dismissed. Then, a few weeks later she received a second letter from the Missionary Secretary. There had been a mistake. Her application was welcome after all and the need was urgent. 'Just three months later on 16th January 1957, at the age of 24, Brenda sailed from England on the Braemar Castle to begin her service with the Elim Missionary Society. She travelled up from Cape Town by train, three slow, hot days through South Africa, across the Kalahari Desert to her final destination – the tiny hamlet of Penhalonga in Eastern Rhodesia.'[4]

On 10th April 1960, a farewell service for Mr Peter Griffiths took place in the Swansea Elim church. Peter's early education had been interrupted by a severe illness. He survived rheumatic fever but was hospitalised for almost a year. He had to repeat a whole year at junior school, but he passed his eleven-plus exams and gained a place at Bishop Gore Grammar School in Swansea. Peter, through the influence, testimony and friendship of Bill Sheehan, a young Irish house-painter, committed his life to Christ at the age of 17 and became a member of the Swansea Elim Church.

Peter also met with the Doctors Brien in 1956 while they were in Britain on their first furlough in seventeen years of hard missionary work. By this time, a network of twenty-five very basic schools had been established along the eastern border of Rhodesia and the Doctors spoke of the great need for more missionary teachers to help in this vital work. Peter eventually left the Steel Company of Wales where he had worked since leaving school and began his teacher training in response to the Briens' guidance in preparation for cross-cultural service. Peter was commissioned for service in Rhodesia under the supervision of the Doctors Brien. This was to have far-reaching ramifications, although no-one could have guessed it then. It was a year after his arrival in the country that Peter met Brenda for the first time. Peter Griffiths arrived at Penhalonga on May Day 1960.

'Peter plunged wholeheartedly into his new life as a school teacher in the Elim Mission Station just outside the village of Penhalonga. Many of the 'children' he was teaching were older than he was. In contrast to his battles with British pupils in inner-city Birmingham, he was deeply impressed with the passionate, almost fanatical approach to learning that the young black people of Rhodesia displayed. Education was seen as a key to unlock a prosperous future as well as a passport out of the drudgery and boredom of subsistence farming, just as it had been a way out of the Welsh coalmines a generation before.'[5]

There were strict rules on courtship amongst missionaries on the field which impacted Peter and Brenda's blossoming romance.

Mention is made by Stephen of the ingenious ways in which his parents conducted their romance, mostly by letters as they were some 200 miles apart at different mission stations. Meanwhile, the political situation in nearby Belgian Congo had become extremely volatile and two Elim missionaries from that country joined the Elim mission in Rhodesia. They were Olive Garbutt (nurse) and Catherine Picken (teacher).

Peter finally informed Cecil and Mary Brien of his interest in Brenda and of the development of their relationship. This was not well received and the Briens expressed their anger at what they saw as Peter's deceit.[6] It took the Doctors a full twelve months before they were willing to give their blessing. They were married on 13th December 1963 by the marriage officer, a Baptist Pastor in Umtali with the most appropriate name for a minister, Reverend Sermon!

In 1964, the Elim Missionary team from both centres (Katerere and Penhalonga) met to discuss the possibility of establishing a secondary school with boarding facilities in the Ruangwe Valley. This met with fierce opposition from Cecil and Mary Brien. 'Cecil Brien was the strongest anyone had yet heard him about any missionary project, as he stated that opening a secondary school would be a distraction to the spiritual work and that "blessing wouldn't come through it."'[7] The Briens were held in such esteem by the missionary group that their opposition to the project caused the rest of the group to leave the matter be. Cecil Brien's prayer life and ministry had been greatly influenced by Rees Howells. It was the Doctor's practice to pray between 3.00 and 4.00 in the morning, at noon and again in the evening. 'In the quietness of his home in Katerere a few days after the conference, Cecil was on his knees when he heard God say, "You are to open a school and you will call it 'Emmanuel', for I will be with you."'[8] So the decision was made to build a Secondary School.

Alan and Anne Renshaw returned to Rhodesia after a period in Tanzania, Alan as manager and Anne as a teacher. 'An important development in the work was the erecting of a secondary school in Inyanga alongside the primary school already established there.

Alan Renshaw had the job of designing and arranging for the construction of this building which stands today as a testimony to the faithfulness of God.'9

There were retirements and additions to the work in Rhodesia. The veteran pioneers and leaders of the work in Rhodesia retired in 1970 and Peter Griffiths became the team leader. Whilst on their first furlough, Peter and Brenda were able to take part in the valedictory service for another new missionary to Rhodesia.[10] Maisie Hopper was a member of Ilford Elim church and had shown great interest in missionary work over the years and taken a number of nursing courses in preparation to serve and had gained invaluable nursing experience whilst waiting to go to the mission field.[11]

The early seventies saw the Elim mission personnel in Rhodesia increase, not only numerically, but also by the professional quality of the staff. These young missionaries were all well qualified in their own special fields of service, usually teaching or medicine. Biographical sketches of the nine missionaries who were martyred together with four of their children will be given in the following chapter.

The new missionaries were aware of the dangers that would face them in Rhodesia. With the granting of independence to Mozambique in 1975, the situation in Rhodesia became far more dangerous for white missionaries working close to the border. The new nationalist government in the former Portuguese colony agreed to host guerrilla bases for those fighting for control in neighbouring countries. 'There was a scramble to move Zimbabwe African National Liberation Army (ZANLA) bases from Zambia and Tanzania into a newly welcoming Mozambique.'[12] Students from many secondary schools along the 1200 kilometres eastern border absconded and went to be trained as freedom fighters. Nine pupils absconded from Emmanuel school.[13]

By the end of 1977, the team of Elim missionaries was comprised of Peter and Brenda Griffiths with their children Stephen and Paul, Catherine Picken, Peter and Sandra McCann with their children Philip and Joy, Philip and Susanne Evans with their children Timothy, Rachel and Rebecca, Joyce Pickering, Roy Lynne, Mary Fisher, Joy Bath and Wendy White. Alan and Anne Renshaw, with their children Timothy, Bethan and Karen, who had been missionaries in Tanzania and Rhodesia since 1960 had to return home due to health problems. Alan's role as station manager was filled by a young man from Cullybackey in Northern Ireland. After a two-year course at Elim Bible College, he became the minister of Brookeborough Elim church in Co Fermanagh before responding to the call to go to Zimbabwe. Roy fitted into the team extremely well. He was one of my fellow-students at the Elim Bible College 1967-1969. Roy joined the team in 1974 where he met and fell in love with Joyce Pickering. They both returned home for a short time in 1977 and were married at the Elim Church in York with Peter Smith the pastor of the Elim church there officiating.

Ron and Nettie Chapman went to Rhodesia in July 1974. Having been Elim's Field Superintendent for six years, Mr Chapman responded to a request from the International Missions Board to go to Southern Africa and serve as Field Overseer of the Elim Missions in Rhodesia and South Africa. Based at Penhalonga, they travelled extensively through the two countries visiting and encouraging the missionaries. There was regular communication between Leslie Wigglesworth together with his successor as Elim Missionary Secretary David Ayling and the British Foreign and Commonwealth Office to ascertain the safety of their workers in Rhodesia. 'One interview took place in the office of Labour Foreign Secretary, David Owen. Sometime later in a television interview which dealt with David Owen's personal faith, he paid tribute to the two Elim ministers. They had asked to pray with the Foreign Secretary and were permitted to do so.'[14]

The decision was made to move the Elim School and hospital from their premises in Katerere to the Vumba for safety reasons. There was an army base a few miles from the school and hospital at Katerere and the Patriotic Front guerillas were increasingly active. John Smyth, Elim's administrator, and a member of the Executive Council was delegated by the International Missions

Board to go to Rhodesia to discuss the situation first-hand with Ron Chapman. The nurses and teachers who served at the mission at Katarere and Penhalonga were consulted and every one of the Elim missionaries bravely opted to stay in the country and carry on with their work. Evacuation plans were put in place in the event of an impending disaster.

Eventually, the situation became such that moving became imperative. The decision was made to move the Elim School to the Eagle School premises in the Vumba hills. Meanwhile, Peter and Brenda Griffiths took a furlough and returned to the UK in August 1977 so that Peter could complete his MA studies. Philip Evans at the very young age of 28 was made Acting Principal in the absence of Peter.

The first impression of the Vumba in the eyes of the newly arrived missionaries was that it was like the English Lake District. It was 15 miles from Mutare which meant ready access to shops and wider Christian fellowship. Elim Headquarters were in constant touch with the missionaries. The move to the Eagle school happened on 21st July 1977. Timothy and Rachel Evans, the two older children of Philip and Susanne were at boarding school in Salisbury (now Harare). Joyce and Roy Lynn's baby daughter, Pamela Grace, was delivered two weeks early by Caesarean section in Mutare on 1st June.

The Elim workers felt safer at the Vumba as it was well protected. 'The main reason for the move was to reduce the risk from landmines which seriously impacted the functioning of Elim Katerere. In the Vumba, the road was tarred nearly all the way which was definitely an improvement. But the missionaries actually refused protection because they were concerned that if there was a firefight between guerrillas and Rhodesian forces, students would die.'[15] The school got under way in the new premises. Joyce Lynn opened four clinics in nearby areas while her husband Roy preached and ministered to the men. Monthly visits were made to the hospital at Katerere. This was due to the marvellous service provided by the Missionary Aviation Fellowship.[16]

The second term at the Vumba proved to be very difficult due to increasing guerrilla activity and influence in the region. Some of the students came under the influence of the guerrillas who made regular incursions from Mozambique. Despite the mounting pressure it was felt that scholastically and spiritually the scholars progressed at the Vumba. The International Missions Board sent Peter Griffiths to the Vumba for a short visit in October 1977. This brief visit resulted in the staff again expressing their desire to stay where they were.

Alarmed by news of the killing of two Salvation Army lady teachers in the region, Leslie Wigglesworth phoned Ron Chapman and it was decided that the staff should move to Mutare and travel to the school every day. The staff had their bags ready to move. Matters were hindered because most of the staff came down with a virus.

Before the move could take place, 21 guerrillas came over the border from Mozambique and attacked our missionaries with axes and other weapons. I will not dwell on the horror that took place on the cricket pitch at Eagle School on that winter night of 23rd June 1978. With immense dignity overshadowing a broken heart, Ron Chapman went to the Eagle School to identify the victims and deal with the immediate aftermath. These innocent victims, among them three small children and a three-week- old baby had been savagely murdered. Altogether there were three men, five women and four children whose bodies were found on that cricket field. A sixth woman, Mary Fisher was cruelly attacked but managed to run down the steep hill on which the school stands, going through agonizingly prickly bushes and trees. She was found many hours later and taken unconscious to hospital in the capital, Harare, where she died on 30th June.

At the College graduation service, despite just having heard of the death of his colleagues Peter Griffiths went on to deliver his prepared sermon despite the willingness of others to take his place. He had chosen for his text the words of Paul to the church at Philippi: 'It is my eager expectation and hope that I shall not be at all ashamed, but that with full courage now as always Christ will be honoured in my body, whether by life or by death. For me to live is

Christ, and to die is gain.'[17] With bloodshot eyes from which tears ran freely, Peter recalled his friends and colleagues one by one and spoke of their determination to follow their Lord.

Peter Griffiths and John Smyth flew to Harare on the Sunday night and went first class by courtesy of South African Airways. Leslie Wigglesworth, David Ayling, John Smyth and Peter Griffiths represented the Movement at the funerals in Mutare. Ron Chapman led the service and David Ayling preached. John Smyth conducted the burial service and Ron Chapman preached.[18] Mary Fisher's funeral was held the following Thursday, this was taken by John Smyth and Ron Chapman.

The Elim work in Zimbabwe was not ended on that brutal night on the playing fields of Eagle school. The immense work done by our colleagues resulted in the church continuing and flourishing led no longer by missionaries from a faraway land, but by indigenous workers trained by our colleagues who gave their lives for Christ.

Notes

[1] Smith, Peter, *Global Warming*, ibid, p171.

[2] Smith, Peter, ibid, p172.

[3] Griffiths, Stephen, *The Axe and the Tree, How bloody persecution sowed the seeds of new life in Zimbabwe*, (Oxford: Monarch Books, 2017) p28.

[4] Griffiths, Stephen, ibid, p30.

[5] Griffiths, Stephen, ibid, p43.

[6] Griffiths, Stephen, ibid, p62.

[7] Griffiths, Stephen, ibid, p65.

[8] Griffiths, Stephen, ibid, p66.

[9] Smith, Peter, ibid, p182.

[10] Smith does not give the dates of the Griffiths' first furlough, but I think it was 1966-7.

[11] Smith, Peter, ibid, p184.

[12] Griffiths, Stephen, ibid, p99

[13] Griffiths, Stephen, ibid, p99

[14] *The Vumba Tragedy*, published by Elim International Missions, De Walden Road, Malvern. NB this interview took place after the massacre. It is included here to show the good relationship between Elim and the Foreign Office, both before and after the tragedy.

[15] Stephen Griffiths comment to Maldwyn Jones, by email, 4th March 1922

[16] *The Vumba Tragedy, A Summary of the tragic Events*. ibid, Elim.org.uk

[17] Phil 1:20,21 (NIV).

[18] *The Vumba Tragedy*, ibid.

37
The Martyrs plus one

I spent almost two weeks reading researching and writing these last two chapters of this book. I have found the experience harrowing. The missionaries brutally murdered were my colleagues. I knew all of them personally with the exception of Wendy White. Writing these brief accounts of their lives and ministry has caused me to rejoice for their ministries and sacrifice, but the tears are still flowing as I write. I have titled this chapter 'The Martyrs plus one' because I have included Joy Bath who was a greatly loved and valued member of the team and would also have died with her colleagues had she not been on furlough.

Peter and Sandra McCann

Peter had graduated from university with B.Sc. (honours) degree and came from the Yorkshire town of Huddersfield. After struggling with Christianity throughout his university years, he finally made a full commitment of his life to Christ. 'After working with a chemical firm for some time, he turned to teaching, but never really felt competent at it and wondered how the Lord had allowed him to go in that direction.'[1] Peter may have had doubts about his teaching ability but, Griffiths states that he was a superb teacher but was 'impossibly chaotic at managing daily life, but Sandra's practicality compensated for this, mixing common sense with good humour. Responding to an appeal for qualified teachers, the McCanns arrived in Katerere in mid-1970 with their toddler son Paul.'[2] Peter took over science teaching and Sandra became the school librarian. Tragically, their young son died during surgery for a foot infection one year after the family moved to Rhodesia. The little boy was buried in the hills behind the mission. Sandra, in a letter to her parents giving details of the funeral service held in the Elim Church on the mission compound in Katerere wrote, 'It will mean a lot to the Africans that we have buried Paul in their soil. This is now a part of Rhodesia that is ours and now a foundation stone has been laid…which cannot be removed. They had two other children Philip aged nearly 6 and Sharon aged 4 and a half who were killed with them.

Catherine Picken

Catherine was the oldest member of the team. Born on 15th March 1923, Cath Picken was a native of Southend-on-Sea and was baptised in the Spirit at one of Elim's Youth Camps. She felt the call of God on her life to go to Congo to serve as a missionary. She studied French and other subjects in Belgium for 2 years from 1956 in preparation for missionary work in Congo. However, due to the growing unrest in the Congo she, along with Olive Garbutt was evacuated to Southern Rhodesia in 1960. Cath soon settled into life in her new sphere of ministry and she became a valued teacher in the Elim schools. Whilst on furlough in 1969, Catherine Picken attended Elim's Annual Conference and made an appeal for graduate teachers for Rhodesia. Sandra McCann was present at the Conference and with great excitement returned home to Huddersfield and shared the call with her husband Peter. Catherine Picken was a lady with great spiritual discernment and this aspect of her ministry was invaluable to the rest of the missions' team in Rhodesia. Catherine was 55 at the time of the Vumba massacre. She was a proficient hockey player and sports teacher, a role she was occupying at the time of her death. She served in Rhodesia for almost 18 years.[3]

Philip and Susanne Evans

I first met Phil at a youth camp in Porthpean, Cornwall in 1963. Both of us responded to the call to serve the Lord and we knelt together in the straw in the Marquee. We met up again at youth camps in Swanage where Phil met his lovely wife Susanne, she chose to be called Susanna. Susanna came from Nuneaton and Philip was from Mansfield. He was the nephew of William Evans the pastor of my home church of Porth. Philip was 29 and Susanna 33 when they were killed. Their daughter Rebecca was killed with them. She was only five years old. They had been in Rhodesia for two and a half years and were still on their first term. Philip was incredibly gifted, he held MSc, MPhil and Teaching Diploma qualifications. The accounts written of him reveal him to have been fearless and brave. He pleaded with the guerrillas to let the women and children go free, his broken body bore witness to the brutal replies. Wendy White shouted to him, 'Phil, they can kill the body but not the soul.'

Roy and Joyce Lynn

Born on 21 September 1941, Roy was 36 when he was killed. He was originally intended as a temporary replacement for missionary Alan Renshaw who was on leave and who was normally in charge of maintenance. Roy had an almost magic touch with all machinery. Due to an accident as a youngster Roy was lame and he became especially loved by the Africans because if he fell over while doing a repair, he got up and laughed. Roy would do anything for anybody. I shared a chalet with him at Conference 1977. There were no showers in the chalet and so I washed my hair in the sink. Roy said, 'Here Taffy, let me help you.' He didn't wash my feet, but Roy did wash my hair. He was a great preacher, a wonderful pastor, an inspiring missionary and a wonderful friend. When he left for Rhodesia in 1975 he had to change planes at Heathrow airport. He was met in from Belfast by P S Brewster and Tom Walker from Elim Headquarters. They were surprised to see him walking towards them with a much more pronounced limp than usual. He was carrying two cases, one a fibre one full of tools. He greeted the men with the remark, 'I have had another road accident and I knew that if I told you about it, you would not let me go to Rhodesia. It's too late now and I'm off.' The men were very moved and even found emotional difficulty in praying for this just before he left.'[4]

Roy met and fell in love with Joyce Pickering in Rhodesia. Joyce was 36 when she was killed. She came from York and was a highly skilled nurse and midwife. She and Roy were married in the UK on 23rd July 1977. Their daughter Pamela Grace was born on 1st June 1978, just 3 weeks before her tragic death. Joyce was the very capable matron of the Hospital, a good organiser and very successful in pursuit of her nursing and midwifery ministry.[5]

Mary E Fisher

Born on 13th August 1946, Mary was 31 when she died in hospital in Harare. Mary was from Caerphilly and taught maths and science. She went to Rhodesia in August 1973 and served for almost 5 years. She had a rich soprano voice and her worship tapes were a great blessing both before and after her tragic death. She survived the initial attack, only to die from her terrible injuries on 30th June 1978. She was buried alongside her colleagues in Mutare.[6]

Elisabeth Wendy H White

Born on 14th June 1940, Wendy was 38 years when she was killed. She was from Kensington Temple and was well experienced in nursing, teaching and social work, holding BA, SRN and a Diploma in Social Studies qualifications. She served in Rhodesia for 1 year and 4 months, and was still in her first term when she was killed.[7] Wendy was a deeply spiritual young lady and went to Rhodesia at a time when the risks to personal safety were enormous. In the short time she was with the team, she was a great spiritual encouragement to her fellow missionaries.

Joy Bath

Joy was a member of the Salisbury Elim Church and was greatly involved in the youth ministry of that church. I first met Joy in one of the youth camps that I attended as a teenager. 'She left Salisbury in Wiltshire to fly to Salisbury in Rhodesia and from there, to the hospital at Inyanga. At twenty-four and a trained midwife, she was an invaluable addition to the team.'[8] Joy was home on furlough when the massacre of our missionaries occurred. She was deeply aware that she would have died alongside her beloved colleagues had she not been on furlough. It is my personal opinion that the name of Joy Bath should be added to the names of our martyred colleagues. She went to India for a short time following the martyrdom of her colleagues but returned to Africa to continue her midwifery work. At the time, HIV was rampant in many African countries and particularly, Zimbabwe[9], and Joy became infected with the aids virus whilst working in the hospital theatre at Katerere.

> In February 1992, Joy was assisting in the operating theatre. A man had mangled his hand in a grinding machine and the surgeon was repairing his fingers. It was a long and delicate procedure and Joy started to feel hungry and dizzy. Suddenly gripped with agonizing abdominal pain, Joy put her head down on the operating table next to the patient's head, keeping him asleep by shooting the anaesthetic into his vein every time he moved while sending for the relief surgical assistant, Debbie Brown. By the time Debbie arrived on the scene, Joy was crumpled over on the floor, still managing to keep the patient asleep! A dose of painkillers and a long sleep helped and Joy was back at work the following day. But she remained chronically unwell over the next month, with recurrent fevers and malaise although she struggled on with her nursing work.[10]

Joy had contracted the aids virus. She was admitted to a hospital in Harare where Peter Griffiths visited her. He was present when the doctor broke the news that Joy's blood test revealed that she had contracted Aids. Peter, sank down on the end of the hospital bed and together they wept. The doctor commented, 'For you, Joy, the fact that you are HIV positive is not a matter for shame, but for pride. You have the virus only through your calling and dedication to service.' I had the immense privilege of meeting Joy in her home in Salisbury together with my wife and children. I was preaching in the Elim church and were hosted by Joy's parents. She talked to us about her ministry in the country where her colleagues had died so brutally. In early 1995, Joy went totally blind but was able to communicate the fact that she knew God was with her. On Good Friday 1995, with her family at her side, 'with unexpected strength Joy flung up her arms and shouted "Hallelujah!". Joy died on Easter Saturday, two days before her forty-fifth birthday'[11]

I have found the writing of these two chapters emotionally harrowing. I wish to pay tribute to Peter and Brenda Griffiths who continued their work in Zimbabwe. Peter died as a result of a brain tumour on the 12th October 1993 aged 55. His wife Brenda is over 90 years of age and lives in southern England. More will be written concerning them in my third volume. Elim is greatly indebted to them for their extraordinary service.

In writing of the sacrifice of my colleagues, my mind went back to our graduation service in Capel in June 1969. Roy Lynn stood next to me in the students' choir. One of the songs we sang that day was Ira Stamphill's famous song 'Follow me'. The last verse is particularly poignant:

Oh, Jesus if I die upon a foreign field some day
'Twould be no more than love demands No less could I repay,
'No greater love hath mortal man than for a friend to die'
These are the words He gently spoke to me,
'If just a cup of water I place within your hand
Then just a cup of water is all that I demand.'
But if by death to living they can my glory see,
I'll take my cross and follow close to Thee.

Notes

1 Smith, Peter, *Global Warming*, p184

2 Griffiths, Stephen, *The Axe and the Tree*, p90.

3 *The Vumba Tragedy*, https//www.elim.org.uk – File accessed 17.2.2022

4 *The Vumba Tragedy*, https//www.elim.org.uk – File accessed 17.2.2022

5 *The Vumba Tragedy*, https//www.elim.org.uk – File accessed 17.2.2022

6 *The Vumba Tragedy*, https//www.elim.org.uk – File accessed 17.2.2022

7 *The Vumba Tragedy*, https//www.elim.org.uk – File accessed 17.2.2022

8 Smith, Peter, ibid, p185.

9 By the time of Joy's return to Africa, Zimbabwe had achieved independence, so I have used the country's present name as opposed to her colonial name.

10 Griffiths, Stephen, ibid, p307.

11 Griffiths, Stephen, ibid, p323

End Note

It had been my intention to have covered the impact of the charismatic renewal and the influence of the Bible Weeks in the seventies and eighties, culminating in the Southport Conference in 1981. This will now be included in my third volume. Also included will be an account of the development and growth of the Elim churches in Ireland during the time of the 'Troubles'. There will also be a chapter on the continuation of Elim missions in Zimbabwe.

The world events in the period that have been covered in this volume caused intense theological debate within Elim. Britain joining the Common Market in 1972 was an issue that sparked great discussions and many articles in the Evangel. This was also the case with the six-day war in 1967 and the threat of nuclear warfare. The variety of eschatological opinion on these subjects varied considerably throughout the Movement. This will be discussed in the third volume.

Perhaps, the most important question that is in my mind as I approach the last volume is one concerning the Pentecostal nature of our Movement? Is Elim still worthy of calling itself 'Elim Pentecostal Church?

Bibliography

Published books

Boulton, E C W, *George Jeffreys – A Ministry of the Miraculous*, (London: Elim Publishing Company), 1928.

Bradford, Sarah, *George VI, the Dutiful King*, (London: Penguin Books, 1989) Kindle Edition

Brown, Becky, *Blitz Spirit: Voices of Britain living through Crisis 1939-1945*: (London: Hodder & Stoughton Ltd 2020)

Cartwright, Chris with Holdaway, Jan and David, *Defining Moments, 100 years of the Elim Pentecostal Church* (Malvern: Elim Pentecostal Church, 2014)

Cartwright, Desmond, *The Great Evangelists, The Remarkable lives of George and Stephen Jeffreys*, (Basingstoke: Marshal, Morgan and Scott, 1986)

Churchill, Winston, *The Gathering Storm: the Second World War Volume 1*: (London: Penguin Classics 2005) p48.

Churchill, Winston, *The Grand Alliance – The Second World War Volume 3*, (London: Penguin Books, 2005)

Churchill, Winston, *Their Finest Hour: The Second World War, Volume II*: (London: Penguin Classics 2005)

Cruikshank, Charles, *The German Occupation of the Channel Islands*: (Stroud: The History Press 2019)

Dunk, Philip, *Occupation: Pastor, the Early life and times of Gilbert T S Dunk*, (Copyright, Philip M Dunk 2012)

England, Edward, *Adventurous Christianity, A journey of discovery*, (London: Victory Press, 1962)

Feeney, Paul, *A 1950's Childhood, From Tin Baths to Bread and Dripping*, (Cheltenham: The History Press, 2020)

Gee, Donald, *The Pentecostal Movement*: (London: Elim Publishing Company Limited, 1949)

Gilbert, Martin: *A History of the Twentieth Century, Volume Two 1933-1935*: (London: Harper-Collins Publishers 1998)

Gilbert, Martin, *Churchill, the Power of Words*, (London: Transworld Publishers, 2012)

Glass, John, *The Best is Yet to Come*, (Kindle edition, Life Publications 2017)

Griffiths, Stephen, *The Axe and the Tree, How bloody persecution sowed the seeds of new life in Zimbabwe*, (Oxford: Monarch Books, 2017)

Hathaway, George William, *A Sound From Heaven*, (Clapham, London: Victory Press 1947)

Hywel-Davies, Jack, *The Kensington Temple Story* (Crowborough: Monarch Books, 1998)

Jones, Maldwyn, *And they came to Elim: Volume 1, 1915-1940; An official history of the Elim Pentecostal Movement in the UK* (Rickmansworth: Instant Apostle, 2021)

Jones, Ron, *Then something remarkable happened, the autobiography of Ron Jones* (with Paul Davis), (Bromsgrove: Crossbridge Books 2005

Kay, William, *George Jeffreys: Pentecostal Apostle and Revivalist*, (Cleveland, Tennessee: CPT Press, 2017)

Kingston, Charles J E, *Fullness of Power, Talks on the gifts of the Holy Spirit* (London: Elim Publishing House, 1965)

Liardon, Roberts, *God's Generals: The Healing Evangelists* (Sarasota, FL: Robert Liardon Ministries),

Palmer, Chris, *The Emergence of Pentecostalism in Wales: A historical, theological evaluation of the early development of the Assemblies of God denomination in South East Wales with special reference to Crosskeys and Newbridge*: (London: Apostolos Publishing Ltd, 2016)

Redemption Hymnal: (Eastbourne: Elim Publishing House, 1966)

Smith, Peter, *Global Warming, An anecdotal history of the work of Elim Missions, 1919-1989*, (Antrim: Antrim Printers, 2006)

Stanbrook, Dominic, *Never had it so Good, A History of Britain from Suez to the Beatles* (London: Abacus, 2006)

Sweet, Leonard, *Summoned to Lead*, (Grand Rapids: Zondervan, 2004)

Taylor, Cyril, *My Life as a Social Entrepreneur*, (Stroud: Camberley Publishing, 2013)

Thompson, David, *The Aims of History: Values of the Historical Attitude*, (London: Thames and Hudson, 1969)

Unpublished Works

A Basis for Unity in Elim: A Statement by the Executive Council of the Elim Foursquare Gospel Alliance: January 1940: (Malvern: Elim Archives)

A Reply to the Pamphlet by Principal George Jeffreys entitled: "Why I resigned from the Elim Movement." (Malvern: Elim Archives)

Conference Minutes, *Elim Pentecostal Church 1933-1969*, (Malvern: Elim Archives)

Conference Minutes, *Elim Pentecostal Church, 1970-1989*, (Malvern: Elim Archives)

Canty, George, *History of Elim 1915-1983*, (Malvern: Elim Archives)

1934 Deed Poll; Deed of Variance 1942, (Malvern: Elim Archives)

1939 Ministerial Conference Minutes, Monday afternoon, 27th November 1939, (Malvern: Elim Archives)

Flett, Linda Mary: *A Search for Resonance: A History of the Elim Churches in New Zealand 1922-2000* (PhD Dissertation, Otago University 1921)

Hudson, Neil, *A Schism and its Aftermath: An Historical Analysis of Denominational Discerption in the Elim Pentecostal Church 1939-1940* (PhD Dissertation, King's College, 1999)

Jeffreys, George, *Why I resigned from the Elim Movement*, (Malvern: Elim Archives)

Jones, Maldwyn, *An Analysis of the Role of E J Phillips and an Assessment of His Leadership in the Establishment of the Elim Pentecostal Church as a Coherent Christian denomination,* (MA Dissertation, Regents Theological College/Bangor University, 2011)

Lewis, I Wynne, *History of Elim Pentecostal Church*, (Malvern: Elim Archives)

Phillips, E J, Speech to 1939 Conference, Tuesday, 21st November, (Malvern: Elim Archives)

Phillips, E J, General Survey, Notes of speech to the 1939 Ministerial Conference, (Malvern: Elim Archives)